D0521771

Less managing. More teaching. Greater learning.

 INSTRUCTORS...

Would you like your **students** to show up for class **more prepared**?
(Let's face it, class is much more fun if everyone is engaged and prepared...)

Want an **easy way to assign** homework online and track student **progress**?
(Less time grading means more time teaching...)

Want an **instant view** of student or class performance? *(No more wondering if students understand...)*

Need to **collect data and generate reports** required for administration or accreditation? *(Say goodbye to manually tracking student learning outcomes...)*

Want to **record and post your lectures** for students to view online?

With **McGraw-Hill's** *Connect® Plus Economics*,

INSTRUCTORS GET:

- Simple **assignment management**, allowing you to spend more time teaching.
- **Auto-graded** assignments, quizzes, and tests.
- **Detailed Visual Reporting** where student and section results can be viewed and analyzed.
- Sophisticated **online testing** capability.
- A **filtering and reporting** function that allows you to easily assign and report on materials that are correlated to accreditation standards, learning outcomes, and Bloom's taxonomy.
- An easy-to-use **lecture capture** tool.
- The option to **upload course documents** for student access.

Want an online, **searchable version** of your textbook?

Wish your textbook could be **available online** while you're doing your assignments?

 ### Connect® Plus Economics eBook

If you choose to use *Connect® Plus Economics*, you have an affordable and searchable online version of your book integrated with your other online tools.

Connect® Plus Economics eBook offers features like:

- Topic search
- Direct links from assignments
- Adjustable text size
- Jump to page number
- Print by section

 Want to get more **value** from your textbook purchase?

Think learning economics should be a bit more **interesting**?

 ### Check out the STUDENT RESOURCES section under the *Connect®* Library tab.

Here you'll find a wealth of resources designed to help you achieve your goals in the course. Every student has different needs, so explore the STUDENT RESOURCES to find the materials best suited to you.

Macroeconomics

BRIEF EDITION

Second Edition

Macroeconomics
BRIEF EDITION

Campbell R. McConnell
University of Nebraska

Sean M. Flynn
Scripps College

Stanley L. Brue
Pacific Lutheran University

With the special assistance of
Randy R. Grant
Linfield College

McGraw-Hill
Irwin

The McGraw-Hill Economics Series

The Six Versions of McConnell, Brue, Flynn

Chapter	Economics	Economics: Brief Edition	Microeconomics	Microeconomics: Brief Edition	Macroeconomics	Macroeconomics: Brief Edition	Essentials of Economics
1. Limits, Alternatives, and Choices	x	x	x	x	x	x	x
2. The Market System and the Circular Flow	x	x	x	x	x	x	x
3. Demand, Supply, and Market Equilibrium	x	x	x	x	x	x	x
4. Elasticity	x	x	x	x	x		
5. Market Failures: Public Goods and Externalities	x	x	x	x	x	x	x
6. Consumer Behavior	x		x				
7. Businesses and the Costs of Production	x	x	x	x			x
8. Pure Competition in the Short Run	x	x	x	x			x
9. Pure Competition in the Long Run	x	x	x	x			
10. Pure Monopoly	x	x	x	x			x
11. Monopolistic Competition and Oligopoly	x	x	x	x			x
11W. Technology, R&D, and Efficiency (Web Chapter)	x		x				
12. The Demand for Resources	x		x				
13. Wage Determination	x	x	x	x			x
14. Rent, Interest, and Profit	x		x				
15. Natural Resource and Energy Economics	x		x				
16. Public Finance: Expenditures and Taxes	x	x	x	x			
17. Asymmetric Information, Voting, and Public Choice	x		x				
18. Antitrust Policy and Regulation	x		x				
19. Agriculture: Economics and Policy	x		x				
20. Income Inequality, Poverty, and Discrimination	x	x	x	x			x
21. Health Care	x		x				
22. Immigration	x		x				
23. An Introduction to Macroeconomics	x				x		
24. Measuring Domestic Output and National Income	x	x			x	x	x
25. Economic Growth	x	x			x	x	x
26. Business Cycles, Unemployment, and Inflation	x	x			x	x	x
27. Basic Macroeconomic Relationships	x				x		
28. The Aggregate Expenditures Model	x				x		
29. Aggregate Demand and Aggregate Supply	x	x			x	x	x
30. Fiscal Policy, Deficits, and Debt	x	x			x	x	x
31. Money, Banking, and Financial Institutions	x	x			x	x	x
32. Money Creation	x				x		
33. Interest Rates and Monetary Policy	x	x			x	x	x
34. Financial Economics	x				x		
35. Extending the Analysis of Aggregate Supply	x	x			x	x	
36. Current Issues in Macro Theory and Policy	x				x		
37. International Trade	x	x	x	x	x	x	x
38. The Balance of Payments, Exchange Rates, and Trade Deficits	x	x	x	x	x	x	x
39W. The Economics of Developing Countries (Web Chapter)	x				x		

*Chapter numbers refer to *Economics: Principles, Problems, and Policies*.

*A Red "X" indicates chapters that combine or consolidate content from two or more *Economics* chapters.

MACROECONOMICS: BRIEF EDITION

ISBN   978-0-07-741640-9
MHID   0-07-741640-6

Vice president and editor-in-chief: *Brent Gordon*
Publisher: *Douglas Reiner*
Executive director of development: *Ann Torbert*
Director of digital content: *Douglas Ruby*
Sponsoring Editor: *Scott Smith*
Development editor: *Noelle Bathurst*
Senior marketing manager: *Melissa Larmon*
Senior marketing manager: *Katie White*
Senior project manager: *Harvey Yep*
Lead production supervisor: *Michael R. McCormick*
Interior designer: *Mary Kazak Sander*
Photo researcher: *Keri Johnson*
Senior media project manager: *Kerry Bowler*
Cover design: *Mary Kazak Sander*
Cover image: *Peter Gridley*
Typeface: *10/12 Janson Text 55 Roman*
Compositor: *Aptara®, Inc.*
Printer: *R. R. Donnelley*

Library of Congress Cataloging-in-Publication Data

McConnell, Campbell R.
    Macroeconomics: brief edition / Campbell R. McConnell, Stanley L. Brue,
  Sean M. Flynn. — 2nd ed.
        p. cm. — (The McGraw-Hill economics series)
    Includes index.
    ISBN-13: 978-0-07-741640-9 (alk. paper)
    ISBN-10: 0-07-741640-6 (alk. paper)
    1. Macroeconomics. I. Brue, Stanley L., 1945- II. Flynn, Sean Masaki. III. Title.
  HB172.5.M3742 2013
  339—dc23

                                                            2011052624

To **Mem**, to **Terri** and **Craig**, and to **past instructors**

About the Authors

CAMPBELL R. MCCONNELL earned his Ph.D. from the University of Iowa after receiving degrees from Cornell College and the University of Illinois. He taught at the University of Nebraska–Lincoln from 1953 until his retirement in 1990. He is coauthor of *Economics*, nineteenth edition (McGraw-Hill/Irwin); *Contemporary Labor Economics*, ninth edition (McGraw-Hill/Irwin); and *Essentials of Economics*, second edition (McGraw-Hill/Irwin) and has edited readers for the principles and labor economics courses. He is a recipient of both the University of Nebraska Distinguished Teaching Award and the James A. Lake Academic Freedom Award and is past president of the Midwest Economics Association. Professor McConnell was awarded an honorary Doctor of Laws degree from Cornell College in 1973 and received its Distinguished Achievement Award in 1994. His primary areas of interest are labor economics and economic education. He has an extensive collection of jazz recordings and enjoys reading jazz history.

STANLEY L. BRUE did his undergraduate work at Augustana College (SD) and received its Distinguished Achievement Award in 1991. He received his Ph.D. from the University of Nebraska–Lincoln. He is a professor at Pacific Lutheran University, where he has been honored as a recipient of the Burlington Northern Faculty Achievement Award. Professor Brue has also received the national Leavey Award for excellence in economic education. He has served as national president and chair of the Board of Trustees of Omicron Delta Epsilon International Economics Honorary. He is coauthor of *Economics*, nineteenth edition (McGraw-Hill/Irwin); *Economic Scenes*, fifth edition (Prentice-Hall); *Contemporary Labor Economics*, ninth edition (McGraw-Hill/Irwin); *Essentials of Economics*, second edition (McGraw-Hill/Irwin); and *The Evolution of Economic Thought*, seventh edition (South-Western). For relaxation, he enjoys international travel, attending sporting events, and skiing with family and friends.

SEAN M. FLYNN did his undergraduate work at the University of Southern California before completing his Ph.D. at U.C. Berkeley, where he served as the Head Graduate Student Instructor for the Department of Economics after receiving the Outstanding Graduate Student Instructor Award. He teaches at Scripps College in Claremont, California and is the author of *Economics for Dummies*, second edition (Wiley) and coauthor of *Economics*, nineteenth edition (McGraw-Hill/Irwin) and *Essentials of Economics*, second edition (McGraw-Hill/Irwin). His research interests include finance and behavioral economics. An accomplished martial artist, he has represented the United States in international aikido tournaments and is the author of *Understanding Shodokan Aikido* (Shodokan Press). Other hobbies include running, traveling, and enjoying ethnic food

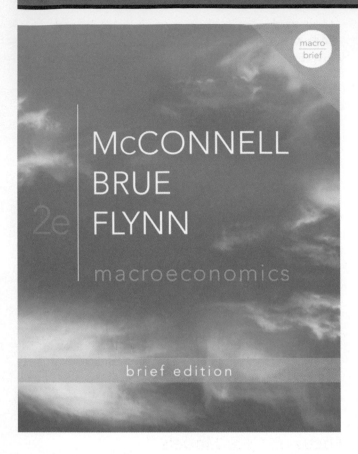

Welcome to *Macroeconomics: Brief Edition*, second edition, the trimmed and edited version of *Economics*, nineteenth edition, the nation's best-selling economics textbook.

Fundamental Objectives

We have three main goals for *Macroeconomics: Brief Edition*:

- Help the beginning student master the principles essential for understanding the economizing problem, specific economic issues, and the policy alternatives.
- Help the student understand and apply the economic perspective and reason accurately and objectively about economic matters.
- Promote a lasting student interest in economics and the economy.

Integrated, Distinct Book

Although *Macroeconomics: Brief Edition* is a spin-off of *Economics*, nineteenth edition, it is not a cut-and-paste book that simply eliminates several chapters of *Economics* and re-orders and renumbers the retained content. We can prepare such books via custom publication. Instead, the *Brief Edition*

is a very concise, highly integrated economics textbook that is distinct in purpose, style, and coverage from *Economics* and its Micro and Macro splits.

What's New and Improved?

One of the benefits of writing a successful text is the opportunity to revise—to delete the outdated and install the new, to rewrite misleading or ambiguous statements, to introduce more relevant illustrations, to improve the organizational structure, and to enhance the learning aids.

We trust that you will agree that we have used this opportunity wisely and fully. Some of the more significant changes include the following:

New and Updated "Illustrating the Idea," "Applying the Analysis," and "Photo Op" Pieces

These examples, applications, and illustrations help drive home central economic ideas in a student-oriented, real-world manner. New content includes a discussion of beekeepers to explain the Coase Theorem, analysis of the effects of rising gas prices on companies like FedEx and Symantec, and an illustration of federal versus state and local spending.

New Discussions of the Financial Crisis and the Recession

In this edition, we have focused on incorporating an analysis of the financial crisis, the recession, and the hesitant recovery into our discussions of macroeconomics. Although we found many ways to work the recession into our macro chapters, we are confident that our basic macroeconomic models will serve equally well in explaining economic recovery and expansion back to the economy's historical growth path. The new inclusions relating to the recession simply help students see the relevance of the models to what they are seeing in the news and perhaps experiencing in their own lives. The overall tone of the book, including the macro, continues to be optimistic with respect to the long-term growth prospects of market economies.

Reworked End-of-Chapter Questions and Problems

We have extensively reworked the end-of-chapter questions, and we have added new problems to each chapter. The questions are analytic and often ask for free responses, whereas the problems are mainly quantitative. We have aligned the questions and problems with the learning objectives presented at the beginning of the chapters. All of the questions and problems are assignable through McGraw Hill's *Connect Economics*, and many contain additional algorithmic variations and can be automatically graded within the system.

Chapter-by-Chapter Changes

In addition to the changes and new features listed above, chapter-specific revisions include:

Chapter 1: Limits, Alternatives, and Choices features updated discussion of the 2007–2009 recession and streamlined coverage of the main concepts.

Chapter 2: The Market System and the Circular Flow includes an improved discussion of the circular flow model, additional coverage of property rights, and updated global data.

Chapter 3: Demand, Supply, and Market Equilibrium begins with a revised introduction to supply and demand and contains additional clarifications of key concepts.

Chapter 4: Market Failures: Public Goods and Externalities features improved coverage of market failures and the distinction between demand-side and supply-side market failures, new topics including consumer and producer surplus and efficiency (deadweight) loss, enhanced discussion of public versus private goods, a new "Illustrating the Idea" piece on the Coase Theorem, and a more complete discussion of correcting for externalities. The coverage of financing public goods and taxation has been moved to Chapter 12 on public finance.

Chapter 5: GDP and Economic Growth includes a revised discussion of GDP accounting and updated coverage of productivity changes.

Chapter 6: Business Cycles, Unemployment, and Inflation contains a new chapter introduction, an improved discussion of business cycles and their causes, and detailed coverage of current unemployment rates and inflation throughout the world.

Chapter 7: Aggregate Demand and Aggregate Supply features detailed discussion, application, and analysis of the recession of 2007–2009.

Chapter 8: Fiscal Policy, Deficits, and Debt includes important updates related to the recession, the subsequent policy response, and the debt debate.

Chapter 9: Money, Banking, and Financial Institutions provides an extensive discussion of the 2007–2008 financial crisis and the postcrisis financial services industry.

Chapter 10: Interest Rates and Monetary Policy features updated coverage of recent U.S. monetary policy, a new explanation of the liquidity trap, a new discussion of the Fed's response to the financial crisis, and a new

"Applying the Analysis" piece on the Fed's balance sheet and its extensive growth.

Chapter 11: Long-Run Aggregate Supply and Aggregate Demand contains streamlined coverage and clarification of the main concepts.

Chapter 12: International Trade and Exchange Rates includes updated material on recent U.S. trade deficits and a revised discussion related to changes in the relative value of the U.S. dollar.

Distinguishing Features

Macroeconomics: Brief Edition includes several features that encourage students to read and retain the content.

Design and Pedagogy

The *Brief Edition* incorporates a single-column design with a host of pedagogical aids, including a strategically placed "To the Student" statement, chapter opening objectives, definitions in the margins, combined tables and graphs, complete chapter summaries, lists of key terms, carefully constructed questions and problems, connections to our website, an appendix on graphs and a web appendix on additional examples of demand and supply, and an extensive glossary.

Focus on Core Models

Macroeconomics: Brief Edition shortens and simplifies explanations where appropriate but stresses the importance of the economic perspective, including explaining and applying core economic models. Our strategy is to develop a limited set of essential models, illustrate them with analogies or anecdotes, explain them thoroughly, and apply them to real-world situations. Eliminating unnecessary graphs and elaborations makes perfect sense in a brief edition, but cutting explanations of the truly fundamental graphs does not. In dealing with the basics, brevity at the expense of clarity is false economy.

We created a student-oriented textbook that draws on the methodological strengths of the discipline and helps students improve their analytical reasoning skills. Regardless of students' eventual occupations, they will discover that such skills are highly valuable in their workplaces.

Illustrating the Idea

Numerous analogies, examples, and anecdotes are included throughout the book to help drive home central economic ideas in a lively, colorful, and easy-to-remember way. For instance, elastic versus inelastic demand is illustrated by comparing the stretch of an Ace bandage and that of a tight rubber tie-down. A piece on Bill Gates, Oprah Winfrey, and Alex Rodriquez illustrates the importance of opportunity costs in decision making. A pizza analogy walks students through the equity-efficiency trade-off, and a discussion of credit cards helps explain what money is and is not. These brief vignettes flow directly from the preceding content and segue to the content that follows, rather than being "boxed off" away from the flow and therefore easily overlooked.

Applying the Analysis

A glance though this book's pages will demonstrate that this is an application-oriented textbook. *Applying the Analysis* pieces immediately follow the development of economic analysis and are part of the flow of the chapters, rather than segregated from the main body discussion in a traditional boxed format. For example, the basics of the economic perspective are applied to why customers choose the shortest checkout lines. McDonald's sandwich "McHits" and "McMisses" over the years apply the concept of consumer sovereignty. The graphics of fiscal policy are followed by a discussion of recent fiscal policy, and the Federal Reserve's role in the economy is demonstrated through an application of its responses to the mortgage debt crisis and the recession. These and many other applications clearly demonstrate the relevance and usefulness of mastering the basic economic principles and models to beginning students.

Photo Ops

Photo sets under the title *Photo Op* are included throughout the book to add visual interest, break up the density, and highlight important distinctions. Just a couple of the many examples are sets of photos on traffic congestion and holiday lighting to contrast negative and positive externalities, and photos of lumber and newly constructed homes to illustrate the difference between intermediate and final goods. Other photo sets illustrate normal versus inferior goods, complements versus substitutes in consumption, homogeneous versus differentiated products, substitute resources versus complementary resources, and more.

Web Buttons

The in-text web buttons (or indicators) merit special mention. Three differing colors of rectangular indicators appear throughout the book, informing readers that complementary content on a subject can be found at our website, **www.mcconnellbrief2e.com.** Scattered throughout the text you'll see:

Worked Problems Written by Norris Peterson of Pacific Lutheran University, these pieces consist of side-by-side computational questions and procedures used

> **WORKED PROBLEMS**
> **W 1.1**
> Budget Lines

to derive the answers. From a student perspective, they provide "cookbook" help for problem solving.

Interactive Graphs These pieces (developed under the supervision of Norris Peterson) depict major graphs and instruct students to shift the curves, observe the outcomes,

> **INTERACTIVE GRAPHS**
> **G 3.1**
> Supply and Demand

and derive relevant generalizations. This hands-on graph work will greatly reinforce the main graphs and their meaning.

Origin of the Ideas These brief histories, written by Randy Grant of Linfield College (OR), examine the origins of major ideas identified in the book. Students will find it interesting to learn about the economists who first

> **ORIGIN OF THE IDEA**
> **O 2.2**
> Specialization/division of labor

developed such ideas as opportunity costs, equilibrium price, elasticity, creative destruction, and comparative advantage.

Global Snapshots

Global Snapshot pieces include bar charts and line graphs that compare data for a particular year or other time period among selected nations. Examples of these lists and comparisons include income per capita, the world's 10 largest corporations, the world's top brand names, the index of economic freedom, the differing economic status of North Korea and South Korea, and so forth. These *Global Snapshots* join other significant international content to help convey that the United States operates in a global economy.

Digital Solutions

McGraw-Hill's *Connect™ Economics*

Less Managing. More Teaching. Greater Learning. McGraw-Hill's *Connect™ Economics* is a web-based assignment and assessment platform that connects students with the tools and resources they'll need to achieve success. *Connect™ Economics* helps prepare students for their future by enabling faster learning, more efficient studying, and higher retention of knowledge. *Connect™ Economics* offers a number of powerful tools and features to make managing assignments easier, so faculty can spend more time teaching. With *Connect™ Economics*, students can engage with their coursework anytime and anywhere, making the learning process more accessible and efficient. *Connect™ Economics* offers the features as described here.

Simple Assignment Management

With *Connect™ Economics*, creating assignments is easier than ever, so you can spend more time teaching and less time managing. The assignment management function enables you to

- Create and deliver assignments easily with selectable end-of-chapter questions and test bank items.
- Streamline lesson planning, student progress reporting, and assignment grading to make classroom management more efficient than ever.
- Go paperless with the e-book and online submission and grading of student assignments.

Smart Grading

When it comes to studying, time is precious. *Connect™ Economics* helps students learn more efficiently by providing feedback and practice material when they need it, where they need it. When it comes to teaching, your time also is precious. The grading function enables you to

- Score assignments automatically, giving students immediate feedback on their work and side-by-side comparisons with correct answers.
- Access and review each response; manually change grades or leave comments for students to review.
- Reinforce classroom concepts with practice tests and instant quizzes.

Instructor Library

The *Connect™ Economics* Instructor Library is your repository for additional resources to improve student engagement in and out of class. You can select and use any asset that enhances your lecture.

Student Study Center

The *Connect™ Economics* Student Study Center is the place for students to access additional resources. The Student Study Center

- Offers students quick access to lectures, practice materials, e-book, and more.
- Provides instant practice material and study questions, easily accessible on the go.
- Gives students access to the Self-Quiz and Study described below.

LearnSmart: Diagnostic and Adaptive Learning of Concepts

Students want to make the best use of their study time. The LearnSmart adaptive self-study technology within *Connect™ Economics* provides students with a seamless combination of practice, assessment, and remediation for every concept in the textbook. LearnSmart's intelligent software adapts to every student response and automatically delivers concepts that advance the student's understanding while reducing time devoted to the concepts already mastered. The result for every student is the fastest path to mastery of the chapter concepts. LearnSmart

- Applies an intelligent concept engine to identify the relationships between concepts and to serve new concepts to each student only when he or she is ready.
- Adapts automatically to each student, so students spend less time on the topics they understand and practice more those they have yet to master.
- Provides continual reinforcement and remediation, but gives only as much guidance as students need.
- Integrates diagnostics as part of the learning experience.
- Enables you to assess which concepts students have efficiently learned on their own, thus freeing class time for more applications and discussion.

Self-Quiz and Study

The Self-Quiz and Study (SQS) connects each student to the learning resources needed for success in the course. For each chapter, students

- Take a practice test to initiate the Self-Quiz and Study.
- Immediately upon completing the practice test, see how their performance compares to chapter Learning Objectives to be achieved within each section of the chapter.
- Receive a Study Plan that recommends specific readings from the text, supplemental study material, and practice work that will improve their understanding and mastery of each learning objective.

Student Progress Tracking

Connect™ Economics keeps instructors informed about how each student, section, and class are performing, allowing for more productive use of lecture and office hours. The progress-tracking function enables you to

- View scored work immediately and track individual or group performance with assignment and grade reports.
- Access an instant view of student or class performance relative to learning objectives.
- Collect data and generate reports required by many accreditation organizations, such as AACSB.

Lecture Capture

Increase the attention paid to lecture discussion by decreasing the attention paid to note taking. For an additional charge, Lecture Capture offers new ways for students to focus on the in-class discussion, knowing they can revisit important topics later. Lecture Capture enables you to

- Record and distribute your lecture with a click of a button.
- Record and index PowerPoint presentations and anything shown on your computer so it is easily searchable, frame by frame.
- Offer access to lectures anytime and anywhere by computer, iPod, or mobile device.
- Increase intent listening and class participation by easing students' concerns about note-taking.

Lecture Capture will make it more likely you will see students' faces, not the tops of their heads.

- To learn more about Tegrity, watch a 2-minute Flash demo at **http://tegritycampus.mhhe.com.**

McGraw-Hill's Connect™ Plus Economics

McGraw-Hill reinvents the textbook learning experience for the modern student with *Connect™ Plus Economics*. A seamless integration of an e-book and *Connect™ Economics*, *Connect™ Plus Economics* provides all of the features mentioned above plus the following:

- An integrated e-book, allowing for anytime, anywhere access to the textbook.
- Dynamic links between the problems or questions you assign to your students and the location in the e-book where that problem or question is covered.
- A powerful search function to pinpoint and connect key concepts in a snap.

In short, *Connect™ Economics* offers you and your students powerful tools and features that optimize your time and energies, enabling you to focus on course content, teaching, and student learning.

For more information about Connect, please visit **www.mcgrawhillconnect.com,** or contact your local McGraw-Hill sales representative.

McGraw-Hill Customer Care Contact Information

At McGraw-Hill, we understand that getting the most from new technology can be challenging. That's why our services don't stop after you purchase our products. You can e-mail our Product Specialists 24 hours a day to get product-training online. Or you can search our knowledge bank of frequently asked questions on our support website. For customer support, call **800-331-5094,** e-mail hmsupport@mcgraw-hill.com, or visit **www.mhhe.com/**

support. One of our technical support analysts will be able to assist you in a timely fashion.

CourseSmart

CourseSmart is a new way for faculty to find and review e-textbooks. It's also a great option for students who are interested in accessing their course materials digitally. CourseSmart offers thousands of the most commonly adopted textbooks across hundreds of courses from a wide variety of higher education publishers. It is the only place for faculty to review and compare the full text of a textbook online. At CourseSmart, students can save up to 50 percent off the cost of a print book, reduce their impact on the environment, and gain access to powerful web tools for learning including full text search, notes and highlighting, and e-mail tools for sharing notes between classmates. Your e-book also includes tech support in case you ever need help. Finding your e-book is easy. Visit **www.CourseSmart.com** and search by title, author, or ISBN.

Online Learning Center

At **www.mcconnellbrief2e.com,** students have access to several learning aids. Along with the Interactive Graphs, Worked Problems, and Origin of the Idea pieces, the student portion of the website includes web-based study questions, self-grading quizzes, and PowerPoint presentations. For math-minded students, there is a "See the Math" section, written by Norris Peterson, where the mathematical details of the concepts in the text can be explored.

The password-protected instructor's side of the Online Learning Center holds all of the supplementary instructor resource materials.

Premium Content

The Premium Content, available at the Online Learning Center, enables students to study and self-test on their computer or on the go.

- One of the world's leading experts on economic education—William Walstad of the University of Nebraska at Lincoln—has prepared the *Study Guide*. Each chapter contains an introductory statement, a checklist of behavioral objectives, an outline, a list of important terms, fill-in questions, problems and projects, objective questions, and discussion questions. Many students will find this "digital tutor" indispensable.

- The Solman Videos, a set of more than 250 minutes of video created by Paul Solman of *The News Hour with Jim Lehrer*, cover core economic concepts such as elasticity, deregulation, and perfect competition.

Study Econ Mobile App

 McGraw-Hill is proud to offer a new mobile study app for students learning economics from McConnell, Brue, and Flynn's *Brief Edition*. The features of the Study Econ app include: flashcards for all key terms, a basic math review, customizable self quizzes, common mistakes, and games. For additional information please refer to the back inside cover of this book. Visit your mobile app store and download a trial version of the McConnell: Brief Edition Study Econ app today!

Supplements for Instructors

Instructor's Manual

Amy Stapp of Cuesta College prepared the Instructor's Manual. It includes chapter learning objectives, outlines, and summaries; numerous teaching suggestions; discussions of "student stumbling blocks;" listings of data and visual aid sources with suggestions for classroom use; and sample chapter quizzes. Available in MS Word on the instructor's side of the website, the manual enables instructors to print portions of the contents, complete with their own additions and alterations, for use as student handouts or in whatever ways they wish.

Test Bank

The *Macroeconomics: Brief Edition* Test Bank, originally written by William Walstad and newly compiled and updated by Mark Wilson of West Virginia University and Jeffrey Phillips of Colby-Sawyer College, contains multiple choice and true-false questions. Each question is tied to a learning objective, topic, and AACSB Assurance of Learning and Bloom's Taxonomy guidelines. While crafting tests in EZTest Online, instructors can use the whole chapter, scramble questions, and narrow the group by selecting the criteria. The Test Bank is also available in MS Word on the instructor's side of the website.

PowerPoint Presentations

Amy Chataginer of Mississippi Gulf Coast Community College created these in-depth slides to accompany lectures. The slides highlight all the main points of each chapter and include all of the figures and key tables from the text, as well as additional discussion notes. Each slide is tied to a learning objective.

Digital Image Library

Every graph and table in the text is available on the website. These figures allow instructors to create their own PowerPoint presentations and lecture materials.

Computerized Test Bank Online

A comprehensive bank of test questions is provided within McGraw-Hill's flexible electronic testing program EZ Test Online, **www.eztestonline.com.** EZ Test Online allows instructors to simply and quickly create tests or quizzes for their students. Instructors can select questions from multiple McGraw-Hill test banks or author their own, and then either print the finalized test or quiz for paper distribution or publish it online for access via the Internet.

This user-friendly program allows instructors to sort questions by format; select questions by learning objectives or Bloom's taxonomy tags; edit existing questions or add new ones; and scramble questions for multiple versions of the same test. Instructors can export their tests for use in WebCT, Blackboard, and PageOut, making it easy to share assessment materials with colleagues, adjuncts, and TAs. Instant scoring and feedback are provided, and EZ Test Online's record book is designed to easily export to instructor gradebooks.

Assurance of Learning Ready

Many educational institutions today are focused on the notion of *assurance of learning*, an important element of many accreditation standards. *Macroeconomics: Brief Edition*, 2nd edition is designed specifically to support your assurance of learning initiatives with a simple, yet powerful, solution.

Each chapter in the book begins with a list of numbered learning objectives, which appear throughout the chapter as well as in the end-of-chapter content. Every Test Bank question for the *Brief Edition* maps to a specific chapter learning objective in the textbook. Each Test Bank question also identifies topic area, level of difficulty, Bloom's Taxonomy level, and AACSB skill area. You can use our Test Bank software, *EZ Test* and *EZ Test Online*, or *Connect Economics* to easily search for learning objectives that directly relate to the learning objectives for your course. You can then use the reporting features of *EZ Test* to aggregate student results in similar fashion, making the collection and presentation of Assurance of Learning data simple and easy.

AACSB Statement

McGraw-Hill/Irwin is a proud corporate member of AACSB International. Understanding the importance and value of AACSB accreditation, *Macroeconomics: Brief Edition* recognizes the curriculum guidelines detailed in the AACSB standards for business accreditation by connecting selected questions in the text and the Test Bank to the general knowledge and skill guidelines in the AACSB standards.

The statements contained in *Macroeconomics: Brief Edition* are provided only as a guide for the users of this textbook. The AACSB leaves content coverage and assessment within the purview of individual schools, the mission of the school, and the faculty. While *Macroeconomics: Brief Edition* and the teaching package make no claim of any specific AACSB qualification or evaluation, we have, within the *Brief Edition*, labeled selected questions according to the six general knowledge and skills areas.

Acknowledgments

We give special thanks to Randy R. Grant of Linfield College, who not only wrote the Origin of the Idea pieces on our website but also served as the content coordinator for the *Brief Edition*. Professor Grant modified and seamlessly incorporated appropriate new content and revisions that the authors made in the nineteenth edition of *Economics* into this second edition of the *Brief Edition*. He also updated the tables and other information in *Macroeconomics: Brief Edition* and made various improvements that he deemed helpful or were suggested to him by the authors, reviewers, and publisher.

We also want to acknowledge Norris Peterson of Pacific Lutheran University, who created the See the Math pieces and the Worked Problem pieces on our website. Professor Peterson also oversaw the development of the Interactive Graph pieces that are on the site. Finally, we wish to acknowledge William Walstad and Tom Barbiero (the coauthor of the Canadian edition of *Economics*) for their ongoing ideas and insights.

We are greatly indebted to an all-star group of professionals at McGraw-Hill—in particular Douglas Reiner, Noelle Bathurst, Harvey Yep, Melissa Larmon, Katie White, and Brent Gordon for their publishing and marketing expertise. We thank Keri Johnson and Michelle Buhr for their selection of Photo Op images. Mary Kazak Sander provided the vibrant interior design and cover.

The second edition has benefited from a number of perceptive formal reviews. The reviewers, listed at the end of the preface, were a rich source of suggestions for this revision. To each of you, and others we may have inadvertently overlooked, thank you for your considerable help in improving *Macroeconomics: Brief Edition*.

Stanley L. Brue
Sean M. Flynn
Campbell R. McConnell

Contributors

Brief Contents

Contents

PART TWO
Price, Quantity, and Efficiency

Chapter 3

Demand, Supply, and Market Equilibrium 52

Chapter 4

Market Failures: Public Goods and Externalities 75

PART THREE
GDP, Growth, and Instability

Chapter 5

GDP and Economic Growth 105

INTRODUCTION

To the Student

This book and its ancillaries contain several features designed to help you learn economics:

- *Icons in the margins*   A glance through the book reveals many pages with web buttons in the margins. Three differing colored rectangular indicators appear throughout the book, alerting you when complementary content on a subject can be found at our Online Learning Center, **www.mcconnellbrief2e.com.** The **Worked Problems** serve as your "cookbook" for problem solving. Numeric problems are presented and then solved, side-by-side, step-by-step. Seeing how the problems are worked will help you solve similar problems on quizzes and exams. Practice hands-on graph work with the **Interactive Graphs** exercises. Manipulate the graphs by clicking on a specific curve and dragging it to a new location. This interaction will enhance your understanding of the underlying concepts. The **Origin of the Idea** pieces trace a particular idea to the person or persons who first developed it.

WORKED PROBLEMS	INTERACTIVE GRAPHS	ORIGIN OF THE IDEA
W 1.1	**G 3.1**	**O 2.2**
Budget lines	Supply and demand	Specialization/division of labor

- *Other Internet aids*   Our Internet site contains many other aids. In the student section at the Online Learning Center, you will find self-testing multiple-choice quizzes, PowerPoint slides, and much more.
- *Appendix on graphs*   To understand the content in this book, you will need to be comfortable with basic graphical analysis and a few quantitative concepts. The appendix (pages 25–30) at the end of Chapter 1 reviews graphing and slopes of curves. Be sure not to skip it.
- *Key terms*   Key terms are set in boldface type within the chapters, defined in the margins, listed at the end of each chapter, and again defined in the Glossary toward the end of the book.
- *"Illustrating the Idea" and "Applying the Analysis"*   These sections flow logically and smoothly from the content that precedes them. They are part and parcel of the development of the ideas and cannot be skipped. Each "Illustrating the Idea" and "Applying the Analysis" section is followed by a question.
- *Questions and Problems*   The end of each chapter features separate sections of Questions and Problems. The Questions are analytic and often ask for free responses, while the Problems are more computational. Each is keyed to a particular learning objective (LO) in the list of LOs at the beginning of the chapter. At the Online Learning Center, there are multiple-choice quizzes and one or more web-based questions for each chapter.
- *Study Guide*   We enthusiastically recommend the *Study Guide* accompanying this text. This "portable tutor" contains not only a broad sampling of various kinds of questions but a host of useful learning aids.

Our two main goals are to help you understand and apply economics and help you improve your analytical skills. An understanding of economics will enable you to comprehend a whole range of economic, social, and political problems that otherwise would seem puzzling and perplexing. Also, your study will enhance reasoning skills that are highly prized in the workplace.

Good luck with your study. We think it will be well worth your time and effort.

After reading this chapter, you should be able to:

1 **Define economics and the features of the economic perspective.**

2 **Describe the role of economic theory in economics.**

3 **Distinguish microeconomics from macroeconomics.**

4 **List the categories of scarce resources and delineate the nature of the economizing problem.**

5 **Apply production possibilities analysis, increasing opportunity costs, and economic growth.**

6 **(Appendix) Understand graphs, curves, and slopes as they relate to economics.**

Limits, Alternatives, and Choices

(An appendix on understanding graphs follows this chapter. If you need a quick review of this mathematical tool, you might benefit by reading the appendix first.)

Economics is about wants and means. Biologically, people need only air, water, food, clothing, and shelter. But in modern society people also desire goods and services that provide a more comfortable or affluent standard of living. We want bottled water, soft drinks, and fruit juices, not just water from the creek. We want salads, burgers, and pizzas, not just berries and nuts. We want jeans, suits, and coats, not just woven reeds. We want apartments, condominiums, or houses, not just mud huts. And, as the saying goes, "That's not the half of it." We also want flat-panel TVs, Internet service, education, homeland security, cell phones, and much more.

Fortunately, society possesses productive resources such as labor and managerial talent, tools and machinery, and land and mineral deposits. These resources, employed in the economic system (or simply the economy), help us produce goods and services that satisfy many of our economic wants. But the blunt reality is that our economic wants far exceed the productive capacity of our scarce (limited) resources. We are forced to make choices. This unyielding truth underlies the definition of **economics,** which is the social science concerned with how individuals, institutions, and society make choices under conditions of scarcity.

The Economic Perspective

economics
The study of how people, institutions, and society make economic choices under conditions of scarcity.

Economists view things through a particular perspective. This **economic perspective,** or economic way of thinking, has several critical and closely interrelated features.

Scarcity and Choice

economic perspective
A viewpoint that envisions individuals and institutions making rational decisions by comparing the marginal benefits and marginal costs of their actions.

From our definition of economics, it is easy to see why economists view the world through the lens of scarcity. Scarce economic resources mean limited goods and services. Scarcity restricts options and demands choices. Because we "can't have it all," we must decide what we will have and what we must forgo.

At the core of economics is the idea that "there is no free lunch." You may be treated to lunch, making it "free" to you, but someone bears a cost. Because all resources are either privately or collectively owned by members of society, ultimately, scarce inputs of land, equipment, farm labor, the labor of cooks and waiters, and managerial talent are required. Because these resources could have been used to produce something else, society sacrifices those other goods and services in making the lunch available. Economists call such sacrifices **opportunity costs:** To obtain more of one thing, society forgoes the opportunity of getting the next best thing. That sacrifice is the opportunity cost of the choice.

opportunity cost
The value of the good, service, or time forgone to obtain something else.

Did Gates, Winfrey, and Rodriguez Make Bad Choices?

The importance of opportunity costs in decision making is illustrated by different choices people make with respect to college. College graduates usually earn about 50 percent more during their lifetimes than persons with just high school diplomas. For most capable students, "Go to college, stay in college, and earn a degree" is very sound advice.

Yet Microsoft cofounder Bill Gates and talk-show host Oprah Winfrey* both dropped out of college, and baseball star Alex Rodriguez ("A-Rod") never even bothered to enroll. What were they thinking? Unlike most students, Gates faced enormous opportunity costs for staying in college. He had a vision for his company, and his starting work young helped ensure Microsoft's success. Similarly, Winfrey landed a spot in local television news when she was a teenager, eventually producing and starring in the *Oprah Winfrey Show* when she was 32 years old. Getting a degree in her twenties might have interrupted the string of successes that made her famous talk show possible. And Rodriguez knew that professional athletes have short careers. Therefore, going to college directly after high school would have taken away 4 years of his peak earning potential.

So Gates, Winfrey, and Rodriguez understood opportunity costs and made their choices accordingly. The size of opportunity costs greatly matters in making individual decisions.

QUESTION: Professional athletes sometimes return to college after they retire from professional sports. How does that college decision relate to opportunity costs?

* Winfrey eventually went back to school and earned a degree from Tennessee State University when she was in her thirties.

Purposeful Behavior

Economics assumes that human behavior reflects "rational self-interest." Individuals look for and pursue opportunities to increase their **utility:** pleasure, happiness, or satisfaction. They allocate their time, energy, and money to maximize their satisfaction. Because they weigh costs and benefits, their decisions are "purposeful" or "rational," not "random" or "chaotic."

Consumers are purposeful in deciding what goods and services to buy. Business firms are purposeful in deciding what products to produce and how to produce them. Government entities are purposeful in deciding what public services to provide and how to finance them.

"Purposeful behavior" does not assume that people and institutions are immune from faulty logic and therefore are perfect decision makers. They sometimes make mistakes. Nor does it mean that people's decisions are unaffected by emotion or the decisions of those around them. People sometimes are impulsive or emulative. "Purposeful behavior" simply means that people make decisions with some desired outcome in mind.

Nor is rational self-interest the same as selfishness. We will find that increasing one's own wage, rent, interest, or profit normally requires identifying and satisfying somebody else's want. Also, many people make personal sacrifices to others without expecting any monetary reward. They contribute time and money to charities because they derive pleasure from doing so. Parents help pay for their children's education for the same reason. These self-interested, but unselfish, acts help maximize the givers' satisfaction as much as any personal purchase of goods or services. Self-interested behavior is simply behavior designed to increase personal satisfaction, however it may be derived.

utility
The satisfaction obtained from consuming a good or service.

ORIGIN OF THE IDEA

O 1.2
Utility

Marginalism: Comparing Benefits and Costs

The economic perspective focuses largely on **marginal analysis**—comparisons of marginal benefits and marginal costs. To economists, "marginal" means "extra," "additional," or "a change in." Most choices or decisions involve changes in the status quo, meaning the existing state of affairs.

Should you attend school for another year? Should you study an extra hour for an exam? Should you supersize your fries? Similarly, should a business expand or reduce its output? Should government increase or decrease its funding for a missile defense system?

Each option involves marginal benefits and, because of scarce resources, marginal costs. In making choices rationally, the decision maker must compare those two amounts. Example: You and your fiancée are shopping for an engagement ring. Should you buy a $\frac{1}{2}$-carat diamond, a $\frac{5}{8}$-carat diamond, a $\frac{3}{4}$-carat diamond, a 1-carat

marginal analysis
The comparison of marginal ("extra" or "additional") benefits and marginal costs, usually for decision making.

ORIGIN OF THE IDEA

O 1.3

Marginal analysis

diamond, or something even larger? The marginal cost of a larger-size diamond is the added expense beyond the cost of the smaller-size diamond. The marginal benefit is the perceived greater lifetime pleasure (utility) from the larger-size stone. If the marginal benefit of the larger diamond exceeds its marginal cost (and you can afford it), buy the larger stone. But if the marginal cost is more than the marginal benefit, you should buy the smaller diamond instead—even if you can afford the larger stone!

In a world of scarcity, the decision to obtain the marginal benefit associated with some specific option always includes the marginal cost of forgoing something else. The money spent on the larger-size diamond means forgoing some other product. An opportunity cost, the value of the next best thing forgone, is always present whenever a choice is made.

APPLYING THE ANALYSIS

Fast-Food Lines

The economic perspective is useful in analyzing all sorts of behaviors. Consider an everyday example: the behavior of fast-food customers. When customers enter the restaurant, they go to the shortest line, believing that line will minimize their time cost of obtaining food. They are acting purposefully; time is limited, and people prefer using it in some way other than standing in a long line.

If one fast-food line is temporarily shorter than other lines, some people will move to that line. These movers apparently view the time saving from the shorter line (marginal benefit) as exceeding the cost of moving from their present line (marginal cost). The line switching tends to equalize line lengths. No further movement of customers between lines occurs once all lines are about equal.

Fast-food customers face another cost-benefit decision when a clerk opens a new station at the counter. Should they move to the new station or stay put? Those who shift to the new line decide that the time saving from the move exceeds the extra cost of physically moving. In so deciding, customers must also consider just how quickly they can get to the new station compared with others who may be contemplating the same move. (Those who hesitate in this situation are lost!)

Customers at the fast-food establishment do not have perfect information when they select lines. Thus, not all decisions turn out as expected. For example, you might enter a short line and find someone in front of you is ordering hamburgers and fries for 40 people in the Greyhound bus parked out back (and the employee is a trainee)! Nevertheless, at the time you made your decision, you thought it was optimal.

Finally, customers must decide what food to order when they arrive at the counter. In making their choices, they again compare marginal costs and marginal benefits in attempting to obtain the greatest personal satisfaction for their expenditure.

Economists believe that what is true for the behavior of customers at fast-food restaurants is true for economic behavior in general. Faced with an array of choices, consumers, workers, and businesses rationally compare marginal costs and marginal benefits in making decisions.

QUESTION: Have you ever gone to a fast-food restaurant only to observe long lines and then leave? Use the economic perspective to explain your behavior.

Theories, Principles, and Models

Like the physical and life sciences, as well as other social sciences, economics relies on the **scientific method.** That procedure consists of several elements:

- Observing real-world behavior and outcomes.
- Based on those observations, formulating a possible explanation of cause and effect (hypothesis).
- Testing this explanation by comparing the outcomes of specific events to the outcome predicted by the hypothesis.
- Accepting, rejecting, or modifying the hypothesis, based on these comparisons.
- Continuing to test the hypothesis against the facts. As favorable results accumulate, the hypothesis evolves into a *theory*. A very well-tested and widely accepted theory is referred to as a *law* or *principle*. Combinations of such laws or principles are incorporated into *models*, which are simplified representations of how something works, such as a market or segment of the economy.

Economists develop theories of the behavior of individuals (consumers, workers) and institutions (businesses, governments) engaged in the production, exchange, and consumption of goods and services. Economic theories and **principles** are statements about economic behavior or the economy that enable prediction of the probable effects of certain actions. They are "purposeful simplifications." The full scope of economic reality itself is too complex and bewildering to be understood as a whole. In developing theories and principles, economists remove the clutter and simplify.

Economic principles and models are highly useful in analyzing economic behavior and understanding how the economy operates. They are the tools for ascertaining cause and effect (or action and outcome) within the economic system. Good theories do a good job of explaining and predicting. They are supported by facts concerning how individuals and institutions actually behave in producing, exchanging, and consuming goods and services.

There are some other things you should know about economic principles:

- *Generalizations*   Economic principles are *generalizations* relating to economic behavior or to the economy itself. Economic principles are expressed as the tendencies of typical or average consumers, workers, or business firms. For example, economists say that consumers buy more of a particular product when its price falls. Economists recognize that some consumers may increase their purchases by a large amount, others by a small amount, and a few not at all. This "price-quantity" principle, however, holds for the typical consumer and for consumers as a group.
- *Other-things-equal assumption*   Like other scientists, economists use the *ceteris paribus* or **other-things-equal assumption** to construct their theories. They assume that all variables except those under immediate consideration are held constant for a particular analysis. For example, consider the relationship between the price of Pepsi and the amount of it purchased. It helps to assume that, of all the factors that might influence the amount of Pepsi purchased (for example, the price of Pepsi, the price of Coca-Cola, and consumer incomes and preferences), only the price of Pepsi varies. The economist can then focus on the relationship between the price of Pepsi and purchases of Pepsi in isolation without being confused by changes in other variables.
- *Graphical expression*   Many economic models are expressed graphically. Be sure to read the special appendix at the end of this chapter as a review of graphs.

scientific method
The systematic pursuit of knowledge by observing facts and formulating and testing hypotheses to obtain theories, principles, and laws.

principles
Statements about economic behavior that enable prediction of the probable effects of certain actions.

other-things-equal assumption
The assumption that factors other than those being considered do not change.

ORIGIN OF THE IDEA

O 1.4

Ceteris paribus

Microeconomics and Macroeconomics

Economists develop economic principles and models at two levels.

Microeconomics

microeconomics
The part of economics concerned with individual decision-making units, such as a consumer, a worker, or a business firm.

Microeconomics is the part of economics concerned with decision making by individual consumers, households, and business firms. At this level of analysis, we observe the details of their behavior under a figurative microscope. We measure the price of a specific product, the number of workers employed by a single firm, the revenue or income of a particular firm or household, or the expenditures of a specific firm, government entity, or family.

Macroeconomics

macroeconomics
The part of economics concerned with the economy as a whole or major components of the economy.

aggregate
A collection of specific economic units treated as if they were one unit.

Macroeconomics examines either the economy as a whole or its basic subdivisions or aggregates, such as the government, household, and business sectors. An **aggregate** is a collection of specific economic units treated as if they were one unit. Therefore, we might lump together the millions of consumers in the U.S. economy and treat them as if they were one huge unit called "consumers."

In using aggregates, macroeconomics seeks to obtain an overview, or general outline, of the structure of the economy and the relationships of its major aggregates. Macroeconomics speaks of such economic measures as total output, total employment, total income, aggregate expenditures, and the general level of prices in analyzing various economic problems. Very little attention is given to specific units making up the various aggregates.

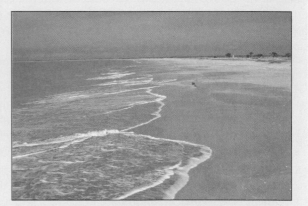

PHOTO OP   Micro versus Macro

Figuratively, microeconomics examines the sand, rock, and shells, not the beach; in contrast, macroeconomics examines the beach, not the sand, rocks, and shells.

Individual's Economic Problem

economic problem
The need for individuals and society to make choices because wants exceed means.

It is clear from our previous discussion that both individuals and society face an **economic problem:** They need to make choices because economic wants are unlimited, but the means (income, time, resources) for satisfying those wants are limited.

Let's first look at the economic problem faced by individuals. To explain the idea, we will construct a very simple microeconomic model.

Limited Income

We all have a finite amount of income, even the wealthiest among us. Sure Bill Gates earns a bit more than the rest of us, but he still has to decide how to spend his money! And the majority of us have much more limited means. Our income comes to us in the form of wages, interest, rent, and profit, although we may also receive money from government programs or family members. As Global Snapshot 1.1 shows, the average income of Americans in 2009 was $46,360. In the poorest nations, it was less than $500.

Unlimited Wants

For better or worse, most people have virtually unlimited wants. We desire various goods and services that provide utility. Our wants extend over a wide range of products, from *necessities* (food, shelter, clothing) to *luxuries* (perfumes, yachts, sports cars). Some wants such as basic food, clothing, and shelter have biological roots. Other wants, for example, specific kinds of food, clothing, and shelter, arise from the conventions and customs of society.

Over time, economic wants tend to change and multiply, fueled by new and improved products. Only recently have people wanted iPods, Internet service, digital cameras, or camera phones because those products did not exist a few decades ago. Also, the satisfaction of certain wants may trigger others: The acquisition of a Ford Focus or a Honda Civic has been known to whet the appetite for a Lexus or a Mercedes.

GLOBAL SNAPSHOT 1.1

Average Income, Selected Nations

Average income (total income/population) and therefore typical budget constraints vary greatly among nations.

Country	Per Capita Income, 2009*
Switzerland	$65,430
United States	46,360
France	42,620
Japan	38,080
South Korea	19,830
Mexico	8,960
Brazil	8,070
China	3,650
Nigeria	1,190
Pakistan	1,000
Rwanda	490
Liberia	160

*U.S. dollars.
Source: World Bank, **www.worldbank.org**.

© Bill Aron/PhotoEdit

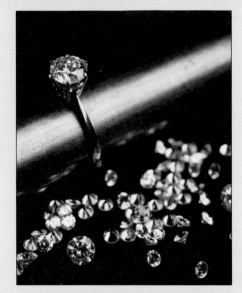

© F. Schussler/PhotoLink/Getty Images

PHOTO OP Necessities versus Luxuries

Economic wants include both necessities and luxuries. Each type of item provides utility to the buyer.

Services, as well as goods, satisfy our wants. Car repair work, the removal of an inflamed appendix, legal and accounting advice, and haircuts all satisfy human wants. Actually, we buy many goods, such as automobiles and washing machines, for the services they render. The differences between goods and services are often smaller than they appear to be.

For most people, the desires for goods and services cannot be fully satisfied. Bill Gates may have all that he wants for himself, but his massive charitable giving suggests that he keenly wants better health care for the world's poor. Our desires for a *particular* good or service can be satisfied; over a short period of time we can surely obtain enough toothpaste or pasta. And one appendectomy is plenty. But our broader desire for more goods and services and higher-quality goods and services seems to be another story.

Because we have only limited income but seemingly insatiable wants, it is in our self-interest to economize: to pick and choose goods and services that maximize our satisfaction, given the limitations we face.

A Budget Line

budget line
A line that shows various combinations of two products a consumer can purchase with a specific money income, given the products' prices.

The economic problem facing individuals can be depicted as a **budget line** (or, more technically, *budget constraint*). It is a schedule or curve that shows various combinations of two products a consumer can purchase with a specific money income.

To understand this idea, suppose that you received a Barnes & Noble gift card as a birthday present. The $120 card is soon to expire. You take the card to the store and confine your purchase decisions to two alternatives: DVDs and paperback books.

FIGURE 1.1 A consumer's budget line. The budget line (or budget constraint) shows all the combinations of any two products that can be purchased, given the prices of the products and the consumer's money income.

The Budget Line: Whole-Unit Combinations of DVDs and Paperback Books Attainable with an Income of $120		
Units of DVDs (Price = $20)	Units of Books (Price = $10)	Total Expenditure
6	0	$120 = ($120 + $0)
5	2	$120 = ($100 + $20)
4	4	$120 = ($80 + $40)
3	6	$120 = ($60 + $60)
2	8	$120 = ($40 + $80)
1	10	$120 = ($20 + $100)
0	12	$120 = ($0 + $120)

DVDs are $20 each, and paperback books are $10 each. Your purchase options are shown in the table in Figure 1.1.

At one extreme, you might spend all of your $120 "income" on 6 DVDs at $20 each and have nothing left to spend on books. Or, by giving up 2 DVDs and thereby gaining $40, you can have 4 DVDs at $20 each and 4 books at $10 each. And so on to the other extreme, at which you could buy 12 books at $10 each, spending your entire gift card on books with nothing left to spend on DVDs.

The graph in Figure 1.1 shows the budget line. As elsewhere in this book, we represent discrete (separate element) numbers in tables as points on continuous-data smooth curves. Therefore, note that the line (curve) in the graph is not restricted to whole units of DVDs and books as is the table. Every point on the line represents a possible combination of DVDs and books, including fractional quantities. The slope of the graphed budget line measures the ratio of the price of books (P_b) to the price of DVDs (P_{dvd}); more precisely, the slope is $P_b/P_{dvd} = \$-10/\$+20 = -\frac{1}{2}$ or $-.5$. So you must forgo 1 DVD (measured on the vertical axis) to buy 2 books (measured on the horizontal axis). This yields a slope of $-\frac{1}{2}$ or $-.5$.

The budget line illustrates several ideas.

Attainable and Unattainable Combinations All the combinations of DVDs and books on or inside the budget line are *attainable* from the $120 of money income. You can afford to buy, for example, 3 DVDs at $20 each and 6 books at $10 each. You also can obviously afford to buy 2 DVDs and 5 books, thereby using up only $90 of the $120 available on your gift card. But to achieve maximum utility, you will want to spend the full $120. The budget line shows all combinations that cost exactly the full $120.

In contrast, all combinations beyond the budget line are *unattainable*. The $120 limit simply does not allow you to purchase, for example, 5 DVDs at $20 each and 5 books at $10 each. That $150 expenditure would clearly exceed the $120 limit. In Figure 1.1, the attainable combinations are on and within the budget line; the unattainable combinations are beyond the budget line.

Trade-offs and Opportunity Costs The budget line in Figure 1.1 illustrates the idea of trade-offs arising from limited income. To obtain more DVDs, you have to

ORIGIN OF THE IDEA

O 1.5

Opportunity cost

give up some books. For example, to acquire the first DVD, you trade off 2 books. So the opportunity cost of the first DVD is 2 books. To obtain the second DVD, the opportunity cost is also 2 books. The straight-line budget constraint, with its constant slope, indicates **constant opportunity cost.** That is, the opportunity cost of 1 extra DVD remains the same (= 2 books) as more DVDs are purchased. And, in reverse, the opportunity cost of 1 extra book does not change (= $\frac{1}{2}$ DVD) as more books are bought.

Choice Limited income forces people to choose what to buy and what to forgo to fulfill wants. You will select the combination of DVDs and paperback books that you think is "best." That is, you will evaluate your marginal benefits and your marginal costs (here, product price) to make choices that maximize your satisfaction. Other people, with the same $120 gift card, would undoubtedly make different choices.

Income Changes The location of the budget line varies with money income. An increase in money income shifts the budget line to the right; a decrease in money income shifts it to the left. To verify this, recalculate the table in Figure 1.1, assuming the card value (income) is (a) $240 and (b) $60, and plot the new budget lines in the graph. No wonder people like to have more income: That shifts their budget lines outward and enables them to buy more goods and services. But even with more income, people will still face spending trade-offs, choices, and opportunity costs.

Society's Economic Problem

Society must also make choices under conditions of scarcity. It, too, faces an economic problem. Should it devote more of its limited resources to the criminal justice system (police, courts, and prisons) or to education (teachers, books, and schools)? If it decides to devote more resources to both, what other goods and services does it forgo? Health care? Homeland security? Energy development?

Scarce Resources

Society's economic resources are limited or scarce. By **economic resources** we mean all natural, human, and manufactured resources that go into the production of goods and services. That includes the entire set of factory and farm buildings and all the equipment, tools, and machinery used to produce manufactured goods and agricultural products; all transportation and communication facilities; all types of labor; and land and mineral resources.

Resource Categories

Economists classify economic resources into four general categories.

Land Land means much more to the economist than it does to most people. To the economist **land** includes all natural resources ("gifts of nature") used in the production process. These include mineral and oil deposits, arable land, forests, and water resources.

Labor The resource **labor** consists of the physical actions and mental activities that people contribute to the production of goods and services. The work-related activities of a logger, retail clerk, machinist, teacher, professional football player, and nuclear physicist all fall under the general heading "labor."

---

constant opportunity cost
An opportunity cost that remains the same as consumers shift purchases from one product to another along a straight-line budget line.

WORKED PROBLEMS

W 1.1
Budget lines

economic resources
The land, labor, capital, and entrepreneurial ability used in the production of goods and services.

land
Natural resources ("gifts of nature") used to produce goods and services.

labor
The physical and mental talents and efforts of people used to produce goods and services.

Capital For economists, **capital** (or *capital goods*) includes all manufactured aids used in producing consumer goods and services. Included are all factory, storage, transportation, and distribution facilities, as well as all tools and machinery. Economists use the term **investment** to describe spending that pays for the production and accumulation of capital goods.

Capital goods differ from consumer goods because consumer goods satisfy wants directly, while capital goods do so indirectly by aiding the production of consumer goods. For example, large commercial baking ovens (capital goods) help make loaves of bread (consumer goods). Note that the term "capital" as used by economists refers not to money but to tools, machinery, and other productive equipment. Because money produces nothing, economists do not include it as an economic resource. Money (or money capital or financial capital) is simply a means for purchasing goods and services, including capital goods.

Entrepreneurial Ability Finally, there is the special human resource, distinct from labor, called **entrepreneurial ability.** The entrepreneur performs several socially useful functions:

- The entrepreneur takes the initiative in combining the resources of land, labor, and capital to produce a good or a service. Both a spark plug and a catalyst, the entrepreneur is the driving force behind production and the agent who combines the other resources in what is hoped will be a successful business venture.
- The entrepreneur makes the strategic business decisions that set the course of an enterprise.
- The entrepreneur innovates. He or she commercializes new products, new production techniques, or even new forms of business organization.
- The entrepreneur bears risk. Innovation is risky, as nearly all new products and ideas are subject to the possibility of failure as well as success. Progress would cease without entrepreneurs who are willing to take on risk by devoting their time, effort, and ability—as well as their own money and the money of others—to commercializing new products and ideas that may enhance society's standard of living.

capital
Human-made resources (buildings, machinery, and equipment) used to produce goods and services.

investment
The purchase of capital resources.

entrepreneurial ability
The human talent that combines the other resources to produce a product, make strategic decisions, and bear risks.

factors of production
Economic resources: land, labor, capital, and entrepreneurial ability.

© Lester Lefkowitz/CORBIS   © Lance Nelson/Stock Photos/zefa/CORBIS   © Creatas/PunchStock   © Neville Elder/Corbis

PHOTO OP Economic Resources

Land, labor, capital, and entrepreneurial ability all contribute to producing goods and services.

Because land, labor, capital, and entrepreneurial ability are combined to produce goods and services, they are called the **factors of production** or simply inputs.

Production Possibilities Model

Society uses its scarce resources to produce goods and services. The alternatives and choices it faces can best be understood through a macroeconomic model of production possibilities. To keep things simple, we assume:

- *Full employment* The economy is employing all of its available resources.
- *Fixed resources* The quantity and quality of the factors of production are fixed.
- *Fixed technology* The state of technology (the methods used to produce output) is constant.
- *Two goods* The economy is producing only two goods: food products and manufacturing equipment. Food products symbolize **consumer goods,** products that satisfy our wants directly; manufacturing equipment symbolizes **capital goods,** products that satisfy our wants indirectly by making possible more efficient production of consumer goods.

consumer goods
Products and services that directly satisfy consumer wants.

capital goods
Items that are used to produce other goods and therefore do not directly satisfy consumer wants.

Production Possibilities Table

A production possibilities table lists the different combinations of two products that can be produced with a specific set of resources, assuming full employment. Figure 1.2 contains such a table for a simple economy that is producing food products and manufacturing equipment; the data are, of course, hypothetical. At alternative A, this economy would be devoting all its available resources to the production of manufacturing equipment (capital goods); at alternative E, all resources would go to food-product production (consumer goods). Those alternatives are unrealistic extremes; an economy typically produces both capital goods and consumer goods, as in B, C, and D. As we move from alternative A to E, we increase the production of food products at the expense of the production of manufacturing equipment.

Because consumer goods satisfy our wants directly, any movement toward E looks tempting. In producing more food products, society increases the satisfaction of its current wants. But there is a cost: More food products mean less manufacturing equipment.

FIGURE 1.2 **The production possibilities curve.** Each point on the production possibilities curve represents some maximum combination of two products that can be produced if resources are fully and efficiently employed. When an economy is operating on the curve, more manufacturing equipment means less food products, and vice versa. Limited resources and a fixed technology make any combination of manufacturing equipment and food products lying outside the curve (such as at *W*) unattainable. Points inside the curve are attainable, but they indicate that full employment is not being realized.

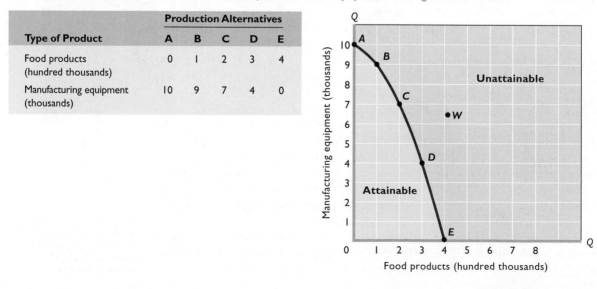

Type of Product	Production Alternatives				
	A	**B**	**C**	**D**	**E**
Food products (hundred thousands)	0	1	2	3	4
Manufacturing equipment (thousands)	10	9	7	4	0

This shift of resources to consumer goods catches up with society over time because the stock of capital goods expands more slowly, thereby reducing potential future production. By moving toward alternative E, society chooses "more now" at the expense of "much more later."

By moving toward A, society chooses to forgo current consumption, thereby freeing up resources that can be used to increase the production of capital goods. By building up its stock of capital this way, society will have greater future production and, therefore, greater future consumption. By moving toward A, society is choosing "more later" at the cost of "less now."

Generalization: At any point in time, a fully employed economy must sacrifice some of one good to obtain more of another good. Scarce resources prohibit such an economy from having more of both goods. Society must choose among alternatives. There is no such thing as a free bag of groceries or a free manufacturing machine. Having more of one thing means having less of something else.

Production Possibilities Curve

The data presented in a production possibilities table can also be shown graphically. We arbitrarily represent the economy's output of capital goods (here, manufacturing equipment) on the vertical axis and the output of consumer goods (here, food products) on the horizontal axis, as shown in Figure 1.2.

Each point on the **production possibilities curve** represents some maximum output of the two products. The curve is a "constraint" because it shows the limit of attainable outputs. Points on the curve are attainable as long as the economy uses all its available resources. Points lying inside the curve are also attainable, but they reflect less total output and therefore are not as desirable as points on the curve. Points inside the curve imply that the economy could have more of both manufacturing equipment and food products if it achieved full employment. Points lying beyond the production possibilities curve, like *W*, would represent a greater output than the output at any point on the curve. Such points, however, are unattainable with the current availability of resources and technology.

Law of Increasing Opportunity Costs

Figure 1.2 clearly shows that more food products mean less manufacturing equipment. The number of units of manufacturing equipment that must be given up to obtain another unit of food products, of course, is the opportunity cost of that unit of food products.

In moving from alternative A to alternative B in the table in Figure 1.2, the cost of 1 additional unit of food products is 1 less unit of manufacturing equipment. But when additional units are considered—B to C, C to D, and D to E—an important economic principle is revealed: The opportunity cost of each additional unit of food products is greater than the opportunity cost of the preceding one. When we move from A to B, just 1 unit of manufacturing equipment is sacrificed for 1 more unit of food products; but in going from B to C, we sacrifice 2 additional units of manufacturing equipment for 1 more unit of food products; then 3 more of manufacturing equipment for 1 more of food products; and finally 4 for 1. Conversely, confirm that as we move from E to A, the cost of an additional unit of manufacturing equipment (on average) is $\frac{1}{4}$, $\frac{1}{3}$, $\frac{1}{2}$, and 1 unit of food products, respectively, for the four successive moves.

Our example illustrates the **law of increasing opportunity costs:** The more of a product that society produces, the greater is the opportunity cost of obtaining an extra unit.

INTERACTIVE GRAPHS

G 1.1

Production possibilities curve

production possibilities curve
A curve showing the different combinations of goods and services that can be produced in a fully employed economy, assuming the available supplies of resources and technology are fixed.

law of increasing opportunity costs
The principle that as the production of a good increases, the opportunity cost of producing an additional unit rises.

Shape of the Curve The law of increasing opportunity costs is reflected in the shape of the production possibilities curve: The curve is bowed out from the origin of the graph. Figure 1.2 shows that when the economy moves from *A* to *E*, it must give up successively larger amounts of manufacturing equipment (1, 2, 3, and 4) to acquire equal increments of food products (1, 1, 1, and 1). This is shown in the slope of the production possibilities curve, which becomes steeper as we move from *A* to *E*.

Economic Rationale The law of increasing opportunity costs is driven by the fact that economic resources are not completely adaptable to alternative uses. Many resources are better at producing one type of good than at producing others. Consider land. Some land is highly suited to growing the ingredients necessary for pizza production. But as pizza production expands, society has to start using land that is less bountiful for farming. Other land is rich in mineral deposits and therefore well-suited to producing the materials needed to make manufacturing equipment. That land will be the first land devoted to the production of manufacturing equipment. But as society steps up the production of manufacturing equipment, it must push resources that are less and less suited to making that equipment into its production.

If we start at *A* and move to *B* in Figure 1.2, we can shift resources whose productivity is relatively high in food production and low in manufacturing equipment. But as we move from *B* to *C*, *C* to *D*, and so on, resources highly productive of food products become increasingly scarce. To get more food products, resources whose productivity in manufacturing equipment is relatively great will be needed. It will take increasingly more of such resources, and hence greater sacrifices of manufacturing equipment, to achieve each 1-unit increase in food products. This lack of perfect flexibility, or interchangeability, on the part of resources is the cause of increasing opportunity costs for society.

Optimal Allocation

Of all the attainable combinations of food products and manufacturing equipment on the curve in Figure 1.2, which is optimal (best)? That is, what specific quantities of resources should be allocated to food products and what specific quantities to manufacturing equipment in order to maximize satisfaction?

Recall that economic decisions center on comparisons of marginal benefits (MB) and marginal costs (MC). Any economic activity should be expanded as long as marginal benefit exceeds marginal cost and should be reduced if marginal cost exceeds marginal benefit. The optimal amount of the activity occurs where MB = MC. Society needs to make a similar assessment about its production decision.

Consider food products. We already know from the law of increasing opportunity costs that the marginal cost of additional units of food products will rise as more units are produced. At the same time, we need to recognize that the extra or marginal benefits that come from producing and consuming food products decline with each successive unit of food products. Consequently, each successive unit of food products brings with it both increasing marginal costs and decreasing marginal benefits.

The optimal quantity of food production is indicated by the intersection of the MB and MC curves: 200,000 units in Figure 1.3. Why is this amount the optimal quantity? If only 100,000 units of food products were produced, the marginal benefit of an extra unit of them would exceed its marginal cost. In money terms, MB is $15, while MC is only $5. When society gains something worth $15 at a marginal cost of only $5, it is better off. In Figure 1.3, net gains of decreasing amounts can be realized until food-product production has been increased to 200,000.

In contrast, the production of 300,000 units of food products is excessive. There the MC of an added unit is $15 and its MB is only $5. This means that 1 unit of food

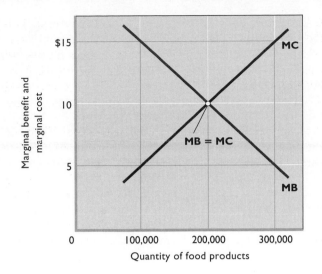

products is worth only $5 to society but costs it $15 to obtain. This is a losing proposition for society!

So resources are being efficiently allocated to any product when the marginal benefit and marginal cost of its output are equal (MB = MC). Suppose that by applying the above analysis to manufacturing equipment, we find its optimal (MB = MC) quantity is 7000. This would mean that alternative *C* (200,000 units of food products and 7000 units of manufacturing equipment) on the production possibilities curve in Figure 1.2 would be optimal for this economy.

The Economics of War

Production possibilities analysis is helpful in assessing the costs and benefits of waging the war on terrorism, including the wars in Afghanistan and Iraq. At the end of 2010, the estimated cost of these efforts exceeded $1.05 trillion.

If we categorize all of U.S. production as either "defense goods" or "civilian goods," we can measure them on the axes of a production possibilities diagram such as that shown in Figure 1.2. The opportunity cost of using more resources for defense goods is the civilian goods sacrificed. In a fully employed economy, more defense goods are achieved at the opportunity cost of fewer civilian goods—health care, education, pollution control, personal computers, houses, and so on. The cost of waging war is the other goods forgone. The benefits of these activities are numerous and diverse but clearly include the gains from protecting against future loss of American lives, assets, income, and well-being.

Society must assess the marginal benefit (MB) and marginal cost (MC) of additional defense goods to determine their optimal amounts—where to locate on the defense goods–civilian goods production possibilities curve. Although estimating marginal benefits and marginal costs is an imprecise art, the MB-MC framework is a useful way of approaching choices. Allocative efficiency requires that society expand production of defense goods until MB = MC.

The events of September 11, 2001, and the future threats they posed increased the perceived marginal benefits of defense goods. If we label the horizontal axis in Figure 1.3 "defense goods," and draw in a rightward shift of the MB curve, you will see that the optimal quantity of defense goods rises. In view of the concerns relating to September 11, the United States allocated more of its resources to defense. But the MB-MC analysis also reminds us we can spend too much on defense, as well as too little. The United States should not expand defense goods beyond the point where MB = MC. If it does, it will be sacrificing civilian goods of greater value than the defense goods obtained.

QUESTION: Would society's costs of war be lower if it drafted soldiers at low pay rather than attracted them voluntarily to the military through market pay?

Unemployment, Growth, and the Future

In the depths of the Great Depression of the 1930s, one-quarter of U.S. workers were unemployed and one-third of U.S. production capacity was idle. Subsequent downturns have been much less severe. During the deep 2007–2009 recession, for instance, production fell by a comparably smaller 5.1 percent, and 1 in 10 workers was without a job.

Almost all nations have experienced widespread unemployment and unused production capacity from business downturns at one time or another. Since 2000, for example, several nations—including Argentina, Japan, Mexico, Germany, and South Korea—have had economic downturns and unemployment.

How do these realities relate to the production possibilities model? Our analysis and conclusions change if we relax the assumption that all available resources are fully employed. The five alternatives in the table of Figure 1.2 represent maximum outputs; they illustrate the combinations of food products and manufacturing equipment that can be produced when the economy is operating at full employment. With unemployment, this economy would produce less than each alternative shown in the table.

Graphically, we represent situations of unemployment by points inside the original production possibilities curve (reproduced in Figure 1.4). Point *U* is one such point. Here the economy is falling short of the various maximum combinations of food products and manufacturing equipment represented by the points on the production possibilities curve. The arrows in Figure 1.4 indicate three possible paths back to full employment. A move toward full employment would yield a greater output of one or both products.

A Growing Economy

When we drop the assumptions that the quantity and quality of resources and technology are fixed, the production possibilities curve shifts positions, and the potential maximum output of the economy changes.

Increases in Resource Supplies Although resource supplies are fixed at any specific moment, they change over time. For example, a nation's growing population brings about increases in the supplies of labor and entrepreneurial ability. Also, labor

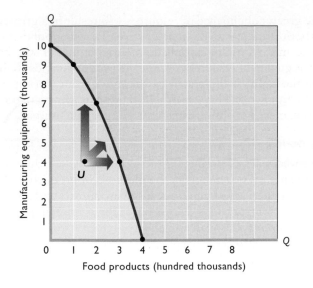

FIGURE 1.4 Unemployment and the production possibilities curve. Any point inside the production possibilities curve, such as *U*, represents unemployment or a failure to achieve full employment. The arrows indicate that, by realizing full employment, the economy could operate on the curve. This means it could produce more of one or both products than it is producing at point *U*.

quality usually improves over time. Historically, the economy's stock of capital has increased at a significant, though unsteady, rate. And although some of our energy and mineral resources are being depleted, new sources are also being discovered. The development of irrigation systems, for example, adds to the supply of arable land.

The net result of these increased supplies of the factors of production is the ability to produce more of both consumer goods and capital goods. Thus, 20 years from now, the production possibilities in Figure 1.5 may supersede those shown in

FIGURE 1.5 Economic growth and the production possibilities curve. The increase in supplies of resources, the improvements in resource quality, and the technological advances that occur in a dynamic economy move the production possibilities curve outward and to the right, allowing the economy to have larger quantities of both types of goods.

	Production Alternatives				
Type of Product	**A'**	**B'**	**C'**	**D'**	**E'**
Food products (hundred thousands)	0	2	4	6	8
Manufacturing equipment (thousands)	14	12	9	5	0

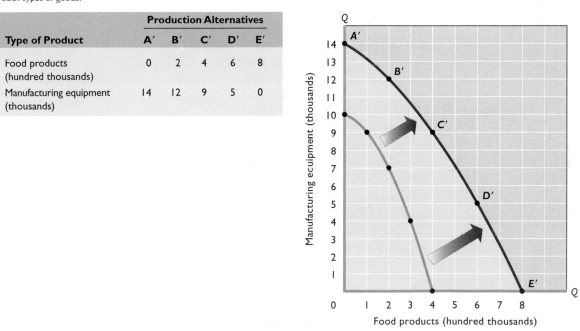

Figure 1.2. The greater abundance of resources will result in a greater potential output of one or both products at each alternative. The economy will have achieved economic growth in the form of expanded potential output. Thus, when an increase in the quantity or quality of resources occurs, the production possibilities curve shifts outward and to the right, as illustrated by the move from the inner curve to curve *A′ B′ C′ D′ E′* in Figure 1.5. This sort of shift represents growth of economic capacity, which, when used, means **economic growth:** a larger total output.

economic growth
An outward shift of the production possibilities curve that results from an increase in resource supplies or quality or an improvement in technology.

Advances in Technology An advancing technology brings both new and better goods and improved ways of producing them. For now, let's think of technological advance as being only improvements in the methods of production, for example, the introduction of computerized systems to manage inventories and schedule production. These advances alter our previous discussion of the economic problem by allowing society to produce more goods with available resources. As with increases in resource supplies, technological advances make possible the production of more manufacturing equipment *and* more food products.

APPLYING THE ANALYSIS

Information Technology and Biotechnology

A real-world example of improved technology is the recent surge of new technologies relating to computers, communications, and biotechnology. Technological advances have dropped the prices of computers and greatly increased their speed. Improved software has greatly increased the everyday usefulness of computers. Cellular phones and the Internet have increased communications capacity, enhancing production and improving the efficiency of markets. Advances in biotechnology have resulted in important agricultural and medical discoveries. These and other new and improved technologies have contributed to U.S. economic growth (outward shifts of the nation's production possibilities curve).

QUESTION: How have technological advances in medicine helped expand production possibilities in the United States?

Conclusion: Economic growth is the result of (1) increases in supplies of resources, (2) improvements in resource quality, and (3) technological advances. The consequence of growth is that a full-employment economy can enjoy a greater output of both consumption goods and capital goods. While static, no-growth economies must sacrifice some of one good to obtain more of another, dynamic, growing economies can have larger quantities of both goods.

Present Choices and Future Possibilities

An economy's current choice of positions on its production possibilities curve helps determine the future location of that curve. Let's designate the two axes of the production possibilities curve as "goods for the future" and "goods for the present," as in Figure 1.6. Goods for the future are such things as capital goods, research and education, and

FIGURE 1.6 **Present choices and future locations of production possibilities curves.** A nation's current choice favoring "present goods," as made by Presentville in (a), will cause a modest outward shift of the production possibilities curve in the future. A nation's current choice favoring "future goods," as made by Futureville in (b), will result in a greater outward shift of the curve in the future.

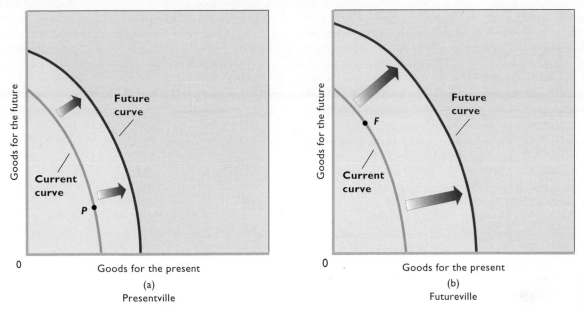

preventive medicine. They increase the quantity and quality of property resources, enlarge the stock of technological information, and improve the quality of human resources. As we have already seen, goods for the future, such as capital goods, are the ingredients of economic growth. Goods for the present are consumer goods such as food, clothing, and entertainment.

Now suppose there are two hypothetical economies, Presentville and Futureville, which are initially identical in every respect except one: Presentville's current choice of positions on its production possibilities curve strongly favors present goods over future goods. Point *P* in Figure 1.6a indicates that choice. It is located quite far down the curve to the right, indicating a high priority for goods for the present, at the expense of less goods for the future. Futureville, in contrast, makes a current choice that stresses larger amounts of future goods and smaller amounts of present goods, as shown by point *F* in Figure 1.6b.

Now, other things equal, we can expect Futureville's future production possibilities curve to be farther to the right than Presentville's future production possibilities curve. By currently choosing an output more favorable to technological advances and to increases in the quantity and quality of resources, Futureville will achieve greater economic growth than Presentville. In terms of capital goods, Futureville is choosing to make larger current additions to its "national factory" by devoting more of its current output to capital than Presentville. The payoff from this choice for Futureville is greater future production capacity and economic growth. The opportunity cost is fewer consumer goods in the present for Futureville to enjoy.

Is Futureville's choice thus necessarily "better" than Presentville's? That, we cannot say. The different outcomes simply reflect different preferences and priorities in the two countries. But each country will have to live with the consequences of its choice.

INTERACTIVE GRAPHS

G 1.2

Present choices and future possibilities

Summary

1. Economics is the social science that studies how people, institutions, and society make choices under conditions of scarcity. Central to economics is the idea of opportunity cost: the value of the good, service, or time forgone to obtain something else.

2. The economic perspective includes three elements: scarcity and choice, purposeful behavior, and marginalism. It sees individuals and institutions making rational decisions based on comparisons of marginal costs and marginal benefits.

3. Economists employ the scientific method, in which they form and test hypotheses of cause-and-effect relationships to generate theories, laws, and principles. Economists often combine theories into representations called models.

4. Microeconomics examines the decision making of specific economic units or institutions. Macroeconomics looks at the economy as a whole or its major aggregates.

5. Individuals face an economic problem. Because their wants exceed their incomes, they must decide what to purchase and what to forgo. Society also faces an economic problem. Societal wants exceed the available resources necessary to fulfill them. Society therefore must decide what to produce and what to forgo.

6. Graphically, a budget line (or budget constraint) illustrates the economic problem for individuals. The line shows the various combinations of two products that a consumer can purchase with a specific money income, given the prices of the two products.

7. Economic resources are inputs into the production process and can be classified as land, labor, capital, and entrepreneurial ability. Economic resources are also known as factors of production or inputs.

8. Society's economic problem can be illustrated through production possibilities analysis. Production possibilities tables and curves show the different combinations of goods and services that can be produced in a fully employed economy, assuming that resource quantity, resource quality, and technology are fixed.

9. An economy that is fully employed and thus operating on its production possibilities curve must sacrifice the output of some types of goods and services to increase the production of others. The gain of one type of good or service is always accompanied by an opportunity cost in the form of the loss of some of the other type.

10. Because resources are not equally productive in all possible uses, shifting resources from one use to another results in increasing opportunity costs. The production of additional units of one product requires the sacrifice of increasing amounts of the other product.

11. The optimal point on the production possibilities curve represents the most desirable mix of goods and is determined by expanding the production of each good until its marginal benefit (MB) equals its marginal cost (MC).

12. Over time, technological advances and increases in the quantity and quality of resources enable the economy to produce more of all goods and services, that is, to experience economic growth. Society's choice as to the mix of consumer goods and capital goods in current output is a major determinant of the future location of the production possibilities curve and thus of the extent of economic growth.

Terms and Concepts

economics	macroeconomics	investment
economic perspective	aggregate	entrepreneurial ability
opportunity cost	economic problem	factors of production
utility	budget line	consumer goods
marginal analysis	constant opportunity cost	capital goods
scientific method	economic resources	production possibilities curve
principles	land	law of increasing opportunity costs
other-things-equal assumption	labor	economic growth
microeconomics	capital	

Questions   connect ECONOMICS

1. Ralph Waldo Emerson once wrote: "Want is a growing giant whom the coat of have was never large enough to cover." How does this statement relate to the definition of economics? LO1

2. "Buy 2, get 1 free." Explain why the "1 free" is free to the buyer but not to society. LO1

3. Which of the following decisions would entail the greater opportunity cost: allocating a square block in the heart of

New York City for a surface parking lot or allocating a square block at the edge of a typical suburb for such a lot? Explain. **LO1**

4. What is meant by the term "utility," and how does it relate to purposeful behavior? **LO1**

5. Cite three examples of recent decisions that you made in which you, at least implicitly, weighed marginal cost and marginal benefit. **LO1**

6. What are the key elements of the scientific method, and how does this method relate to economic principles and laws? **LO2**

7. Indicate whether each of the following statements applies to microeconomics or macroeconomics: **LO3**
   a. The unemployment rate in the United States was 9.0% in April 2011.
   b. A U.S. software firm discharged 15 workers last month and transferred the work to India.
   c. An unexpected freeze in central Florida reduced the citrus crop and caused the price of oranges to rise.
   d. U.S. output, adjusted for inflation, grew by 2.9% in 2010.
   e. Last week Wells Fargo Bank lowered its interest rate on business loans by one-half of 1 percentage point.
   f. The consumer price index rose by 1.6% in 2010.

8. What are economic resources? What categories do economists use to classify them? Why are resources also called factors of production? Why are they called inputs? **LO4**

9. Why isn't money considered a capital resource in economics? Why is entrepreneurial ability considered a category of economic resource, distinct from labor? What are the major functions of the entrepreneur? **LO4**

10. Specify and explain the typical shapes of marginal-benefit and marginal-cost curves. How are these curves used to determine the optimal allocation of resources to a particular product? If current output is such that marginal cost exceeds marginal benefit, should more or fewer resources be allocated to this product? Explain. **LO5**

11. Explain how (if at all) each of the following events affects the location of a country's production possibilities curve: **LO5**
    a. The quality of education increases.
    b. The number of unemployed workers increases.
    c. A new technique improves the efficiency of extracting copper from ore.
    d. A devastating earthquake destroys numerous production facilities.

12. Suppose that, on the basis of a nation's production possibilities curve, an economy must sacrifice 10,000 pizzas domestically to get the 1 additional industrial robot it desires but that it can get the robot from another country in exchange for 9000 pizzas. Relate this information to the following statement: "Through international specialization and trade, a nation can reduce its opportunity cost of obtaining goods and thus 'move outside its production possibilities curve.'" **LO5**

Problems

1. Potatoes cost Janice $1 per pound, and she has $5.00 that she could possibly spend on potatoes or other items. If she feels that the first pound of potatoes is worth $1.50, the second pound is worth $1.14, the third pound is worth $1.05, and all subsequent pounds are worth $0.30, how many pounds of potatoes will she purchase? What if she only had $2 to spend? **LO1**

2. Pham can work as many or as few hours as she wants at the college bookstore for $9 per hour. But due to her hectic schedule, she has just 15 hours per week that she can spend working at either the bookstore or at other potential jobs. One potential job, at a café, will pay her $12 per hour for up to 6 hours per week. She has another job offer at a garage that will pay her $10 an hour for up to 5 hours per week. And she has a potential job at a day care center that will pay her $8.50 per hour for as many hours as she can work. If her goal is to maximize the amount of money she can make each week, how many hours will she work at the bookstore? **LO1**

3. Suppose you won $15 on a lotto ticket at the local 7-Eleven and decided to spend all the winnings on candy bars and bags of peanuts. The price of candy bars is $.75 and the price of peanuts is $1.50. **LO4**
   a. Construct a table showing the alternative combinations of the two products that are available.

   b. Plot the data in your table as a budget line in a graph. What is the slope of the budget line? What is the opportunity cost of one more candy bar? Of one more bag of peanuts? Do these opportunity costs rise, fall, or remain constant as each additional unit of the product is purchased?
   c. How, in general, would you decide which of the available combinations of candy bars and bags of peanuts to buy?
   d. Suppose that you had won $30 on your ticket, not $15. Show the $30 budget line in your diagram. Why would this budget line be preferable to the old one?

4. Suppose that you are on a desert island and possess exactly 20 coconuts. Your neighbor, Friday, is a fisherman, and he is willing to trade 2 fish for every 1 coconut that you are willing to give him. Another neighbor, Kwame, is also a fisherman, and he is willing to trade 3 fish for every 1 coconut. **LO4**
   a. On a single figure, draw budget lines for trading with Friday and for trading with Kwame. (Put coconuts on the vertical axis.)
   b. What is the slope of the budget line from trading with Friday?
   c. What is the slope of the budget line from trading with Kwame?

d. Which budget line features a larger set of attainable combinations of coconuts and fish?

e. If you are going to trade coconuts for fish, would you rather trade with Friday or Kwame?

5. Below is a production possibilities table for consumer goods (automobiles) and capital goods (forklifts): **LO5**

Type of Production	Production Alternatives				
	A	**B**	**C**	**D**	**E**
Automobiles	0	2	4	6	8
Forklifts	30	27	21	12	0

a. Show these data graphically. Upon what specific assumptions is this production possibilities curve based?

b. If the economy is at point *C*, what is the cost of two more automobiles? Of six more forklifts? Explain how the production possibilities curve reflects the law of increasing opportunity costs.

c. If the economy characterized by this production possibilities table and curve were producing 3 automobiles and 20 forklifts, what could you conclude about its use of its available resources?

d. What would production at a point outside the production possibilities curve indicate? What must occur before the economy can attain such a level of production?

6. Referring to the table in problem 5, suppose improvement occurs in the technology of producing forklifts but not in the technology of producing automobiles. Draw the new production possibilities curve. Now assume that a technological advance occurs in producing automobiles but not in producing forklifts. Draw the new production possibilities curve. Now draw a production possibilities curve that reflects technological improvement in the production of both goods. **LO5**

7. On average, households in China save 40 percent of their annual income each year, whereas households in the United States save less than 5 percent. Production possibilities are growing at roughly 9 percent annually in China and 3.5 percent in the United States. Use graphical analysis of "present goods" versus "future goods" to explain the differences in growth rates. **LO5**

FURTHER TEST YOUR KNOWLEDGE AT
www.mcconnellbrief2e.com

At the text's Online Learning Center, **www.mcconnellbrief2e.com**, you will find one or more web-based questions that require information from the Internet to answer. We urge you to check them out, since they will familiarize you with websites that may be helpful in other courses and perhaps even in your career. The OLC also features multiple-choice quizzes that give instant feedback and provides other helpful ways to further test your knowledge of the chapter.

**Visit your mobile app store and download the
McConnell Brief Edition: Study Econ app** *today!*

Chapter One Appendix

Graphs and Their Meaning

If you glance quickly through this text, you will find many graphs. These graphs are included to help you visualize and understand economic relationships. Most of our principles or models explain relationships between just two sets of economic data, which can be conveniently represented with two-dimensional graphs.

Construction of a Graph

A graph is a visual representation of the relationship between two variables. The table in Figure 1 is a hypothetical illustration showing the relationship between income and consumption for the economy as a whole. Because people tend to buy more goods and services when their incomes go up, it is not surprising to find in the table that total consumption in the economy increases as total income increases.

The information in the table is also expressed graphically in Figure 1. Here is how it is done: We want to show visually or graphically how consumption changes as income changes. Since income is the determining factor, we follow mathematical custom and represent it on the horizontal axis of the graph. And because consumption depends on income, it is represented on the vertical axis of the graph.

The vertical and horizontal scales of the graph reflect the ranges of values of consumption and income, marked in convenient increments. As you can see, the values on the scales cover all the values in the table.

Because the graph has two dimensions, each point within it represents an income value and its associated consumption value. To find a point that represents one of the five income-consumption combinations in the table, we draw lines from the appropriate values on the vertical and horizontal axes. For example, to plot point *c* (the $200 income–$150 consumption point), lines are drawn up from the horizontal (income) axis at $200 and across from the vertical (consumption) axis at $150. These lines intersect at point *c*, which represents this particular income-consumption combination. You should verify that the other income-consumption combinations shown in the table in Figure 1 are properly located in the graph that is there.

Finally, by assuming that the same general relationship between income and consumption prevails for all other incomes, we draw a line or smooth curve to connect these points. That line or curve represents the income-consumption relationship.

If the graph is a straight line, as in Figure 1, the relationship is said to be *linear*.

Direct and Inverse Relationships

The line in Figure 1 slopes upward to the right, so it depicts a **direct relationship** between income and consumption. A direct relationship, or positive relationship, means that two variables (here, consumption and income) change in the same direction. An increase in consumption is associated with an increase in income; a decrease in consumption accompanies a decrease in income. When two sets of data are positively or directly related, they always graph as an upsloping line, as in Figure 1.

direct relationship The (positive) relationship between two variables that change in the same direction.

FIGURE 1 Graphing the direct relationship between consumption and income. Two sets of data that are positively or directly related, such as consumption and income, graph as an upsloping line.

Income per Week	Consumption per Week	Point
$ 0	$ 50	a
100	100	b
200	150	c
300	200	d
400	250	e

FIGURE 2 **Graphing the inverse relationship between ticket prices and game attendance.** Two sets of data that are negatively or inversely related, such as ticket price and the attendance at basketball games, graph as a downsloping line.

Ticket Price	Attendance, Thousands	Point
$50	0	a
40	4	b
30	8	c
20	12	d
10	16	e
0	20	f

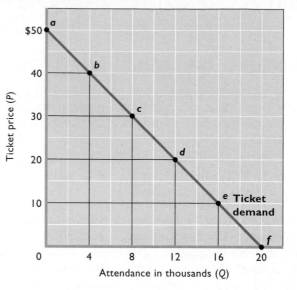

In contrast, two sets of data may be inversely related. Consider the table in Figure 2, which shows the relationship between the price of basketball tickets and game attendance for Big Time University (BTU). Here there is an **inverse relationship,** or negative relationship, because the two variables change in opposite directions. When ticket prices for the games decrease, attendance increases. When ticket prices increase, attendance decreases. The six data points in the table are plotted in the graph in Figure 2. This inverse relationship graphs as a downsloping line.

inverse relationship
The (negative) relationship between two variables that change in opposite directions.

Dependent and Independent Variables

Economists seek to determine which variable is the "cause" and which the "effect." Or, more formally, they seek the independent variable and the dependent variable. The **independent variable** is the cause or source; it is the variable that changes first. The **dependent variable** is the effect or outcome; it is the variable that changes because of the change in the independent variable. As in our income-consumption example, income generally is the independent variable and consumption the dependent variable. Income causes consumption to be what it is rather than the other way around. Similarly, ticket prices (set in

independent variable
The variable causing a change in some other (dependent) variable; the "causal variable."

dependent variable
The variable that changes as a result of a change in some other (independent) variable; the "outcome variable."

advance of the season and printed on the ticket) determine attendance at BTU basketball games; attendance at games does not determine the printed ticket prices for those games. Ticket price is the independent variable, and the quantity of tickets purchased is the dependent variable.

Mathematicians always put the independent variable (cause) on the horizontal axis and the dependent variable (effect) on the vertical axis. Economists are less tidy; their graphing of independent and dependent variables is more arbitrary. Their conventional graphing of the income-consumption relationship is consistent with mathematical convention, but economists historically put price and cost data on the vertical axis of their graphs. Contemporary economists have followed the tradition. So economists' graphing of BTU's ticket price–attendance data differs from normal mathematical procedure. This does not present a problem, but we want you to be aware of this fact to avoid any possible confusion.

Other Things Equal

Our simple two-variable graphs purposely ignore many other factors that might affect the amount of consumption occurring at each income level or the number of people who attend BTU basketball games at each possible ticket price. When economists plot the relationship between any two variables, they employ the *ceteris paribus* (other-things-equal) assumption. Thus, in Figure 1 all factors other than income that might affect the amount of consumption are presumed to be constant or unchanged. Similarly, in Figure 2 all factors other than ticket price that might influence attendance at BTU basketball games are assumed constant. In reality, "other things" are not equal; they often change, and when they do, the relationship represented in our two tables and graphs will change. Specifically, the lines we have plotted would *shift* to new locations.

Consider a stock market "crash." The dramatic drop in the value of stocks might cause people to feel less wealthy and therefore less willing to consume at each level of income. The result might be a downward shift of the consumption line. To see this, you should plot a new consumption line in Figure 1, assuming that consumption is, say, $20 less at each income level. Note that the relationship remains direct; the line merely shifts downward to reflect less consumption spending at each income level.

Similarly, factors other than ticket prices might affect BTU game attendance. If BTU loses most of its games, attendance at BTU games might be less at each ticket price. To see this, redraw Figure 2, assuming that 2000 fewer fans attend BTU games at each ticket price.

Slope of a Line

Lines can be described in terms of their slopes. The **slope of a straight line** is the ratio of the vertical change (the rise or drop) to the horizontal change (the run) between any two points of the line.

> **slope (of a straight line)** The ratio of the vertical change (the rise or fall) to the horizontal change (the run) between any two points on a line.

Positive Slope Between point *b* and point *c* in the graph in Figure 1, the rise or vertical change (the change in consumption) is +$50 and the run or horizontal change (the change in income) is +$100. Therefore:

$$\text{Slope} = \frac{\text{vertical change}}{\text{horizontal change}} = \frac{+50}{+100} = \frac{1}{2} = .5$$

Note that our slope of $\frac{1}{2}$ or .5 is positive because consumption and income change in the same direction; that is, consumption and income are directly or positively related.

Negative Slope Between any two of the identified points in the graph of Figure 2, say, point *c* and point *d*, the vertical change is −10 (the drop) and the horizontal change is +4 (the run). Therefore:

$$\text{Slope} = \frac{\text{vertical change}}{\text{horizontal change}} = \frac{-10}{+4} = -2\frac{1}{2} = -2.5$$

This slope is negative because ticket price and attendance have an inverse relationship.

Slopes and Marginal Analysis Economists are largely concerned with changes in values. The concept of slope is important in economics because it reflects marginal changes—those involving 1 more (or 1 fewer) unit. For example, in Figure 1 the .5 slope shows that $.50 of extra or marginal consumption is associated with each $1 change in income. In this example, people collectively will consume $.50 of any $1 increase in their incomes and reduce their consumption by $.50 for each $1 decline in income. Careful inspection of Figure 2 reveals that every $1 increase in ticket price for BTU games will decrease game attendance by 400 people and every $1 decrease in ticket price will increase game attendance by 400 people.

Infinite and Zero Slopes Many variables are unrelated or independent of one another. For example, the quantity of wristwatches purchased is not related to the price of bananas. In Figure 3a the price of bananas is measured on the vertical axis and the quantity of watches demanded on the horizontal axis. The graph of their relationship is the line parallel to the vertical axis, indicating that the same quantity of watches is

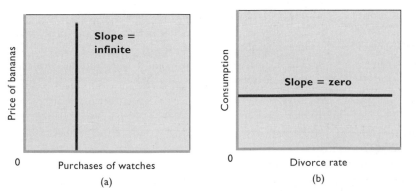

FIGURE 3 Infinite and zero slopes. (a) A line parallel to the vertical axis has an infinite slope. Here, purchases of watches remain the same no matter what happens to the price of bananas. (b) A line parallel to the horizontal axis has a slope of zero. In this case, total consumption remains the same no matter what happens to the divorce rate. In both (a) and (b), the two variables are totally unrelated to one another.

purchased no matter what the price of bananas. The slope of such a line is infinite.

Similarly, aggregate consumption is completely unrelated to the nation's divorce rate. In Figure 3b we put consumption on the vertical axis and the divorce rate on the horizontal axis. The line parallel to the horizontal axis represents this lack of relatedness. This line has a slope of zero.

Slope of a Nonlinear Curve We now move from the simple world of linear relationships (straight lines) to the somewhat more complex world of nonlinear relationships. The slope of a straight line is the same at all its points. The slope of a line representing a nonlinear relationship changes from one point to another. Such lines are always referred to as *curves*.

Consider the downsloping curve in Figure 4. Its slope is negative throughout, but the curve flattens as we move down along it. Thus, its slope constantly changes; the curve has a different slope at each point.

To measure the slope at a specific point, we draw a straight line tangent to the curve at that point. A line is tangent at a point if it touches, but does not intersect, the curve at that point. So line *aa* is tangent to the curve in Figure 4 at point *A*. The slope of the curve at that point is equal to the slope of the tangent line. Specifically, the total vertical change (drop) in the tangent line *aa* is −20 and the total horizontal change (run) is +5. Because the slope of the tangent line *aa* is −20/+5, or −4, the slope of the curve at point *A* is also −4.

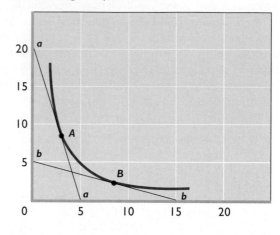

FIGURE 4 **Determining the slopes of curves.** The slope of a nonlinear curve changes from point to point on the curve. The slope at any point (say, B) can be determined by drawing a straight line that is tangent to that point (line bb) and calculating the slope of that line.

Line *bb* in Figure 4 is tangent to the curve at point *B*. Using the same procedure, we find the slope at *B* to be −5/+15, or −$\frac{1}{3}$. Thus, in this flatter part of the curve, the slope is less negative.

Several of the Appendix questions are of a "workbook" variety, and we urge you to go through them carefully to check your understanding of graphs and slopes.

Appendix Summary

1. Graphs are a convenient and revealing way to represent economic relationships.

2. Two variables are positively or directly related when their values change in the same direction. The line (curve) representing two directly related variables slopes upward.

3. Two variables are negatively or inversely related when their values change in opposite directions. The curve representing two inversely related variables slopes downward.

4. The value of the dependent variable (the "effect") is determined by the value of the independent variable (the "cause").

5. When the "other factors" that might affect a two-variable relationship are allowed to change, the graph of the relationship will likely shift to a new location.

6. The slope of a straight line is the ratio of the vertical change to the horizontal change between any two points. The slope of an upsloping line is positive; the slope of a downsloping line is negative.

7. The slope of a line or curve is especially relevant for economics because it measures marginal changes.

8. The slope of a horizontal line is zero; the slope of a vertical line is infinite.

9. The slope of a curve at any point is determined by calculating the slope of a straight line tangent to the curve at that point.

Appendix Terms and Concepts

direct relationship

inverse relationship

independent variable

dependent variable

slope of a straight line

Appendix Questions

1. Briefly explain the use of graphs as a way to represent economic relationships. What is an inverse relationship? How does it graph? What is a direct relationship? How does it graph? **LO6**
2. Describe the graphical relationship between ticket prices and the number of people choosing to visit amusement parks. Is that relationship consistent with the fact that, historically, park attendance and ticket prices have both risen? Explain. **LO6**
3. Look back at Figure 2, which shows the inverse relationship between ticket prices and game attendance at Big Time University. (a) Interpret the meaning of the slope. (b) If the slope of the line were steeper, what would that say about the amount by which ticket sales respond to increases in ticket prices? **LO6**

Appendix Problems

1. Graph and label as either direct or indirect the relationships you would expect to find between (a) the number of inches of rainfall per month and the sale of umbrellas, (b) the amount of tuition and the level of enrollment at a university, and (c) the popularity of an entertainer and the price of her concert tickets. **LO6**
2. Indicate how each of the following might affect the data shown in the table and graph in Figure 2 of this appendix: **LO6**
   a. BTU's athletic director hires away the coach from a perennial champion.
   b. An NBA team locates in the city where BTU plays.
   c. BTU contracts to have all its home games televised.
3. The following table contains data on the relationship between saving and income. Rearrange these data into a meaningful order and graph them on the accompanying grid. What is the slope of the line? What would you predict saving to be at the $12,500 level of income? **LO6**

Income per Year	Saving per Year
$15,000	$1,000
0	−500
10,000	500
5,000	0
20,000	1,500

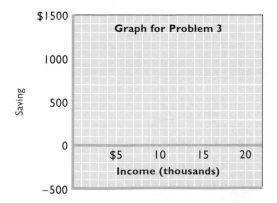

4. Construct a table from the data shown on the graph below. Which is the dependent variable and which the independent variable? **LO6**

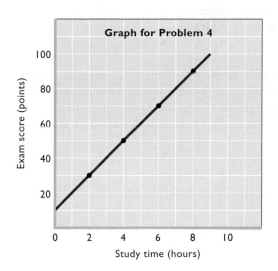

5. Suppose that when the price of gold is $100 an ounce, gold producers find it unprofitable to sell gold. However, when the price is $200 an ounce, 5000 ounces of output (production) is profitable. At $300, a total of 10,000 ounces of output is profitable. Similarly, total production increases by 5000 ounces for each successive $100 increase in the price of gold. Describe the relevant relationship between the price of gold and the production of gold in a table and on a graph. Put the price of gold on the vertical axis and the output of gold on the horizontal axis. **LO6**

6. The accompanying graph shows curve XX' and tangents to the curve at points A, B, and C. Calculate the slope of the curve at each of these three points. **LO6**

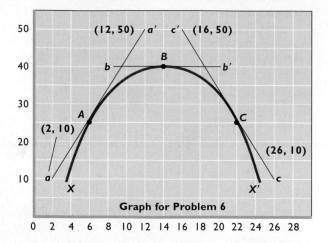

Graph for Problem 6

7. In the accompanying graph, is the slope of curve AA' positive or negative? Does the slope increase or decrease as we move along the curve from A to A'? Answer the same two questions for curve BB'. **LO6**

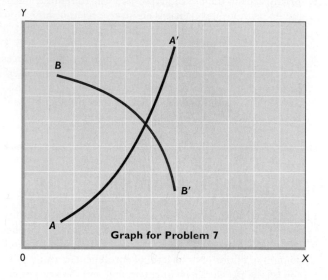

Graph for Problem 7

After reading this chapter, you should be able to:

1 Differentiate between a command system and a market system.

2 List the main characteristics of the market system.

3 Explain how the market system answers the four fundamental questions.

4 Discuss how the market system adjusts to change and promotes progress.

5 Describe the mechanics of the circular flow model.

The Market System and the Circular Flow

You are at the mall. Suppose you were assigned to compile a list of all the individual goods and services there, including the different brands and variations of each type of product. That task would be daunting and the list would be long! And even though a single shopping mall contains a remarkable quantity and variety of goods, it is only a tiny part of the national economy.

Who decided that the particular goods and services available at the mall and in the broader economy should be produced? How did the producers determine which technology and types of resources to use in producing these particular goods? Who will obtain these products? What accounts for the new and improved products among these goods? This chapter will answer these questions.

Economic Systems

economic system
A particular set of institutional arrangements and a coordinating mechanism for producing goods and services.

Every society needs to develop an **economic system**—a particular set of institutional arrangements and a coordinating mechanism—to respond to the economic problem. The economic system has to determine what goods are produced, how they are produced, who gets them, and how to promote technological progress.

Economic systems differ as to (1) who owns the factors of production and (2) the method used to motivate, coordinate, and direct economic activity. There are two general types of economic systems: the command system and the market system.

The Command System

command system
An economic system in which most property resources are owned by the government and economic decisions are made by a central government body.

The **command system** is also known as *socialism* or *communism*. In a command system, government owns most property resources and economic decision making occurs through a central economic plan. A central planning board appointed by the government makes nearly all the major decisions concerning the use of resources, the composition and distribution of output, and the organization of production. The government owns most of the business firms, which produce according to government directives. The central planning board determines production goals for each enterprise and specifies the amount of resources to be allocated to each enterprise so that it can reach its production goals. The division of output between capital and consumer goods is centrally decided, and capital goods are allocated among industries on the basis of the central planning board's long-term priorities.

A pure command economy would rely exclusively on a central plan to allocate the government-owned property resources. But, in reality, even the preeminent command economy—the Soviet Union—tolerated some private ownership and incorporated some markets before its collapse in 1992. Recent reforms in Russia and most of the eastern European nations have to one degree or another transformed their command economies to capitalistic, market-oriented systems. China's reforms have not gone as far, but they have greatly reduced the reliance on central planning. Although there is still extensive government ownership of resources and capital in China, the nation has increasingly relied on free markets to organize and coordinate its economy. North Korea and Cuba are the last remaining examples of largely centrally planned economies. Global Snapshot 2.1 reveals how North Korea's centrally planned economy compares to the market economy of its neighbor, South Korea. Later in this chapter, we will explore the main reasons for the general demise of the command systems.

The Market System

market system
An economic system in which property resources are privately owned and markets and prices are used to direct and coordinate economic activities.

The polar alternative to the command system is the **market system,** or *capitalism*. The system is characterized by the private ownership of resources and the use of markets and prices to coordinate and direct economic activity. Participants act in their own self-interest. Individuals and businesses seek to achieve their economic goals through their own decisions regarding work, consumption, or production. The system allows for the private ownership of capital, communicates through prices, and coordinates economic activity through *markets*—places where buyers and sellers come together to buy and sell goods, services, and resources. Goods and services are produced and resources are supplied by whoever is willing and able to do so. The result is competition among independently acting buyers and sellers of each product and resource. Thus, economic decision making is widely dispersed. Also, the high potential monetary rewards create powerful incentives for existing firms to innovate and entrepreneurs to pioneer new products and processes.

ORIGIN OF THE IDEA

O 2.1
Laissez-faire

GLOBAL SNAPSHOT 2.1

The Two Koreas

North Korea is one of the few command economies still standing. After the Second World War, Korea was divided into North Korea and South Korea. North Korea, under the influence of the Soviet Union, established a command economy that emphasized government ownership and central government planning. South Korea, protected by the United States, established a market economy based upon private ownership and the profit motive. Today, the differences in the economic outcomes of the two systems are striking:

	North Korea	South Korea
GDP	$40 billion*	$1.3 trillion*
GDP per capita	$1800*	$27,700*
Exports	$2.0 billion	$355 billion
Imports	$3.5 billion	$313 billion
Agriculture as % of GDP	23 percent	3 percent

*Based on purchasing power equivalencies to the U.S. dollar.
Source: CIA World Fact Book, 2010, **www.cia.gov**.

In *pure* capitalism—or *laissez-faire* capitalism—government's role would be limited to protecting private property and establishing an environment appropriate to the operation of the market system. The term "laissez-faire" means "let it be," that is, keep government from interfering with the economy. The idea is that such interference will disturb the efficient working of the market system.

But in the capitalism practiced in the United States and most other countries, government plays a substantial role in the economy. It not only provides the rules for economic activity but also promotes economic stability and growth, provides certain goods and services that would otherwise be underproduced or not produced at all, and modifies the distribution of income. The government, however, is not the dominant economic force in deciding what to produce, how to produce it, and who will get it. That force is the market.

Characteristics of the Market System

It will be very instructive to examine some of the key features of the market system in more detail.

Private Property

In a market system, private individuals and firms, not the government, own most of the property resources (land and capital). It is this extensive private ownership of capital that gives capitalism its name. This right of **private property,** coupled with the freedom to negotiate binding legal contracts, enables individuals and businesses to obtain, use, and dispose of property resources as they see fit. The right of property owners to designate who will receive their property when they die sustains the institution of private property.

The most important consequence of property rights is that they encourage people to cooperate by helping to ensure that only *mutually agreeable* economic transactions

private property
The right of persons and firms to obtain, own, control, employ, dispose of, and bequeath land, capital, and other property.

take place. In a world without legally enforceable property rights, the strong could simply take whatever they wanted from the weak without giving them any compensation. But in a world of legally enforceable property rights, any person wanting something from you has to get you to agree to give it to them. And you can say no. The result is that if that person really wants what you have, she must offer you something that you value more highly in return. That is, she must offer you a mutually agreeable economic transaction—one that benefits you as well as her.

Property rights also encourage investment, innovation, exchange, maintenance of property, and economic growth. Why would anyone stock a store, build a factory, or clear land for farming if someone else, or the government itself, could take that property for his or her own benefit?

Property rights also extend to intellectual property through patents, copyrights, and trademarks. Such long-term protection encourages people to write books, music, and computer programs and to invent new products and production processes without fear that others will steal them and the rewards they may bring.

Moreover, property rights facilitate exchange. The title to an automobile or the deed to a cattle ranch assures the buyer that the seller is the legitimate owner. Also, property rights encourage owners to maintain or improve their property so as to preserve or increase its value. Finally, property rights enable people to use their time and resources to produce more goods and services, rather than using them to protect and retain the property they have already produced or acquired.

Freedom of Enterprise and Choice

Closely related to private ownership of property is freedom of enterprise and choice. The market system requires that various economic units make certain choices, which are expressed and implemented in the economy's markets:

freedom of enterprise
The freedom of firms to obtain economic resources, to use those resources to produce products of the firms' own choosing, and to sell their products in markets of their choice.

freedom of choice
The freedom of owners of resources to employ or dispose of their resources as they see fit, and the freedom of consumers to spend their incomes in a manner they think is appropriate.

self-interest
The most-advantageous outcome as viewed by each firm, property owner, worker, or consumer.

- **Freedom of enterprise** ensures that entrepreneurs and private businesses are free to obtain and use economic resources to produce their choice of goods and services and to sell them in their chosen markets.
- **Freedom of choice** enables owners to employ or dispose of their property and money as they see fit. It also allows workers to enter any line of work for which they are qualified. Finally, it ensures that consumers are free to buy the goods and services that best satisfy their wants.

These choices are free only within broad legal limitations, of course. Illegal choices such as selling human organs or buying illicit drugs are punished through fines and imprisonment. (Global Snapshot 2.2 reveals that the degree of economic freedom varies greatly from nation to nation.)

Self-Interest

In the market system, **self-interest** is the motivating force of the various economic units as they express their free choices. Self-interest simply means that each economic unit tries to achieve its own particular goal, which usually requires delivering something of value to others. Entrepreneurs try to maximize profit or minimize loss. Property owners try to get the highest price for the sale or rent of their resources. Workers try to maximize their utility (satisfaction) by finding jobs that offer the best combination of wages, hours, fringe benefits, and working conditions. Consumers try to obtain the products they want at the lowest possible price and apportion their expenditures to maximize their utility. The motive of self-interest gives direction and consistency to what might otherwise be a chaotic economy.

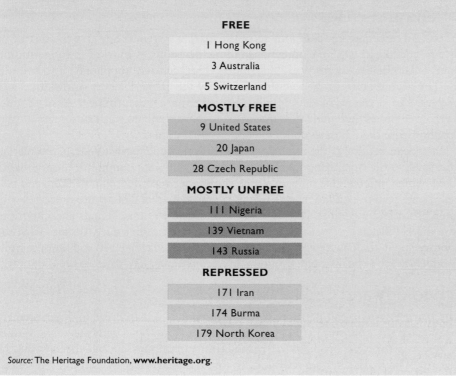

GLOBAL SNAPSHOT 2.2

Index of Economic Freedom, Selected Economies

The Index of Economic Freedom measures economic freedom using 10 broad categories such as trade policy, property rights, and government intervention, with each category containing more than 50 specific criteria. The index then ranks 183 economies according to their degree of economic freedom. A few selected rankings for 2011 are listed below.

FREE

1 Hong Kong

3 Australia

5 Switzerland

MOSTLY FREE

9 United States

20 Japan

28 Czech Republic

MOSTLY UNFREE

111 Nigeria

139 Vietnam

143 Russia

REPRESSED

171 Iran

174 Burma

179 North Korea

Source: The Heritage Foundation, **www.heritage.org**.

Competition

The market system depends on **competition** among economic units. The basis of this competition is freedom of choice exercised in pursuit of a monetary return. Very broadly defined, competition requires:

- Independently acting sellers and buyers operating in a particular product or resource market.
- Freedom of sellers and buyers to enter or leave markets, on the basis of their economic self-interest.

Competition diffuses economic power within the businesses and households that make up the economy. When there are independently acting sellers and buyers in a market, no one buyer or seller is able to dictate the price of the product or resource because others can undercut that price.

Competition also implies that producers can enter or leave an industry; there are no insurmountable barriers to an industry's expanding or contracting. This freedom of an industry to expand or contract provides the economy with the flexibility needed to remain efficient over time. Freedom of entry and exit enables the economy to adjust to changes in consumer tastes, technology, and resource availability.

competition
The presence in a market of independent buyers and sellers vying with one another, and the freedom of buyers and sellers to enter and leave the market.

ORIGIN OF THE IDEA

O 2.2

Self-interest

The diffusion of economic power inherent in competition limits the potential abuse of that power. A producer that charges more than the competitive market price will lose sales to other producers. An employer who pays less than the competitive market wage rate will lose workers to other employers. A firm that fails to exploit new technology will lose profits to firms that do. And a firm that produces shoddy products will be punished as customers switch to higher-quality items made by rival firms. Competition is the basic regulatory force in the market system.

Markets and Prices

market
An institution or mechanism that brings buyers and sellers together.

Markets and prices are key components of the market system. They give the system its ability to coordinate millions of daily economic decisions. A **market** is an institution or mechanism that brings buyers ("demanders") and sellers ("suppliers") into contact. A market system conveys the decisions made by buyers and sellers of products and resources. The decisions made on each side of the market determine a set of product and resource prices that guide resource owners, entrepreneurs, and consumers as they make and revise their choices and pursue their self-interest.

Just as competition is the regulatory mechanism of the market system, the market system itself is the organizing mechanism. It is an elaborate communication network through which innumerable individual free choices are recorded, summarized, and balanced. Those who respond to market signals and heed market dictates are rewarded with greater profit and income; those who do not respond to those signals and choose to ignore market dictates are penalized. Through this mechanism society decides what the economy should produce, how production can be organized efficiently, and how the fruits of production are to be distributed among the various units that make up the economy.

Technology and Capital Goods

In the market system, competition, freedom of choice, self-interest, and personal reward provide the opportunity and motivation for technological advance. The monetary rewards for new products or production techniques accrue directly to the innovator. The market system therefore encourages extensive use and rapid development of complex capital goods: tools, machinery, large-scale factories, and facilities for storage, communication, transportation, and marketing.

Advanced technology and capital goods are important because the most direct methods of production are often the least efficient. The only way to avoid that inefficiency is to rely on capital goods. It would be ridiculous for a farmer to go at production with bare hands. There are huge benefits to be derived from creating and using such capital equipment as plows, tractors, storage bins, and so on. The more efficient production means much more abundant outputs.

Specialization

specialization
The use of resources of an individual, region, or nation to produce one or a few goods and services rather than the entire range of goods and services.

The extent to which market economies rely on **specialization** is extraordinary. Specialization is using the resources of an individual, region, or nation to produce one or a few goods or services rather than the entire range of goods and services. Those goods and services are then exchanged for a full range of desired products. The majority of consumers produce virtually none of the goods and services they consume, and they consume little or nothing of the items they produce. The person working nine to five installing windows in commercial aircraft may rarely fly. Many farmers sell their milk to the local dairy and then buy margarine at the local grocery store. Society learned long ago that self-sufficiency breeds inefficiency. The jack-of-all-trades may be a very colorful individual but is certainly not an efficient producer.

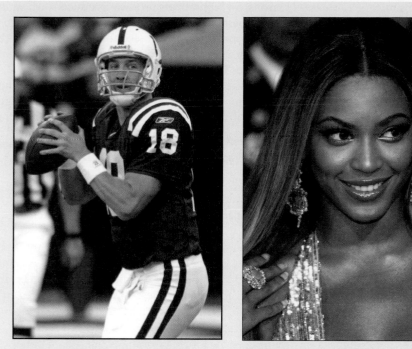

© Brent Smith/Reuters/Corbis   © PRNewsFoto/Diamond information Center

PHOTO OP   Peyton Manning and Beyoncé Knowles

It makes economic sense for Peyton Manning and Beyoncé Knowles to specialize in what they do best.

Division of Labor   Human specialization—called the **division of labor**—contributes to a society's output in several ways:

- ***Specialization makes use of differences in ability***   Specialization enables individuals to take advantage of existing differences in their abilities and skills. If Peyton is strong, athletic, and good at throwing a football and Beyoncé is beautiful, agile, and can sing, their distribution of talents can be most efficiently used if Peyton plays professional football and Beyoncé records songs and gives concerts.
- ***Specialization fosters learning by doing***   Even if the abilities of two people are identical, specialization may still be advantageous. By devoting time to a single task rather than working at a number of different tasks, a person is more likely to develop the skills required and to improve techniques. You learn to be a good lawyer by studying and practicing law.
- ***Specialization saves time***   By devoting time to a single task, a person avoids the loss of time incurred in shifting from one job to another.

For all these reasons, specialization increases the total output society derives from limited resources.

Geographic Specialization   Specialization also works on a regional and international basis. It is conceivable that oranges could be grown in Nebraska, but because of the unsuitability of the land, rainfall, and temperature, the costs would be very high. And it is conceivable that wheat could be grown in Florida, but such production would

division of labor
The separation of the work required to produce a product into a number of different tasks that are performed by different workers.

ORIGIN OF THE IDEA

O 2.3

Specialization: Division of labor

be costly for similar geographical reasons. So Nebraskans produce products—wheat in particular—for which their resources are best suited, and Floridians do the same, producing oranges and other citrus fruits. By specializing, both economies produce more than is needed locally. Then, very sensibly, Nebraskans and Floridians swap some of their surpluses—wheat for oranges, oranges for wheat.

Similarly, on an international scale, the United States specializes in producing such items as commercial aircraft and computers, which it sells abroad in exchange for video recorders from Japan, bananas from Honduras, and woven baskets from Thailand. Both human specialization and geographic specialization are needed to achieve efficiency in the use of limited resources.

Use of Money

A rather obvious characteristic of any economic system is the extensive use of money. Money performs several functions, but first and foremost it is a **medium of exchange.** It makes trade easier.

Specialization requires exchange. Exchange can, and sometimes does, occur through **barter**—swapping goods for goods, say, wheat for oranges. But barter poses serious problems because it requires a *coincidence of wants* between the buyer and the seller. In our example, we assumed that Nebraskans had excess wheat to trade and wanted oranges. And we assumed that Floridians had excess oranges to trade and wanted wheat. So an exchange occurred. But if such a coincidence of wants is missing, trade is stymied.

Suppose that Nebraska has no interest in Florida's oranges but wants potatoes from Idaho. And suppose that Idaho wants Florida's oranges but not Nebraska's wheat. And, to complicate matters, suppose that Florida wants some of Nebraska's wheat but none of Idaho's potatoes. We summarize the situation in Figure 2.1.

In none of the cases shown in the figure is there a coincidence of wants. Trade by barter clearly would be difficult. Instead, people in each state use **money,** which is simply a convenient social invention to facilitate exchanges of goods and services. Historically, people have used cattle, cigarettes, shells, stones, pieces of metal, and many other commodities, with varying degrees of success, as money. To serve as money, an item needs to pass only one test: It must be generally acceptable to sellers in exchange for their goods and services. Money is socially defined; whatever society accepts as a medium of exchange *is* money.

medium of exchange
Any item sellers generally accept and buyers generally use to pay for goods and services.

barter
The exchange of one good or service for another good or service.

money
Any item that is generally acceptable to sellers in exchange for goods and services.

FIGURE 2.1 **Money facilitates trade when wants do not coincide.** The use of money as a medium of exchange permits trade to be accomplished despite a noncoincidence of wants. (1) Nebraska trades the wheat that Florida wants for money from Floridians; (2) Nebraska trades the money it receives from Florida for the potatoes it wants from Idaho; (3) Idaho trades the money it receives from Nebraska for the oranges it wants from Florida.

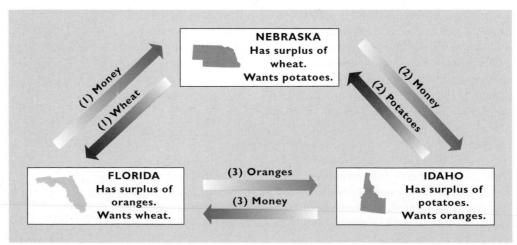

Today, most economies use pieces of paper as money. The use of paper dollars (currency) as a medium of exchange is what enables Nebraska, Florida, and Idaho to overcome their trade stalemate, as demonstrated in Figure 2.1.

On a global basis, specialization and exchange are complicated by the fact that different nations have different currencies. But markets in which currencies are bought and sold make it possible for people living in different countries to exchange goods and services without resorting to barter.

Active, but Limited, Government

An active, but limited, government is the final characteristic of market systems in real-life advanced industrial economies. Although a market system promotes a high degree of efficiency in the use of its resources, it has certain inherent shortcomings. We will discover in Chapter 5 that government can increase the overall effectiveness of the economic system in several ways.

Four Fundamental Questions

The key features of the market system help explain how market economies respond to four fundamental questions:

- What goods and services will be produced?
- How will the goods and services be produced?
- Who will get the goods and services?
- How will the system promote progress?

These four questions highlight the economic choices underlying the production possibilities curve discussed in Chapter 1. They reflect the reality of scarce resources in a world of unlimited wants. All economies, whether market or command, must address these four questions.

What Will Be Produced?

How will a market system decide on the specific types and quantities of goods to be produced? The simple answer is this: The goods and services that can be produced at a continuing profit will be produced, while those whose production generates a continuing loss will be discontinued. Profits and losses are the difference between the total revenue (TR) a firm receives from the sale of its products and the total cost (TC) of producing those products. (For economists, total costs include not only wage and salary payments to labor, and interest and rental payments for capital and land, but also payments to the entrepreneur for organizing and combining the other resources to produce a product.)

Continuing economic profit (TR > TC) in an industry results in expanded production and the movement of resources toward that industry. The industry expands. Continuing losses (TC > TR) in an industry leads to reduced production and the exit of resources from that industry. The industry contracts.

In the market system, consumers are sovereign (in command). **Consumer sovereignty** is crucial in determining the types and quantities of goods produced. Consumers spend their income on the goods they are most willing and able to buy. Through these **"dollar votes"** they register their wants in the market. If the dollar votes for a certain product are great enough to create a profit, businesses will produce that product and offer it for sale. In contrast, if the dollar votes do not create sufficient revenues to cover costs, businesses will not produce the product. So the consumers are sovereign. They collectively direct resources to industries that are meeting consumer wants and away from industries that are not meeting consumer wants.

consumer sovereignty
Determination by consumers of the types and quantities of goods and services that will be produced with the economy's scarce resources.

dollar votes
The "votes" that consumers and entrepreneurs cast for the production of consumer and capital goods when they purchase them in product and resource markets.

McHits and McMisses

McDonald's has introduced several new menu items over the decades. Some have been profitable "hits," while others have been "misses." Ultimately, consumers decide whether a menu item is profitable and therefore whether it stays on the McDonald's menu.

- Hulaburger (1962)—McMiss
- Filet-O-Fish (1963)—McHit
- Strawberry shortcake (1966)—McMiss
- Big Mac (1968)—McHit
- Hot apple pie (1968)—McHit
- Egg McMuffin (1975)—McHit
- Drive-thru (1975)—McHit
- Chicken McNuggets (1983)—McHit
- Extra Value Meal (1991)—McHit
- McLean Deluxe (1991)—McMiss
- Arch Deluxe (1996)—McMiss
- 55-cent special (1997)—McMiss
- Big Xtra (1999)—McHit
- McSalad Shaker (2000)—McMiss
- McGriddle (2003)—McHit
- Snack Wrap (2006)—McHit

QUESTION: Do you think McDonald's premium salads will be a lasting McHit, or do you think they eventually will become a McMiss?

Source: Dyan Machan, "Polishing the Golden Arches," *Forbes*, June 15, 1998, pp. 42–43, updated. Used with permission of Forbes Media LLC © 2011.

The dollar votes of consumers determine not only which industries will continue to exist but also which products will survive or fail. Only profitable industries, firms, and products survive.

How Will the Goods and Services Be Produced?

What combinations of resources and technologies will be used to produce goods and services? How will the production be organized? The answer: In combinations and ways that minimize the cost per unit of output. This is true because inefficiency drives up costs and lowers profits. As a result, any firm wishing to maximize its profits will make great efforts to minimize production costs. These efforts will include using the right mix of labor and capital, given the prices and productivity of those resources. They also mean locating production facilities optimally to hold down production and transportation expenses. Finally, it means using the most appropriate technology in producing and distributing output.

Those efforts will be intensified if the firm faces competition, as consumers strongly prefer low prices and will shift their purchases over to the firms that can produce a quality product at the lowest possible price. Any firm foolish enough to use higher-cost production methods will go bankrupt as it is undersold by its more efficient competitors who can still make a profit when selling at a lower price. Simply stated: Competition eliminates high-cost producers.

Who Will Get the Output?

The market system enters the picture in two ways when determining the distribution of total output. Generally, any product will be distributed to consumers on the basis of their ability and willingness to pay its existing market price. If the price of some product, say, a small sailboat, is $3000, then buyers who are willing and able to pay that price will "sail, sail away." Consumers who are unwilling or unable to pay the price will "sit on the dock of the bay."

The ability to pay the prices for sailboats and other products depends on the amount of income that consumers have, along with the prices of, and preferences for, various goods. If consumers have sufficient income and want to spend their money on a particular good, they can have it. And the amount of income they have depends on (1) the quantities of the property and human resources they supply and (2) the prices those resources command in the resource market. Resource prices (wages, interest, rent, profit) are key in determining the size of each household's income and therefore each household's ability to buy part of the economy's output.

How Will the System Promote Progress?

Society desires economic growth (greater output) and higher standards of living (greater output *per person*). How does the market system promote technological improvements and capital accumulation, both of which contribute to a higher standard of living for society?

Technological Advance   The market system provides a strong incentive for technological advance and enables better products and processes to supplant inferior ones. An entrepreneur or firm that introduces a popular new product will gain revenue and economic profit at the expense of rivals. Firms that are highly profitable one year may find they are in financial trouble just a few years later.

Technological advance also includes new and improved methods that reduce production or distribution costs. By passing part of its cost reduction on to the consumer through a lower product price, the firm can increase sales and obtain economic profit at the expense of rival firms.

Moreover, the market system promotes the *rapid spread* of technological advance throughout an industry. Rival firms must follow the lead of the most innovative firm or else suffer immediate losses and eventual failure. In some cases, the result is **creative destruction:** The creation of new products and production methods completely destroys the market positions of firms that are wedded to existing products and older ways of doing business. Example: The advent of compact discs largely demolished long-play vinyl records, and iPods and other digital technologies are now supplanting CDs.

creative destruction
The idea that the creation of new products and production methods may simultaneously destroy the market power of existing firms.

Capital Accumulation   Most technological advances require additional capital goods. The market system provides the resources necessary to produce additional capital through increased dollar votes for those goods. That is, the market system acknowledges dollar voting for capital goods as well as for consumer goods.

But who counts the dollar votes for capital goods? Answer: Entrepreneurs and business owners. As receivers of profit income, they often use part of that income to purchase capital goods. Doing so yields even greater profit income in the future if the technological innovation that required the additional capital goods is successful. Also, by paying interest or selling ownership shares, the entrepreneur and firm can attract some of the income of households to cast dollar votes for the production of more capital goods.

"invisible hand"
The tendency of firms and resource suppliers that are seeking to further their own self-interest in competitive markets to also promote the interest of society as a whole.

The "Invisible Hand"

In his 1776 book *The Wealth of Nations*, Adam Smith first noted that the operation of a market system creates a curious unity between private interests and social interests. Firms and resource suppliers, seeking to further their own self-interest and operating within the framework of a highly competitive market system, will simultaneously, as though guided by an **"invisible hand,"** promote the public or social interest. For example, we have seen that in a competitive environment, businesses seek to build new and improved products to increase profits. Those enhanced products increase society's well-being. Businesses also use the least costly combination of resources to produce a specific output because it is in their self-interest to do so. To act otherwise would be to forgo profit or even to risk business failure. But, at the same time, to use scarce resources in the least costly way is clearly in the social interest as well. It "frees up" resources to produce something else that society desires.

Self-interest, awakened and guided by the competitive market system, is what induces responses appropriate to the changes in society's wants. Businesses seeking to make higher profits and to avoid losses, and resource suppliers pursuing greater monetary rewards, negotiate changes in the allocation of resources and end up with the output that society wants. Competition controls or guides self-interest such that self-interest automatically and quite unintentionally furthers the best interest of society. The invisible hand ensures that when firms maximize their profits and resource suppliers maximize their incomes, these groups also help maximize society's output and income.

QUESTION: Are "doing good for others" and "doing well for oneself" conflicting ideas, according to Adam Smith?

The Demise of the Command Systems

Now that you know how the market system answers the four fundamental questions, you can easily understand why command systems of the Soviet Union, eastern Europe, and prereform China failed. Those systems encountered two insurmountable problems.

The first difficulty was the *coordination problem*. The central planners had to coordinate the millions of individual decisions by consumers, resource suppliers, and businesses. Consider the setting up of a factory to produce tractors. The central planners had to establish a realistic annual production target, for example, 1000 tractors. They then had to make available all the necessary inputs—labor, machinery, electric power, steel, tires, glass, paint, transportation—for the production and delivery of those 1000 tractors.

Because the outputs of many industries serve as inputs to other industries, the failure of any single industry to achieve its output target caused a chain reaction of repercussions. For example, if iron mines, for want of machinery or labor or transportation, did not supply the steel industry with the required inputs of iron ore, the steel mills were unable to fulfill the input needs of the many industries that depended on steel. Those steel-using industries (such as tractor, automobile, and transportation) were unable to fulfill their planned production goals. Eventually the chain reaction spread to all firms that used steel as an input and from there to other input buyers or final consumers.

The coordination problem became more difficult as the economies expanded. Products and production processes grew more sophisticated, and the number of industries requiring planning increased. Planning techniques that worked for the simpler economy proved highly inadequate and inefficient for the larger economy. Bottlenecks and production stoppages became the norm, not the exception.

A lack of a reliable success indicator added to the coordination problem in the Soviet Union and prereform China. We have seen that market economies rely on profit as a success indicator. Profit depends on consumer demand, production efficiency, and product quality. In contrast, the major success indicator for the command economies usually was a quantitative production target that the central planners assigned. Production costs, product quality, and product mix were secondary considerations. Managers and workers often sacrificed product quality because they were being awarded bonuses for meeting quantitative, not qualitative, targets. If meeting production goals meant sloppy assembly work, so be it.

It was difficult at best for planners to assign quantitative production targets without unintentionally producing distortions in output. If the production target for an enterprise manufacturing nails was specified in terms of *weight* (tons of nails), the producer made only large nails. But if its target was specified as a *quantity* (thousands of nails), the producer made all small nails, and lots of them!

The command economies also faced an *incentive problem*. Central planners determined the output mix. When they misjudged how many automobiles, shoes, shirts, and chickens were wanted at the government-determined prices, persistent shortages and surpluses of those products arose. But as long as the managers who oversaw the production of those goods were rewarded for meeting their assigned production goals, they had no incentive to adjust production in response to the shortages and surpluses. And there were no fluctuations in prices and profitability to signal that more or less of certain products was desired. Thus, many products were unavailable or in short supply, while other products were overproduced and sat for months or years in warehouses.

The command systems of the Soviet Union and prereform China also lacked entrepreneurship. Central planning did not trigger the profit motive, nor did it reward innovation and enterprise. The route for getting ahead was through participation in the political hierarchy of the Communist Party. Moving up the hierarchy meant better housing, better access to health care, and the right to shop in special stores. Meeting production targets and maneuvering through the minefields of party politics were measures of success in "business." But a definition of business success based solely on political savvy is not conducive to technological advance, which is often disruptive to existing products, production methods, and organizational structures.

QUESTION: In market economies, firms rarely worry about the availability of inputs to produce their products, whereas in command economies input availability was a constant concern. Why the difference?

FIGURE 2.2 The circular flow diagram. Products flow from businesses to households through the product market, and resources flow from households to businesses through the resource market. Opposite those real flows are monetary flows. Households receive income from businesses (their costs) through the resource market, and businesses receive revenue from households (their expenditures) through the product market.

The Circular Flow Model

circular flow diagram
The flow of resources from households to firms and of products from firms to households.

The dynamic market economy creates continuous, repetitive flows of goods and services, resources, and money. The **circular flow diagram,** shown in Figure 2.2, illustrates those flows for a simplified economy in which there is no government. Observe that in the diagram we group this economy's decision makers into *businesses* and *households*. Additionally, we divide this economy's markets into the *resource market* and the *product market*.

Households

households
One or more persons occupying a housing unit that provide resources to the economy and use income received to purchase goods and services that satisfy economic wants.

The blue rectangle on the right side of the circular flow diagram in Figure 2.2 represents **households,** which are defined as one or more persons occupying a housing unit. There are currently about 116 million households in the U.S. economy. Households buy the goods and services that businesses make available in the product market. Households obtain the income needed to buy those products by selling resources in the resource market.

All the resources in our no-government economy are ultimately owned or provided by households. For instance, the members of one household or another directly provide all of the labor and entrepreneurial ability in the economy. Households also own all of the land and all of the capital in the economy either directly, as personal property, or indirectly, as a consequence of owning all of the businesses in the economy (and thereby controlling all of the land and capital owned by businesses). Thus, all of the income in the economy—all wages, rents, interest, and profits—flows to households because they provide the economy's labor, land, capital, and entrepreneurial ability.

Businesses

businesses
Firms that purchase resources and provide goods and services to the economy.

The blue rectangle on the left side of the circular flow diagram represents **businesses,** which are commercial establishments that attempt to earn profits for their owners by offering goods and services for sale. Businesses sell goods and services in the product market in order to obtain revenue, and they incur costs in the resource markets when they purchase the labor, land, capital, and entrepreneurial ability that they need to produce their respective goods and services.

Product Market

The red rectangle at the bottom of the diagram represents the **product market,** the place where goods and services produced by businesses are bought and sold. Households use the income they receive from the sale of resources to buy goods and services. The money that consumers spend on goods and services flows to businesses as revenue. Businesses compare those revenues to their costs in determining profitability and whether or not a particular good or service should continue to be produced.

product market
A market in which goods and services (products) are sold by firms and bought by households.

Resource Market

Finally, the red rectangle at the top of the circular flow diagram represents the **resource market** in which households sell resources to businesses. The households sell resources to generate income, and the businesses buy resources to produce goods and services. The funds that businesses pay for resources are costs to businesses but are flows of wage, rent, interest, and profit income to the household. Productive resources therefore flow from households to businesses, and money flows from businesses to households.

resource market
A market in which households sell and firms buy economic resources.

The circular flow model depicts a complex, interrelated web of decision making and economic activity involving businesses and households. For the economy, it is the circle of life. Businesses and households are both buyers and sellers. Businesses buy resources and sell products. Households buy products and sell resources. As shown in Figure 2.2, there is a counterclockwise *real flow* of economic resources and finished goods and services and a clockwise *money flow* of income and consumption expenditures.

ORIGIN OF THE IDEA

O 2.4
Circular flow diagram

© T. O'Keefe/PhotoLink/Getty Images

© Royalty Free/CORBIS

PHOTO OP Resource Markets and Product Markets

The sale of a grove of orange trees would be a transaction in the resource market; the sale of oranges to final consumers would be a transaction in the product market.

Some Facts about U.S. Businesses

Businesses constitute one part of the private sector. The business population is extremely diverse, ranging from giant corporations such as Walmart, with 2010 sales of $405 billion and 2.1 million employees, to neighborhood specialty shops with one or two employees and sales of only $200 to $300 per day. There are three major legal forms of businesses: sole proprietorships, partnerships, and corporations.

A *sole proprietorship* is a business owned and operated by one person. Usually, the proprietor (the owner) personally supervises its operation. In a *partnership*, two or more individuals (the partners) agree to own and operate a business together.

A *corporation* is a legal creation that can acquire resources, own assets, produce and sell products, incur debts, extend credit, sue and be sued, and perform the functions of any other type of enterprise. A corporation sells stocks (ownership shares) to raise funds but is legally distinct and separate from the individual stockholders. The stockholders' legal and financial liability is limited to the loss of the value of their shares. Hired executives and managers operate corporations on a day-to-day basis.

Figure 2.3a shows how the business population is distributed among the three major legal forms. About 72% of firms are sole proprietorships, whereas only 18% are corporations. But as Figure 2.3b indicates, corporations account for 82% of total sales revenue (and therefore total output) in the United States. Virtually all the nation's largest business enterprises are corporations. Global Snapshot 2.3 lists the world's largest corporations.

QUESTION: Why do you think sole proprietorships and partnerships typically incorporate (become corporations) when they experience rapid and sizable increases in their production, sales, and profits?

FIGURE 2.3   The business population and shares of total revenue. (a) Sole proprietorships dominate the business population numerically, but (b) corporations dominate total sales revenue (total output). *Source:* U.S. Census Bureau, **www.census.gov**.

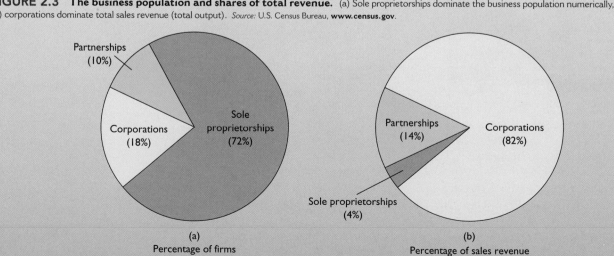

(a)
Percentage of firms

(b)
Percentage of sales revenue

GLOBAL SNAPSHOT 2.3

The World's 10 Largest Corporations

Two of the world's ten largest corporations, based on dollar revenue in 2010, were headquartered in the United States. For the first time, China was home to the most, with three of the top ten.

Walmart (USA) $408 billion	
Royal Dutch Shell (Netherlands) $285 billion	
ExxonMobil (USA) $285 billion	
BP (Britain) $246 billion	
Toyota Motor (Japan) $204 billion	
Japan Post Holdings (Japan) $202 billion	
Sinopec (China) $188 billion	
State Grid (China) $184 billion	
AXA (France) $175 billion	
China National Petroleum (China) $165 billion	

Source: "Global 500," *Fortune Magazine,* July 26, 2010. © Time Inc., used under license.

APPLYING THE ANALYSIS

Some Facts about U.S. Households

Households constitute the second part of the private sector. The U.S. economy currently has about 114 million households. These households consist of one or more persons occupying a housing unit and are both the ultimate suppliers of all economic resources *and* the major spenders in the economy.

The nation's earned income is apportioned among wages, rents, interest, and profits. *Wages* are paid to labor; *rents* and *interest* are paid to owners of property resources; and *profits* are paid to the owners of corporations and unincorporated businesses.

Figure 2.4a shows the categories of U.S. income earned in 2010. The largest source of income for households is the wages and salaries paid to workers. Notice that the bulk of total U.S. income goes to labor, not to capital. Proprietors' income—the income of doctors, lawyers, small-business owners, farmers, and owners of other unincorporated enterprises—also has a "wage" element. Some of this income is payment for one's own labor, and some of it is profit from one's own business.

The other three types of income are self-evident: Some households own corporate stock and receive dividend incomes as their share of corporate profits. Many households also own bonds and savings accounts that yield interest income. And some households receive rental income by providing buildings and natural resources (including land) to businesses and other individuals.

U.S. households use their income to buy (spend), save, and pay taxes. Figure 2.4b shows how households divide their spending among three broad categories of goods and services: *consumer durables* (goods such as cars, refrigerators, and personal computers that have expected lives of 3 years or longer), *nondurables* (goods such as food, clothing, and gasoline that have lives of less than 3 years), and *services* (the work done by people such as lawyers, physicians, and recreational workers). Observe that approximately 65% of consumer spending is on services. For this reason, the United States is known as a *service-oriented economy*.

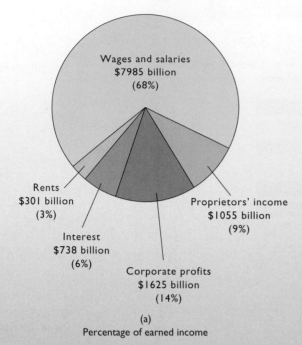

Wages and salaries
$7985 billion
(68%)

Rents
$301 billion
(3%)

Interest
$738 billion
(6%)

Corporate profits
$1625 billion
(14%)

Proprietors' income
$1055 billion
(9%)

(a)
Percentage of earned income

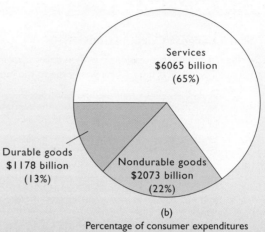

Services
$6065 billion
(65%)

Durable goods
$1178 billion
(13%)

Nondurable goods
$2073 billion
(22%)

(b)
Percentage of consumer expenditures

FIGURE 2.4 Sources of U.S. income and the composition of spending. (a) Sixty-eight percent of U.S. income is received as wages and salaries. Income to property owners—corporate profit, interest, and rents—accounts for about 23% of total income. (b) Consumers divide their spending among durable goods, nondurable goods, and services. Roughly 65% of consumer spending is for services; the rest is for goods. *Source:* Bureau of Economic Analysis, **www.bea.gov.**

Question: Over the past several decades, the service share of spending in the United States has increased relative to the goods share. Why do you think that trend has occurred?

© PRNewsFoto/Whirlpool Corporation   © Ed Carey/Cole Group/Getty Images   © Royalty-Free/CORBIS

PHOTO OP Durable Goods, Nondurable Goods, and Services

Consumers collectively spend their income on durable goods (such as the washer-dryer combo), nondurable goods (such as the pizza), and services (such as hair care).

Summary

1. The market system and the command system are the two broad types of economic systems used to address the economic problem. In the market system (or capitalism), private individuals own most resources, and markets coordinate most economic activity. In the command system (or socialism or communism), government owns most resources, and central planners coordinate most economic activity.

2. The market system is characterized by the private ownership of resources, including capital, and the freedom of individuals to engage in economic activities of their choice to advance their material well-being. Self-interest is the driving force of such an economy, and competition functions as a regulatory or control mechanism.

3. In the market system, markets, prices, and profits organize and make effective the many millions of individual economic decisions that occur daily.

4. Specialization, use of advanced technology, and the extensive use of capital goods are common features of market systems. Functioning as a medium of exchange, money eliminates the problems of bartering and permits easy trade and greater specialization, both domestically and internationally.

5. Every economy faces four fundamental questions: (a) What goods and services will be produced? (b) How will the goods and services be produced? (c) Who will get the goods and services? (d) How will the system promote progress?

6. The market system produces products whose production and sale yield total revenue sufficient to cover total cost. It does not produce products for which total revenue continuously falls short of total cost. Competition forces firms to use the lowest-cost production techniques.

7. Economic profit (total revenue minus total cost) indicates that an industry is prosperous and promotes its expansion. Losses signify that an industry is not prosperous and hasten its contraction.

8. Consumer sovereignty means that both businesses and resource suppliers are subject to the wants of consumers. Through their dollar votes, consumers decide on the composition of output.

9. The prices that a household receives for the resources it supplies to the economy determine that household's income. This income determines the household's claim on the economy's output. Those who have income to spend get the products produced in the market system.

10. The market system encourages technological advance and capital accumulation, both of which raise a nation's standard of living.

11. Competition, the primary mechanism of control in the market economy, promotes a unity of self-interest and social interests. As if directed by an invisible hand, competition harnesses the self-interested motives of businesses and resource suppliers to further the social interest.

12. The circular flow model illustrates the flows of resources and products from households to businesses and from businesses to households, along with the corresponding monetary flows. Businesses are on the buying side of the resource market and the selling side of the product market. Households are on the selling side of the resource market and the buying side of the product market.

Terms and Concepts

economic system	self-interest	barter	circular flow diagram
command system	competition	money	households
market system	market	consumer sovereignty	businesses
private property	specialization	dollar votes	product market
freedom of enterprise	division of labor	creative destruction	resource market
freedom of choice	medium of exchange	"invisible hand"	

Questions Mc Graw Hill **connect** | ECONOMICS

1. Contrast how a market system and a command economy try to cope with economic scarcity. **LO1**

2. How does self-interest help achieve society's economic goals? Why is there such a wide variety of desired goods and services in a market system? In what way are entrepreneurs and businesses at the helm of the economy but commanded by consumers? **LO2**

3. Why is private property, and the protection of property rights, so critical to the success of the market system? How do property rights encourage cooperation? **LO2**

4. What are the advantages of using capital in the production process? What is meant by the term "division of labor"? What are the advantages of specialization in the use of human and material resources? Explain why exchange is the necessary consequence of specialization. **LO2**

5. What problem does barter entail? Indicate the economic significance of money as a medium of exchange. What is meant by the statement "We want money only to part with it"? **LO2**

6. Evaluate and explain the following statements: **LO2**
   a. The market system is a profit-and-loss system.

b. Competition is the disciplinarian of the market economy.

7. In the 1990s thousands of "dot-com" companies emerged with great fanfare to take advantage of the Internet and new information technologies. A few, like Google, eBay, and Amazon, have generally thrived and prospered, but many others struggled and eventually failed. Explain these varied outcomes in terms of how the market system answers the question "What goods and services will be produced?" **LO3**

8. Some large hardware stores such as Home Depot boast of carrying as many as 20,000 different products in each store. What motivated the producers of those individual products to make them and offer them for sale? How did the producers decide on the best combinations of resources to use? Who made those resources available, and why? Who decides whether these particular hardware products should continue to be produced and offered for sale? **LO3**

9. What is meant by the term "creative destruction"? How does the emergence of MP3 (or iPod) technology relate to this idea? **LO3**

10. In a sentence, describe the meaning of the phrase "invisible hand." **LO4**

11. Distinguish between the resource market and the product market in the circular flow model. In what way are businesses and households both sellers and buyers in this model? What are the flows in the circular flow model? **LO5**

12. What are the three major legal forms of business enterprises? Which form is the most prevalent in terms of numbers? Which form is dominant in terms of total sales revenues? **LO5**

13. What are the major forms of household income? Contrast the wage and salary share to the profit share in terms of relative size. Distinguish between a durable consumer good and a nondurable consumer good. How does the combined spending on both types of consumer goods compare to the spending on services? **LO5**

Problems

1. Suppose Natasha currently makes $50,000 per year working as a manager at a cable TV company. She then develops two possible entrepreneurial business opportunities. In one, she will quit her job to start an organic soap company. In the other, she will try to develop an Internet-based competitor to the local cable company. For the soap-making opportunity, she anticipates annual revenue of $465,000 and costs for the necessary land, labor, and capital of $395,000 per year. For the Internet opportunity, she anticipates costs for land, labor, and capital of $3,250,000 per year as compared to revenues of $3,275,000 per year. (a) Should she quit her current job to become an entrepreneur? (b) If she does quit her current job, which opportunity would she pursue? **LO3**

2. With current technology, suppose a firm is producing 400 loaves of banana bread daily. Also assume that the least-cost combination of resources in producing those loaves is 5 units of labor, 7 units of land, 2 units of capital, and 1 unit of entrepreneurial ability, selling at prices of $40, $60, $60, and $20, respectively. If the firm can sell these 400 loaves at $2 per unit, what is its total revenue? Its total cost? Its profit or loss? Will it continue to produce banana bread? If this firm's situation is typical for the other makers of banana bread, will resources flow toward or away from this bakery good? **LO3**

3. Let's put dollar amounts on the flows in the circular flow diagram of Figure 2.2. **LO5**

   a. Suppose that businesses buy a total of $100 billion of the four resources (labor, land, capital, and entrepreneurial ability) from households. If households receive $60 billion in wages, $10 billion in rent, and $20 billion in interest, how much are households paid for providing entrepreneurial ability?

   b. If households spend $55 billion on goods and $45 billion on services, how much in revenues do businesses receive in the product market?

FURTHER TEST YOUR KNOWLEDGE AT
www.mcconnellbrief2e.com

At the text's Online Learning Center, **www.mcconnellbrief2e.com**, you will find one or more web-based questions that require information from the Internet to answer. We urge you to check them out, since they will familiarize you with websites that may be helpful in other courses and perhaps even in your career. The OLC also features multiple-choice quizzes that give instant feedback and provides other helpful ways to further test your knowledge of the chapter.

Visit your mobile app store and download the McConnell Brief Edition: Study Econ app *today*!

PART TWO

PRICE, QUANTITY, AND EFFICIENCY

3

After reading this chapter, you should be able to:

1 Describe *demand* and explain how it can change.

2 Describe *supply* and explain how it can change.

3 Relate how supply and demand interact to determine market equilibrium.

4 Explain how changes in supply and demand affect equilibrium prices and quantities.

5 Identify what government-set prices are and how they can cause product surpluses and shortages.

Demand, Supply, and Market Equilibrium

The model of supply and demand is the economics profession's greatest contribution to human understanding because it explains the operation of the markets on which we depend for nearly everything that we eat, drink, or consume. The model is so powerful and so widely used that to many people it *is* economics.

Markets bring together buyers ("demanders") and sellers ("suppliers") and exist in many forms. The corner gas station, an e-commerce site, the local music store, a farmer's roadside stand—all are familiar markets. The New York Stock Exchange and the Chicago Board of Trade are markets where buyers and sellers of stocks and bonds and farm commodities from all over the world communicate with one another to buy and sell. Auctioneers bring together potential buyers and sellers of art, livestock, used farm equipment, and, sometimes, real estate.

Some markets are local, while others are national or international. Some are highly personal, involving face-to-face contact between demander and supplier; others are faceless, with buyer and seller never seeing or knowing each other. But all competitive markets involve demand and supply, and this chapter discusses how the model works to explain both the *quantities* that are bought and sold in markets as well as the *prices* at which they trade.

ORIGIN OF THE IDEA

O 3.1

Demand and supply

Demand

Demand is a schedule or a curve that shows the various amounts of a product that consumers will purchase at each of several possible prices during a specified period of time.[1] The table in Figure 3.1 is a hypothetical demand schedule for a *single consumer* purchasing a particular product, in this case, lattes. (For simplicity, we will categorize all espresso drinks as "lattes" and assume a highly competitive market.)

The table reveals that, if the price of lattes were $5 each, Joe Java would buy 10 lattes per month; if it were $4, he would buy 20 lattes per month; and so forth.

The table does not tell us which of the five possible prices will actually exist in the market. That depends on the interaction between demand and supply. Demand is simply a statement of a buyer's plans, or intentions, with respect to the purchase of a product.

To be meaningful, the quantities demanded at each price must relate to a specific period—a day, a week, a month. Here that period is 1 month.

demand
A schedule or curve that shows the various amounts of a product that consumers will buy at each of a series of possible prices during a specific period.

Law of Demand

A fundamental characteristic of demand is this: Other things equal, as price falls, the quantity demanded rises, and as price rises, the quantity demanded falls. In short, there

ORIGIN OF THE IDEA

O 3.2

Law of demand

---

[1]This definition obviously is worded to apply to product markets. To adjust it to apply to resource markets, substitute the word "resource" for "product" and the word "businesses" for "consumers."

FIGURE 3.1 Joe Java's demand for lattes. Because price and quantity demanded are inversely related, an individual's demand schedule graphs as a downsloping curve such as *D*. Other things equal, consumers will buy more of a product as its price declines and less of the product as its price rises. (Here and in later figures, *P* stands for price and *Q* stands for quantity demanded or supplied.)

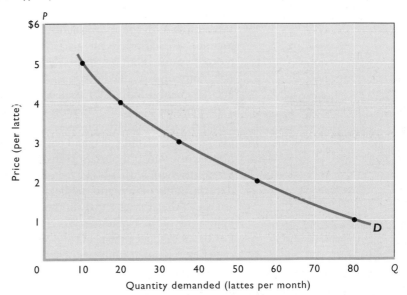

Joe Java's Demand for Lattes	
Price per Latte	**Quantity Demanded per Month**
$5	10
4	20
3	35
2	55
1	80

is an *inverse* relationship between price and quantity demanded. Economists call this inverse relationship the **law of demand.**

law of demand
The principle that, other things equal, as price falls, the quantity demanded rises, and as price rises, the quantity demanded falls.

The other-things-equal assumption is critical here. Many factors other than the price of the product being considered affect the amount purchased. The quantity of lattes purchased will depend not only on the price of lattes but also on the prices of such substitutes as tea, soda, fruit juice, and bottled water. The law of demand in this case says that fewer lattes will be purchased if the price of lattes rises while the prices of tea, soda, fruit juice, and bottled water all remain constant.

The law of demand is consistent with both common sense and observation. People ordinarily *do* buy more of a product at a low price than at a high price. Price is an obstacle that deters consumers from buying. The higher that obstacle, the less of a product they will buy; the lower the obstacle, the more they will buy. The fact that businesses reduce prices to clear out unsold goods is evidence of their belief in the law of demand.

The Demand Curve

demand curve
A curve illustrating the inverse relationship between the price of a product and the quantity of it demanded, other things equal.

The inverse relationship between price and quantity demanded for any product can be represented on a simple graph, in which, by convention, we measure *quantity demanded* on the horizontal axis and *price* on the vertical axis. In Figure 3.1 we have plotted the five price-quantity data points listed in the table and connected the points with a smooth curve, labeled *D.* This is a **demand curve.** Its downward slope reflects the law of demand: People buy more of a product, service, or resource as its price falls. They buy less as its price rises. There is an inverse relationship between price and quantity demanded.

The table and graph in Figure 3.1 contain exactly the same data and reflect the same inverse relationship between price and quantity demanded.

Market Demand

So far, we have concentrated on just one consumer, Joe Java. But competition requires that more than one buyer be present in each market. By adding the quantities demanded by all consumers at each of the various possible prices, we can get from *individual* demand to *market* demand. If there are just three buyers in the market (Joe Java, Sarah Coffee, and Mike Cappuccino), as represented by the table and graph in Figure 3.2, it is relatively easy to determine the total quantity demanded at each price. We simply sum the individual quantities demanded to obtain the total quantity demanded at each price. The particular price and the total quantity demanded are then plotted as one point on the market demand curve in Figure 3.2.

Competition, of course, ordinarily entails many more than three buyers of a product. To avoid hundreds or thousands of additions, let's simply suppose that the table and curve D_1 in Figure 3.3 show the amounts all the buyers in this market will purchase at each of the five prices.

determinants of demand
Factors other than price that locate the position of a demand curve.

In constructing a demand curve such as D_1 in Figure 3.3, economists assume that price is the most important influence on the amount of any product purchased. But economists know that other factors can and do affect purchases. These factors, called **determinants of demand,** are held constant when a demand curve like D_1 is drawn. They are the "other things equal" in the relationship between price and quantity demanded. When any of these determinants changes, the demand curve will shift to the right or left. For this reason, determinants of demand are sometimes referred to as *demand shifters.*

The basic determinants of demand are (1) consumers' tastes (preferences), (2) the number of consumers in the market, (3) consumers' incomes, (4) the prices of related goods, and (5) expected prices.

FIGURE 3.2 Market demand for lattes, three buyers. We establish the market demand curve D by adding horizontally the individual demand curves (D_1, D_2, and D_3) of all the consumers in the market. At the price of $3, for example, the three individual curves yield a total quantity demanded of 100 lattes.

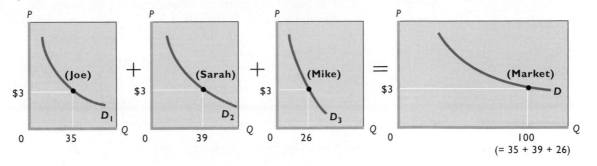

			Market Demand for Lattes, Three Buyers				
Price per Latte		**Quantity Demanded**					**Total Quantity Demanded per Month**
	Joe Java		**Sarah Coffee**		**Mike Cappuccino**		
$5	10	+	12	+	8	=	30
4	20	+	23	+	17	=	60
3	35	+	39	+	26	=	100
2	55	+	60	+	39	=	154
1	80	+	87	+	54	=	221

FIGURE 3.3 Changes in the demand for lattes. A change in one or more of the determinants of demand causes a change in demand. An increase in demand is shown as a shift of the demand curve to the right, as from D_1 to D_2. A decrease in demand is shown as a shift of the demand curve to the left, as from D_1 to D_3. These changes in demand are to be distinguished from a change in *quantity demanded*, which is caused by a change in the price of the product, as shown by a movement from, say, point a to point b on fixed demand curve D_1.

Market Demand for Lattes (D)	
(1)	**(2)**
Price per Latte	**Total Quantity Demanded per Month**
$5	2,000
4	4,000
3	7,000
2	11,000
1	16,000

Quantity demanded (thousands of lattes per month)

Changes in Demand

A change in one or more of the determinants of demand will change the underlying demand data (the demand schedule in the table) and therefore the location of the demand curve in Figure 3.3. A change in the demand schedule or, graphically, a shift in the demand curve is called a *change in demand*.

If consumers desire to buy more lattes at each possible price, that *increase in demand* is shown as a shift of the demand curve to the right, say, from D_1 to D_2. Conversely, a *decrease in demand* occurs when consumers buy fewer lattes at each possible price. The leftward shift of the demand curve from D_1 to D_3 in Figure 3.3 shows that situation.

Now let's see how changes in each determinant affect demand.

Tastes   A favorable change in consumer tastes (preferences) for a product means more of it will be demanded at each price. Demand will increase; the demand curve will shift rightward. For example, greater concern about the environment has increased the demand for hybrid cars and other "green" technologies. An unfavorable change in consumer preferences will decrease demand, shifting the demand curve to the left. For example, the recent popularity of low-carbohydrate diets has reduced the demand for bread and pasta.

Number of Buyers   An increase in the number of buyers in a market increases product demand. For example, the rising number of older persons in the United States in recent years has increased the demand for motor homes and retirement communities. In contrast, the migration of people away from many small rural communities has reduced the demand for housing, home appliances, and auto repair in those towns.

Income   The effect of changes in income on demand is more complex. For most products, a rise in income increases demand. Consumers collectively buy more airplane tickets, projection TVs, and gas grills as their incomes rise. Products whose demand increases or decreases *directly* with changes in income are called *superior goods*, or **normal goods.**

Although most products are normal goods, there are a few exceptions. As incomes increase beyond some point, the demand for used clothing, retread tires, and soy-enhanced hamburger may decline. Higher incomes enable consumers to buy new clothing, new tires, and higher-quality meats. Goods whose demand increases or decreases *inversely* with money income are called **inferior goods.** (This is an economic term; we are not making personal judgments on specific products.)

Prices of Related Goods   A change in the price of a related good may either increase or decrease the demand for a product, depending on whether the related good is a substitute or a complement:

- A **substitute good** is one that can be used in place of another good.
- A **complementary good** is one that is used together with another good.

Beef and chicken are substitute goods or, simply, *substitutes*. When two products are substitutes, an increase in the price of one will increase the demand for the other. For example, when the price of beef rises, consumers will buy less beef and increase their demand for chicken. So it is with other product pairs such as Nikes and Reeboks, Budweiser and Miller beer, or Colgate and Crest toothpaste. They are *substitutes in consumption*.

normal good
A good (or service) whose consumption rises when income increases and falls when income decreases.

inferior good
A good (or service) whose consumption declines when income rises and rises when income decreases.

substitute good
A good (or service) that can be used in place of some other good (or service).

complementary good
A good (or service) that is used in conjunction with some other good (or service).

© Bambu Producoes/Getty Images   © Doug Menuez/Getty Images

PHOTO OP   Normal versus Inferior Goods

New television sets are normal goods. People buy more of them as their incomes rise. Hand-pushed lawn mowers are inferior goods. As incomes rise, people purchase gas-powered mowers instead.

Complementary goods (or, simply, *complements*) are products that are used together and thus are typically demanded jointly. Examples include computers and software, cell phones and cellular service, and snowboards and lift tickets. If the price of a complement (for example, lettuce) goes up, the demand for the related good (salad dressing) will decline. Conversely, if the price of a complement (for example, tuition) falls, the demand for a related good (textbooks) will increase.

The vast majority of goods that are unrelated to one another are called *independent goods*. There is virtually no demand relationship between bacon and golf balls or pickles and ice cream. A change in the price of one will have virtually no effect on the demand for the other.

Expected Prices   Changes in expected prices may shift demand. A newly formed expectation of a higher price in the future may cause consumers to buy now in order to "beat" the anticipated price rise, thus increasing current demand. For example, when freezing weather destroys much of Brazil's coffee crop, buyers may conclude that the price of coffee beans will rise. They may purchase large quantities now to stock up on beans. In contrast, a newly formed expectation of falling prices may decrease current demand for products.

© Michael Newman/PhotoEdit

© John A. Rizzo/Getty Images

PHOTO OP   Substitutes versus Complements

Different brands of soft drinks are substitute goods; goods consumed jointly such as hot dogs and mustard are complementary goods.

Changes in Quantity Demanded

change in demand
A change in the quantity demanded of a product at every price; a shift of the demand curve to the left or right.

Be sure not to confuse a *change in demand* with a *change in quantity demanded*. A **change in demand** is a shift of the demand curve to the right (an increase in demand) or to the left (a decrease in demand). It occurs because the consumer's state of mind about purchasing the product has been altered in response to a change in one or more of the determinants of demand. Recall that "demand" is a schedule or a curve; therefore, a "change in demand" means a change in the schedule and a shift of the curve.

change in quantity demanded
A movement from one point to another on a fixed demand curve.

In contrast, a **change in quantity demanded** is a movement from one point to another point—from one price-quantity combination to another—on a fixed demand curve. The cause of such a change is an increase or decrease in the price of the product under consideration. In the table in Figure 3.3, for example, a decline in the price of lattes from $5 to $4 will increase the quantity of lattes demanded from 2000 to 4000.

In the graph in Figure 3.3, the shift of the demand curve D_1 to either D_2 or D_3 is a change in demand. But the movement from point *a* to point *b* on curve D_1 represents a change in quantity demanded: Demand has not changed; it is the entire curve, and it remains fixed in place.

Supply

supply
A schedule or curve that shows the amounts of a product that producers are willing to make available for sale at each of a series of possible prices during a specific period.

Supply is a schedule or curve showing the amounts of a product that producers will make available for sale at each of a series of possible prices during a specific period.[2] The table in Figure 3.4 is a hypothetical supply schedule for Star Buck, a single supplier of lattes. Curve *S* incorporates the data in the table and is called a *supply curve*. The

---

[2]This definition is worded to apply to product markets. To adjust it to apply to resource markets, substitute "resource" for "product" and "owners" for "producers."

FIGURE 3.4 Star Buck's supply of lattes. Because price and quantity supplied are directly related, the supply curve for an individual producer graphs as an upsloping curve. Other things equal, producers will offer more of a product for sale as its price rises and less of the product for sale as its price falls.

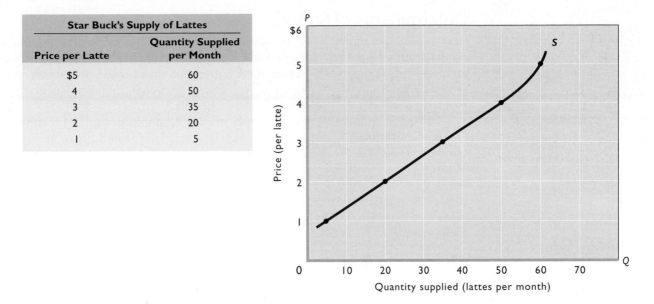

Star Buck's Supply of Lattes	
Price per Latte	Quantity Supplied per Month
$5	60
4	50
3	35
2	20
1	5

schedule and curve show the quantities of lattes that will be supplied at various prices, other things equal.

Law of Supply

Figure 3.4 shows a positive or direct relationship that prevails between price and quantity supplied. As price rises, the quantity supplied rises; as price falls, the quantity supplied falls. This relationship is called the **law of supply.** A supply schedule or curve reveals that, other things equal, firms will offer for sale more of their product at a high price than at a low price. This, again, is basically common sense.

 Price is an obstacle from the standpoint of the consumer (for example, Joe Java), who is on the paying end. The higher the price, the less the consumer will buy. But the supplier (for example, Star Buck) is on the receiving end of the product's price. To a supplier, price represents *revenue*, which is needed to cover costs and earn a profit. Higher prices therefore create a profit incentive to produce and sell more of a product. The higher the price, the greater this incentive and the greater the quantity supplied.

law of supply
The principle that, other things equal, as price rises, the quantity supplied rises, and as price falls, the quantity supplied falls.

Market Supply

Market supply is derived from individual supply in exactly the same way that market demand is derived from individual demand (Figure 3.2). We sum (not shown) the quantities supplied by each producer at each price. That is, we obtain the market **supply curve** by "horizontally adding" (also not shown) the supply curves of the individual producers. The price and quantity-supplied data in the table in Figure 3.5 are for an assumed 200 identical producers in the market, each willing to supply lattes according to the supply schedule shown in Figure 3.4. Curve S_1 is a graph of the market supply data. Note that the axes in Figure 3.5 are the same as those used in our

supply curve
A curve illustrating the direct relationship between the price of a product and the quantity of it supplied, other things equal.

graph of market demand (Figure 3.3). The only difference is that we change the label on the horizontal axis from "quantity demanded" to "quantity supplied."

Determinants of Supply

determinants of supply
Factors other than price that locate the position of the supply curve.

In constructing a supply curve, we assume that price is the most significant influence on the quantity supplied of any product. But other factors (the "other things equal") can and do affect supply. The supply curve is drawn on the assumption that these other things are fixed and do not change. If one of them does change, a *change in supply* will occur, meaning that the entire supply curve will shift.

The basic **determinants of supply** are (1) resource prices, (2) technology, (3) taxes and subsidies, (4) prices of other goods, (5) expected price, and (6) the number of sellers in the market. A change in any one or more of these determinants of supply, or *supply shifters*, will move the supply curve for a product either right or left. A shift to the *right*, as from S_1 to S_2 in Figure 3.5, signifies an *increase* in supply: Producers supply larger quantities of the product at each possible price. A shift to the *left*, as from S_1 to S_3, indicates a *decrease* in supply: Producers offer less output at each price.

Changes in Supply

Let's consider how changes in each of the determinants affect supply. The key idea is that costs are a major factor underlying supply curves; anything that affects costs (other than changes in output itself) usually shifts the supply curve.

Resource Prices   The prices of the resources used in the production process help determine the costs of production incurred by firms. Higher *resource* prices raise production costs and, assuming a particular *product* price, squeeze profits. That reduction

FIGURE 3.5   Changes in the supply of lattes. A change in one or more of the determinants of supply causes a change in supply. An increase in supply is shown as a rightward shift of the supply curve, as from S_1 to S_2. A decrease in supply is depicted as a leftward shift of the curve, as from S_1 to S_3. In contrast, a change in the *quantity supplied* is caused by a change in the product's price and is shown by a movement from one point to another, as from *a* to *b* on fixed supply curve S_1.

Market Supply of Lattes (S_1)	
(1) Price per Latte	(2) Total Quantity Supplied per Month
$5	12,000
4	10,000
3	7000
2	4000
1	1000

in profits reduces the incentive for firms to supply output at each product price. For example, an increase in the prices of coffee beans and milk will increase the cost of making lattes and therefore reduce their supply.

In contrast, lower *resource* prices reduce production costs and increase profits. So when resource prices fall, firms supply greater output at each product price. For example, a decrease in the prices of sand, gravel, and limestone will increase the supply of concrete.

Technology   Improvements in technology (techniques of production) enable firms to produce units of output with fewer resources. Because resources are costly, using fewer of them lowers production costs and increases supply. Example: Technological advances in producing flat-panel computer monitors have greatly reduced their cost. Thus, manufacturers will now offer more such monitors than previously at the various prices; the supply of flat-panel monitors has increased.

Taxes and Subsidies   Businesses treat sales and property taxes as costs. Increases in those taxes will increase production costs and reduce supply. In contrast, subsidies are "taxes in reverse." If the government subsidizes the production of a good, it in effect lowers the producers' costs and increases supply.

Prices of Other Goods   Firms that produce a particular product, say, soccer balls, can usually use their plant and equipment to produce alternative goods, say, basketballs and volleyballs. The higher prices of these "other goods" may entice soccer ball producers to switch production to those other goods in order to increase profits. This *substitution in production* results in a decline in the supply of soccer balls. Alternatively, when basketballs and volleyballs decline in price relative to the price of soccer balls, firms will produce fewer of those products and more soccer balls, increasing the supply of soccer balls.

Expected Prices   Changes in expectations about the future price of a product may affect the producer's current willingness to supply that product. It is difficult, however, to generalize about how a new expectation of higher prices affects the present supply of a product. Farmers anticipating a higher wheat price in the future might withhold some of their current wheat harvest from the market, thereby causing a decrease in the current supply of wheat. In contrast, in many types of manufacturing industries, newly formed expectations that price will increase may induce firms to add another shift of workers or to expand their production facilities, causing current supply to increase.

Number of Sellers   Other things equal, the larger the number of suppliers, the greater the market supply. As more firms enter an industry, the supply curve shifts to the right. Conversely, the smaller the number of firms in the industry, the less the market supply. This means that as firms leave an industry, the supply curve shifts to the left. Example: The United States and Canada have imposed restrictions on haddock fishing to replenish dwindling stocks. As part of that policy, the federal government has bought the boats of some of the haddock fishers as a way of putting them out of business and decreasing the catch. The result has been a decline in the market supply of haddock.

Changes in Quantity Supplied

The distinction between a *change in supply* and a *change in quantity supplied* parallels the distinction between a change in demand and a change in quantity demanded. Because

change in supply
A change in the quantity supplied of a product at every price; a shift of the supply curve to the left or right.

change in quantity supplied
A movement from one point to another on a fixed supply curve.

supply is a schedule or curve, a **change in supply** means a change in the schedule and a shift of the curve. An increase in supply shifts the curve to the right; a decrease in supply shifts it to the left. The cause of a change in supply is a change in one or more of the determinants of supply.

In contrast, a **change in quantity supplied** is a movement from one point to another on a fixed supply curve. The cause of such a movement is a change in the price of the specific product being considered. In Figure 3.5, a decline in the price of lattes from $4 to $3 decreases the quantity of lattes supplied per month from 10,000 to 7000. This movement from point *b* to point *a* along S_1 is a change in quantity supplied, not a change in supply. Supply is the full schedule of prices and quantities shown, and this schedule does not change when the price of lattes changes.

Market Equilibrium

With our understanding of demand and supply, we can now show how the decisions of Joe Java and other buyers of lattes interact with the decisions of Star Buck and other sellers to determine the price and quantity of lattes. In the table in Figure 3.6, columns 1 and 2 repeat the market supply of lattes (from Figure 3.5), and columns 2 and 3 repeat the market demand for lattes (from Figure 3.3). We assume this is a competitive market, so neither buyers nor sellers can set the price.

Equilibrium Price and Quantity

equilibrium price
The price in a competitive market at which the quantity demanded and quantity supplied of a product are equal.

equilibrium quantity
The quantity demanded and quantity supplied that occur at the equilibrium price in a competitive market.

We are looking for the equilibrium price and equilibrium quantity. The **equilibrium price** (or *market-clearing price*) is the price at which the intentions of buyers and sellers match. It is the price at which quantity demanded equals quantity supplied. The table in Figure 3.6 reveals that at $3, *and only at that price*, the number of lattes that sellers wish to sell (7000) is identical to the number that consumers want to buy (also 7000). At $3 and 7000 lattes, there is neither a shortage nor a surplus of lattes. So 7000 lattes is the **equilibrium quantity:** the quantity at which the intentions of buyers and sellers match so that the quantity demanded and the quantity supplied are equal.

Graphically, the equilibrium price is indicated by the intersection of the supply curve and the demand curve in Figure 3.6. (The horizontal axis now measures both quantity demanded and quantity supplied.) With neither a shortage nor a surplus at $3, the market is *in equilibrium*, meaning "in balance" or "at rest."

surplus
The amount by which the quantity supplied of a product exceeds the quantity demanded at a specific (above-equilibrium) price.

To better understand the uniqueness of the equilibrium price, let's consider other prices. At any above-equilibrium price, quantity supplied exceeds quantity demanded. For example, at the $4 price, sellers will offer 10,000 lattes, but buyers will purchase only 4000. The $4 price encourages sellers to offer lots of lattes but discourages many consumers from buying them. The result is a **surplus** or *excess supply* of 6000 lattes. If latte sellers made them all, they would find themselves with 6000 unsold lattes.

Surpluses drive prices down. Even if the $4 price existed temporarily, it could not persist. The large surplus would prompt competing sellers to lower the price to encourage buyers to stop in and take the surplus off their hands. As the price fell, the incentive to produce lattes would decline and the incentive for consumers to buy lattes would increase. As shown in Figure 3.6, the market would move to its equilibrium at $3.

Any price below the $3 equilibrium price would create a shortage; quantity demanded would exceed quantity supplied. Consider a $2 price, for example. We see in column 4 of the table in Figure 3.6 that quantity demanded exceeds quantity

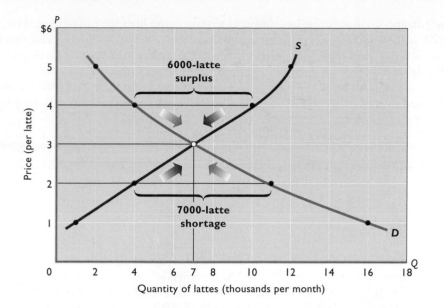

FIGURE 3.6 Equilibrium price and quantity. The intersection of the downsloping demand curve D and the upsloping supply curve S indicates the equilibrium price and quantity, here $3 and 7000 lattes. The shortages of lattes at below-equilibrium prices (for example, 7000 at $2) drive up price. The higher prices increase the quantity supplied and reduce the quantity demanded until equilibrium is achieved. The surpluses caused by above-equilibrium prices (for example, 6000 lattes at $4) push price down. As price drops, the quantity demanded rises and the quantity supplied falls until equilibrium is established. At the equilibrium price and quantity, there are neither shortages nor surpluses of lattes.

Market Supply of and Demand for Lattes			
(1) Total Quantity Supplied per Month	(2) Price per Latte	(3) Total Quantity Demanded per Month	(4) Surplus (+) or Shortage (−)*
12,000	$5	2000	+10,000 ↓
10,000	4	4000	+6000 ↓
7000	**3**	**7000**	**0**
4000	2	11,000	−7000 ↑
1000	1	16,000	−15,000 ↑

*Arrows indicate the effect on price.

supplied at that price. The result is a **shortage** or *excess demand* of 7000 lattes. The $2 price discourages sellers from devoting resources to lattes and encourages consumers to desire more lattes than are available. The $2 price cannot persist as the equilibrium price. Many consumers who want to buy lattes at this price will not obtain them. They will express a willingness to pay more than $2 to get them. Competition among these buyers will drive up the price, eventually to the $3 equilibrium level. Unless disrupted by supply or demand changes, this $3 price of lattes will continue.

Rationing Function of Prices

The ability of the competitive forces of supply and demand to establish a price at which selling and buying decisions are consistent is called the *rationing function of prices*. In our case, the equilibrium price of $3 clears the market, leaving no

shortage
The amount by which the quantity demanded of a product exceeds the quantity supplied at a specific (below-equilibrium) price.

INTERACTIVE GRAPHS

G 3.1

Supply and demand

burdensome surplus for sellers and no inconvenient shortage for potential buyers. And it is the combination of freely made individual decisions that sets this market-clearing price. In effect, the market outcome says that all buyers who are willing and able to pay $3 for a latte will obtain one; all buyers who cannot or will not pay $3 will go without one. Similarly, all producers who are willing and able to offer a latte for sale at $3 will sell it; all producers who cannot or will not sell for $3 will not sell their product.

APPLYING THE ANALYSIS

Ticket Scalping

Ticket prices for athletic events and musical concerts are usually set far in advance of the events. Sometimes the original ticket price is too low to be the equilibrium price. Lines form at the ticket window, and a severe shortage of tickets occurs at the printed price. What happens next? Buyers who are willing to pay more than the original price bid up the equilibrium price in resale ticket markets. The price rockets upward.

Tickets sometimes get resold for much greater amounts than the original price—market transactions known as "scalping." For example, an original buyer may resell a $75 ticket to a concert for $200. The media sometimes denounce scalpers for "ripping off" buyers by charging "exorbitant" prices.

But is scalping really a rip-off? We must first recognize that such ticket resales are voluntary transactions. If both buyer and seller did not expect to gain from the exchange, it would not occur! The seller must value the $200 more than seeing the event, and the buyer must value seeing the event at $200 or more. So there are no losers or victims here: Both buyer and seller benefit from the transaction. The "scalping" market simply redistributes assets (game or concert tickets) from those who would rather have the money (other things) to those who would rather have the tickets.

Does scalping impose losses or injury on the sponsors of the event? If the sponsors are injured, it is because they initially priced tickets below the equilibrium level. Perhaps they did this to create a long waiting line and the attendant media publicity. Alternatively, they may have had a genuine desire to keep tickets affordable for lower-income, ardent fans. In either case, the event sponsors suffer an opportunity cost in the form of less ticket revenue than they might have otherwise received. But such losses are self-inflicted and quite separate and distinct from the fact that some tickets are later resold at a higher price.

So is ticket scalping undesirable? Not on economic grounds! It is an entirely voluntary activity that benefits both sellers and buyers.

QUESTION: Why do you suppose some professional sports teams are setting up legal "ticket exchanges" (at buyer- and seller-determined prices) at their Internet sites? (*Hint:* For the service, the teams charge a percentage of the transaction price of each resold ticket.)

Changes in Demand, Supply, and Equilibrium

We know that prices can and do change in markets. For example, demand might change because of fluctuations in consumer tastes or incomes, changes in expected price, or variations in the prices of related goods. Supply might change in response to changes in resource prices, technology, or taxes. How will such changes in demand and supply affect equilibrium price and quantity?

Changes in Demand

Suppose that the supply of some good (for example, health care) is constant and the demand for the good increases, as shown in Figure 3.7a. As a result, the new intersection of the supply and demand curves is at higher values on both the price and the quantity axes. Clearly, an increase in demand raises both equilibrium price and equilibrium quantity. Conversely, a decrease in demand, such as that shown in Figure 3.7b, reduces both equilibrium price and equilibrium quantity.

Changes in Supply

What happens if the demand for some good (for example, cell phones) is constant but the supply increases, as in Figure 3.7c? The new intersection of supply and demand is located at a lower equilibrium price but at a higher equilibrium quantity. An increase in supply reduces equilibrium price but increases equilibrium quantity. In contrast, if supply decreases, as in Figure 3.7d, equilibrium price rises while equilibrium quantity declines.

Complex Cases

When both supply and demand change, the effect is a combination of the individual effects.

Supply Increase; Demand Decrease   What effect will a supply increase for some good (for example, apples) and a demand decrease have on equilibrium price? Both changes decrease price, so the net result is a price drop greater than that resulting from either change alone.

What about equilibrium quantity? Here the effects of the changes in supply and demand are opposed: The increase in supply increases equilibrium quantity, but the decrease in demand reduces it. The direction of the change in equilibrium quantity depends on the relative sizes of the changes in supply and demand. If the increase in supply is larger than the decrease in demand, the equilibrium quantity will increase. But if the decrease in demand is greater than the increase in supply, the equilibrium quantity will decrease.

Supply Decrease; Demand Increase   A decrease in supply and an increase in demand for some good (for example, gasoline) both increase price. Their combined effect is an increase in equilibrium price greater than that caused by either change separately. But their effect on the equilibrium quantity is again indeterminate, depending on the relative sizes of the changes in supply and demand. If the decrease in supply is larger than the increase in demand, the equilibrium quantity will decrease. In contrast, if the increase in demand is greater than the decrease in supply, the equilibrium quantity will increase.

FIGURE 3.7 **Changes in demand and supply and the effects on price and quantity.** The increase in demand from D_1 to D_2 in (a) increases both equilibrium price and equilibrium quantity. The decrease in demand from D_3 to D_4 in (b) decreases both equilibrium price and equilibrium quantity. The increase in supply from S_1 to S_2 in (c) decreases equilibrium price and increases equilibrium quantity. The decrease in supply from S_3 to S_4 in (d) increases equilibrium price and decreases equilibrium quantity. The boxes in the top right summarize the respective changes and outcomes. The upward arrows in the boxes signify increases in equilibrium price (P) and equilibrium quantity (Q); the downward arrows signify decreases in these items.

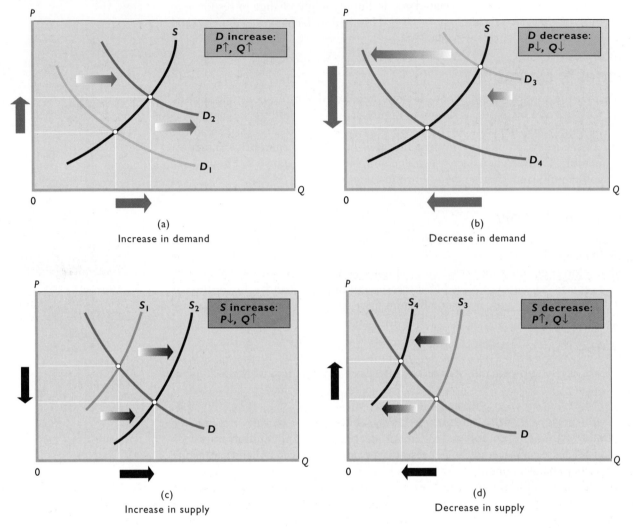

Supply Increase; Demand Increase What if supply and demand both increase for some good (for example, sushi)? A supply increase drops equilibrium price, while a demand increase boosts it. If the increase in supply is greater than the increase in demand, the equilibrium price will fall. If the opposite holds, the equilibrium price will rise. If the two changes are equal and cancel out, price will not change.

The effect on equilibrium quantity is certain: The increases in supply and in demand both raise the equilibrium quantity. Therefore, the equilibrium quantity will increase by an amount greater than that caused by either change alone.

Supply Decrease; Demand Decrease What about decreases in both supply and demand for some good (for example, new homes)? If the decrease in supply is greater than the decrease in demand, equilibrium price will rise. If the reverse is true, equilibrium price will fall. If the two changes are of the same size and cancel out, price will not change. Because the decreases in supply and demand both reduce equilibrium quantity, we can be sure that equilibrium quantity will fall.

Government-Set Prices

In most markets, prices are free to rise or fall with changes in supply or demand, no matter how high or low those prices might be. However, government occasionally concludes that changes in supply and demand have created prices that are unfairly high to buyers or unfairly low to sellers. Government may then place legal limits on how high or low a price or prices may go. Our previous analysis of shortages and surpluses helps us evaluate the wisdom of government-set prices.

APPLYING THE ANALYSIS

Price Ceilings on Gasoline

A **price ceiling** sets the maximum legal price a seller may charge for a product or service. A price at or below the ceiling is legal; a price above it is not. The rationale for establishing price ceilings (or ceiling prices) on specific products is that they purportedly enable consumers to obtain some "essential" good or service that they could not afford at the equilibrium price.

Figure 3.8 shows the effects of price ceilings graphically. Let's look at a hypothetical situation. Suppose that rapidly rising world income boosts the purchase of automobiles and increases the demand for gasoline so that the equilibrium or market price reaches $3.50 per gallon. The rapidly rising price of gasoline greatly burdens low- and moderate-income households, which pressure government to "do something." To keep gasoline prices down, the government imposes a ceiling price of $3 per gallon. To impact the market, a price ceiling must be below the equilibrium price. A ceiling price of $4, for example, would have no effect on the price of gasoline in the current situation.

What are the effects of this $3 ceiling price? The rationing ability of the free market is rendered ineffective. Because the $3 ceiling price is below the $3.50 market-clearing price, there is a lasting shortage of gasoline. The quantity of gasoline demanded at $3 is Q_d and the quantity supplied is only Q_s; a persistent excess demand or shortage of amount $Q_d - Q_s$ occurs.

The $3 price ceiling prevents the usual market adjustment in which competition among buyers bids up the price, inducing more production and rationing some buyers out of the market. That process would normally continue until the shortage disappeared at the equilibrium price and quantity, $3.50 and Q_0.

How will sellers apportion the available supply Q_s among buyers, who want the greater amount Q_d? Should they distribute gasoline on a first-come, first-served basis, that is, to those willing and able to get in line the soonest or stay in line the longest? Or should gas stations distribute it on the basis of favoritism? Since an unregulated shortage does not lead to an equitable distribution of gasoline, the government must establish some formal system for rationing it to consumers. One option is to issue ration coupons, which authorize bearers to purchase a fixed amount of gasoline per

price ceiling
A legally established maximum (below-equilibrium) price for a product.

FIGURE 3.8   A price ceiling.
A price ceiling is a maximum legal price, such as $3, that is below the equilibrium price. It results in a persistent product shortage, here shown by the distance between Q_d and Q_s.

month. The rationing system might entail first the printing of coupons for Q_s gallons of gasoline and then the equal distribution of the coupons among consumers so that the wealthy family of four and the poor family of four both receive the same number of coupons.

But ration coupons would not prevent a second problem from arising. The demand curve in Figure 3.8 reveals that many buyers are willing to pay more than the $3 ceiling price. And, of course, it is more profitable for gasoline stations to sell at prices above the ceiling. Thus, despite a sizable enforcement bureaucracy that would have to accompany the price controls, *black markets* in which gasoline is illegally bought and sold at prices above the legal limits will flourish. Counterfeiting of ration coupons will also be a problem. And since the price of gasoline is now "set by government," there might be political pressure on government to set the price even lower.

QUESTION: Why is it typically difficult to end price ceilings once they have been in place for a long time?

APPLYING THE ANALYSIS

Rent Controls

About 200 cities in the United States, including New York City, Boston, and San Francisco, have at one time or another enacted price ceilings in the form of rent controls—maximum rents established by law—or, more recently, have set maximum rent increases for existing tenants. Such laws are well intended. Their goals are to protect low-income families from escalating rents caused by demand increases that outstrip supply increases. Rent controls are designed to alleviate perceived housing shortages and make housing more affordable.

What have been the actual economic effects? On the demand side, the below-equilibrium rents attract a larger number of renters. Some are locals seeking to move into their own places after sharing housing with friends or family. Others are outsiders attracted into the area by the artificially lower rents. But a large problem occurs on the supply side. Price controls make it less attractive for landlords to offer housing on the rental market. In the short run, owners may sell their rental units or convert them to condominiums. In the long run, low rents make it unprofitable for owners to repair or renovate their rental units. (Rent controls are one cause of the many abandoned apartment buildings found in some larger cities.) Also, insurance companies, pension funds, and other potential new investors in housing will find it more profitable to invest in office buildings, shopping malls, or motels, where rents are not controlled.

In brief, rent controls distort market signals, and thus resources are misallocated: Too few resources are allocated to rental housing, and too many to alternative uses. Ironically, although rent controls are often legislated to lessen the effects of perceived shortages, controls in fact are a primary cause of such shortages. For that reason, most American cities either have abandoned rent controls or are gradually phasing them out.

QUESTION: Why does maintenance tend to diminish in rent-controlled apartment buildings relative to maintenance in buildings where owners can charge market-determined rents?

Price Floors on Wheat

A **price floor** is a minimum price fixed by the government. A price at or above the price floor is legal; a price below it is not. Price floors above equilibrium prices are usually invoked when society feels that the free functioning of the market system has not provided a sufficient income for certain groups of resource suppliers or producers. Supported prices for agricultural products and current minimum wages are two examples of price (or wage) floors. Let's look at the former.

Suppose that many farmers have extremely low incomes when the price of wheat is at its equilibrium value of $2 per bushel. The government decides to help out by establishing a legal price floor (or "price support") of $3 per bushel.

What will be the effects? At any price above the equilibrium price, quantity supplied will exceed quantity demanded—that is, there will be a persistent surplus of the product. Farmers will be willing to produce and offer for sale more wheat than private buyers are willing to buy at the $3 price floor. As we saw with a price ceiling, an imposed legal price disrupts the rationing ability of the free market.

Figure 3.9 illustrates the effect of a price floor graphically. Suppose that S and D are the supply and demand curves for wheat. Equilibrium price and quantity are $2 and Q_0, respectively. If the government imposes a price floor of $3, farmers will produce Q_s but private buyers will purchase only Q_d. The surplus is the excess of Q_s over Q_d.

price floor
A legally established minimum (above-equilibrium) price for a product.

FIGURE 3.9 A price floor. A price floor is a minimum legal price, such as $3, that results in a persistent product surplus, here shown by the distance between Q_s and Q_d.

The government may cope with the surplus resulting from a price floor in two ways:

- It can restrict supply (for example, by instituting acreage allotments by which farmers agree to take a certain amount of land out of production) or increase demand (for example, by researching new uses for the product involved). These actions may reduce the difference between the equilibrium price and the price floor and that way reduce the size of the resulting surplus.
- If these efforts are not wholly successful, then the government must purchase the surplus output at the $3 price (thereby subsidizing farmers) and store or otherwise dispose of it.

Price floors such as $3 in Figure 3.9 not only disrupt the rationing ability of prices but also distort resource allocation. Without the price floor, the $2 equilibrium price of wheat would cause financial losses and force high-cost wheat producers to plant other crops or abandon farming altogether. But the $3 price floor allows them to continue to grow wheat and remain farmers. So society devotes too many scarce resources to wheat production and too few to producing other, more valuable, goods and services. It fails to achieve an optimal allocation of resources.

That's not all. Consumers of wheat-based products pay higher prices because of the price floor. Taxpayers pay higher taxes to finance the government's purchase of the surplus. Also, the price floor causes potential environmental damage by encouraging wheat farmers to bring hilly, erosion-prone "marginal land" into production. The higher price also prompts imports of wheat. But, since such imports would increase the quantity of wheat supplied and thus undermine the price floor, the government needs to erect tariffs (taxes on imports) to keep the foreign wheat out. Such tariffs usually prompt other countries to retaliate with their own tariffs against U.S. agricultural or manufacturing exports.

QUESTION: To maintain price floors on milk, the U.S. government has at times bought out and destroyed entire dairy herds from dairy farmers. What's the economic logic of these actions?

It is easy to see why economists "sound the alarm" when politicians advocate imposing price ceilings or price floors such as price controls, rent controls, interest-rate lids, or agricultural price supports. In all these cases, good intentions lead to bad economic outcomes. Government-controlled prices lead to shortages or surpluses, distort resource allocations, and cause negative side effects.

For additional examples of demand and supply, view the Chapter 3 Web appendix at **www.mcconnellbrief2e.com.** *There, you will find examples relating to such diverse products as lettuce, corn, salmon, gasoline, sushi, and Olympic tickets. Several of the examples depict simultaneous shifts in demand and supply curves—circumstances that often show up in exam questions!*

INTERACTIVE GRAPHS

G 3.2

Price floors and ceilings

Summary

1. Demand is a schedule or curve representing the willingness of buyers in a specific period to purchase a particular product at each of various prices. The law of demand implies that consumers will buy more of a product at a low price than at a high price. So, other things equal, the relationship between price and quantity demanded is inverse and is graphed as a downsloping curve.

2. Market demand curves are found by adding horizontally the demand curves of the many individual consumers in the market.

3. Changes in one or more of the determinants of demand (consumer tastes, the number of buyers in the market, the money incomes of consumers, the prices of related goods, and expected prices) shift the market demand curve. A shift to the right is an increase in demand; a shift to the left is a decrease in demand. A change in demand is different from a change in the quantity demanded, the latter being a movement from one point to another point on a fixed demand curve because of a change in the product's price.

4. Supply is a schedule or curve showing the amounts of a product that producers are willing to offer in the market at each possible price during a specific period. The law of supply states that, other things equal, producers will offer more of a product at a high price than at a low price. Thus, the relationship between price and quantity supplied is positive or direct, and supply is graphed as an upsloping curve.

5. The market supply curve is the horizontal summation of the supply curves of the individual producers of the product.

6. Changes in one or more of the determinants of supply (resource prices, production techniques, taxes or subsidies, the prices of other goods, expected prices, or the number of suppliers in the market) shift the supply curve

of a product. A shift to the right is an increase in supply; a shift to the left is a decrease in supply. In contrast, a change in the price of the product being considered causes a change in the quantity supplied, which is shown as a movement from one point to another point on a fixed supply curve.

7. The equilibrium price and quantity are established at the intersection of the supply and demand curves. The interaction of market demand and market supply adjusts the price to the point at which the quantities demanded and supplied are equal. This is the equilibrium price. The corresponding quantity is the equilibrium quantity.

8. A change in either demand or supply changes the equilibrium price and quantity. Increases in demand raise both equilibrium price and equilibrium quantity; decreases in demand lower both equilibrium price and equilibrium quantity. Increases in supply lower equilibrium price and raise equilibrium quantity; decreases in supply raise equilibrium price and lower equilibrium quantity.

9. Simultaneous changes in demand and supply affect equilibrium price and quantity in various ways, depending on their direction and relative magnitudes.

10. A price ceiling is a maximum price set by government and is designed to help consumers. Effective price ceilings produce persistent product shortages, and if an equitable distribution of the product is sought, government must ration the product to consumers.

11. A price floor is a minimum price set by government and is designed to aid producers. Price floors lead to persistent product surpluses; the government must either purchase the product or eliminate the surplus by imposing restrictions on production or increasing private demand.

12. Legally fixed prices stifle the rationing function of prices and distort the allocation of resources.

Terms and Concepts

demand	change in demand	change in quantity supplied
law of demand	change in quantity demanded	equilibrium price
demand curve	supply	equilibrium quantity
determinants of demand	law of supply	surplus
normal good	supply curve	shortage
inferior good	determinants of supply	price ceiling
substitute good	change in supply	price floor
complementary good		

Questions connect

| ECONOMICS

1. Explain the law of demand. Why does a demand curve slope downward? How is a market demand curve derived from individual demand curves? **LO1**
2. What are the determinants of demand? What happens to the demand curve when any of these determinants changes? Distinguish between a change in demand and a change in the quantity demanded, noting the cause(s) of each. **LO1**
3. What effect will each of the following have on the demand for small automobiles such as the Mini Cooper and Smart car? **LO1**
   a. Small automobiles become more fashionable.
   b. The price of large automobiles rises (with the price of small autos remaining the same).
   c. Income declines and small autos are an inferior good.
   d. Consumers anticipate that the price of small autos will greatly come down in the near future.
   e. The price of gasoline substantially drops.
4. Explain the law of supply. Why does the supply curve slope upward? How is the market supply curve derived from the supply curves of individual producers? **LO2**
5. What are the determinants of supply? What happens to the supply curve when any of these determinants changes? Distinguish between a change in supply and a change in the quantity supplied, noting the cause(s) of each. **LO2**
6. What effect will each of the following have on the supply of auto tires? **LO2**
   a. A technological advance in the methods of producing tires.
   b. A decline in the number of firms in the tire industry.
   c. An increase in the price of rubber used in the production of tires.
   d. The expectation that the equilibrium price of auto tires will be lower in the future than currently.
   e. A decline in the price of the large tires used for semi trucks and earth-hauling rigs (with no change in the price of auto tires).
   f. The levying of a per-unit tax on each auto tire sold.
   g. The granting of a 50-cent-per-unit subsidy for each auto tire produced.
7. "In the latte market, demand often exceeds supply and supply sometimes exceeds demand." "The price of a latte rises and falls in response to changes in supply and demand." In

which of these two statements are the concepts of supply and demand used correctly? Explain. **LO4**
8. In 2001 an outbreak of hoof-and-mouth disease in Europe led to the burning of millions of cattle carcasses. What impact do you think this had on the supply of cattle hides, hide prices, the supply of leather goods, and the price of leather goods? **LO4**
9. Critically evaluate: "In comparing the two equilibrium positions in Figure 3.7a, I note that a larger amount is actually demanded at a higher price. This refutes the law of demand." **LO4**
10. For each stock in the stock market, the number of shares sold daily equals the number of shares purchased. That is, the quantity of each firm's shares demanded equals the quantity supplied. So, if this equality always occurs, why do the prices of stock shares ever change? **LO4**
11. Suppose the total demand for wheat and the total supply of wheat per month in the Kansas City grain market are as shown in the table below. Suppose that the government establishes a price ceiling of $3.70 for wheat. What might prompt the government to establish this price ceiling? Explain carefully the main effects. Demonstrate your answer graphically. Next, suppose that the government establishes a price floor of $4.60 for wheat. What will be the main effects of this price floor? Demonstrate your answer graphically. **LO5**

Thousands of Bushels Demanded	Price per Bushel	Thousands of Bushels Supplied
85	$3.40	72
80	3.70	73
75	4.00	75
70	4.30	77
65	4.60	79
60	4.90	81

12. What do economists mean when they say "price floors and ceilings stifle the rationing function of prices and distort resource allocation"? **LO5**

Problems

1. Suppose there are three buyers of candy in a market: Tex, Dex, and Rex. The market demand and the individual demands of Tex, Dex, and Rex are shown below. **LO1**
   a. Fill in the table for the missing values.
   b. Which buyer demands the least at a price of $5? The most at a price of $7?
   c. Which buyer's quantity demanded increases the most when the price is lowered from $7 to $6?
   d. Which direction would the market demand curve shift if Tex withdrew from the market? What if Dex doubled his purchases at each possible price?
   e. Suppose that at a price of $6, the total quantity demanded increases from 19 to 38. Is this a "change in the quantity demanded" or a "change in demand"?

Price per Candy	Individual Quantities Demanded						Total Quantity Demanded
	Tex		Dex		Rex		
$8	3	+	1	+	0	=	___
7	8	+	2	+	___	=	12
6	___	+	3	+	4	=	19
5	17	+	___	+	6	=	27
4	23	+	5	+	8	=	___

2. The figure below shows the supply curve for tennis balls, S_1, for Drop Volley Tennis, a producer of tennis equipment. Use the figure and the table below to give your answers to the following questions. **LO2**

a. Use the figure to fill in the quantity supplied on supply curve S_1 for each price in the table below.

Price	S_1 Quantity Supplied	S_2 Quantity Supplied	Change in Quantity Supplied
$3	___	4	___
2	___	2	___
1	___	0	___

b. If production costs were to increase, the quantities supplied at each price would be as shown by the third column of the table ("S_2 Quantity Supplied"). Use that data to draw supply curve S_2 on the same graph as supply curve S_1.
   c. In the fourth column of the table, enter the amount by which the quantity supplied at each price changes due to the increase in product costs. (Use positive numbers for increases and negative numbers for decreases.)
   d. Did the increase in production costs cause a "decrease in supply" or a "decrease in quantity supplied"?

3. Refer to the expanded table below from question 11. **LO3**
   a. What is the equilibrium price? At what price is there neither a shortage nor a surplus? Fill in the surplus-shortage column and use it to confirm your answers.
   b. Graph the demand for wheat and the supply of wheat. Be sure to label the axes of your graph correctly. Label equilibrium price P and equilibrium quantity Q.
   c. How big is the surplus or shortage at $3.40? At $4.90? How big a surplus or shortage results if the price is 60 cents higher than the equilibrium price? 30 cents lower than the equilibrium price?

Thousands of Bushels Demanded	Price per Bushel	Thousands of Bushels Supplied	Surplus (+) or Shortage (−)
85	$3.40	72	_____
80	3.70	73	_____
75	4.00	75	_____
70	4.30	77	_____
65	4.60	79	_____
60	4.90	81	

4. How will each of the following changes in demand and/or supply affect equilibrium price and equilibrium quantity in a competitive market; that is, do price and quantity rise, fall, or remain unchanged, or are the answers indeterminate because they depend on the magnitudes of the shifts? Use supply and demand to verify your answers. **LO4**
   a. Supply decreases and demand is constant.
   b. Demand decreases and supply is constant.
   c. Supply increases and demand is constant.
   d. Demand increases and supply increases.
   e. Demand increases and supply is constant.
   f. Supply increases and demand decreases.
   g. Demand increases and supply decreases.
   h. Demand decreases and supply decreases.

5. Use two market diagrams to explain how an increase in state subsidies to public colleges might affect tuition and enrollments in both public and private colleges. **LO4**

6. **ADVANCED ANALYSIS** Assume that demand for a commodity is represented by the equation $P = 10 - .2Q_d$ and supply by the equation $P = 2 + .2Q_s$, where Q_d and Q_s are quantity demanded and quantity supplied, respectively, and P is price. Using the equilibrium condition $Q_s = Q_d$, solve the equations to determine equilibrium price. Now determine equilibrium quantity. LO4

7. Suppose that the demand and supply schedules for rental apartments in the city of Gotham are as given in the table below. LO5

Monthly Rent	Apartments Demanded	Apartments Supplied
$2500	10,000	15,000
2000	12,500	12,500
1500	15,000	10,000
1000	17,500	7500
500	20,000	5000

a. What is the market equilibrium rental price per month and the market equilibrium number of apartments demanded and supplied?

b. If the local government can enforce a rent-control law that sets the maximum monthly rent at $1500, will there be a surplus or a shortage? Of how many units? And how many units will actually be rented each month?

c. Suppose that a new government is elected that wants to keep out the poor. It declares that the minimum rent that can be charged is $2500 per month. If the government can enforce that price floor, will there be a surplus or a shortage? Of how many units? And how many units will actually be rented each month?

d. Suppose that the government wishes to decrease the market equilibrium monthly rent by increasing the supply of housing. Assuming that demand remains unchanged, by how many units of housing would the government have to increase the supply of housing in order to get the market equilibrium rental price to fall to $1500 per month? To $1000 per month? To $500 per month?

FURTHER TEST YOUR KNOWLEDGE AT
www.mcconnellbrief2e.com

At the text's Online Learning Center, **www.mcconnellbrief2e.com**, you will find one or more web-based questions that require information from the Internet to answer. We urge you to check them out, since they will familiarize you with websites that may be helpful in other courses and perhaps even in your career. The OLC also features multiple-choice quizzes that give instant feedback and provides other helpful ways to further test your knowledge of the chapter.

Visit your mobile app store and download the McConnell Brief Edition: Study Econ app *today*!

7

After reading this chapter, you should be able to:

1 **Differentiate between demand-side market failures and supply-side market failures.**

2 **Explain consumer surplus and producer surplus, and discuss how properly functioning markets maximize their sum while optimally allocating resources.**

3 **Identify how public goods are distinguished from private goods, and explain the method for determining the optimal quantity of a public good.**

4 **Explain how positive and negative externalities cause under- and overallocations of resources, and how they might be corrected.**

5 **Show why we normally won't want to pay what it would cost to eliminate every last bit of a negative externality.**

4

Market Failures: Public Goods and Externalities

Competitive markets usually do a remarkable job of allocating society's scarce resources to their highest-valued uses. But markets have certain limitations. In some circumstances, economically desirable goods are not produced at all. In other situations, they are either overproduced or underproduced. This chapter examines **market failure,** which occurs when the competitive market system (1) does not allocate any resources whatsoever to the production of certain goods or (2) either underallocates or overallocates resources to the production of certain goods.

> **market failure**
> The inability of a market to produce a desirable product or produce it in the "right" amount.

Where private markets fail, an economic role for government may arise. In this chapter, we will examine that role as it relates to public goods and so-called externalities—situations where market failures lead to suboptimal outcomes that the government may be able to improve upon by using its powers to tax, spend, and regulate. We conclude the chapter by noting potential government inefficiencies that can hinder government's economic efforts.

Market Failures in Competitive Markets[1]

Competitive markets usually produce an assignment of resources that is "right" from an economic perspective. Unfortunately, the presence of robust competition involving many buyers and many sellers may not be enough to guarantee that a market will allocate resources correctly. Market failures sometimes happen in competitive markets. The focus of this chapter is to explain how and why such market failures can arise, and how they might be corrected.

Fortunately, the broad picture is simple. Market failures in competitive markets fall into just two categories:

- **Demand-side market failures** happen when demand curves do not reflect consumers' full willingness to pay for a good or service.
- **Supply-side market failures** occur when supply curves do not reflect the full cost of producing a good or service.

Demand-Side Market Failures

demand-side market failures Underallocations of resources that occur when private demand curves understate consumers' full willingness to pay for a good or service.

Demand-side market failures arise because it is impossible in certain cases to charge consumers what they are willing to pay for a product. Consider outdoor fireworks displays. People enjoy fireworks and would therefore be *willing* to pay to see a fireworks display if the only way to see it was to have to pay for the right to do so. But because such displays are outdoors and in public, people don't actually *have* to pay to see the display because there is no way to exclude those who haven't paid from also enjoying the show. Private firms will therefore be unwilling to produce outdoor fireworks displays, as it will be nearly impossible for them to raise enough revenue to cover production costs.

Supply-Side Market Failures

supply-side market failures Overallocations of resources that occur when private supply curves understate the full cost of producing a good or service.

Supply-side market failures arise in situations in which a firm does not have to pay the full cost of producing its output. Consider a coal-burning power plant. The firm running the plant will have to pay for all of the land, labor, capital, and entrepreneurship that it uses to generate electricity by burning coal. But if the firm is not charged for the smoke that it releases into the atmosphere, it will fail to pay another set of costs—the costs that its pollution imposes on other people. These include future harm from global warming, toxins that affect wildlife, and possible damage to agricultural crops downwind.

A market failure arises because it is not possible for the market to correctly weigh costs and benefits in a situation in which some of the costs are completely unaccounted for. The coal-burning power plant produces more electricity and generates more pollution than it would if it had to pay for each ton of smoke that it released into the atmosphere. The extra units that are produced are units of output for which the costs are *greater than* the benefits. Obviously, these units should not be produced.

---

[1]Other market failures arise when there are not enough buyers or sellers to ensure competition. In those situations, the lack of competition allows either buyers or sellers to restrict purchases or sales below optimal levels for their own benefit. As an example, a monopoly—a firm that is the only producer in its industry—can restrict the amount of output that it supplies in order to drive up the market price and thereby increase its own profit.

Efficiently Functioning Markets

The best way to understand market failure is to first understand how properly functioning competitive markets achieve economic efficiency.

A competitive market not only makes private goods available to consumers but also allocates society's resources efficiently to the particular product. Competition among producers forces them to use the best technology and right mix of productive resources. Otherwise, lower-cost producers will drive them out of business. The result is **productive efficiency**: the production of any particular good in the least costly way. When society produces, say, bottled water at the lowest achievable per-unit cost, it is expending the smallest amount of resources to produce that product and therefore is making available the largest amount of resources to produce other desired goods. Suppose society has only $100 worth of resources available. If it can produce a bottle of water using only $1 of those resources, then it will have available $99 of resources to produce other goods. This is clearly better than producing the bottle of water for $5 and having only $95 of resources available for alternative uses.

productive efficiency
The production of a good in the least costly way.

Competitive markets also produce **allocative efficiency**: the *particular mix* of goods and services most highly valued by society (minimum-cost production assumed). For example, society wants high-quality mineral water to be used for bottled water, not for gigantic blocks of refrigeration ice. It wants MP3 players (such as iPods), not phonographs and 45-rpm records. Moreover, society does not want to devote all its resources to bottled water and MP3 players. It wants to assign some resources to automobiles and personal computers. Competitive markets make those proper assignments, as we will demonstrate.

allocative efficiency
The production of the "right" mix of goods and services (minimum-cost production assumed).

Two conditions must hold if a competitive market is to produce efficient outcomes: The demand curve in the market must reflect consumers' full willingness to pay and the supply curve in the market must reflect all the costs of production. If these conditions hold, then the market will produce only units for which benefits are at least equal to costs. It also will maximize the amount of "benefit surpluses" that are shared between consumers and producers.

Consumer Surplus

The benefit surplus received by a consumer or consumers in a market is called **consumer surplus**. It is defined as the difference between the maximum price a consumer is (or consumers are) willing to pay for a product and the actual price that they do pay.

consumer surplus
The difference between the maximum price a consumer is (or consumers are) willing to pay for a product and the actual price they do pay.

Suppose that the maximum Ted is willing to pay for an apple is $1.25. If Ted is charged any market price less than $1.25, he will receive a consumer surplus equal to the difference between the $1.25 maximum price that he would have been willing to pay and the lower market price. For instance, if the market price is $.50 per apple, Ted will receive a consumer surplus of $.75 per apple (= $1.25 − $.50). In nearly all markets, consumers individually and collectively gain greater total utility or satisfaction in dollar terms from their purchases than the amount of their expenditures (= product price × quantity). This utility surplus arises because each consumer who buys the product only has to pay the equilibrium price even though many of them would have been willing to pay more than the equilibrium price to obtain the product.

The concept of maximum willingness to pay also gives us another way to understand demand curves. Consider Table 4.1, where the first two columns show the maximum amounts that six consumers would each be willing to pay for a bag of oranges. Bob, for instance, would be willing to pay a maximum of $13 for a bag of oranges. Betty, by contrast, would only be willing to pay a maximum of $8 for a bag of oranges.

TABLE 4.1 Consumer Surplus

(1) Person	(2) Maximum Price Willing to Pay	(3) Actual Price (Equilibrium Price)	(4) Consumer Surplus
Bob	$13	$8	$5 (= $13 − $8)
Barb	12	8	4 (= $12 − $8)
Bill	11	8	3 (= $11 − $8)
Bart	10	8	2 (= $10 − $8)
Brent	9	8	1 (= $9 − $8)
Betty	8	8	0 (= $8 − $8)

The maximum prices that these individuals are willing to pay represent points on a demand curve because the lower the market price, the more bags of oranges will be demanded. At a price of $12.50, for instance, Bob will be the only person listed in the table who will purchase a bag. But at a price of $11.50, both Bob and Barb will want to purchase a bag. The lower the price, the greater the total quantity demanded as the market price falls below the maximum prices of more and more consumers.

Lower prices also imply larger consumer surpluses. When the price is $12.50, Bob only gets $.50 in consumer surplus because his maximum willingness to pay of $13 is only $.50 higher than the market price of $12.50. But if the market price were to fall to $8, then his consumer surplus would be $5 (= $13 − $8). The third and fourth columns of Table 4.1 show how much consumer surplus each of our six consumers will receive if the market price of a bag of oranges is $8. Only Betty receives no consumer surplus because her maximum willingness to pay exactly matches the $8 equilibrium price.

It is easy to show on a graph the consumer surplus received by buyers in a market. Consider Figure 4.1, which shows the market equilibrium price P_1 = $8 as well as the downsloping demand curve D for bags of oranges. Demand curve D includes not only the six consumers named in Table 4.1 but also every other consumer of oranges in the market. The individual consumer surplus of each particular person who is willing to buy at the $8 market price is simply the vertical distance from the horizontal line that marks the $8 market price up to that particular buyer's maximum willingness to pay. The collective consumer surplus obtained by all of our named and unnamed buyers is found by adding together each of their individual consumer surpluses. To obtain the Q_1 bags of oranges represented, consumers collectively are willing to pay the total

FIGURE 4.1 Consumer surplus.
Consumer surplus—shown as the green triangle—is differences between the maximum prices consumers are willing to pay for a product and the lower equilibrium price, here assumed to be $8. For quantity Q_1, consumers are willing to pay the sum of the amounts represented by the green triangle and the yellow rectangle. Because they need to pay only the amount shown as the yellow rectangle, the green triangle shows consumer surplus.

amount shown by the sum of the green triangle and yellow rectangle under the demand curve and to the left of Q_1. But consumers need pay only the amount represented by the yellow rectangle (= $P_1 \times Q_1$). So the green triangle is the consumer surplus in this market. It is the sum of the vertical distances between the demand curve and the $8 equilibrium price at each quantity up to Q_1. Thus, consumer surplus can also be defined as the area that lies below the demand curve and above the price line that extends horizontally from P_1.

Consumer surplus and price are inversely (negatively) related. Given the demand curve, higher prices reduce consumer surplus; lower prices increase it. When price goes up, the gap narrows between the maximum willingness to pay and the actual price; a price decline widens the gap.

Producer Surplus

Like consumers, producers also receive a benefit surplus in markets. This **producer surplus** is the difference between the actual price a producer receives (or producers receive) and the minimum acceptable price that a consumer would have to pay the producer to make a particular unit of output available.

A producer's minimum acceptable price for a particular unit will equal the producer's marginal cost of producing that particular unit. That marginal cost will be the sum of the rent, wages, interest, and profit that the producer will need to pay in order to obtain the land, labor, capital, and entrepreneurship required to produce that particular unit. In this section, we are assuming that the marginal cost of producing a unit will include *all* of the costs of production. Unlike the coal-burning power plant mentioned previously, the producer must pay for all of its costs, including the cost of pollution. In later sections, we will explore the market failures that arise in situations where firms do not have to pay all their costs.

The size of the producer surplus earned on any particular unit will be the difference between the market price that the producer actually receives and the producer's minimum acceptable price. Consider Table 4.2, which shows the minimum acceptable prices of six different orange growers. With a market price of $8, Carlos, for instance, has a producer surplus of $5, which is equal to the market price of $8 minus his minimum acceptable price of $3. Chad, by contrast, receives no producer surplus because his minimum acceptable price of $8 just equals the market equilibrium price of $8.

Carlos's minimum acceptable price is lower than Chad's minimum acceptable price because Carlos is a more efficient producer than Chad, by which we mean that Carlos produces oranges using a less-costly combination of resources than Chad uses. The differences in efficiency between Carlos and Chad are likely due to differences in the type and quality of resources available to them.

producer surplus
The difference between the actual price a producer receives (or producers receive) and the minimum acceptable price.

TABLE 4.2 Producer Surplus

(1) Person	(2) Minimum Acceptable Price	(3) Actual Price (Equilibrium Price)	(4) Producer Surplus
Carlos	$3	$8	$5 (= $8 − $3)
Courtney	4	8	4 (= $8 − $4)
Chuck	5	8	3 (= $8 − $5)
Cindy	6	8	2 (= $8 − $6)
Craig	7	8	1 (= $8 − $7)
Chad	8	8	0 (= $8 − $8)

FIGURE 4.2 Producer surplus.
Producer surplus—shown as the blue triangle—is the differences between the actual price producers receive for a product (here $8) and the lower minimum payments they are willing to accept. For quantity Q_1, producers receive the sum of the amounts represented by the blue triangle plus the yellow area. Because they need receive only the amount shown by the yellow area to produce Q_1, the blue triangle represents producer surplus.

The minimum acceptable prices that producers are willing to accept form points on a supply curve because the higher the price, the more bags of oranges will be supplied. At a price of $3.50, for instance, only Carlos would be willing to supply a bag of oranges. But at a price of $5.50, Carlos, Courtney, and Chuck would all be willing to supply a bag of oranges. The higher the market price, the more oranges will be supplied, as the market price surpasses the marginal costs and minimum acceptable prices of more and more producers. Thus, supply curves shown in this competitive market are both marginal-cost curves and minimum-acceptable-price curves.

The supply curve in Figure 4.2 includes not only the six producers named in Table 4.2 but also every other producer of oranges in the market. At the market price of $8 per bag, Q_1 bags are produced because only those producers whose minimum acceptable prices are less than $8 per bag will choose to produce oranges with their resources. Those lower acceptable prices for each of the units up to Q_1 are shown by the portion of the supply curve lying to the left of and below the assumed $8 market price.

The individual producer surplus of each of these sellers is thus the vertical distance from each seller's respective minimum acceptable price on the supply curve up to the $8 market price. Their collective producer surplus is shown by the blue triangle in Figure 4.2. In that figure, producers collect revenues of $P_1 \times Q_1$, which is the sum of the blue triangle and the yellow area. As shown by the supply curve, however, revenues of only those illustrated by the yellow area would be required to entice producers to offer Q_1 bags of oranges for sale. The sellers therefore receive a producer surplus shown by the blue triangle. That surplus is the sum of the vertical distances between the supply curve and the $8 equilibrium price at each of the quantities to the left of Q_1.

There is a direct (positive) relationship between equilibrium price and the amount of producer surplus. Given the supply curve, lower prices reduce producer surplus; higher prices increase it. The gaps between minimum acceptable payments and actual prices widen when the price increases.

Efficiency Revisited

In Figure 4.3 we bring together the demand and supply curves of Figures 4.1 and 4.2 to show the equilibrium price and quantity and the previously described regions of consumer and producer surplus. All markets that have downsloping demand curves and upsloping supply curves yield consumer and producer surplus.

Because we are assuming in Figure 4.3 that the demand curve reflects buyers' full willingness to pay and the supply curve reflects all of the costs facing sellers, the

WORKED PROBLEMS

W 4.1

Consumer and producer surplus

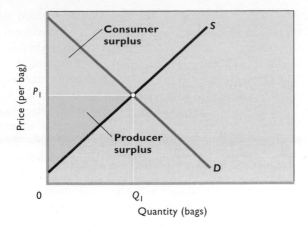

**FIGURE 4.3 Efficiency:
maximum combined consumer
and producer surplus.** At quantity
Q_1 the combined amount of consumer
surplus, shown as the green triangle, and
producer surplus, shown as the blue
triangle, is maximized. Efficiency occurs
because, at Q_1, maximum willingness to
pay, indicated by the points on the demand
curve, equals minimum acceptable price,
shown by the points on the supply curve.

equilibrium quantity in Figure 4.3 reflects both components of economic efficiency: productive efficiency and allocative efficiency.

- *Productive efficiency* is achieved because competition forces orange growers to use the best technologies and combinations of resources available. Doing so minimizes the per-unit cost of the output produced.
- *Allocative efficiency* is achieved because the correct quantity of oranges—Q_1—is produced relative to other goods and services.

There are two ways to understand why Q_1 is the correct quantity of oranges. Both involve realizing that any resources directed toward the production of oranges are resources that could have been used to produce other products. Thus, the only way to justify taking any amount of any resource (land, labor, capital, entrepreneurship) away from the production of other products is if it brings more utility or satisfaction when devoted to the production of oranges than it would if it were used to produce other products.

The first way to see why Q_1 is the allocatively efficient quantity of oranges is to note that demand and supply curves can be interpreted as measuring marginal benefit (MB) and marginal cost (MC). Recall from the discussion relating to Figure 1.3 that optimal allocation is achieved at the output level where MB = MC. We have already seen that supply curves are marginal cost curves. As it turns out, demand curves are marginal benefit curves. This is true because the maximum price that a consumer would be willing to pay for any particular unit is equal to the benefit that she would get if she were to consume that unit. Thus, each point on a demand curve represents both some consumer's maximum willingness to pay as well as the marginal benefit that he or she would get from consuming the particular unit in question.

Combining the fact that supply curves are MC curves with the fact that demand curves are MB curves, we see that points on the demand curve in Figure 4.3 measure the marginal benefit of oranges at each level of output, while points on the supply curve measure the marginal cost of oranges at each level of output. As a result, MB = MC where the demand and supply curves intersect—which means that the equilibrium quantity Q_1 must be allocatively efficient.

The second way to see why Q_1 is the correct quantity of oranges is based on our analysis of consumer and producer surplus and the fact that we can interpret demand and supply curves in terms of maximum willingness to pay and minimum acceptable price. In Figure 4.3, the maximum willingness to pay on the demand curve for each bag of oranges up to Q_1 exceeds the corresponding minimum acceptable price on the supply curve. Thus, each of these bags adds a positive amount (= maximum willingness to pay *minus* minimum acceptable price) to the *total* of consumer and producer surplus.

The fact that maximum willingness to pay exceeds minimum acceptable price for every unit up to Q_1 means that people gain more utility from producing and consuming those units than they would if they produced and consumed anything else that could be made with the resources that went into making those units. Only at the equilibrium quantity Q_1—where the maximum willingness to pay exactly equals the minimum acceptable price—does society exhaust all opportunities to produce units for which benefits exceed costs (including opportunity costs). Producing Q_1 units therefore achieves allocative efficiency because the market is producing and distributing only those units that make people happier with bags of oranges than they would be with anything else that could be produced with the same resources.

Geometrically, producing Q_1 units maximizes the combined area of consumer and producer surplus in Figure 4.3. In this context, the combined area is referred to as *total surplus*. Thus, when Q_1 units are produced, total surplus is equal to the large triangle formed by the green consumer-surplus triangle and the blue producer-surplus triangle.

When demand curves reflect buyers' full willingness to pay and when supply curves reflect all the costs facing sellers, competitive markets produce equilibrium quantities that maximize the sum of consumer and producer surplus. Allocative efficiency occurs at the market equilibrium quantity where three conditions exist simultaneously:

- MB = MC (Figure 1.3).
- Maximum willingness to pay = minimum acceptable price.
- Total surplus (= sum of consumer and producer surplus) is at a maximum.

Economists are enamored of markets because properly functioning markets automatically achieve allocative efficiency. Other methods of allocating resources—such as government central planning—do exist. But because other methods cannot do any better than properly functioning markets—and may in many cases do much worse—economists usually prefer that resources be allocated through markets whenever properly functioning markets are available.

Efficiency Losses (or Deadweight Losses)

efficiency (or deadweight) losses Reductions in combined consumer and producer surplus caused by an underallocation or overallocation of resources to the production of a good or service.

Figures 4.4a and 4.4b demonstrate that **efficiency losses**—reductions of combined consumer and producer surplus—result from both underproduction and overproduction. First, consider Figure 4.4a, which analyzes the case of underproduction by considering what happens if output falls from the efficient level Q_1 to the smaller amount Q_2. When that happens, the sum of consumer and producer surplus, previously *abc*, falls to *adec*. So the combined consumer and producer surplus declines by the amount of the gray triangle to the left of Q_1. That triangle represents an efficiency loss to buyers and sellers. And because buyers and sellers are members of society, it represents an efficiency loss (or a so-called **deadweight loss**) to society.

For output levels from Q_2 to Q_1, consumers' maximum willingness to pay (as reflected by points on the demand curve) exceeds producers' minimum acceptable price (as reflected by points on the supply curve). By failing to produce units of this product for which a consumer is willing to pay more than a producer is willing to accept, society suffers a loss of net benefits. As a concrete example, consider a particular unit for which a consumer is willing to pay $10 and a producer is willing to accept $6. The $4 difference between those values is a net benefit that will not be realized if this unit is not produced. In addition, the resources that should have gone to producing this unit will go instead to producing other products that will not generate as much utility as if those resources had been used here to produce this unit of this product. The triangle

FIGURE 4.4 Efficiency losses (or deadweight losses). Quantity levels either less than or greater than the efficient quantity Q_1 create efficiency losses. In (a), triangle *dbe* shows the efficiency loss associated with underproduction at output Q_2. Triangle *bfg* in (b) illustrates the efficiency loss associated with overproduction at output level Q_3.

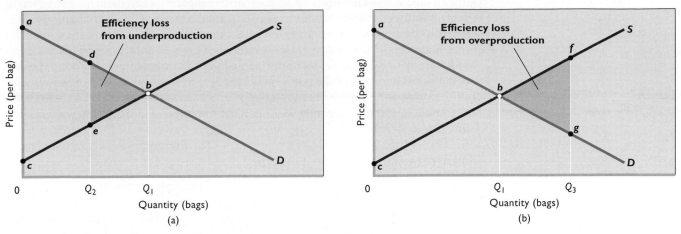

(a)   (b)

dbe in Figure 4.4a shows the total loss of net benefits that results from failing to produce the units from Q_2 to Q_1.

In contrast, consider the case of overproduction shown in Figure 4.4b, in which the number of oranges produced is Q_3 rather than the efficient level Q_1. In Figure 4.4b the combined consumer and producer surplus therefore declines by *bfg*—the gray triangle to the right of Q_1. This triangle subtracts from the total consumer and producer surplus of *abc* that would occur if the quantity had been Q_1. That is, for all units from 0 to Q_1, benefits exceed costs, so that those units generate the economic surplus shown by triangle *abc*. But the units from Q_1 to Q_3 are such that costs exceed benefits. Thus, they generate an economic loss shown by triangle *bfg*. The total economic surplus for all units from 0 to Q_3 is therefore the economic surplus given by *abc* for the units from 0 to Q_1 *minus* the economic loss given by *bfg* for the units from Q_1 to Q_3.

Producing any unit beyond Q_1 generates an economic loss because the willingness to pay for such units on the part of consumers is less than the minimum acceptable price to produce such units on the part of producers. As a concrete example, note that producing an item for which the maximum willingness to pay is, say, $7 and the minimum acceptable price is, say, $10 subtracts $3 from society's net benefits. Such production is uneconomical and creates an efficiency loss (or deadweight loss) for society. Because the net benefit of each bag of oranges from Q_1 to Q_3 is negative, we know that the benefits from these units are smaller than the opportunity costs of the other products that could have been produced with the resources that were used to produce these bags of oranges. The resources used to produce the bags from Q_1 to Q_3 could have generated net benefits instead of net losses if they had been directed toward producing other products. The gray triangle *bfg* to the right of Q_1 in Figure 4.4b shows the total efficiency loss from overproduction at Q_3.

The magic of markets is that when demand reflects consumers' full willingness to pay and when supply reflects all costs, the market equilibrium quantity will automatically equal the allocatively efficient output level. Under these conditions, the market equilibrium quantity will ensure that there are neither efficiency losses from underproduction nor efficiency losses from overproduction. As we are about to see, however, such losses do happen when either demand does not reflect consumers' full willingness to pay or supply does not reflect all costs.

Private and Public Goods

Demand-side market failures arise in competitive markets when demand curves fail to reflect consumers' full willingness to pay for a good or service. In such situations, markets fail to produce all of the units for which there are net benefits because demand curves underreport how much consumers are willing and able to pay. This underreporting problem reaches its most extreme form in the case of a public good: Markets may fail to produce *any* of the public good because its demand curve may reflect *none* of its consumers' willingness to pay.

To understand public goods, we first need to understand the characteristics that define private goods.

Private Goods Characteristics

private goods
Goods that people individually buy and consume and that private firms can profitably provide because they keep people who do not pay from receiving the benefits.

Certain goods called **private goods** are produced through the market system. Private goods encompass the full range of goods offered for sale in stores and shops. Examples include automobiles, clothing, personal computers, household appliances, and sporting goods. Private goods have two characteristics: rivalry and excludability.

- *Rivalry* (in consumption) means that when one person buys and consumes a product, it is not available for another person to buy and consume. When Adams purchases and drinks a bottle of mineral water, it is not available for Benson to purchase and consume.
- *Excludability* means that sellers can keep people who do not pay for a product from obtaining its benefits. Only people who are willing and able to pay the market price for bottles of water can obtain these drinks and the benefits they confer.

Profitable Provision

Consumers fully express their personal demands for private goods in the market. If Adams likes bottled mineral water, that fact will be known by her desire to purchase the product. Other things equal, the higher the price of bottled water, the fewer bottles she will buy. So Adams' demand for bottled water will reflect an inverse relationship between the price of bottled water and the quantity of it demanded. This is simply *individual* demand, as described in Chapter 3.

The *market* demand for a private good is the horizontal summation of the individual demand schedules (review Figure 3.2). Suppose there are just two consumers in the market for bottled water and the price is $1 per bottle. If Adams will purchase 3 bottles and Benson will buy 2, the market demand will reflect that consumers demand 5 bottles at the $1 price. Similar summations of quantities demanded at other prices will generate the market demand schedule and curve.

Suppose the equilibrium price of bottled water is $1. Adams and Benson will buy a total of 5 bottles, and the sellers will obtain total revenue of $5 (= $1 × 5). If the sellers' cost per bottle is $.80, their total cost will be $4 (= $.80 × 5). So sellers charging $1 per bottle will obtain $5 of total revenue, incur $4 of total cost, and earn $1 of profits for the 5 bottles sold.

Because firms can profitably "tap market demand" for private goods, they will produce and offer them for sale. Consumers demand private goods, and profit-seeking suppliers produce goods that satisfy the demand. Consumers willing to pay the market price obtain the goods; nonpayers go without. A competitive market not only makes private goods available to consumers but also allocates society's resources efficiently to the particular product. There is neither underproduction nor overproduction of the product.

Public Goods Characteristics

Public goods have the opposite characteristics of private goods. Public goods are distinguished by nonrivalry and nonexcludability.

- *Nonrivalry* (in consumption) means that one person's consumption of a good does not preclude consumption of the good by others. Everyone can simultaneously obtain the benefit from a public good such as a global positioning system, national defense, street lighting, and environmental protection.

- *Nonexcludability* means there is no effective way of excluding individuals from the benefit of the good once it comes into existence.

These two characteristics create a **free-rider problem.** Once a producer has provided a public good, everyone including nonpayers can obtain the benefit. Because most people do not voluntarily pay for something that they can obtain for free, most people become free riders. Free riders would be willing to pay for the public good if producers could somehow force them to pay—but nonexcludability means that there is no way for producers to withhold the good from the free riders without also denying it to the few who do pay. As a result, free riding means that the willingness to pay of the free riders is not expressed in the market. From the viewpoint of producers, free riding reduces demand. The more free riding, the less demand. And if all consumers free ride, demand will collapse all the way to zero.

public goods
Goods that everyone can simultaneously consume and from which no one can be excluded, even if they do not pay.

free-rider problem
The inability of a firm to profitably provide a good because everyone, including nonpayers, can obtain the benefit.

© Steven P. Lynch/The McGraw-Hill Companies, Inc.   © S. Solum/PhotoLink/Getty Images

PHOTO OP Private versus Public Goods

Apples, distinguished by rivalry (in consumption) and excludability, are examples of private goods. In contrast, streetlights, distinguished by nonrivalry (in consumption) and nonexcludability, are examples of public goods.

The low or even zero demand caused by free riding makes it virtually impossible for private firms to profitably provide public goods. With little or no demand, firms cannot effectively "tap market demand" for revenues and profits. As a result, they will not produce public goods. Society will therefore suffer efficiency losses because goods for which marginal benefits exceed marginal costs are not produced. Thus, if society wants a public good to be produced, it will have to direct government to provide it. Because the public good will still feature nonexcludability, the government won't have any better luck preventing free riding or charging people for it. But because the government can finance the provision of the public good through the taxation of other things, the government does not have to worry about profitability. It can therefore provide the public good even when private firms can't.

A significant example of a public good is homeland defense. The vast majority of Americans think this public good is economically justified because they perceive the benefits as exceeding the costs. Once homeland defense efforts are undertaken, however, the benefits accrue to all Americans (nonrivalry). And there is no practical way to exclude any American from receiving those benefits (nonexcludability).

No private firm will undertake overall homeland defense because the free-rider problem means that benefits cannot be profitably sold. So here we have a service that yields substantial net benefits but to which the market system will not allocate sufficient resources. Like national defense in general, homeland defense is a public good. Society signals its desire for such goods by voting for particular political candidates who support their provision. Because of the free-rider problem, government provides these goods and finances them through compulsory charges in the form of taxes.

Optimal Quantity of a Public Good If consumers need not reveal their true demand for a public good in the marketplace, how can society determine the optimal amount of that good? The answer is that the government has to try to estimate the demand for a public good through surveys or public votes. It can then compare the marginal benefit of an added unit of the good against the government's marginal cost of providing it. Adhering to the MB = MC rule, it can provide the "right" amount of the public good.

ILLUSTRATING THE IDEA

Art for Art's Sake

Suppose an enterprising sculptor creates a piece of art costing $600 and, with permission, places it in the town square. Also suppose that Jack gets $300 of enjoyment from the art and Diane gets $400. Sensing this enjoyment and hoping to make a profit, the sculptor approaches Jack for a donation equal to his satisfaction. Jack falsely says that, unfortunately, he does not particularly like the piece. The sculptor then tries Diane, hoping to get $400 or so. Same deal: Diane professes not to like the piece either. Jack and Diane have become free riders. Although feeling a bit guilty, both reason that it makes no sense to pay for something when anyone can receive the benefits without paying for them. The artist is a quick learner; he vows never to try anything like that again.

QUESTION: What is the rationale for government funding for art placed in town squares and other public spaces?

TABLE 4.3 Optimal Quantity of a Public Good, Two Individuals

(1) Quantity of Public Good	(2) Adams' Willingness to Pay (Price)		(3) Benson's Willingness to Pay (Price)		(4) Collective Willingness to Pay (Price)	(5) Marginal Cost
1	$4	+	$5	=	$9	$3
2	3	+	4	=	7	4
3	2	+	3	=	5	5
4	1	+	2	=	3	6
5	0	+	1	=	1	7

Measuring Demand Suppose that Adams and Benson are the only two people in the society and that their willingness to pay for a public good, this time the war on terrorism, is as shown in columns 1 and 2 and columns 1 and 3 in Table 4.3. Economists might have discovered these schedules through a survey asking hypothetical questions about how much each citizen was willing to pay for various types and amounts of public goods rather than go without them.

Notice that the schedules in the first four columns of Table 4.3 are price-quantity schedules, meaning they are demand schedules. Rather than depicting demand in the usual way—the quantity of a product someone is willing to buy at each possible price—these schedules show the price someone is willing to pay for the extra unit of each possible quantity. That is, Adams is willing to pay $4 for the first unit of the public good, $3 for the second, $2 for the third, and so on.

Suppose the government produces 1 unit of this public good. Because of nonrivalry, Adams' consumption of the good does not preclude Benson from also consuming it, and vice versa. So both people consume the good, and neither volunteers to pay for it. But from Table 4.3 we can find the amount these two people would be willing to pay, together, rather than do without this 1 unit of the good. Columns 1 and 2 show that Adams would be willing to pay $4 for the first unit of the public good, whereas columns 1 and 3 reveal that Benson would be willing to pay $5 for it. Adams and Benson therefore are jointly willing to pay $9 (= $4 + $5) for this first unit.

For the second unit of the public good, the collective price they are willing to pay is $7 (= $3 from Adams + $4 from Benson); for the third unit they will pay $5 (= $2 + $3); and so on. By finding the collective willingness to pay for each additional unit (column 4), we can construct a collective demand schedule (a willingness-to-pay schedule) for the public good. Here we are *not* adding the quantities demanded at each possible price, as with the market demand for a private good. Instead, we are adding the prices that people are willing to pay for the last unit of the public good at each possible quantity demanded.

What does it mean in columns 1 and 4 of Table 4.3 that, for example, Adams and Benson are collectively willing to pay $7 for the second unit of the public good? It means that they jointly expect to receive $7 of extra benefit or utility from that unit. Column 4, in effect, reveals the collective marginal benefit of each unit of the public good.

Comparing Marginal Benefit and Marginal Cost

Now let's suppose the marginal cost of providing the public good is as shown in column 5 of Table 4.3. As explained in Chapter 1, marginal cost tends to rise as more of a good is produced. In view of the marginal-cost data shown, how much of the good

WORKED PROBLEMS

W 4.2

Optimal amount of a public good

should government provide? The optimal amount occurs at the quantity where marginal benefit equals marginal cost. In Table 4.3 that quantity is 3 units, where the collective willingness to pay for the third unit—the $5 marginal benefit—just matches that unit's $5 marginal cost. As we saw in Chapter 1, equating marginal benefit and marginal cost efficiently allocates society's scarce resources.

APPLYING THE ANALYSIS

cost-benefit analysis
The formal comparison of marginal costs and marginal benefits of a government project to decide whether it is worth doing and to what extent resources should be devoted to it.

Cost-Benefit Analysis

The above example suggests a practical means, called **cost-benefit analysis,** for deciding whether to provide a particular public good and how much of it to provide. Like our example, cost-benefit analysis (or marginal-benefit–marginal-cost analysis) involves a comparison of marginal costs and marginal benefits.

Suppose the federal government is contemplating a highway construction plan. Because the economy's resources are limited, any decision to use more resources in the public sector will mean fewer resources for the private sector. There will be both a cost and a benefit. The cost is the loss of satisfaction resulting from the accompanying decline in the production of private goods; the benefit is the extra satisfaction resulting from the output of more public goods. Should the needed resources be shifted from the private to the public sector? The answer is yes if the benefit from the extra public goods exceeds the cost that results from having fewer private goods. The answer is no if the cost of the forgone private goods is greater than the benefit associated with the extra public goods.

Cost-benefit analysis, however, can indicate more than whether a public program is worth doing. It can also help the government decide on the extent to which a project should be pursued. Real economic questions cannot usually be answered simply by "yes" or "no" but, rather, involve questions such as "how much" or "how little."

Roads and highways can be run privately, as excludability is possible with toll gates. However, the federal highway system is almost entirely nonexclusive because anyone with a car can get on and off most federal highways without restriction anytime they want. Federal highways therefore satisfy one characteristic of a public good: nonexcludability. The other characteristic, nonrivalry, is also satisfied by the the fact that unless a highway is already extremely crowded, one person's driving on the highway does not preclude another person's driving on the highway. Thus, the federal highway system is effectively a public good. This leads us to ask: Should the federal government expand the federal highway system? If so, what is the proper size or scope for the overall project?

Table 4.4 lists a series of increasingly ambitious and increasingly costly highway projects: widening existing two-lane highways; building new two-lane highways; building new four-lane highways; building new six-lane highways. The extent to which government should undertake highway construction depends on the costs and benefits. The costs are largely the costs of constructing and maintaining the highways; the benefits are improved flows of people and goods throughout the nation.

The table shows that total annual benefit (column 4) exceeds total annual cost (column 2) for plans A, B, and C, indicating that some highway construction is economically justifiable. We see this directly in column 6, where total costs (column 2) are subtracted from total annual benefits (column 4). Net benefits are positive for plans A, B, and C. Plan D is not economically justifiable because net benefits are negative.

But the question of optimal size or scope for this project remains. Comparing the marginal cost (the change in total cost) and the marginal benefit (the change in total

TABLE 4.4 Cost-Benefit Analysis for a National Highway Construction Project (in Billions)

(1) Plan	(2) Total Cost of Project	(3) Marginal Cost	(4) Total Benefit	(5) Marginal Benefit	(6) Net Benefit (4) − (2)
No new construction	$ 0		$ 0		$ 0
A: Widen existing highways	4	$ 4	5	$ 5	1
B: New 2-lane highways	10	6	13	8	3
C: New 4-lane highways	18	8	23	10	5
D: New 6-lane highways	28	10	26	3	−2

benefit) relating to each plan determines the answer. The guideline is well known to you from previous discussions: Increase an activity, project, or output as long as the marginal benefit (column 5) exceeds the marginal cost (column 3). Stop the activity at, or as close as possible to, the point at which the marginal benefit equals the marginal cost. Do not undertake a project for which marginal cost exceeds marginal benefit.

In this case plan C (building new four-lane highways) is the best plan. Plans A and B are too modest; the marginal benefits exceed the marginal costs. Plan D's marginal cost ($10 billion) exceeds the marginal benefit ($3 billion) and therefore cannot be justified; it overallocates resources to the project. Plan C is closest to the theoretical optimum because its marginal benefit ($10 billion) still exceeds marginal cost ($8 billion) but approaches the MB = MC (or MC = MB) ideal.

This marginal-cost–marginal-benefit rule tells government which plan provides the maximum excess of total benefits over total costs or, in other words, the plan that provides society with the maximum net benefit. You can confirm directly in column 6 that the maximum net benefit ($5 billion) is associated with plan C.

QUESTION: Do you think it is generally easier to measure the costs of public goods or their benefits? Explain your reasoning.

Externalities

In addition to providing public goods, governments also can improve the allocation of resources in the economy by correcting for market failures caused by externalities. An *externality* occurs when some of the costs or the benefits of a good or service are passed onto or "spill over" to someone other than the immediate buyer or seller. Such spillovers are called externalities because they are benefits or costs that accrue to some third party that is external to the market transaction.

Negative Externalities

Production or consumption costs inflicted on a third party without compensation are called **negative externalities** or *spillover costs*. Environmental pollution is an example. When a chemical manufacturer or a meatpacking plant dumps its wastes into a lake or river, water users such as swimmers, fishers, and boaters suffer negative externalities. When a petroleum refinery pollutes the air with smoke or a paper mill creates obnoxious odors, the community experiences negative externalities for which it is not compensated.

negative externalities
Spillover production or consumption costs imposed on third parties without compensation to them.

FIGURE 4.5 Negative externalities and positive externalities. (a) With negative externalities borne by society, the producers' supply curve S is to the right of (below) the total-cost supply curve S_t. Consequently, the equilibrium output Q_e is greater than the optimal output Q_o, and the efficiency loss is *abc*. (b) When positive externalities accrue to society, the market demand curve D is to the left of (below) the total-benefit demand curve D_t. As a result, the equilibrium output Q_e is less than the optimal output Q_o, and the efficiency loss is *xyz*.

(a) Negative externalities

(b) Positive externalities

INTERACTIVE GRAPHS

G 4.1

Externalities

Figure 4.5a illustrates how negative externalities affect the allocation of resources. When producers shift some of their costs onto the community as spillover costs, producers' marginal costs are lower than they would be if they had to pay for these costs. So their supply curves do not include or "capture" all the costs legitimately associated with the production of their goods. A supply curve such as S in Figure 4.5a therefore understates the total cost of production for a polluting firm. Its supply curve lies to the right of (or below) the full-cost supply curve S_t, which would include the negative externality. Through polluting and thus transferring cost to society, the firm enjoys lower production costs and has the supply curve S.

The resource allocation outcome is shown in Figure 4.5a, where equilibrium output Q_e is larger than the optimal output Q_o. This is a market failure because resources are *overallocated* to the production of this commodity; too many units of it are produced. In fact, there is a net loss to society for every unit from Q_0 to Q_e because, for those units, the supply curve that accounts for all costs, S_t, lies above the demand curve. Therefore, MC exceeds MB for those units. The resources that went into producing those units should have been used elsewhere in the economy to produce other things.

In terms of our previous analysis, the negative externality results in an efficiency loss represented by triangle *abc*.

Positive Externalities

Sometimes spillovers appear as external benefits. The production or consumption of certain goods and services may confer spillover or external benefits on third parties or on the community at large without compensating payment. Immunization against measles and polio results in direct benefits to the immediate consumer of those vaccines. But it also results in widespread substantial positive externalities to the entire community.

positive externalities Spillover production or consumption benefits conferred on third parties without compensation from them.

Education is another example of **positive externalities.** Education benefits individual consumers: Better-educated people generally achieve higher incomes than less-well-educated people. But education also benefits society through a more versatile and more productive labor force, on the one hand, and smaller outlays for crime prevention, law enforcement, and welfare programs, on the other.

Figure 4.5b shows the impact of positive externalities on resource allocation. When positive externalities occur, the market demand curve D lies to the left of (or below) the full-benefits demand curve, D_t. That is, D does not include the positive externalities of the product, whereas D_t does. Consider inoculations against a communicable disease. When John gets vaccinated against a disease, this is a benefit not only to himself (because he can no longer contract the disease) but also to everyone else around him (because they know that in the future he will never be able to infect them). These other people would presumably be willing to pay some positive amount of money for the benefit they receive when John is vaccinated. But because there is no way to make them pay, the market demand curve reflects only the direct, private benefits to John. It does not reflect the positive externalities—the spillover benefits—to those around John, which are included in D_t.

The outcome, as shown in Figure 4.5b, is that the equilibrium output Q_e is less than the optimal output Q_o. The market fails to produce enough vaccinations, and resources are *underallocated* to this product. The underproduction implies that society is missing out on potential net benefits. For every unit from Q_e to Q_0, the demand curve that accounts for all benefits, D_t, lies above the supply curve that accounts for all costs—including the opportunity cost of producing other items with the resources that would be needed to produce these units. Therefore, MB exceeds MC for each of these units and society should redeploy some of its resources away from the production of other things in order to produce these units that generate net benefits.

In terms of our previous analysis, the positive externality results in an efficiency loss represented by triangle *xyz*.

Economists have explored several approaches to the problems of negative and positive externalities. Sometimes private parties work out their own solutions to externality problems; other times government intervention is warranted.

ORIGIN OF THE IDEA

O 4.2

Externalities

© Paul Taylor/Photolibrary

© Charles Smith/Corbis

PHOTO OP Positive and Negative Consumption Externalities

Homeowners create positive externalities when they put up nice holiday lighting displays. Not only does the homeowner benefit from consuming the sight, but so do people who pass by the house. In contrast, when people consume roads (drive) during rush hour, it creates a negative externality. This takes the form of traffic congestion, imposing time and fuel costs on other drivers.

Coase theorem
The idea that externality problems can be resolved through private negotiations by the affected parties when property rights are clearly established.

ORIGIN OF THE IDEA

O 4.3
Coase theorem

Beekeepers and the Coase Theorem

Economist Ronald Coase received the Nobel Prize for his so-called **Coase theorem,** which pointed out that under the right conditions, private individuals could often negotiate their own mutually agreeable solutions to externality problems through *private bargaining* without the need for government interventions like pollution taxes.

This is a very important insight because it means that we shouldn't automatically call for government intervention every time we see a potential externality problem. Consider the positive externalities that bees provide by pollinating farmers' crops. Should we assume that beekeeping will be underprovided unless the government intervenes with, for instance, subsidies to encourage more hives and hence more pollination?

As it turns out, no. Research has shown that farmers and beekeepers long ago used private bargaining to develop customs and payment systems that avoid free riding by farmers and encourage beekeepers to keep the optimal number of hives. Free riding is avoided by the custom that all farmers in an area simultaneously hire beekeepers to provide bees to pollinate their crops. And farmers always pay the beekeepers for their pollination services because if they didn't, then no beekeeper would ever work with them in the future—a situation that would lead to massively reduced crop yields due to a lack of pollination.

The "Fable of the Bees" is a good reminder that it is a fallacy to assume that the government must always get involved to remedy externalities. In many cases, the private sector can solve both positive and negative externality problems on its own.

QUESTIONS: Suppose that in a town a large number of home gardeners need pollination services for their fruit and vegetable crops, but none can individually afford to pay a professional beekeeper. How might that affect the contracting of beekeepers? Would it suggest a possible role for government?

Government Intervention

Government intervention may be called upon to achieve economic efficiency when externalities affect large numbers of people or when community interests are at stake. Government can use direct controls and taxes to counter negative externalities (spillover costs); it may provide subsidies or public goods to deal with positive externalities (spillover benefits).

Direct Controls The direct way to reduce negative externalities from a certain activity is to pass legislation limiting that activity. Such direct controls force the offending firms to incur the actual costs of the offending activity. To date, this approach has dominated public policy in the United States. Clean-air legislation has

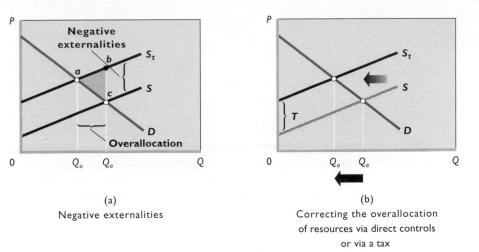

FIGURE 4.6 **Correcting for negative externalities.** (a) Negative externalities (spillover costs) result in an overallocation of resources. (b) Government can correct this overallocation in two ways: (1) using direct controls, which would shift the supply curve from S to S_t and reduce output from Q_e to Q_o, or (2) imposing a specific tax T, which would also shift the supply curve from S to S_t, eliminating the overallocation of resources and thus the efficiency loss.

created uniform emission standards—limits on allowable pollution—and has forced factories and businesses to install "maximum achievable control technology" to reduce emissions of toxic chemicals. It has also mandated reductions in (1) tailpipe emissions from automobiles, (2) use of chlorofluorocarbons (CFCs) that deplete the ozone layer, and (3) emissions of sulfur dioxide by coal-burning utilities to prevent the acid-rain destruction of lakes and forests. Also, clean-water legislation has limited the amounts of heavy metals and detergents that firms can discharge into rivers and bays. Toxic-waste laws dictate special procedures and dump sites for disposing of contaminated soil and solvents. Violating these laws means fines and, in some cases, imprisonment.

Direct controls raise the marginal cost of production because the firms must operate and maintain pollution-control equipment. The supply curve S in Figure 4.6b, which does not reflect the negative externalities, shifts leftward (upward) to the full-cost supply curve, S_t. Product price increases, equilibrium output falls from Q_e to Q_o, and the initial overallocation of resources shown in Figure 4.6a is corrected. Observe that the efficiency loss shown by triangle *abc* in Figure 4.6a disappears after the overallocation is corrected in Figure 4.6b.

Specific Taxes A second policy approach to negative externalities is for government to levy taxes or charges specifically on the related good. For example, the government has placed a manufacturing excise tax on CFCs, which deplete the stratospheric ozone layer protecting the earth from excessive solar ultraviolet radiation. Facing such an excise tax, manufacturers must decide whether to pay the tax or expend additional funds to purchase or develop substitute products. In either case, the tax raises the marginal cost of producing CFCs, shifting the private supply curve for this product leftward (or upward).

In Figure 4.6b, a tax equal to T per unit increases the firm's marginal cost, shifting the supply curve from S to S_t. The equilibrium price rises, and the equilibrium output declines from Q_e to the economically efficient level Q_o. The tax thus eliminates the initial overallocation of resources, and therefore the efficiency loss, associated with the negative externality.

FIGURE 4.7 Correcting for positive externalities. (a) Positive externalities (spillover benefits) result in an underallocation of resources. (b) Government can correct this underallocation through a subsidy to consumers, which shifts market demand from D to D_t and increases output from Q_e to Q_o. (c) Alternatively, government can eliminate the underallocation by giving producers a subsidy of U, which shifts their supply curve from S_t to S'_t, increasing output from Q_e to Q_o.

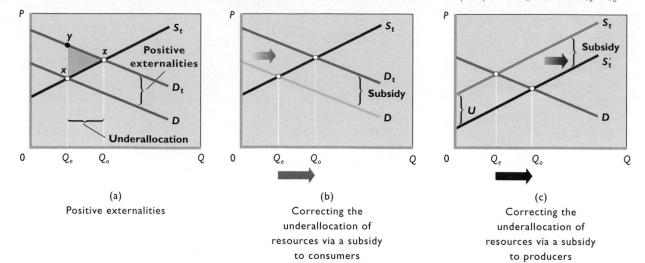

(a)
Positive externalities

(b)
Correcting the
underallocation of
resources via a subsidy
to consumers

(c)
Correcting the
underallocation of
resources via a subsidy
to producers

Subsidies and Government Provision   What policies might be useful in dealing with *positive* externalities? Where positive externalities are large and diffuse, as in our earlier example of inoculations, government has three options for correcting the underallocation of resources:

- **Subsidies to buyers**   Figure 4.7a again shows the supply-demand situation for positive externalities. Government could correct the underallocation of resources, for example, to inoculations, by subsidizing consumers of the product. It could give each new mother in the United States a discount coupon to be used to obtain a series of inoculations for her child. The coupon would reduce the "price" to the mother by, say, 50 percent. As shown in Figure 4.7b, this program would shift the demand curve for inoculations from too low D to the appropriate D_t. The number of inoculations would rise from Q_e to the economically optimal Q_o, eliminating the underallocation of resources and efficiency loss shown in Figure 4.7a.

- **Subsidies to producers**   A subsidy to producers is a tax in reverse. Taxes impose an extra cost on producers, while subsidies reduce producers' costs. As shown in Figure 4.7c, a subsidy of U per inoculation to physicians and medical clinics would reduce their marginal costs and shift their supply curve rightward from S_t to S'_t. The output of inoculations would increase from Q_e to the optimal level Q_o, correcting the underallocation of resources and efficiency loss shown in Figure 4.7a.

- **Government provision**   Finally, where positive externalities are extremely large, the government may decide to provide the product for free or for a minimal charge. Government provides many goods that could be produced and delivered in such a way that exclusion would be possible. Such goods, called **quasi-public goods,** include education, streets and highways, police and fire protection, libraries and museums, preventive medicine, and sewage disposal. They could all be priced and provided by private firms through the market system because the free-rider problem would be minimal. But, because spillover benefits extend well beyond the individual buyer, the market system may underproduce them. Therefore, government often provides quasi-public goods.

quasi-public goods
Goods for which exclusion could occur but which government provides because of perceived widespread and diffuse benefits.

Lojack: A Case of Positive Externalities

Economists Ayres and Levitt point out that some forms of private crime prevention simply redistribute crime rather than reduce it. For example, car alarm systems that have red blinking warning lights may simply divert professional auto thieves to vehicles that do not have such lights and alarms. The owner of a car with such an alarm system benefits through reduced likelihood of theft but imposes a cost on other car owners who do not have such alarms. Their cars are more likely to be targeted for theft by thieves because other cars have visible security systems.

In contrast, some private crime prevention measures actually reduce crime, rather than simply redistribute it. One such measure is installation of a Lojack (or some similar) car retrieval system. Lojack is a tiny radio transmitter that is hidden in one of many possible places within the car. When an owner reports a stolen car, the police can remotely activate the transmitter. Police then can determine the car's precise location and track its subsequent movements.

The owner of the car benefits because the 95 percent retrieval rate on cars with the Lojack system is higher than the 60 percent retrieval rate for cars without the system. But, according to a study by Ayres and Levitt, the benefit to the car owner is only 10 percent of the total benefit. Ninety percent of the total benefit is external; it is a spillover benefit to other car owners in the community.

There are two sources of this positive externality. First, the presence of the Lojack device sometimes enables police to intercept the car while the thief is still driving it. For example, in California the arrest rate for cars with Lojack was three times greater than that for cars without it. The arrest puts the car thief out of commission for a time and thus reduces subsequent car thefts in the community. Second, and far more important, the device enables police to trace cars to "chop shops," where crooks disassemble cars for resale of the parts. When police raid the chop shop, they put the entire theft ring out of business. In Los Angeles alone, Lojack has eliminated 45 chop shops in just a few years. The purging of the chop shop and theft ring reduces auto theft in the community. So auto owners who do not have Lojack devices in their cars benefit from car owners who do. Ayres and Levitt estimate the *marginal social benefit* of Lojack—the marginal benefit to the Lojack car owner *plus* the spillover benefit to other car owners—is 15 times greater than the marginal cost of the device.

We saw in Figure 4.7a that the existence of positive externalities causes an insufficient quantity of a product and thus an underallocation of scarce resources to its production. The two general ways to correct the outcome are to subsidize the consumer, as shown in Figure 4.7b, or to subsidize the producer, as shown in Figure 4.7c. Currently, there is only one form of government intervention in place: state-mandated insurance discounts for people who install auto retrieval systems such as Lojack. In effect, those discounts on insurance premiums subsidize the consumer by lowering the "price" of the system to consumers. The lower price raises the number of systems installed. But, on the basis of their research, Ayres and Levitt contend that the current levels of insurance discounts are far too small to correct the underallocation that results from the positive externalities created by Lojack.

QUESTION: Other than mandating lower insurance premiums for Lojack users, what might government do to increase the use of Lojack devices in automobiles?

Source: Based on Ian Ayres and Steven D. Levitt, "Measuring Positive Externalities from Unobservable Victim Precaution: An Empirical Analysis of Lojack," *Quarterly Journal of Economics*, February 1998, pp. 43–77. The authors point out that Lojack did not fund their work; nor do they have any financial stake in Lojack.

Reducing Greenhouse Gases

Climate change, to the extent it is caused by human-generated greenhouse gases, is a negative externality problem. Suggested policies to reduce carbon emissions, a major greenhouse gas, include carbon taxes and a cap-and-trade program.

A tax imposed on each ton of carbon emitted would increase the marginal cost of production to all firms that release carbon into the air through their production processes. Because of the added marginal cost, the supply curves within affected markets would shift to the left (as illustrated by the move from S to S_t in Figure 4.5). The reduced market supply would increase equilibrium price and reduce equilibrium quantity. With the lower output, carbon emissions in these industries would fall.

A carbon tax would require minimum government interference in the economy once the tax was in place. The federal government could direct the revenues from the tax to research on cleaner production technologies or simply use the new revenues to reduce other taxes. But there would be no free lunch here: According to a 2007 study, a proposed $15 tax per ton of carbon dioxide emitted would add an estimated 14 cents to a gallon of gasoline, 1.63 cents to a kilowatt hour of electricity, $28.50 to a ton of coal, and $6.48 to a barrel of crude oil.

An alternative approach is a cap-and-trade program, which creates a market for the right to discharge a particular pollutant into the air or water. These rights, allocated in the form of a fixed quantity of pollution permits, can be bought or sold in a permit market. Each permit specifies the amount of the pollutant that can be emitted. The decision to buy or sell permits depends on how costly it is for a company to reduce its pollution relative to the market price of the permits. Permit buyers, for example, are those whose costs to reduce emissions exceed the costs of the permits that allow them to pollute.

As it currently does with sulfur dioxide emissions, the federal government could place a cap or lid on total carbon emissions and then either hand out emission rights or auction them off. In ways previously discussed, the cap-and-trade program would reduce society's overall cost of lowering carbon emissions. In that regard, it would be more efficient than direct controls requiring each producer of greenhouse gas to reduce emissions by a fixed percentage amount. Existing cap-and-trade programs—including current European markets for carbon certificates—prove that this program can work. But such programs require considerable government oversight and enforcement of the rules.

QUESTION: Why would rising prices of emission rights increase the incentive for firms to use cleaner production methods?

Table 4.5 lists several methods for correcting externalities, including those we have discussed thus far.

Society's Optimal Amount of Externality Reduction

Negative externalities such as pollution reduce the utility of those affected. These spillovers are not economic goods but economic "bads." If something is bad, shouldn't society eliminate it? Why should society allow firms or municipalities to discharge *any* impure waste into public waterways or to emit *any* pollution into the air?

TABLE 4.5 Methods for Dealing with Externalities

Problem	Resource Allocation Outcome	Ways to Correct
Negative externalities (spillover costs)	Overproduction of output and therefore overallocation of resources	1. Private bargaining 2. Liability rules and lawsuits 3. Tax on producers 4. Direct controls 5. Market for externality rights
Positive externalities (spillover benefits)	Underproduction of output and therefore underallocation of resources	1. Private bargaining 2. Subsidy to consumers 3. Subsidy to producers 4. Government provision

Economists answer these questions by pointing out that reducing pollution and negative externalities is not free. There are costs as well as benefits to reducing pollution. As a result, the correct question to ask when it comes to cleaning up negative externalities is not, "Do we pollute a lot or pollute zero?" That is an all-or-nothing question that ignores marginal costs and marginal benefits. Instead, the correct question is, "What is the optimal amount to clean up—the amount that equalizes the marginal cost of cleaning up with the marginal benefit of a cleaner environment?"

Reducing a negative externality has a "price." Society must decide how much of a reduction it wants to "buy." High costs may mean that totally eliminating pollution might not be desirable, even if it is technologically feasible. Because of the law of diminishing returns, cleaning up the second 10 percent of pollutants from an industrial smokestack normally is more costly than cleaning up the first 10 percent. Eliminating the third 10 percent is more costly than cleaning up the second 10 percent, and so on. Therefore, cleaning up the last 10 percent of pollutants is the most costly reduction of all.

The marginal cost (MC) to the firm and hence to society—the opportunity cost of the extra resources used—rises as pollution is reduced more and more. At some point MC may rise so high that it exceeds society's marginal benefit (MB) of further pollution abatement (reduction). Additional actions to reduce pollution will therefore lower society's well-being; total cost will rise more than total benefit.

MC, MB, and Equilibrium Quantity Figure 4.8 shows both the rising marginal-cost curve, MC, for pollution reduction and the downsloping marginal-benefit curve, MB, for pollution reduction. MB slopes downward because of the law of diminishing marginal utility: The more pollution reduction society accomplishes, the lower the utility (and benefit) of the next unit of pollution reduction.

The **optimal reduction of an externality** occurs when society's marginal cost and marginal benefit of reducing that externality are equal (MC = MB). In Figure 4.8 this optimal amount of pollution abatement is Q_1 units. When MB exceeds MC, additional abatement moves society toward economic efficiency; the added benefit of cleaner air or water exceeds the benefit of any alternative use of the required resources. When MC exceeds MB, additional abatement reduces economic efficiency; there would be greater benefits from using resources in some other way than to further reduce pollution.

In reality, it is difficult to measure the marginal costs and benefits of pollution control. Figure 4.8 demonstrates that some pollution may be economically efficient. This is so not because pollution is desirable but because beyond some level of control,

optimal reduction of an externality The reduction of a negative externality to the level at which the marginal benefit and marginal cost of reduction are equal.

FIGURE 4.8 Society's optimal amount of pollution abatement. The optimal amount of externality reduction—in this case, pollution abatement—occurs at Q_1, where society's marginal cost MC and marginal benefit MB of reducing the spillover are equal.

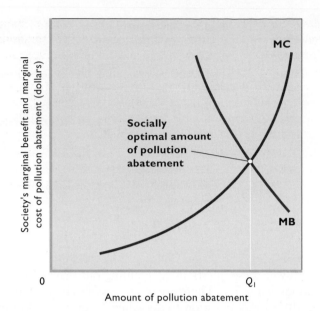

further abatement may reduce society's net well-being. As an example, it would cost the government billions of dollars to clean up every last piece of litter in America. Thus, it would be better to tolerate some trash blowing around if the money saved by picking up less trash would yield larger net benefits when spent on other things.

Shifts in Locations of the Curves The locations of the marginal-cost and marginal-benefit curves in Figure 4.8 are not forever fixed. They can, and probably do, shift over time. For example, suppose that the technology of pollution-control equipment improved noticeably. We would expect the cost of pollution abatement to fall, society's MC curve to shift rightward, and the optimal level of abatement to rise. Or suppose that society were to decide that it wanted cleaner air and water because of new information about the adverse health effects of pollution. The MB curve in Figure 4.8 would shift rightward, and the optimal level of pollution control would increase beyond Q_1. Test your understanding of these statements by drawing the new MC and MB curves in Figure 4.8.

Government's Role in the Economy

Market failures can be used to justify government interventions in the economy. The inability of private-sector firms to break even when attempting to provide public goods and the over- and underproduction problems caused by positive and negative externalities mean that government can have an important role to play if society's resources are to be efficiently allocated to the goods and services that people most highly desire.

Correcting for market failures is not, however, an easy task. To begin with, government officials must correctly identify the existence and the cause of any given market failure. That by itself may be difficult, time-consuming, and costly. But even if a market failure is correctly identified and diagnosed, government may still fail to take appropriate corrective action due to the fact that government undertakes its economic role in the context of politics.

To serve the public, politicians need to get elected. To stay elected, officials (presidents, senators, representatives, mayors, council members, school board members) need to satisfy their particular constituencies. At best, the political realities complicate government's role in the economy; at worst, they produce undesirable economic outcomes.

In the political context, overregulation can occur in some cases; underregulation, in others. Some public goods and quasi-public goods can be produced not because their benefits exceed their costs but because their benefits accrue to firms located in states served by powerful elected officials. Inefficiency can easily creep into government activities because of the lack of a profit incentive to hold down costs. Policies to correct negative externalities can be politically blocked by the very parties that are producing the spillovers. In short, the economic role of government, although critical to a well-functioning economy, is not always perfectly carried out.

Economists use the term "government failure" to describe economically inefficient outcomes caused by shortcomings in the public sector.

Summary

1. A market failure happens in a particular market when the market produces an equilibrium level of output that either overallocates or underallocates resources to the product being traded in the market. In competitive markets that feature many buyers and many sellers, market failures can be divided into two types: Demand-side market failures occur when demand curves do not reflect consumers' full willingness to pay; supply-side market failures occur when supply curves do not reflect all production costs, including those that may be borne by third parties.

2. Properly functioning competitive markets ensure that private goods are (a) available, (b) produced in the least costly way, and (c) produced and sold in the "right" amounts.

3. Consumer surplus is the difference between the maximum price that a consumer is willing to pay for a product and the lower price actually paid; producer surplus is the difference between the minimum price that a producer is willing to accept for a product and the higher price actually received. Collectively, consumer surplus is represented by the triangle under the demand curve and above the actual price, whereas producer surplus is shown by the triangle above the supply curve and below the actual price.

4. Graphically, the combined amount of producer and consumer surplus is represented by the triangle to the left of the intersection of the supply and demand curves that is below the demand curve and above the supply curve. At the equilibrium price and quantity in competitive markets, marginal benefit equals marginal cost, maximum willingness to pay equals minimum acceptable price, and the combined amount of consumer surplus and producer surplus is maximized.

5. Output levels that are either less than or greater than the equilibrium output create efficiency losses, also called deadweight losses. These losses are reductions in the combined amount of consumer surplus and producer surplus. Underproduction creates efficiency losses because output is not being produced for which maximum willingness to pay exceeds minimum acceptable price. Overproduction creates efficiency losses because output is being produced for which minimum acceptable price exceeds maximum willingness to pay.

6. Public goods are distinguished from private goods. Private goods are characterized by rivalry (in consumption) and excludability. One person's purchase and consumption of a private good precludes others from also buying and consuming it. Producers can exclude nonpayers (free riders) from receiving the benefits. In contrast, public goods are characterized by nonrivalry (in consumption) and nonexcludability. Public goods are not profitable to private firms because nonpayers (free riders) can obtain and consume those goods without paying. Government can, however, provide desirable public goods, financing them through taxation.

7. The collective demand schedule for a particular public good is found by summing the prices that each individual is willing to pay for an additional unit. The optimal quantity of a public good occurs where the society's willingness to pay for the last unit—the marginal benefit of the good—equals the marginal cost of the good.

8. Externalities cause the output of certain goods to vary from society's optimal output. Negative externalities (spillover costs) result in an overallocation of resources to a particular product. Positive externalities (spillover benefits) are accompanied by an underallocation of resources to a particular product.

9. Direct controls and specific taxes can improve resource allocation in situations where negative externalities affect many people and community resources. Both direct controls (for example, smokestack emission standards) and specific taxes (for example, taxes on firms producing toxic chemicals) increase production costs and hence product price. As product price rises, the externality, overallocation

of resources, and efficiency loss are reduced since less of the output is produced.

10. Government can correct the underallocation of resources and therefore the efficiency losses that result from positive externalities in a particular market either by subsidizing consumers (which increases market demand) or by subsidizing producers (which increases market supply). Such subsidies increase the equilibrium output, reducing or eliminating the positive externality and consequent underallocation of resources and efficiency loss.

11. The Coase theorem suggests that under the right circumstances private bargaining can solve externality problems. Thus, government intervention is not always needed to deal with externality problems.

12. The socially optimal amount of externality abatement occurs where society's marginal cost and marginal benefit of reducing the externality are equal. With pollution, for example, this optimal amount of pollution abatement is likely to be less than a 100 percent reduction. Changes in technology or changes in society's attitudes toward pollution can affect the optimal amount of pollution abatement.

13. Market failures present government with opportunities to improve the allocation of society's resources and thereby enhance society's total well-being. But even when government correctly identifies the existence and cause of a market failure, political pressures may make it difficult or impossible for government officials to implement a proper solution.

Terms and Concepts

market failures

demand-side market failures

supply-side market failures

productive efficiency

allocative efficiency

consumer surplus

producer surplus

efficiency losses (or deadweight losses)

private goods

public goods

free-rider problem

cost-benefit analysis

negative externality

positive externality

Coase theorem

quasi-public goods

optimal reduction of an externality

Questions ![McGraw Hill Connect ECONOMICS]

1. Explain the two causes of market failures. Given their definitions, could a market be affected by both types of market failures simultaneously? **LO1**

2. Draw a supply and demand graph and identify the areas of consumer surplus and producer surplus. Given the demand curve, what impact will an increase in supply have on the amount of consumer surplus shown in your diagram? Explain why. **LO2**

3. Use the ideas of consumer surplus and producer surplus to explain why economists say competitive markets are efficient. Why are below- or above-equilibrium levels of output inefficient, according to these two sets of ideas? **LO2**

4. Contrast the characteristics of public goods with those of private goods. Why won't private firms produce public goods? **LO3**

5. Draw a production possibilities curve with public goods on the vertical axis and private goods on the horizontal axis. Assuming the economy is initially operating on the curve, indicate how the production of public goods might be increased. How might the output of public goods be increased if the economy is initially operating at a point inside the curve? **LO3**

6. Use the distinction between the characteristics of private and public goods to determine whether the following should be produced through the market system or provided by government: (a) French fries, (b) airport screening, (c) court systems, (d) mail delivery, and (e) medical care. State why you answered as you did in each case. **LO3**

7. What divergences arise between equilibrium output and efficient output when (a) negative externalities and (b) positive externalities are present? How might government correct these divergences? Cite an example (other than the text examples) of an external cost and an external benefit. **LO4**

8. Why are spillover costs and spillover benefits also called negative and positive externalities? Show graphically how a tax can correct for a negative externality and how a subsidy to producers can correct for a positive externality. How does a subsidy to consumers differ from a subsidy to producers in correcting for a positive externality? **LO4**

9. An apple grower's orchard provides nectar to a neighbor's bees, while the beekeeper's bees help the apple grower by pollinating his apple blossoms. Use Figure 4.5b to explain why this situation of dual positive externalities might lead to

an underallocation of resources to both apple growing and beekeeping. How might this underallocation get resolved via the means suggested by the Coase theorem? **LO4**

10. Explain the following statement, using the MB curve in Figure 4.8 to illustrate: "The optimal amount of pollution abatement for some substances, say, dirty water from storm drains, is very low; the optimal amount of abatement for other substances, say, cyanide poison, is close to 100 percent." **LO5**

11. Explain why zoning laws, which allow certain land uses only in specific locations, might be justified in dealing with a problem of negative externalities. Explain why in areas where buildings sit close together tax breaks to property owners for installing extra fire prevention equipment might be justified in view of positive externalities. Explain why excise taxes on beer might be justified in dealing with a problem of external costs. **LO5**

Problems

1. Refer to Table 4.1. If the six people listed in the table are the only consumers in the market and the equilibrium price is $11 (not the $8 shown), how much consumer surplus will the market generate? **LO2**

2. Refer to Table 4.2. If the six people listed in the table are the only producers in the market and the equilibrium price is $6 (not the $8 shown), how much producer surplus will the market generate? **LO2**

3. Look at Tables 4.1 and 4.2 together. What is the total surplus if Bob buys a unit from Carlos? If Barb buys a unit from Courtney? If Bob buys a unit from Chad? If you match up pairs of buyers and sellers so as to maximize the total surplus of all transactions, what is the largest total surplus that can be achieved? **LO2**

4. **ADVANCED ANALYSIS** Assume the following values for Figures 4.4a and 4.4b. Q_1 = 20 bags. Q_2 = 15 bags. Q_3 = 27 bags. The market equilibrium price is $45 per bag. The price at a is $85 per bag. The price at c is $5 per bag. The price at f is $59 per bag. The price at g is $31 per bag. Apply the formula for the area of a triangle (Area = ½ × Base × Height) to answer the following questions. **LO2**

   a. What is the dollar value of the total surplus (producer surplus plus consumer surplus) when the allocatively efficient output level is being produced? How large is the dollar value of the consumer surplus at that output level?

   b. What is the dollar value of the deadweight loss when output level Q_2 is being produced? What is the total surplus when output level Q_2 is being produced?

   c. What is the dollar value of the deadweight loss when output level Q_3 is produced? What is the dollar value of the total surplus when output level Q_3 is produced?

5. The accompanying table relating to a public good provides information on the prices Young and Zorn are willing to pay for various quantities of that public good. These two people are the only members of society. Determine the price that society is willing to pay for the public good at each quantity of output. If the government's marginal cost of providing this public good is constant at $7,

how many units of the public good should government provide? **LO3**

Young		Zorn		Society	
P	**Q_d**	**P**	**Q_d**	**P**	**Q_d**
$8	0	$8	1	$ __	1
7	0	7	2	__	2
6	0	6	3	__	3
5	1	5	4	__	4
4	2	4	5	__	5
3	3	3	6	__	6
2	4	2	7	__	7
1	5	1	8	__	8

6. The table below shows the total costs and total benefits in billions for four different antipollution programs of increasing scope. Use cost-benefit analysis to determine which program should be undertaken. **LO3**

Program	Total Cost	Total Benefit
A	$ 3	$ 7
B	7	12
C	12	16
D	18	19

7. On the basis of the three individual demand schedules at the top of the next page, and assuming these three people are the only ones in the society, determine (a) the market demand schedule on the assumption that the good is a private

good and (b) the collective demand schedule on the assumption that the good is a public good. **LO3**

P	$Q_d(D_1)$	$Q_d(D_2)$	$Q_d(D_3)$
$8	0	1	0
7	0	2	0
6	0	3	1
5	1	4	2
4	2	5	3
3	3	6	4
2	4	7	5
1	5	8	6

8. Use your demand schedule for a public good, determined in problem 7, and the following supply schedule to ascertain the optimal quantity of this public good. **LO3**

P	Q_s
$19	10
16	8
13	6
10	4
7	2
4	1

9. Look at Tables 4.1 and 4.2, which show, respectively, the willingness to pay and willingness to accept of buyers and sellers of bags of oranges. For the following questions, assume that the equilibrium price and quantity will depend on the indicated changes in supply and demand. Assume that the only market participants are those listed by name in the two tables. **LO4**

   a. What are the equilibrium price and quantity for the data displayed in the two tables?

   b. What if, instead of bags of oranges, the data in the two tables dealt with a public good like fireworks displays? If all the buyers free ride, what will be the quantity supplied by private sellers?

   c. Assume that we are back to talking about bags of oranges (a private good), but that the government has decided that tossed orange peels impose a negative externality on the public that must be rectified by imposing a $2-per-bag tax on sellers. What are the new equilibrium price and quantity? If the new equilibrium quantity is the optimal quantity, by how many bags were oranges being overproduced before?

FURTHER TEST YOUR KNOWLEDGE AT
www.mcconnellbrief2e.com

At the text's Online Learning Center, **www.mcconnellbrief2e.com**, you will find one or more web-based questions that require information from the Internet to answer. We urge you to check them out, since they will familiarize you with websites that may be helpful in other courses and perhaps even in your career. The OLC also features multiple-choice quizzes that give instant feedback and provides other helpful ways to further test your knowledge of the chapter.

Visit your mobile app store and download the McConnell Brief Edition: Study Econ app *today*!

GDP, GROWTH, AND INSTABILITY

After reading this chapter, you should be able to:

1 Explain how gross domestic product (GDP) is defined and measured.

2 Describe how economists distinguish between nominal GDP and real GDP.

3 List two ways that economic growth is measured.

4 Identify the general supply, demand, and efficiency forces that give rise to economic growth.

5 Describe "growth accounting" and the specific factors accounting for economic growth in the United States.

6 Explain why the trend rate of U.S. productivity growth has increased since the earlier 1973–1995 period.

7 Discuss differing perspectives as to whether growth is desirable and sustainable.

GDP and Economic Growth

As you learned in Chapter 2, economists represent the economy as a circular flow of output (goods and services), income, and spending (Figure 2.2, p. 44). In our discussion of microeconomics, we examined how society can maximize output and income at any point in time by using the market system and government decisions to allocate society's limited resources to their highest valued uses.

We now want to turn to macroeconomics: the part of economics concerned with the economy as a whole. In this chapter we are interested in how economists measure the overall (aggregate) flow of goods and services in the circular flow diagram, both in total and on a per-person basis. Once that is established, we can examine the factors that expand the flow of goods and services over time and thus improve a society's standard of living. What are the main sources of such economic growth? Is economic growth desirable?

Gross Domestic Product

To examine the level of total output, total income, and total spending, we need to combine and measure the production, income, and spending of all the participants in the economy. The Bureau of Economic Analysis (BEA), an agency of the Commerce Department, does just that when it compiles the **national income and product accounts (NIPA)** for the U.S. economy. The BEA derives the NIPA data from Census Bureau surveys and information available from government agencies.

The primary measure of the economy's performance is its annual total output of goods and services. This output is called **gross domestic product (GDP):** the total market value of all final goods and services produced within the borders of a country during a specific period of time, typically a year. GDP includes all goods and services produced by either citizen-supplied or foreign-supplied resources employed within the country. If a final good or service is produced in the United States, it is part of U.S. GDP.[1]

A Monetary Measure

If the economy produces three sofas and two computers in year 1 and two sofas and three computers in year 2, in which year is output greater? We can't answer that question until we attach a price tag to each of the two products to indicate how society evaluates their relative worth.

That's what GDP does. It is a *monetary measure*. Without such a measure we would have no way of comparing the relative values of the vast number of goods and services produced in different years. In Table 5.1 the price of sofas is $500 and the price of computers is $2000. GDP would gauge the output of year 2 ($7000) as greater than the output of year 1 ($5500) because society places a higher monetary value on the output of year 2. Society is willing to pay $1500 more for the combination of goods produced in year 2 than for the combination of goods produced in year 1.

Avoiding Multiple Counting

To measure aggregate output accurately, all goods and services produced in a particular year must be counted once and only once. Because most products go through a series of production stages before they reach the market, some of their components are bought and sold many times. To avoid counting those components each time, GDP includes only the market value of *final goods* and ignores *intermediate goods* altogether.

Intermediate goods are goods and services that are purchased for resale or for further processing or manufacturing. **Final goods** are products that are purchased by their end users. Crude oil is an intermediate good; gasoline used for personal transportation is

---

[1]In contrast to GDP, U.S. gross *national* product (GNP) consists of the total value of all the final goods and services produced by American-supplied resources, whether those goods and services are produced within the borders of the United States or abroad. The United States switched from GNP to GDP accounting in 1992 to match the type of accounting used by other countries worldwide.

national income and product accounts (NIPA)
The national accounts that measure the overall production and income of the economy for the nation as a whole.

gross domestic product (GDP)
The total market value of all final goods and services produced annually within the borders of the United States, whether by U.S. or foreign-supplied resources.

intermediate goods
Products that are purchased for resale or further processing or manufacturing.

final goods
Products, capital goods, and services that have been purchased for final use and not for resale or further processing or manufacturing.

TABLE 5.1 Comparing Heterogeneous Output by Using Money Prices

Year	Annual Output	Market Value
1	3 sofas and 2 computers	3 at $500 + 2 at $2000 = $5500
2	2 sofas and 3 computers	2 at $500 + 3 at $2000 = $7000

© Brand X Pictures/Punchstock   © Royalty-Free/CORBIS

PHOTO OP Intermediate versus Final Goods

Lumber is an intermediate good, and a new townhouse is a final good.

a final good. Steel beams are intermediate goods; completed high-rise apartments are final goods. Lettuce, carrots, and vinegar in restaurant salads are intermediate goods; restaurant salads are final goods. Other examples of final goods are sunglasses bought by consumers, assembly machinery purchased by businesses, surveillance satellites bought by government, and smart phones purchased by foreign buyers.

Including the value of intermediate goods in calculating GDP would amount to *multiple counting*, and that would distort the value of GDP. For example, suppose that among other inputs an automobile manufacturer uses $4000 of steel, $2000 of glass, and $1000 of tires in producing a new automobile that sells for $20,000. The $20,000 final good already includes the $7000 of steel, glass, and tires. We would be greatly overstating GDP if we added the $7000 of components to the $20,000 price of the auto and obtained $27,000 of output.

Excluding Secondhand Sales and Financial Transactions

Secondhand sales do not contribute to current production and therefore are excluded from GDP. If you sell your 1965 Ford Mustang to a friend, that transaction would be ignored in determining this year's GDP because it generates no current production. The same would be true if you sold a brand-new Mustang to a neighbor a week after you purchased it. It has already been counted in GDP.

Likewise, purely financial transactions do not contribute to current production. These transactions include public transfer payments, such as social security and welfare payments, and private transfers, including the cash gifts that parents give children. Money changes hands but not in exchange for anything produced in the present. The sales of stocks and bonds are also excluded from GDP as they simply transfer pieces of paper that represent company ownership (stocks) or loans (bonds). Note, however, that the services of the stockbroker who facilitates the exchange of stock are included in GDP, as those services are part of the economy's current production.

© PhotoLink/Getty Images   © Colin Young-Wolff/PhotoEdit

PHOTO OP New Goods versus Secondhand Goods

The goods offered for sale at a shopping mall are new goods and therefore included in current GDP. In contrast, many of the goods sold through eBay are secondhand items and thus not part of current GDP.

Measuring GDP

The simplest way to measure GDP is to add up all that was spent to buy total output in a certain year. Economists use precise terms for the four categories of spending.

Personal Consumption Expenditures (C)

personal consumption expenditures (C)
Expenditures by households for durable goods, nondurable goods, and services.

The symbol C designates the **personal consumption expenditures** component of GDP. That term covers all expenditures by households on *durable consumer goods* (automobiles, refrigerators, cameras) that have lives of more than 3 years, *nondurable consumer goods* (bread, milk, toothpaste), and *consumer expenditures for services* (of lawyers, doctors, mechanics).

Gross Private Domestic Investment (I_g)

gross private domestic investment (I_g)
Expenditures for newly produced capital goods (such as plant and equipment) and for additions to inventories.

Under the heading **gross private domestic investment** are included (1) all final purchases of machinery, equipment, and tools by business enterprises; (2) all construction; and (3) changes in inventories.

Notice that this list, except for the first item, includes more than we have meant by "economic investment" so far. The second item includes residential construction as well as the construction of new factories, warehouses, and stores. Why is residential construction investment rather than consumption? Because apartment buildings and houses, like factories and stores, earn income when they are rented or leased. Owner-occupied houses are treated as investment goods because they *could be* rented to bring in an income return. So all residential construction is treated as investment. Finally, an increase in inventories (unsold goods) is investment because it is "unconsumed output." For economists, all new output either is consumed or is capital. An increase in inventories is an addition (although temporary) to the stock of capital goods, and such additions are precisely how we define investment.

Positive and Negative Changes in Inventories We need to look at changes in inventories more closely. Inventories can either increase or decrease over some period. Suppose inventories rose by $10 billion between December 31, 2010, and December 31, 2011. That means the economy produced $10 billion more output than was purchased in 2011. We need to count all output produced in 2011 as part of that year's GDP, even though some of it remained unsold at the end of the year. This is accomplished by including the $10 billion increase in inventories as investment in 2011. That way the expenditures in 2011 will correctly measure the output produced that year.

Alternatively, suppose inventories fell by $10 billion in 2011. This "drawing down of inventories" means that the economy sold $10 billion more of output in 2011 than it produced that year. It did this by selling goods produced in prior years—goods already counted as GDP in those years. Unless corrected, expenditures in 2011 will overstate GDP for 2011. So in 2011 we consider the $10 billion decline in inventories as "negative investment" and subtract it from total investment that year. Thus, expenditures in 2011 will correctly measure the output produced in 2011.

Noninvestment Transactions So much for what investment *is*. You also need to know what it *isn't*. For economists and NIPA accountants, investment does *not* include noninvestment transactions such as the transfer of paper assets (stocks, bonds) or the resale of tangible assets (houses, factories). Such financial transactions merely transfer the ownership of existing assets. The investment in the GDP accounts is economic investment—the creation of *new* capital assets. The mere transfer (sale) of claims to existing capital goods does not produce new capital goods. Therefore, such transactions (so-called financial investments) are not included as investment in the GDP accounts.

Gross Investment As we have seen, the category "gross private domestic investment" includes (1) all final purchases of machinery, equipment, and tools; (2) all construction; and (3) changes in inventories. The words "private" and "domestic" mean that we are speaking of spending by private businesses, not by government (public) agencies, and that the investment is taking place inside the country, not abroad.

The word "gross" means that we are referring to *all* investment goods—both those that replace machinery, equipment, and buildings that were used up (worn out or made obsolete) in producing the current year's output and any net additions to the economy's stock of capital. Gross investment includes investment in replacement capital *and* in added capital [as opposed to net investment, for which replacement capital (depreciation) is subtracted from gross investment].

The symbol I represents private domestic investment spending, along with the subscript g to signify gross investment.

Government Purchases (G)

The third category of expenditures in the national income accounts is **government purchases,** officially labeled "government consumption expenditures and gross investment." These expenditures have two components: (1) expenditures for goods and services that government consumes in providing public services and (2) expenditures for *publicly owned capital* such as schools and highways, which have long lifetimes. Government purchases (federal, state, and local) include all government expenditures on final goods and all direct purchases of resources, including labor. It does *not* include

government purchases (G) Government expenditures on final goods, services, and publicly owned capital.

government transfer payments such as Social Security payments, unemployment compensation, and veterans' benefits because they merely transfer government receipts to certain households and generate no *current* production. The symbol G signifies government purchases.

Net Exports (X_n)

International trade transactions are a significant item in national income accounting. But when calculating U.S. GDP, we must keep in mind that we want to total up only those expenditures that are used to purchase goods and services produced *within the borders of the United States.* Thus, we must add in the value of exports, X, since exports are by definition goods and services produced within the borders of the United States. Don't be confused by the fact that the expenditures made to buy up our exports are made by foreigners. The definition of GDP does not care about *who* is making expenditures on U.S.-made goods and services—only that the goods and services that they buy are made within the borders of the United States. Thus, foreign spending on our exports must be included in GDP.

At this point, you might incorrectly think that GDP should be equal to the sum of $C + I_g + G + X$. But this sum overstates GDP. The problem is that, once again, we must consider only expenditures made on *domestically produced* goods and services. As it stands, C, I_g, and G count up expenditures on consumption, investment, and government purchases regardless of where those goods and services are made. Crucially, not all of the C, I_g, or G expenditures are for domestically produced goods and services. Some of the expenditures are for imports—goods and services produced outside of the United States. Thus, since we wish to count *only* the part of C, I_g, and G that goes to purchasing domestically produced goods and services, we must subtract off the spending that goes to imports, M. Doing so yields the correct formula for calculating gross domestic product:

$$GDP = C + I_g + G + X - M$$

net exports (X_n)
Exports minus imports.

Accountants simplify this formula for GDP by defining **net exports,** X_n, to be equal to exports minus imports:

$$\text{Net exports } (X_n) = \text{exports } (X) - \text{imports } (M)$$

Using this definition of net exports, the formula for gross domestic product simplifies to

$$GDP = C + I_g + G + X_n$$

In 2010 Americans spent $516 billion more on imports than foreigners spent on U.S. exports. That is, net exports in 2010 were a negative $516 billion.

Adding It Up: GDP $= C + I_g + G + X_n$

Taken together, these four categories of expenditures provide a measure of the market value of a given year's total output—its GDP. For the United States in 2010,

$$GDP = \$10{,}349 + 1827 + 3000 - 516 = \$14{,}660 \text{ billion (or } \$14.66 \text{ trillion)}$$

Global Snapshot 5.1 compares GDP in the United States to GDP in several other countries for 2010.

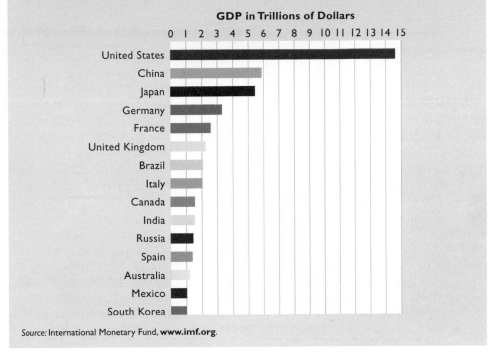

GLOBAL SNAPSHOT 5.1

Comparative GDPs in Trillions of U.S. Dollars, Selected Nations, 2010

The United States, China, and Japan have the world's highest GDPs. The GDP data charted below have been converted to dollars via international exchange rates.

GDP in Trillions of Dollars

Source: International Monetary Fund, **www.imf.org**.

Nominal GDP versus Real GDP

Recall that GDP is a measure of the market or money value of all final goods and services produced by the economy in a given year. We use money or nominal values as a common denominator in order to sum that heterogeneous output into a meaningful total. But that creates a problem: How can we compare the market values of GDP from year to year if the value of money itself changes in response to inflation or deflation? After all, we determine the value of GDP by multiplying total output by market prices.

Whether there is a 5 percent increase in output with no change in prices or a 5 percent increase in prices with no change in output, the change in the monetary value of GDP will be the same. And yet it is the *quantity* of goods that get produced and distributed to households that affects our standard of living, not the price of the goods. The McDonald's hamburger that sold for 99 cents in 2011 yielded the same satisfaction as the nearly identical McDonald's hamburger that sold for 18 cents in 1967.

The way around this problem is to *deflate* GDP when prices rise and to *inflate* GDP when prices fall. These adjustments give us a measure of GDP for various years as if the value of the dollar had always been the same as it was in some reference year. A GDP based on the prices that prevailed when the output was produced is called *unadjusted GDP*, or **nominal GDP**. A GDP that has been deflated or inflated to reflect changes in the price level is called *adjusted GDP*, or **real GDP.**

nominal GDP
Gross domestic product measured in terms of the price level at the time of measurement (i.e., GDP that is unadjusted for inflation).

real GDP
Gross domestic product measured in terms of the price level in a base period (i.e., GDP that is adjusted for inflation).

TABLE 5.2 Calculating Real GDP (Base Year = Year 1)

Year	(1) Units of Output	(2) Price of Pizza per Unit	(3) Unadjusted, or Nominal, GDP, (1) × (2)	(4) Adjusted, or Real, GDP
1	5	$10	$ 50	$50
2	7	20	140	70
3	8	25	200	80
4	10	30	___	___
5	11	28	___	___

Let's see how real GDP can be found. For simplicity, suppose the economy produces only one good, pizza, in the amounts indicated in Table 5.2 for years 1, 2, 3, 4, and 5. Also assume that we gather output and price data directly from the pizza business in various years. That is, we collect separate data on physical outputs (as in column 1) and their prices (as in column 2).

We can then determine the unadjusted, or nominal, GDP in each year by multiplying the number of units of output by the price per unit. Nominal GDP—here, the market value of pizza—is shown for each year in column 3.

We can also determine adjusted, or real, GDP from the data in Table 5.2. We want to know the market value of outputs in successive years *if the base-year price ($10) had prevailed*. In year 2, the 7 units of pizza would have a value of $70 (= 7 units × $10) at the year-1 price. As column 4 shows, that $70 worth of output is year 2's real GDP. Similarly, we can determine the real GDP for year 3 by multiplying the 8 units of output that year by the $10 price in the base year. You should check your understanding of nominal versus real GDP by completing columns 3 and 4, where we purposely left the last rows blank.

Let's return to the real economy. As previously determined, nominal GDP in the United States was $14,660 billion in 2010. What was real GDP that year? Because prices rose between the 2005 base year and 2010, real GDP in 2010 turned out to be $13,248 billion. Or, in the language of economics, "GDP in 2010 was $13,248 billion in 2005 (base-year) prices."

WORKED PROBLEMS

W 5.1

Real GDP and price indexes

APPLYING THE ANALYSIS

The Underground Economy

Real GDP is a reasonably accurate and highly useful measure of how well or how poorly the economy is performing. But some production never shows up in GDP, which measures only the *market value* of output. Embedded in the U.S. economy is a flourishing, productive underground sector. Some of the people who conduct business there are gamblers, smugglers, prostitutes, "fences" of stolen goods, drug producers, and drug dealers. They have good reason to conceal their economic activities. When they do, their "contributions" to output do not show up in GDP.

Most participants in the underground economy, however, engage in perfectly legal activities but choose not to report their full incomes to the Internal Revenue Service (IRS). A bell captain at a hotel may report just a portion of the tips received from customers. Storekeepers may report only a portion of their sales receipts. Workers who want to hold on to their unemployment compensation benefits may take an "off-the-books" or "cash-only" job. A brick mason may agree to rebuild a neighbor's fireplace in exchange for the neighbor's repairing his boat engine. The value of none of these transactions shows up in GDP.

The value of underground transactions is estimated to be about 8 percent of the recorded GDP in the United States. That would mean that GDP in 2010 was understated by about $1.17 trillion. Global Snapshot 5.2 shows estimates of the relative sizes of underground economies in selected nations.

QUESTION: How would decriminalization of drugs instantly increase a nation's real GDP? What might be the downside of decriminalization of drugs for growth of real GDP over time?

Economic Growth

The NIPA data enable economists to calculate and analyze economic growth rates. Economists define and measure **economic growth** as either an *increase in real GDP* occurring over time or an *increase in real GDP per capita* occurring over time. **Real GDP per capita** (or output per person) is found by dividing real GDP by the size of the population. With either definition, economic growth is calculated as a percentage rate of growth per quarter (3-month period) or per year.

economic growth
The expansion of real GDP (or real GDP per capita) over time.

real GDP per capita
Real output divided by population.

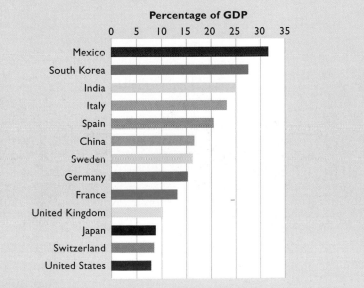

GLOBAL SNAPSHOT 5.2

The Underground Economy as a Percentage of GDP, Selected Nations

Underground economies vary in size worldwide. Three factors that help explain the variation are (1) the extent and complexity of regulation, (2) the type and degree of taxation, and (3) the effectiveness of law enforcement.

Percentage of GDP

Mexico
South Korea
India
Italy
Spain
China
Sweden
Germany
France
United Kingdom
Japan
Switzerland
United States

Source: Friedrich Schneider, "Shadow Economies and Corruption All over the World: New Estimates for 145 Countries," *Economics: The Open Access—Open Assessment, E-Journal,* vol. 1, 2007–9. Used with permission of Friedrich Schneider.

For measuring expansion of military potential or political preeminence, the growth of real GDP is more useful. Unless specified otherwise, growth rates reported in the news and by international agencies use this definition of economic growth. For comparing living standards, however, the second definition is superior. While China's GDP in 2008 was $4326 billion compared with Denmark's $343 billion, Denmark's real GDP per capita was $62,118 compared with China's $3267.

Growth as a Goal

Economic growth is a widely held economic goal. The expansion of total output relative to population results in rising real wages and incomes and thus higher standards of living. An economy that is experiencing economic growth is better able to meet people's wants and resolve socioeconomic problems. Rising real wages and income provide richer opportunities to individuals and families—a vacation trip, a personal computer, a higher education—without sacrificing other opportunities and pleasures. A growing economy can undertake new programs to alleviate poverty and protect the environment without impairing existing levels of consumption, investment, and public goods production.

In short, *growth lessens the burden of scarcity*. A growing economy, unlike a static economy, can consume more today while increasing its capacity to produce more in the future. By easing the burden of scarcity—by relaxing society's constraints on production—economic growth enables a nation to attain its economic goals more readily and to undertake new endeavors that require the use of goods and services to be accomplished.

Arithmetic of Growth

WORKED PROBLEMS

W 5.2

GDP growth

The mathematical approximation called the *rule of 70* shows the effect of compounding of economic growth rates over time. It tells us that we can find the number of years it will take for some measure to double, given its annual percentage increase, by dividing that percentage increase into the number 70. So

$$\text{Approximate number of years required to double real GDP} = \frac{70}{\text{annual percentage rate of growth}}$$

Examples: A 3 percent annual rate of growth will double real GDP in about 23 (= 70/3) years. Growth of 8 percent per year will double it in about 9 (= 70/8) years.

ILLUSTRATING THE IDEA

Growth Rates Matter!

Small absolute differences in rates of economic growth add up to substantial differences in real GDP and standards of living. Consider three hypothetical countries—Slogo, Sumgo, and Speedo. Suppose that in 2008 these countries have identical levels of real GDP ($6 trillion), population (200 million), and real GDP per capita ($30,000). Also, assume that annual real GDP growth is 2 percent in Slogo, 3 percent in Sumgo, and 4 percent in Speedo.

How will these alternative growth rates affect real GDP and real GDP per capita over a long period, say, the 70-year average life span of an American? By 2078 the 2, 3, and 4 percent growth rates would boost real GDP from $6 trillion to $24 trillion in Slogo, $47 trillion in Sumgo, and $93 trillion in Speedo.

For illustration, let's assume that each country experienced an average annual population growth of 1 percent over the 70 years. Then, in 2078 real GDP per capita would be about $60,000 in Slogo, $118,000 in Sumgo, and $233,000 in Speedo.

No wonder economists pay so much attention to small changes in the rate of economic growth. For the United States, with a current real GDP of about $12 trillion, the difference between a 3 percent and a 4 percent rate of growth is about $120 billion of output each year. For a poor country, a difference of one-half of a percentage point in the rate of growth may mean the difference between starvation and mere hunger. Economic growth rates matter!

QUESTION: Why would gaps in GDP per capita for Slogo and Speedo be even more dramatic if population growth was faster in Slogo than in Speedo?

Growth in the United States

Table 5.3 gives an overview of economic growth in the United States over past periods. Column 2 reveals strong growth as measured by increases in real GDP. Note that real GDP increased more than sixfold between 1950 and 2010. But the U.S. population also increased over these years. Nevertheless, in column 4 we find that real GDP per capita rose more than threefold.

What has been the *rate* of U.S. growth? Real GDP grew at an annual rate of about 3.2 percent between 1950 and 2010. Real GDP per capita increased about 2 percent per year over that time.

Viewed from the perspective of the last half-century, economic growth in the United States lagged behind that in Japan, Germany, Italy, Canada, and France. Japan's annual growth rate, in fact, averaged twice that of the United States. But economic growth since 2000 is quite another matter. As shown in Global Snapshot 5.3, until 2007, the U.S. growth rate generally topped the rates of growth in Japan and other major industrial nations.

(1) Year	(2) Real GDP, Billions of 2005 $	(3) Population, Millions	(4) Real per Capita GDP, 2005 $ (2) ÷ (3)
1950	$ 2006	152	$13,197
1960	2831	181	15,640
1970	4270	205	20,829
1980	5839	228	25,610
1990	8034	250	32,136
2000	11,226	282	39,809
2010	13,248	309	43,456

TABLE 5.3 Real GDP and per Capita Real GDP, Selected Years, 1950–2010

Source: Bureau of Economic Analysis, **www.bea.doc.gov,** and U.S. Census Bureau, **www.census.gov.**

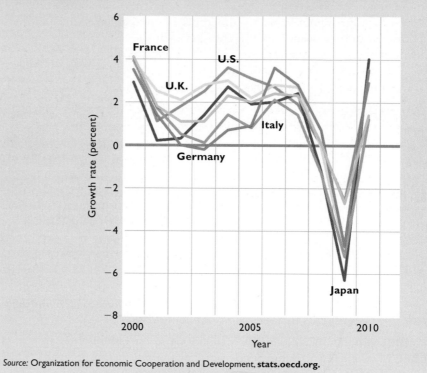

GLOBAL SNAPSHOT 5.3

Average Annual Growth Rates, 2000–2010, Selected Nations

Between 2000 and 2006, economic growth in the United States exceeded that of several other major countries. U.S. economic growth greatly slowed in 2001 and 2002 before rising again in 2003 and 2004. U.S. growth slowed again in 2007, and many countries experienced recession in 2008 and 2009.

Source: Organization for Economic Cooperation and Development, **stats.oecd.org.**

Determinants of Growth

There are six main determinants of economic growth. We can group them as supply, demand, and efficiency factors.

Supply Factors

Four of the determinants of economic growth relate to the physical ability of the economy to expand. They are:

- Increases in the quantity and quality of natural resources.
- Increases in the quantity and quality of human resources.
- Increases in the supply (or stock) of capital goods.
- Improvements in technology.

These *supply factors*—changes in the physical and technical agents of production—enable an economy to expand its potential GDP.

Demand Factor

The fifth determinant of economic growth is the *demand factor:*

- To achieve the higher production potential created by the supply factors, households, businesses, and government must *purchase* the economy's expanding output of goods and services.

When that occurs, there will be no unplanned increases in inventories and resources will remain fully employed. Economic growth requires increases in total spending to realize the output gains made available by increased production capacity.

Efficiency Factor

The sixth determinant of economic growth is the *efficiency factor:*

- To reach its full production potential, an economy must achieve economic efficiency as well as full employment.

The economy must use its resources in the least costly way (productive efficiency) to produce the specific mix of goods and services that maximizes people's well-being (allocative efficiency). The ability to expand production, together with the full use of available resources, is not sufficient for achieving maximum possible growth. Also required is the efficient use of those resources.

The supply, demand, and efficiency factors in economic growth are related. Unemployment caused by insufficient total spending (the demand factor) may lower the rate of new capital accumulation (a supply factor) and delay expenditures on research (also a supply factor). Conversely, low spending on investment (a supply factor) may cause insufficient spending (the demand factor) and unemployment. Widespread inefficiency in the use of resources (the efficiency factor) may translate into higher costs of goods and services and thus lower profits, which in turn may slow innovation and reduce the accumulation of capital (supply factors). Economic growth is a dynamic process in which the supply, demand, and efficiency factors all interact.

> **ORIGIN OF THE IDEA**
>
> **O 5.1**
> Growth theory

Production Possibilities Analysis

To put the six factors affecting the rate of economic growth into better perspective, let's use the production possibilities analysis introduced in Chapter 1.

Growth and Production Possibilities

Recall that a curve like *AB* in Figure 5.1 is a production possibilities curve. It indicates the various *maximum* combinations of products an economy can produce with its fixed quantity and quality of natural, human, and capital resources and its stock of technological knowledge. An improvement in any of the supply factors will push the production possibilities curve outward, as from *AB* to *CD*.

But the demand factor reminds us that an increase in total spending is needed to move the economy from a point like *a* on curve *AB* to any of the points on the higher curve *CD*. And the efficiency factor reminds us that we need least-cost production and an optimal location on *CD* for the resources to make their maximum possible dollar contribution to total output. You will recall from Chapter 1 that this "best allocation" is determined by expanding production of each good until its marginal cost equals its marginal benefit. Here, we assume that this optimal combination of capital and consumer goods occurs at point *b*.

FIGURE 5.1 Economic growth and the production possibilities curve. Economic growth is made possible by the four supply factors that shift the production possibilities curve outward, as from *AB* to *CD*. Economic growth is realized when the demand factor and the efficiency factor move the economy from point *a* to *b*.

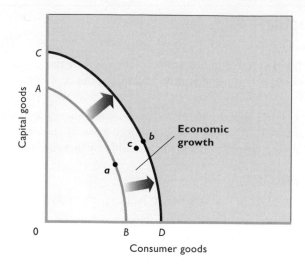

Example: The net increase in the size of the labor force in the United States in recent years has been 1.5 million to 2 million workers per year. That increment raises the economy's production capacity. But obtaining the extra output that these added workers could produce depends on their success in finding jobs. It also depends on whether or not the jobs are in firms and industries where the workers' talents are fully and optimally used. Society does not want new labor-force entrants to be unemployed. Nor does it want pediatricians working as plumbers or pediatricians producing services for which marginal costs exceed marginal benefits.

Normally, increases in total spending match increases in production capacity, and the economy moves from a point on the previous production possibilities curve to a point on the expanded curve. Moreover, the competitive market system tends to drive the economy toward productive and allocative efficiency. Occasionally, however, the economy may end up at some point such as *c* in Figure 5.1. That kind of outcome occurred in the United States during the severe recession of 2007–2009. Real output fell far below the real output that the economy would have produced if it had achieved full employment and operated on its production possibilities curve.

WORKED PROBLEMS

W 5.3

Productivity and economic growth

labor productivity
Real output per hour of work.

Inputs and Productivity

Society can increase its output and income in two fundamental ways: (1) by increasing its inputs of resources and (2) by raising the productivity of those inputs. Figure 5.2 concentrates on the input of *labor* and provides a useful framework for discussing the role of supply factors in growth. A nation's real GDP in any year depends on the input of labor (measured in hours of work) multiplied by **labor productivity** (measured as real output per hour of work).

So, thought of this way, a nation's economic growth from one year to the next depends on its *increase* in labor inputs (if any) and its *increase* in labor productivity (if any).

Illustration: Assume that the cool economy of Rapland has 10 workers in year 1, each working 2000 hours per year (50 weeks at 40 hours per week). The total input of labor therefore is 20,000 hours. If productivity (average real output per hour of work) is $10, then real GDP in Rapland will be $200,000 (= 20,000 × $10). If work hours rise to 20,200 and labor productivity rises to $10.40, Rapland's real GDP will increase to $210,080 in year 2. Rapland's rate of economic growth will be about 5 percent [= ($210,080 − $200,000)/$200,000] for the year.

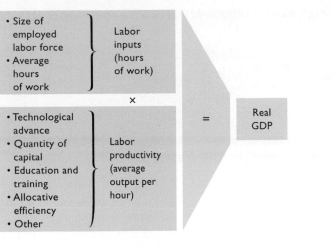

FIGURE 5.2 The supply determinants of real output. Real GDP is usefully viewed as the product of the quantity of labor inputs (hours of work) multiplied by labor productivity.

Hours of Work What determines the number of hours worked each year? As shown in Figure 5.2, the hours of labor input depend on the size of the employed labor force and the length of the average workweek. Labor-force size depends on the size of the working-age population and the **labor-force participation rate**—the percentage of the working-age population actually in the labor force. The length of the average workweek is governed by legal and institutional considerations and by collective bargaining.

Labor Productivity Figure 5.2 tells us that labor productivity is determined by technological progress, the quantity of capital goods available to workers, the quality of the labor itself, and the efficiency with which inputs are allocated, combined, and managed. Productivity rises when the health, training, education, and motivation of workers improve, when workers have more and better machinery and natural resources with which to work, when production is better organized and managed, and when labor is reallocated from less efficient industries to more efficient industries.

> **labor-force participation rate** The percentage of the working-age population actually in the labor force.

Accounting for Growth

The Council of Economic Advisers uses a system called **growth accounting** to assess the relative importance of the supply-side elements that contribute to changes in real GDP. This system groups these elements into the two main categories we have just discussed:

- Increases in hours of work.
- Increases in labor productivity.

> **growth accounting** The bookkeeping of the supply-side elements that contribute to changes in real GDP.

Labor Inputs versus Labor Productivity

Table 5.4 provides the relevant data for four periods. The symbol "Q" in the table stands for "quarter" of the year. The beginning points for three of the four periods are business-cycle peaks, and the last column includes future projections by the Council of Economic Advisers. It is clear from the table that both increases in the quantity of labor and rises in labor productivity are important sources of economic growth. Between 1953 and 2011, the labor force increased from 63 million to 154 million workers. Over that period the average length of the workweek remained relatively stable. Falling birthrates slowed the growth of the native population, but increased immigration partly offset that slowdown. Of particular significance was a surge of women's participation in the labor force, from 34 percent in 1953 to 59 percent in

TABLE 5.4 Accounting for the Growth of U.S. Real GDP, 1953–2007 Plus Projection from 2010 to 2021 (Average Annual Percentage Changes)

Item	Actual				Projected
	1953 Q2 to 1973 Q4	1973 Q4 to 1995 Q2	1995 Q2 to 2001 Q1	2001 Q1 to 2007 Q3	2010 Q1 to 2021 Q4
Increase in real GDP	3.6	2.8	3.8	2.6	2.5
Increase in quantity of labor	1.1	1.3	1.4	−0.1	0.2
Increase in labor productivity	2.5	1.5	2.4	2.7	2.3

Source: Derived from *Economic Report of the President, 2008*, p. 45; and *Economic Report of the President, 2011*, p. 52.

2010. Partly as a result, U.S. labor-force growth averaged about 1.6 million workers per year over the past 58 years.

The growth of labor productivity has also been important to economic growth. In fact, productivity growth has usually been the more significant factor, with the exception of 1973–1995 when productivity growth greatly slowed. For example, between 2001 and 2007, productivity growth was responsible for all of the 2.6 percent average annual economic growth. Productivity growth is projected to account for 92 percent of the growth of real GDP between 2010 and 2021.

Because increases in labor productivity are so important to economic growth, economists go to the trouble of investigating and assessing the relative importance of the factors that contribute to productivity growth. There are five factors that, together, appear to explain changes in productivity growth rates. They are technological advance, the amount of capital each worker has to work with, education and training, economies of scale, and resource allocation. We will examine each factor in turn, noting how much each factor contributes to productivity growth.

Technological Advance

The largest contributor to productivity growth is technological advance, which is thought to account for about 40 percent of productivity growth. As economist Paul Romer has stated, "Human history teaches us that economic growth springs from better recipes, not just from more cooking."

Technological advance includes not only innovative production techniques but new managerial methods and new forms of business organization that improve the process of production. Generally, technological advance is generated by the discovery of new knowledge, which allows resources to be combined in improved ways that increase output. Once discovered and implemented, new knowledge soon becomes available to entrepreneurs and firms at relatively low cost. Technological advance therefore eventually spreads through the entire economy, boosting productivity and economic growth.

Technological advance and capital formation (investment) are closely related because technological advance usually promotes investment in new machinery and equipment. In fact, technological advance is often *embodied* within new capital. For example, the purchase of new computers brings into industry speedier, more powerful computers that incorporate new technology.

Technological advance has been both rapid and profound. Gas and diesel engines, conveyor belts, and assembly lines are significant developments of the past. So, too, are fuel-efficient commercial aircraft, integrated microcircuits, personal computers, digital photography, and containerized shipping. More recently, technological advance has exploded, particularly in the areas of computers, wireless communications, and the Internet. Other fertile areas of recent innovation are medicine and biotechnology.

Quantity of Capital

A second major contributor to productivity growth is increased capital, which explains roughly 30 percent of productivity growth. More and better plant and equipment make workers more productive. And a nation acquires more capital by saving some of its income and using that saving to invest in plant and equipment.

Although some capital substitutes for labor, most capital is complementary to labor—it makes labor more productive. A key determinant of labor productivity is the amount of capital goods available *per worker*. If both the aggregate stock of capital goods and the size of the labor force increase over a given period, the individual worker is not necessarily better equipped and productivity will not necessarily rise. But the quantity of capital equipment available per U.S. worker has increased greatly over time. (In 2008 it was about $118,200 per worker.)

Public investment in the U.S. **infrastructure** (highways and bridges, public transit systems, water and sewage systems, airports, industrial parks, educational facilities, and so on) has also grown over the years. This publicly owned capital complements private capital. Investments in new highways promote private investment in new factories and retail stores along their routes. Industrial parks developed by local governments attract manufacturing and distribution firms.

Private investment in infrastructure also plays a large role in economic growth. One example is the tremendous growth of private capital relating to communications systems over the years.

infrastructure
Public and private capital goods that buttress an economy's production capacity (for example, highways, bridges, airports, public transit systems, wastewater treatment facilities, educational facilities, and telecommunications systems that complement private capital).

© Medioimages/Superstock   © Royalty-Free/CORBIS

PHOTO OP Public and Private Investment in Infrastructure

Both public infrastructure investments (such as highways and bridges) and private infrastructure investments (such as wireless communications systems) have increased the nation's stock of private and public capital and help expand real GDP.

FIGURE 5.3 Changes in the educational attainment of the U.S. adult population. The percentage of the U.S. adult population, age 25 or more, completing high school and college has been rising over recent decades. Source: U.S. Census Bureau, **www.census.gov**.

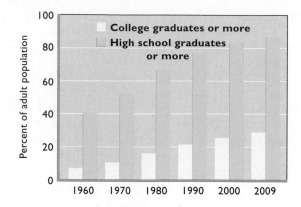

Education and Training

human capital
The knowledge and skills that make a worker productive.

Ben Franklin once said, "He that hath a trade hath an estate," meaning that education and training contribute to a worker's stock of **human capital**—the knowledge and skills that make a worker productive. Investment in human capital includes not only formal education but also on-the-job training. Like investment in physical capital, investment in human capital is an important means of increasing labor productivity and earnings. An estimated 15 percent of productivity growth derives from investments in people's education and skills.

One measure of a nation's quality of labor is its level of educational attainment. Figure 5.3 shows large gains in educational attainment over the past several decades. In 1960 only 41 percent of the U.S. population age 25 or older had at least a high school education; and only 8 percent had a college education or more. By 2009, those numbers had increased to 87 and 29 percent, respectively. Clearly, more people are receiving an education than ever before.

But all is not upbeat with education in the United States. Many observers think that the quality of education in the United States has declined. For example, U.S. students in science and mathematics perform poorly on tests on those subjects relative to students in many other nations. The United States has been producing fewer native-born engineers and scientists, a problem that may trace back to inadequate training in math and science in elementary and high schools. For these reasons, much recent public policy discussion and legislation have been directed toward improving the quality of the U.S. education and training system.

Economies of Scale and Resource Allocation

Economies of scale and improved resource allocation are a fourth and fifth source of productivity growth, and together they explain about 15 percent of productivity growth.

economies of scale
Reductions in per-unit production costs that result from increases in the size of markets and firms.

Economies of Scale Reductions in per-unit production costs that result from increases in output levels are called **economies of scale.** Markets have increased in size over time, allowing firms to increase output levels and thereby achieve production advantages associated with greater size. As firms expand their size and output, they are able to use larger, more productive equipment and employ methods of manufacturing and delivery that increase productivity. They also are better able to recoup substantial investments in developing new products and production methods. Examples: A large manufacturer of autos can use elaborate assembly lines with computerization and robotics, while smaller producers must settle for less-advanced technologies using more labor inputs. Large pharmaceutical firms greatly reduce the average amount of labor (researchers, production workers) needed to produce each pill as they increase the number of pills produced. Accordingly, economies of scale result in greater real GDP and thus contribute to economic growth.

Improved Resource Allocation Improved resource allocation means that workers over time have moved from low-productivity employment to high-productivity employment. Historically, many workers have shifted from agriculture, where labor productivity is low, to manufacturing, where it is quite high. More recently, labor has shifted away from some manufacturing industries to even higher-productivity industries such as computer software, business consulting, and pharmaceuticals. As a result of such shifts, the average productivity of U.S. workers has increased.

Also, things such as tariffs, import quotas, and other barriers to international trade tend to relegate resources to relatively unproductive pursuits. The long-run movement toward liberalized international trade through international agreements has improved the allocation of resources, increased labor productivity, and expanded real output, both here and abroad.

Finally, discrimination in education and the labor market has historically deterred some women and minorities from entering high-productivity jobs. With the decline of such discrimination over time, many members of those groups have shifted from low-productivity jobs to higher-productivity jobs. The result has been higher overall labor productivity and real GDP.

Institutional Structures That Promote Growth

Economic historians have identified several institutional structures that promote and sustain modern economic growth. Some structures increase the savings and investment that are needed to fund the construction and maintenance of the huge amounts of infrastructure required to run modern economies. Other institutional structures promote the development of new technologies. And still others act to ensure that resources flow efficiently to their most productive uses. These growth-promoting institutional structures include

- *Strong property rights* These appear to be absolutely necessary for rapid and sustained economic growth. People will not invest if they believe that thieves, bandits, or a rapacious and tyrannical government will steal their investments or their expected returns.
- *Patents and copyrights* These are necessary if a society wants a constant flow of innovative new technologies and sophisticated new ideas. Before patents and copyrights were first issued and enforced, inventors and authors usually saw their ideas stolen before they could profit from them. By giving inventors and authors the exclusive right to market and sell their creations, patents and copyrights give a strong financial incentive to invent and create.
- *Efficient financial institutions* These are needed to channel the savings generated by households towards the businesses, entrepreneurs, and inventors that do most of society's investing and inventing. Banks as well as stock and bond markets appear to be institutions crucial to modern economic growth.
- *Free trade* Free trade promotes economic growth by allowing countries to specialize so that different types of output can be produced in the countries where

they can be made most efficiently. In addition, free trade promotes the rapid spread of new ideas so that innovations made in one country quickly spread to other countries.

- *A competitive market system* Under a market system, prices and profits serve as the signals that tell firms what to make and how much of it to make. Rich leader countries vary substantially in terms of how much government regulation they impose on markets, but in all cases, firms have substantial autonomy to follow market signals not only in terms of current production but also in terms of the investments they will currently make to produce what they believe consumers will demand in the future.

Other Factors

Several other difficult-to-measure factors also influence a nation's capacity for economic growth. The overall social-cultural-political environment of the United States, for example, has encouraged economic growth. Beyond the market system that has prevailed in the United States, the nation also has had a stable political system characterized by democratic principles, internal order, the right of property ownership, the legal status of enterprise, and the enforcement of contracts. Economic freedom and political freedom have been "growth-friendly."

In addition, and unlike some nations, there are virtually no social or moral taboos on production and material progress in the United States. The nation's social philosophy has embraced wealth creation as an attainable and desirable goal and the inventor, the innovator, and the businessperson are accorded high degrees of prestige and respect in American society. Finally, Americans have a positive attitude toward work and risk taking, resulting in an ample supply of willing workers and innovative entrepreneurs. A flow of energetic immigrants has greatly augmented that supply.

The Rise in the Average Rate of Productivity Growth

Figure 5.4 shows the growth of labor productivity (as measured by changes in the index of labor productivity for the full business sector) in the United States from 1973 to 2009, along with separate trend lines for 1973–1995 and 1995–2009. Labor

FIGURE 5.4 Growth of labor productivity in the United States, 1973–2009. U.S. labor productivity (here, for the business sector) increased at an average annual rate of only 1.5 percent from 1973 to 1995. But between 1995 and 2009, it rose to an annual rate of 2.8 percent.
Source: U.S. Bureau of Labor Statistics, **www.bls.gov**.

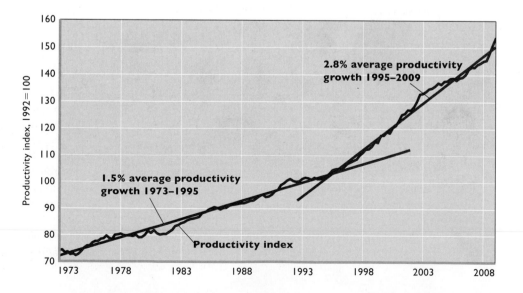

productivity in the business sector grew by an average of only 1.5 percent yearly over the 1973–1995 period. But productivity growth averaged 2.8 percent between 1995 and 2009. Many economists believe that this higher productivity growth resulted from a significant new wave of technological advance, coupled with global competition. Some economists think there is a good chance that the higher trend rates of productivity growth could continue for many years to come.

This increase in productivity growth is important because real output, real income, and real wages are linked to labor productivity. To see why, suppose you are alone on an uninhabited island. The number of fish you can catch or coconuts you can pick per hour—your productivity—is your real wage (or real income) per hour. By *increasing* your productivity, you can improve your standard of living because greater output per hour means there are more fish and coconuts (goods) available to consume.

So it is for the economy as a whole: Over long periods, the economy's labor productivity determines its average real hourly wage, which includes fringe benefits such as health care insurance and contributions to pensions. The economy's income per hour is equal to its output per hour. So productivity growth is the economy's main route for improving the living standards for its workers.

Reasons for the Rise in the Average Rate of Productivity Growth

Why has productivity growth increased relative to earlier periods?

The Microchip and Information Technology The core element of the productivity speedup is an explosion of entrepreneurship and innovation based on the microprocessor, or *microchip*, which bundles transistors on a piece of silicon. Some observers liken the invention of the microchip to that of electricity, the automobile, air travel, the telephone, and television in importance and scope.

The microchip has found its way into thousands of applications. It has helped create a wide array of new products and services and new ways of doing business. Its immediate results were the pocket calculator, the bar-code scanner, the personal computer, the laptop computer, and more powerful business computers. But the miniaturization of electronic circuits also advanced the development of many other products such as cell phones and pagers, computer-guided lasers, deciphered genetic codes, global positioning equipment, energy conservation systems, Doppler radar, and digital cameras.

Perhaps of greatest significance, the widespread availability of personal and laptop computers stimulated the desire to tie them together. That desire promoted rapid development of the Internet and all its many manifestations, such as business-to-household and business-to-business electronic commerce (*e-commerce*). The combination of the computer, fiber optic cable, wireless technology, and the Internet constitutes a spectacular advance in **information technology,** which has been used to connect all parts of the world.

New Firms and Increasing Returns Hundreds of new **start-up firms** advanced various aspects of the new information technology. Many of these firms created more "hype" than goods and services and quickly fell by the wayside. But a number of firms flourished, eventually to take their places among the nation's largest firms. Examples of those firms include Intel (microchips); Apple and Dell (personal computers); Microsoft and Oracle (computer software); Cisco Systems (Internet switching systems); Yahoo and Google (Internet search engines); and Amazon.com (electronic commerce). There are scores more! Most of these firms were either "not on the radar"

information technology
New and more efficient methods of delivering and receiving information through use of computers, fax machines, wireless phones, and the Internet.

start-up firms
New firms focused on creating and introducing particular new products or employing specific new production or distribution methods.

or "a relatively small blip on the radar" 30 years ago. Today each of them has large annual revenue and employs thousands of workers.

increasing returns
A firm's output increases by a larger percentage than the increase in its inputs.

Successful new firms often experience **increasing returns,** a situation in which a given percentage increase in the amount of inputs a firm uses leads to an even larger percentage increase in the amount of output the firm produces. For example, suppose that a company called Techco decides to double the size of its operations to meet the growing demand for its services. After doubling its plant and equipment and doubling its workforce, say, from 100 workers to 200 workers, it finds that its total output has tripled from 8000 units to 24,000 units. Techco has experienced increasing returns; its output has increased by 200 percent, while its inputs have increased by only 100 percent. That is, its labor productivity has gone up from 80 units per worker (= 8000 units/100 workers) to 120 units per worker (= 24,000 units/200 workers). Increasing returns boost labor productivity and lower per-unit production costs. Since these cost reductions result from increases in output levels, they are examples of *economics of scale*.

Both emerging firms as well as established firms can exploit several different sources of increasing returns and economies of scale:

- *More specialized inputs*   Firms can use more specialized and thus more productive capital and workers as they expand their operations. A growing new e-commerce business, for example, can purchase highly specialized inventory management systems and hire specialized personnel such as accountants, marketing managers, and system maintenance experts.

- *Spreading of development costs*   Firms can spread high product development costs over greater output. For example, suppose that a new software product costs $100,000 to develop and only $2 per unit to manufacture and sell. If the firm sells 1000 units of the software, its cost per unit will be $102 [= ($100,000 + $2000)/1000], but if it sells 500,000 units, that cost will drop to only $2.20 [= ($100,000 + $1 million)/500,000].

- *Simultaneous consumption*   Many recently developed products and services can satisfy large numbers of customers at the same time. Unlike a gallon of gas that needs to be produced for each buyer, a software program needs to be produced only once. It then becomes available at very low expense to thousands or even millions of buyers. The same is true of books delivered to electronic reading devices, movies distributed on DVDs, and information disseminated through the Internet.

network effects
Increases in the value of a product to each user, including existing users, as the total number of users rises.

- *Network effects*   Software and Internet service become more beneficial to a buyer the greater the number of households and businesses that also buy them. When others have Internet service, you can send e-mail messages to them. And when they also have software that allows display of documents and photos, you can attach those items to your e-mail messages. These system advantages are called **network effects,** which are increases in the value of the product to each user, including existing users, as the total number of users rises. The domestic and global expansion of the Internet in particular has produced network effects, as have cell phones, pagers, palm computers, and other aspects of wireless communication. Network effects magnify the value of output well beyond the costs of inputs.

learning by doing
Achieving greater productivity and lower average total costs through gains in knowledge and skill that accompany repetition of a task.

- *Learning by doing*   Finally, firms that produce new products or pioneer new ways of doing business experience increasing returns through **learning by doing.** Tasks that initially may have taken firms hours may take them only minutes once the methods are perfected.

Whatever the particular source of increasing returns, the result is higher productivity, which tends to reduce the per-unit cost of producing and delivering products.

Global Competition The recent economy is characterized not only by information technology and increasing returns but also by heightened global competition. The collapse of the socialist economies in the late 1980s and early 1990s, together with the success of market systems, has led to a reawakening of capitalism throughout the world. The new information technologies have "shrunk the globe" and made it imperative for all firms to lower their costs and prices and to innovate in order to remain competitive. Free-trade zones such as those created by the North American Free Trade Agreement (NAFTA) and the European Union (EU) also have heightened competition internationally by removing trade protection from domestic firms. So, too, has trade liberalization through the World Trade Organization (WTO). The larger geographic markets and lower tariffs, in turn, have enabled emerging and old-line firms to expand beyond their national borders.

Implications for Economic Growth

Other things equal, stronger productivity growth and heightened global competition allow the economy to achieve a higher rate of economic growth. A glance back at Figure 5.1 will help make this point. Suppose that the shift of the production possibilities curve from *AB* to *CD* reflects annual changes in potential output levels before the recent increase in growth rates. Then the higher growth rates of the more recent period of accelerated productivity growth would be depicted by a *larger* outward shift of the economy's production possibilities from *AB* to a curve beyond *CD*. When coupled with economic efficiency and increased total spending, the economy's real GDP would rise by more than that shown.

Two cautions: Although the trend line of productivity growth seems to be steeper than in the past and bodes well for long-term economic growth, fluctuations of the rate of economic growth will still occur. Because of demand factors, real output periodically deviates below and above the growth trend—as it certainly did during the very severe recession of 2007–2009. Also, you need to know that the growth of the U.S. labor force may be declining. That slowing may offset some or all of the extra potential for economic growth that would arise from greater productivity growth.

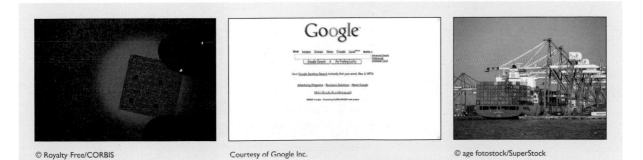

© Royalty Free/CORBIS   Courtesy of Google Inc.   © age fotostock/SuperStock

PHOTO OP Key Elements of the Rise in U.S. Productivity

A combination of information technology, emerging new firms, and globalization helps explain the speedup in U.S. productivity growth since 1995.

Skepticism about Longevity

Although most macroeconomists have revised their forecasts for long-term productivity growth upward, at least slightly, others are still skeptical and urge a "wait-and-see" approach. These macroeconomists acknowledge that the economy has experienced a rapid advance of new technology, some new firms have experienced increasing returns, and global competition has increased. But they wonder if these factors are sufficiently profound to produce a 15- to 20-year period of substantially higher rates of productivity growth and real GDP growth.

They also point out that productivity surged between 1975 and 1978 and between 1983 and 1986 but in each case soon reverted to its lower long-run trend. The higher trend line of productivity inferred from the short-run spurt of productivity could prove to be an illusion. Only by looking backward over long periods can economists distinguish the start of a new long-run trend from a shorter-term boost in productivity related to the business cycle and temporary factors.

What Can We Conclude?

Given the different views on the recent productivity acceleration, what should we conclude? Perhaps the safest conclusions are these:

- The prospects for a lasting increase in productivity growth are good (see Global Snapshot 5.4). Studies indicate that productivity increases related to information technology have spread to a wide range of industries, including services. Even in

GLOBAL SNAPSHOT 5.4

Global Competitiveness Index

The Global Competitiveness Index published annually by the World Economic Forum measures each country's potential for economic growth. The index uses various factors—such as innovativeness, the capability to transfer technology among sectors, the efficiency of the financial system, rates of investment, and the degree of integration with the rest of the world—to measure a country's ability to achieve economic growth over time. Here is the top 10 list for 2010–2011.

Country	Global Competitiveness Ranking, 2010–2011
Switzerland	1
Singapore	2
Sweden	3
Finland	4
United States	5
Germany	6
Netherlands	7
Denmark	8
Japan	9
United Kingdom	10

Source: Copyright World Economic Forum, *The Global Competitiveness Report*, 2011–2012, **www.weforum.org.**

the recession year 2001 and in 2002, when the economy was sluggish, productivity growth remained strong. Specifically, it averaged about 3.3 percent in the business sector over those two years. Productivity rose by 3.8 percent in 2003, 2.9 percent in 2004, and 2.0 percent in 2005 as the economy vigorously expanded.

- Time will tell. Productivity growth was 1.0 percent in 2006, 1.8 percent in 2007, 2.7 percent in 2008, and 2.1 percent in 2009. The average for these rates for the latest four years is lower than the 2.8 percent rate shown by the trend line in Figure 5.4, but it is higher than the 1.5 percent rate for the 1973–1995 period. Clearly many more years must elapse before economists will be ready to declare the post-1995 productivity acceleration to be a sustained, long-term trend.

Is Growth Desirable and Sustainable?

Economists typically see economic growth as desirable and sustainable. But not all social observers agree.

The Antigrowth View

Critics of growth say industrialization and growth result in pollution, climate change, ozone depletion, and other environmental problems. These adverse spillover costs occur because inputs in the production process reenter the environment as some form of waste. The more rapid our growth and the higher our standard of living, the more waste the environment must absorb—or attempt to absorb. In an already wealthy society, further growth usually means satisfying increasingly trivial wants at the cost of mounting threats to the ecological system.

Critics of growth also argue that there is little compelling evidence that economic growth has solved sociological problems such as poverty, homelessness, and discrimination. Consider poverty: In the antigrowth view, American poverty (and, for that matter, world poverty) is a problem of distribution, not production. The requisite for solving the problem is commitment and political courage to redistribute wealth and income, not further increases in output.

Antigrowth sentiment also says that while growth may permit us to "make a better living," it does not give us "the good life." We may be producing more and enjoying it less. Growth means frantic paces on jobs, worker burnout, and alienated employees who have little or no control over decisions affecting their lives. The changing technology at the core of growth poses new anxieties and new sources of insecurity for workers. Both high-level and low-level workers face the prospect of having their hard-earned skills and experience rendered obsolete by an onrushing technology. High-growth economies are high-stress economies, which may impair our physical and mental health.

Finally, critics of high rates of growth doubt that they are sustainable. The planet Earth has finite amounts of natural resources available, and they are being consumed at alarming rates. Higher rates of economic growth simply speed up the degradation and exhaustion of the earth's resources. In this view, slower economic growth that is sustainable is preferable to faster growth.

In Defense of Economic Growth

The primary defense of growth is that it is the path to the greater material abundance and higher living standards desired by the vast majority of people. Rising output and incomes allow people to buy

more education, recreation, and travel, more medical care, closer communications, more skilled personal and professional services, and better-designed as well as more numerous products. It also means more art, music, and poetry, theater, and drama. It can even mean more time and resources devoted to spiritual growth and human development.[2]

Growth also enables society to improve the nation's infrastructure, enhance the care of the sick and elderly, provide greater access for the disabled, and provide more police and fire protection. Economic growth may be the only realistic way to reduce poverty, since there is little political support for greater redistribution of income. The way to improve the economic position of the poor is to increase household incomes through higher productivity and economic growth. Also, a no-growth policy among industrial nations might severely limit growth in poor nations. Foreign investment and development assistance in those nations would fall, keeping the world's poor in poverty longer.

Economic growth has not made labor more unpleasant or hazardous, as critics suggest. New machinery is usually less taxing and less dangerous than the machinery it replaces. Air-conditioned workplaces are more pleasant than steamy workshops. Furthermore, why would an end to economic growth reduce materialism or alienation? The loudest protests against materialism are heard in those nations and groups that now enjoy the highest levels of material abundance! The high standard of living that growth provides has increased our leisure and given us more time for reflection and self-fulfillment.

Does growth threaten the environment? The connection between growth and environment is tenuous, say growth proponents. Increases in economic growth need not mean increases in pollution. Pollution is not so much a by-product of growth as it is a "problem of the commons." Much of the environment—streams, lakes, oceans, and the air—is treated as "common property," with insufficient or no restrictions on its use. The commons have become our dumping grounds; we have overused and debased them. Environmental pollution is a case of spillover or external costs, and correcting this problem involves regulatory legislation, specific taxes ("effluent charges"), or market-based incentives to remedy misuse of the environment.

Those who support growth admit there are serious environmental problems but say that limiting growth is the wrong solution. Growth has allowed economies to reduce pollution, be more sensitive to environmental considerations, set aside wilderness, create national parks and monuments, and clean up hazardous waste, while still enabling rising household incomes.

Is growth sustainable? Yes, say the proponents of growth. If we were depleting natural resources faster than their discovery, we would see the prices of those resources rise. That has not been the case for most natural resources; in fact, the prices of most of them have declined. And if one natural resource becomes too expensive, another resource will be substituted for it. Moreover, say economists, economic growth has to do with the expansion and application of human knowledge and information, not of extractable natural resources. In this view, economic growth—and solving any problems it may create—is limited only by human imagination.

---

[2]Alice M. Rivlin, Reviving the American Dream (Washington, D.C.: Brookings Institution, 1992), p. 36.

Summary

1. Gross domestic product (GDP) is the market value of all final goods and services produced within the borders of a nation in a year. Intermediate goods and secondhand sales are purposely excluded in calculating GDP.

2. GDP can be calculated by adding consumer purchases of goods and services, gross investment spending by businesses, government purchases, and net exports: $GDP = C + I_g + G + X_n$.

3. Nominal (current-dollar) GDP measures each year's output valued in terms of the prices prevailing in that year. Real (constant-dollar) GDP measures each year's output in terms of the prices that prevailed in a selected base year. Because real GDP is adjusted for price-level changes, differences in real GDP are due only to differences in output.

4. Economic growth is either (a) an increase of real GDP over time or (b) an increase in real GDP per capita over time. Growth lessens the burden of scarcity and provides increases in real GDP that can be used to resolve socioeconomic problems.

5. The supply factors in economic growth are (a) the quantity and quality of a nation's natural resources, (b) the quantity and quality of its human resources, (c) its stock of capital facilities, and (d) its technology. Two other factors—a sufficient level of aggregate demand and economic efficiency—are necessary for the economy to realize its growth potential.

6. The growth of production capacity is shown graphically as an outward shift of a nation's production possibilities curve. Growth is realized when total spending rises sufficiently to match the growth of production capacity.

7. U.S. real GDP has grown partly because of increased inputs of labor and primarily because of increases in the productivity of labor. The increases in productivity have resulted mainly from technological progress, increases in the quantity of capital per worker, improvements in the quality of labor, economies of scale, and an improved allocation of labor.

8. Over long time periods, the growth of labor productivity underlies an economy's growth of real wages and its standard of living.

9. Productivity rose by 2.8 percent annually between 1995 and 2009, compared to 1.5 percent annually between 1973 and 1995. Some economists think this productivity acceleration will be long-lasting and allow the economy to experience greater noninflationary economic growth.

10. The post-1995 increase in the average rate of productivity growth is based on (a) rapid technological change in the form of the microchip and information technology, (b) increasing returns and lower per-unit costs, and (c) heightened global competition that holds down prices.

11. The main sources of increasing returns in recent years are (a) the use of more specialized inputs as firms grow, (b) the spreading of development costs, (c) simultaneous consumption by consumers, (d) network effects, and (e) learning by doing. Increasing returns mean higher productivity and lower per-unit production costs.

12. Some economists wonder if the recent rise in the average rate of productivity growth is permanent, and therefore they urge a wait-and-see approach. They point out that surges in productivity and real GDP growth have previously occurred but do not necessarily represent long-lived trends.

13. Critics of rapid growth say that it adds to environmental degradation, increases human stress, and exhausts the earth's finite supply of natural resources. Defenders of rapid growth say that it is the primary path to the rising living standards nearly universally desired by people, that it need not debase the environment, and that there are no indications that we are running out of resources. Growth is based on the expansion and application of human knowledge, which is limited only by human imagination.

Terms and Concepts

national income and product accounts (NIPA)

gross domestic product (GDP)

intermediate goods

final goods

personal consumption expenditures (C)

gross private domestic investment (I_g)

government purchases (G)

net exports (X_n)

nominal GDP

real GDP

economic growth

real GDP per capita

labor productivity

labor-force participation rate

growth accounting

infrastructure

human capital

economies of scale

information technology

start-up firms

increasing returns

network effects

learning by doing

Questions ![McGraw Hill connect ECONOMICS]

1. Why do national income accountants compare the market value of the total outputs in various years rather than actual physical volumes of production? What problem is posed by any comparison over time of the market values of various total outputs? How is this problem resolved? **LO1**

2. Why are only final goods counted in measuring GDP for a particular year? Why is the value of used furniture that's bought and sold not counted? **LO1**

3. What are the three main types of consumption expenditures? Why are purchases of new houses considered to be investment expenditures rather than consumption expenditures? **LO1**

4. Why are changes in inventories included as part of investment spending? Suppose inventories declined by $1 billion during 2012. How would this affect the size of gross private domestic investment and gross domestic product in 2012? Explain. **LO1**

5. Define net exports. Explain how U.S. exports and imports each affects domestic production. How are net exports determined? Explain how net exports might be a negative amount. **LO1**

6. Which of the following are included in this year's GDP? Explain your answer in each case. **LO1**
   a. The services of a commercial painter in painting the family home.
   b. An auto dealer's sale of a new car to a nonbusiness customer.
   c. The money received by Smith when she sells her biology textbook to a used-book buyer.
   d. The publication and sale of a new economics textbook.
   e. A $2 billion increase in business inventories.
   f. Government purchases of newly produced aircraft.

7. What are the four supply factors of economic growth? What is the demand factor? What is the efficiency factor? Illustrate these factors in terms of the production possibilities curve. **LO4**

8. To what extent have increases in U.S. real GDP resulted from more labor inputs? From higher labor productivity? Rearrange the following contributors to the growth of real GDP in order of their quantitative importance: economies of scale, quantity of capital, improved resource allocation, education and training, technological advance. **LO5**

9. True or false? If false, explain why. **LO5**
   a. Technological advance, which to date has played a relatively small role in U.S. economic growth, is destined to play a more important role in the future.
   b. Many public capital goods are complementary to private capital goods.
   c. Immigration has slowed economic growth in the United States.

10. Explain why there is such a close relationship between changes in a nation's rate of productivity growth and changes in its average real hourly wage. **LO6**

11. Relate each of the following to the recent productivity speedup: **LO6**
   a. Information technology
   b. Increasing returns
   c. Network effects
   d. Global competition

12. Provide three examples of products or services that can be simultaneously consumed by many people. Explain why labor productivity greatly rises as the firm sells more units of the product or service. Explain why the higher level of sales greatly reduces the per-unit cost of the product. **LO6**

Problems

1. Suppose that annual output in year 1 in a 3-good economy is 3 quarts of ice cream, 1 bottle of shampoo, and 3 jars of peanut butter. In year 2, the output mix changes to 5 quarts of ice cream, 2 bottles of shampoo, and 2 jars of peanut butter. If the prices in both years are $4 per quart for ice cream, $3 per bottle of shampoo, and $2 per jar of peanut butter, what was the economy's GDP in year 1? What was its GDP in year 2? **LO1**

2. If in some country personal consumption expenditures in a specific year are $50 billion, purchases of stocks and bonds are $30 billion, net exports are −$10 billion, government

purchases are $20 billion, sales of secondhand items are $8 billion, and gross investment is $25 billion, what is the country's GDP for the year? **LO1**

3. Assume that a grower of flower bulbs sells its annual output of bulbs to an Internet retailer for $70,000. The retailer, in turn, brings in $160,000 from selling the bulbs directly to final customers. What amount would these two transactions add to personal consumption expenditures and thus to GDP during the year? **LO1**

4. Using the NIPA data at the top of the next page, compute GDP. All figures are in billions. **LO1**

Personal consumption expenditures	$245
Wages and salaries	223
Imports	18
Corporate profits	42
Depreciation	28
Gross private domestic investment	86
Government purchases	82
Exports	9

5. Suppose that in 1984 the total output in a single-good economy was 7000 buckets of chicken. Also suppose that in 1984 each bucket of chicken was priced at $10. Finally, assume that in 2004 the price per bucket of chicken was $16 and that 22,000 buckets were produced. Determine real GDP for 1984 and 2004, in 1984 prices. **LO2**

6. Suppose an economy's real GDP is $30,000 in year 1 and $31,200 in year 2. What is the growth rate of its real GDP?

Assume that population is 100 in year 1 and 102 in year 2. What is the growth rate of GDP per capita? **LO3**

7. What annual growth rate is needed for a country to double its output in 7 years? In 35 years? In 70 years? In 140 years? **LO3**

8. Assume that a "leader country" has real GDP per capita of $40,000, whereas a "follower country" has real GDP per capita of $20,000. Next suppose that the growth of real GDP per capita falls to zero percent in the leader country and rises to 7 percent in the follower country. If these rates continue for long periods of time, how many years will it take for the follower country to catch up to the living standard of the leader country? **LO3**

9. Suppose that work hours in New Zombie are 200 in year 1 and productivity is $8 per hour worked. What is New Zombie's real GDP? If work hours increase to 210 in year 2 and productivity rises to $10 per hour, what is New Zombie's rate of economic growth? **LO5**

FURTHER TEST YOUR KNOWLEDGE AT
www.mcconnellbrief2e.com

At the text's Online Learning Center, **www.mcconnellbrief2e.com**, you will find one or more web based questions that require information from the Internet to answer. We urge you to check them out, since they will familiarize you with websites that may be helpful in other courses and perhaps even in your career. The OLC also features multiple-choice quizzes that give instant feedback and provides other helpful ways to further test your knowledge of the chapter.

Visit your mobile app store and download the McConnell Brief Edition: Study Econ app *today!*

6

After reading this chapter, you should be able to:

1 Describe the business cycle and its primary phases.

2 Illustrate how unemployment and inflation are measured.

3 Explain the types of unemployment and inflation and their various economic impacts.

Business Cycles, Unemployment, and Inflation

As indicated in Chapter 5, the United States has experienced remarkable economic growth over time. But this growth has not been smooth, steady, or predictable from year to year. At various times the United States has experienced recessions, high unemployment rates, or high inflation rates. For example, U.S. unemployment rose by 8 million workers and the unemployment rate increased from 4.7 percent to 10.1 percent during the Great Recession. Other nations also have suffered high unemployment rates at times. As just one example, Spain's unemployment rate was nearly 20 percent in 2009. Also, inflation has occasionally plagued the United States and other nations. For instance, the U.S. inflation rate in 1980 was 13.5 percent. Zimbabwe's inflation soared to 26,000 percent in 2007!

Our goal in this chapter is to examine the concepts, terminology, and facts relating to macroeconomic instability. Specifically, we want to discuss the business cycle, unemployment, and inflation. The concepts discussed are extremely important for understanding subsequent chapters on economic theory and economic policy.

Business Cycles

The long-run growth trend of the U.S. economy is one of expansion, as stylized by the upsloping line labeled "Growth Trend" in Figure 6.1. But growth has been interrupted by periods of economic instability usually associated with *business cycles*. **Business cycles** are alternating rises and declines in the level of economic activity, sometimes over several years. Individual cycles (one "up" followed by one "down") vary substantially in duration and intensity.

As shown in Figure 6.1, the two primary phases of business cycles are recessions and expansions ("peaks" and "troughs" are merely turning points). A **recession** is a period of decline in total output, income, and employment. This downturn, which lasts 6 months or more, is marked by the widespread contraction of business activity in many sectors of the economy. Along with declines in real GDP, significant increases in unemployment occur. Table 6.1 documents the 10 recessions in the United States since 1950.

A recession is usually followed by a recovery and **expansion,** a period in which real GDP, income, and employment rise. At some point, full employment is again achieved. If spending then expands more rapidly than does production capacity, prices of nearly all goods and services will rise. In other words, inflation will occur.

The Business Cycle Dating Committee of the National Bureau of Economic Research (NBER)—a nonprofit economic research organization—declares the start and end of recessions in the United States. Citing evidence of declining real output and falling employment, the NBER officially declared that the latest recession, the Great Recession, began in December 2007. The NBER subsequently declared that this recession ended in June 2009, 18 months after it began. In making this announcement, the NBER pointed out that its declaration was not a forecast for the future path of the economy.

ORIGIN OF THE IDEA

O 6.1

Business cycles

business cycles
Recurring increases and decreases in the level of economic activity over periods of time.

recession
A period of declining real GDP, accompanied by lower income and higher unemployment.

expansion
A generalized increase in output, income, and business activity.

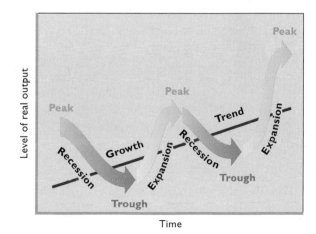

FIGURE 6.1 The business cycle. Economists distinguish two primary phases of the business cycle (recession and expansion); the duration and strength of each phase may vary.

TABLE 6.1 U.S. Recessions since 1950

Period	Duration, Months	Depth (Decline in Real Output)
1953–54	10	−3.7%
1957–58	8	−3.9
1960–61	10	−1.6
1969–70	11	−1.0
1973–75	16	−4.9
1980	6	−2.3
1981–82	16	−3.3
1990–91	8	−1.8
2001	8	−0.5
2007–2009	18	−3.7

Source: National Bureau of Economic Research, **www.nber.org,** and Minneapolis Federal Reserve Bank, "The Recession and Recovery in Perspective," **www.minneapolis-fed.gov.** Output data are in 2000 dollars.

Causes of Business Cycles

The long-run trend of the U.S. economy is expansion and growth. That is why the business cycles in Figure 6.1 are drawn against a trend of economic growth. A key issue in macroeconomics is why the economy sees business cycle fluctuations rather than slow, smooth growth. In terms of Figure 6.1, why does output go up and down rather than just staying on the smooth growth trend line?

shocks
Situations in which events don't meet expectations.

Economists have developed several possible explanations for business cycles. These theories are founded on the idea that fluctuations are driven by **shocks**—situations in which individuals and firms were expecting one thing to happen but then something else happened. For instance, consider a situation in which a firm decides to build a high-speed railroad that will shuttle passengers between Washington, D.C., and New York. They do so expecting it to be very popular and make a handsome profit. But if it unexpectedly turns out to be unpopular and loses money, the railroad must figure out how to respond. Should the railroad go out of business, change the service it provides, or spend millions on a massive advertising campaign? These sorts of decisions are necessitated by the shock and surprise of having to deal with an unexpected situation.

demand shocks
Unexpected changes in the demand for goods and services.

supply shocks
Unexpected changes in the supply of goods and services.

Economies are exposed to both demand shocks and supply shocks. **Demand shocks** are unexpected changes in the demand for goods and services. **Supply shocks** are unexpected changes in the supply of goods and services. Please note that the word *shock* only tells us that something unexpected has happened. It does not tell us whether what has happened is unexpectedly good or unexpectedly bad. To make things more clear, economists use more specific terms. For instance, a *positive demand shock* refers to a situation in which demand turns out to be higher than expected, while a *negative demand shock* refers to a situation in which demand turns out to be lower than expected.

Shocks to the economy, particularly those with significant negative impacts, often lead to calls for government action. But why are shocks a big enough problem to justify calling in the government for help? Why can't firms deal with shocks on their own? Why don't product and resource markets respond quickly to correct imbalances?

The answer to these questions is that the prices of many goods and services are inflexible (slow to change, also known as **sticky prices**) in the short run. This implies that price changes do not quickly equalize the quantities demanded of such goods and services with their respective quantities supplied. Instead, because prices are inflexible, the economy is forced to respond in the short run to demand shocks primarily through changes in output and employment rather than through changes in prices. If negative effects on output and employment effects are severe and/or long-lasting, government is generally called upon to take corrective action. We will address government policy options in upcoming chapters; for now we resume our focus on business cycles.

Economists cite several possible general sources of shocks that can cause business cycles.

- *Irregular innovation* Significant new products or production methods, such as those associated with the railroad, automobile, computer, and the Internet, can rapidly spread through the economy, sparking sizable increases in investment, consumption, output, and employment. After the economy has largely absorbed the new innovation, the economy may for a time slow down or possibly decline. Because such innovations occur irregularly and unexpectedly, they may contribute to the variability of economic activity.

- *Productivity changes* When productivity—output per unit of input—unexpectedly increases, the economy booms; when productivity unexpectedly decreases, the economy recedes. Such changes in productivity can result from unexpected changes in resource availability (of, say, oil or agricultural commodities) or from unexpected changes in the general rate of technological advance.

- *Monetary factors* Some economists see business cycles as purely monetary phenomena. When a nation's central bank shocks the economy by creating more money than people were expecting, an inflationary boom in output occurs. By contrast, printing less money than people were expecting triggers an output decline and, eventually, a price-level fall.

- *Political events* Unexpected political events, such as peace treaties, new wars, or the 9/11 terrorist attacks, can create economic opportunities or strains. In adjusting to these shocks, the economy may experience upswings or downswings.

- *Financial instability* Unexpected financial bubbles (rapid asset price increases) or bursts (abrupt asset price decreases) can spill over to the general economy by expanding or contracting lending, and boosting or eroding the confidence of consumers and businesses. Booms and busts in the rest of the economy may follow.

The severe recession of 2007–2009 was precipitated by a combination of excessive money and a financial frenzy that led to overvalued real estate and unsustainable mortgage debt. Institutions bundled this debt into new securities ("derivatives") that were sold to financial investors. Some of the investors, in turn, bought insurance against losses that might arise from the securities. As real estate prices plummeted and mortgage defaults unexpectedly rocketed, the securitization and insurance structure buckled and nearly collapsed. Credit markets froze, pessimism prevailed, and spending by businesses and households declined.

Whatever the source of economic shocks, most economists agree that the *immediate* cause of the large majority of cyclical changes in the levels of real output and employment is unexpected changes in the level of total spending. If total spending unexpectedly sinks and firms cannot lower prices, firms will find themselves selling fewer units of output (since, with prices fixed, a decreased amount of spending implies fewer items purchased). Slower sales will cause firms to cut back on production.

sticky prices
A situation where prices of goods and services are slow to respond to changes in supply and demand.

As they do, GDP will fall. And because fewer workers will be needed to produce less output, employment also will fall. The economy will contract and enter a recession.

By contrast, if the level of spending unexpectedly rises, output, employment, and incomes will rise. This is true because with prices sticky, the increased spending will mean that consumers will be buying a larger volume of goods and services (since, with prices fixed, more spending means more items purchased). Firms will respond by increasing output. This will increase GDP. And because they will need to hire more workers to produce the larger volume of output, employment also will increase. The economy will boom and enjoy an expansion. Eventually, as time passes and prices become more flexible, prices are also likely to rise as a result of the increased spending.

Cyclical Impact: Durables and Nondurables

Although the business cycle is felt everywhere in the economy, it affects different segments in different ways and to different degrees.

Firms and industries producing *capital goods* (for example, housing, commercial buildings, heavy equipment, and farm implements) and *consumer durables* (for example, automobiles, personal computers, refrigerators) are affected most by the business cycle. Within limits, firms can postpone the purchase of capital goods. For instance, when the economy goes into recession, producers frequently delay the purchase of new equipment and the construction of new plants. The business outlook simply does not warrant increases in the stock of capital goods. In good times, capital goods are usually replaced before they depreciate completely. But when recession strikes, firms patch up their old equipment and make do. As a result, investment in capital goods declines sharply. Firms that have excess plant capacity may not even bother to replace all the capital that is depreciating. For them, net investment may be negative. The pattern is much the same for consumer durables such as automobiles and major appliances. When recession occurs and households must trim their budgets, purchases of these goods are often deferred. Families repair their old cars and appliances rather than buy new ones, and the firms producing these products suffer. (Of course, producers of capital goods and consumer durables also benefit most from expansions.)

In contrast, *service* industries and industries that produce *nondurable consumer goods* are somewhat insulated from the most severe effects of recession. People find it difficult to cut back on needed medical and legal services, for example. And a recession actually helps some service firms, such as pawnbrokers and law firms that specialize in bankruptcies. Nor are the purchases of many nondurable goods such as food and clothing easy to postpone. The quantity and quality of purchases of nondurables will decline, but not so much as will purchases of capital goods and consumer durables.

APPLYING THE ANALYSIS

Stock Prices and Macroeconomic Instability

Every day, the individual stocks (ownership shares) of thousands of corporations are bought and sold in the stock market. The owners of the individual stocks receive dividends—a portion of the firm's profit. Supply and demand in the stock market determine the price of each firm's stock, with individual stock prices generally rising and falling in concert with the collective expectations for each firm's profits. Greater profits normally result in higher dividends to the stock owners, and, in anticipation of higher dividends, people are willing to pay a higher price for the stock.

The media closely monitor and report stock market averages such as the Dow Jones Industrial Average (DJIA)—the weighted-average price of the stocks of 30 major U.S. industrial firms. It is common for these price averages to change over time or even to rise or fall sharply during a single day. On "Black Monday," October 19, 1987, the DJIA fell by 20 percent. In contrast, the stock market averages rose spectacularly in 1998 and 1999, with the DJIA rising 16 and 25 percent in those two years. In 2002, the DJIA fell 17 percent. In 2003, it rose by 25 percent. In the last three months of 2008, the DJIA plummeted by 34 percent, the steepest decline since the 1930s.

The volatility of the stock market raises this question: Do changes in stock price averages and thus stock market wealth cause macroeconomic instability? Linkages between the stock market and the economy might lead us to answer "yes." Consider a sharp increase in stock prices. Feeling wealthier, stock owners respond by increasing their spending (the *wealth effect*). Firms react by increasing their purchases of new capital goods because they can finance such purchases through issuing new shares of high-valued stock (the *investment effect*). Of course, sharp declines in stock prices would produce the opposite results.

Studies find that changes in stock prices do affect consumption and investment but that these consumption and investment impacts are relatively weak. For example, a 10 percent sustained increase in stock market values in 1 year is associated with a 4 percent increase in consumption spending over the next 3 years. The investment response is even weaker. So typical day-to-day and year-to-year changes in stock market values have little impact on the macroeconomy.

In contrast, *stock market bubbles* can be detrimental to an economy. Such bubbles are huge run-ups of overall stock prices, caused by excessive optimism and frenzied buying. The rising stock values are unsupported by realistic prospects of the future strength of the economy and the firms operating in it. Rather than slowly decompress, such bubbles may burst and cause harm to the economy. The free fall of stock values, if long-lasting, causes reverse wealth effects. The stock market crash also may create an overall pessimism about the economy that undermines consumption and investment spending even further. Indeed, the plunge of the stock market in 2007 and 2008 contributed to the severe recession of 2007–2009 by stressing financial institutions and creating a tremendous amount of pessimism about the direction of the economy.

QUESTION: Suppose that your college savings fund of $100,000, all invested in stocks, was reduced in value to $25,000 because of a stock market crash. Explain how that would affect your spending for college (including your choice of school) and spending for other goods and services.

Unemployment

Two problems that arise over the course of the business cycle are unemployment and inflation. Let's look at unemployment first.

Measurement of Unemployment

The U.S. Bureau of Labor Statistics (BLS) conducts a nationwide random survey of some 60,000 households each month to determine who is employed and who is not employed. In a series of questions it asks which members of the household are working,

FIGURE 6.2 The labor force, employment, and unemployment, 2010. The labor force consists of persons 16 years of age or older who are not in institutions and who are (1) employed or (2) unemployed but seeking employment. Source: Bureau of Labor Statistics, **www.bls.gov** (civilian labor force data, which excludes military employment).

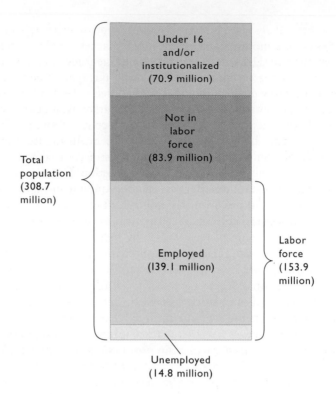

Under 16 and/or institutionalized (70.9 million)

Not in labor force (83.9 million)

Total population (308.7 million)

Employed (139.1 million)

Labor force (153.9 million)

Unemployed (14.8 million)

labor force
Persons 16 years and older who are not in institutions and who are either employed or unemployed and seeking work.

unemployment rate
The percentage of the labor force unemployed.

WORKED PROBLEMS

W 6.1

Unemployment rate

unemployed and looking for work, not looking for work, and so on. From the answers it determines an unemployment rate for the entire nation.

Figure 6.2 helps explain the mathematics. It divides the total U.S. population into three groups. One group is made up of people less than 16 years of age and people who are institutionalized, for example, in mental hospitals or correctional institutions. Such people are not considered potential members of the labor force. A second group, labeled "Not in labor force," is composed of adults who are potential workers but are not employed and are not seeking work. For example, they are homemakers, full-time students, or retirees. The third group is the **labor force** which constituted about 50 percent of the total population in 2010. The labor force consists of people who are able and willing to work. Both those who are employed full-time and part-time and those who are unemployed but actively seeking work are counted as being in the labor force. The **unemployment rate** is the percentage of the labor force unemployed:

$$\text{Unemployment rate} = \frac{\text{unemployed}}{\text{labor force}} \times 100$$

The statistics underlying the rounded numbers in Figure 6.2 show that in 2010 the unemployment rate averaged

$$\frac{14,825,000}{153,889,000} \times 100 = 9.6\%$$

Types of Unemployment

There are three *types* of unemployment: frictional, structural, and cyclical.

Frictional Unemployment At any moment some workers are "between jobs." Some of them will be moving voluntarily from one job to another. Others will have been fired and will be seeking reemployment. Still others will have been laid off temporarily because of seasonal demand. In addition to those between jobs, many young workers will be searching for their first jobs.

As these unemployed people find jobs or are called back from temporary layoffs, other job seekers and laid-off workers will replace them in the "unemployment pool." It is important to keep in mind that while the pool itself persists because there are always newly unemployed workers flowing into it, most workers do *not* stay in the unemployment pool for very long. Indeed, when the economy is strong, the majority of unemployed workers find new jobs within a couple of months. One should be careful not to make the mistake of confusing the permanence of the pool itself with the false ideal that the pool's membership is permanent, too. On the other hand, there *are* workers who do remain unemployed and in the pool for very long periods of time—sometimes for many years. As we discuss the different types of unemployment below, notice that certain types tend to be transitory while others are associated with much longer spells of unemployment.

Economists use the term **frictional unemployment**—consisting of *search unemployment* and *wait unemployment*—for workers who are either searching for jobs or waiting to take jobs in the near future. The word "frictional" implies that the labor market does not operate perfectly and instantaneously (without friction) in matching workers and jobs.

Frictional unemployment is inevitable and, at least in part, desirable. Many people who are frictionally unemployed are moving into the labor force or from low-paying, low-productivity jobs to higher-paying, higher-productivity positions. That means greater income for the workers, a better allocation of labor resources, and a larger real GDP for the economy.

frictional unemployment
Unemployment that is associated with people searching for jobs or waiting to take jobs in the near future.

Structural Unemployment
Frictional unemployment blurs into a category called **structural unemployment.** Here, economists use "structural" in the sense of "compositional." Changes over time in consumer demand and in technology alter the "structure" of the total demand for labor, both occupationally and geographically.

Occupationally, the demand for certain skills (for example, sewing clothes or working on farms) may decline or even vanish. The demand for other skills (for example, designing software or maintaining computer systems) will intensify. Unemployment results because the composition of the labor force does not respond immediately or completely to the new structure of job opportunities. Workers who find that their skills and experience have become obsolete or unneeded thus find that they have no marketable talents. They are structurally unemployed until they adapt or develop skills that employers want.

Geographically, the demand for labor also changes over time. An example: migration of industry and thus of employment opportunities from the Snow Belt to the Sun Belt over the past few decades. Another example is the movement of jobs from inner-city factories to suburban industrial parks. And a final example is the so-called *offshoring* of jobs that occurs when the demand for a particular type of labor shifts from domestic firms to foreign firms. As job opportunities shift from one place to another, some workers become structurally unemployed.

structural unemployment
Unemployment that is associated with a mismatch between available jobs and the skills or locations of those unemployed.

Cyclical Unemployment
Unemployment caused by a decline in total spending is called **cyclical unemployment** and typically begins in the recession phase of the business cycle. As the demand for goods and services decreases, employment falls and unemployment rises. The 25 percent unemployment rate in 1933 reflected mainly cyclical unemployment, as did significant parts of the 9.7 percent unemployment rate in 1982, the 7.5 percent rate in 1992, and the 9.6 percent rate in 2010.

Cyclical unemployment is a very serious problem when it occurs. To understand its costs, we need to define "full employment."

cyclical unemployment
Unemployment that is associated with the recessionary phase of a business cycle.

Definition of Full Employment

Because frictional and structural unemployment are largely unavoidable in a dynamic economy, *full employment* is something less than 100 percent employment of the labor force. Economists say that the economy is "fully employed" when it is experiencing only frictional and structural unemployment. That is, full employment occurs when there is no cyclical unemployment. Today, most economists believe that the economy is fully employed when the unemployment rate is less than 5 percent. The level of real GDP that would occur precisely at "full employment" is called **potential output** (or *potential GDP*).

potential output
The level of real GDP that would occur if there was full employment.

Economic Cost of Unemployment

The basic economic cost of unemployment is forgone output. When the economy fails to create enough jobs for all who have the necessary skills and are willing to work, potential production of goods and services is irretrievably lost. In terms of Chapter 1's analysis, cyclical unemployment means that society is operating at some point inside its production possibilities curve. Economists call this sacrifice of output a **GDP gap**—the difference between actual and potential GDP. That is:

GDP gap
The negative or positive difference between actual GDP and potential GDP.

$$\text{GDP gap} = \text{actual GDP} - \text{potential GDP}$$

The GDP gap can be either a negative number (actual GDP is less than potential GDP) or a positive number (actual GDP exceeds potential GDP). There is a close correlation between the actual unemployment rate and the GDP gap. The higher the unemployment rate, the greater is the negative GDP gap.

Society's cost of unemployment—its forgone output—translates to forgone income for individuals. This loss of income is borne unequally. Some groups have higher unemployment rates than others and bear the brunt of rising rates during recessions. For instance, workers in lower-skilled occupations (for example, laborers) have higher unemployment rates than workers in higher-skilled occupations (for example, professionals). Lower-skilled workers have more and longer spells of structural unemployment than higher-skilled workers. They also are less likely to be self-employed than are higher-skilled workers. Moreover, lower-skilled workers usually bear the brunt of recessions. Businesses generally retain most of their higher-skilled workers, in whom they have invested the expense of training.

Also, teenagers have much higher unemployment rates than adults. Teenagers have lower skill levels, quit their jobs more frequently, are more frequently "fired," and have less geographic mobility than adults. Many unemployed teenagers are new in the labor market, searching for their first jobs. Male African-American teenagers, in particular, have very high unemployment rates.

Finally, the overall unemployment rate for African Americans and Hispanics is higher than that for whites and Asians. The causes of the higher rates include lower rates of educational attainment, greater concentration in lower-skilled occupations, and discrimination in the labor market. In general, the unemployment rate for African Americans is twice that of whites.

International Comparisons

Unemployment rates differ greatly among nations at any given time. One reason is that nations have different unemployment rates when their economies are fully employed. Another is that nations may be in recessions or expansions. Global Snapshot 6.1 shows unemployment rates for five industrialized nations for the years 2000 through 2010. Prior to the Great Recession, the U.S. unemployment rate was considerably lower than that of countries such as France and Germany.

GLOBAL SNAPSHOT 6.1

Unemployment Rates in Five Industrial Nations, 2000–2010

Prior to the severe recession of 2007–2009, compared with France and Germany, the United States had a relatively low unemployment rate. For many years Japan has had one of the lowest unemployment rates among industrial nations.

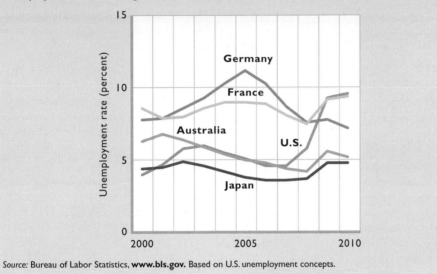

Source: Bureau of Labor Statistics, **www.bls.gov.** Based on U.S. unemployment concepts.

Inflation

We now turn to inflation, another aspect of macroeconomic instability. The problems inflation poses are subtler than those posed by unemployment.

Meaning of Inflation

Inflation is a rise in the *general level of prices.* When inflation occurs, each dollar of income will buy fewer goods and services than before. Inflation reduces the "purchasing power" of money. But inflation does not mean that *all* prices are rising. Even during periods of rapid inflation, some prices may be relatively constant and others may even fall. For example, although the United States experienced high rates of inflation in the 1970s and early 1980s, the prices of video recorders, digital watches, and personal computers declined.

inflation
A rise in the general level of prices in an economy.

Measurement of Inflation

The main measure of inflation in the United States is the **Consumer Price Index (CPI),** compiled by the Bureau of Labor Statistics (BLS). The government uses this index to report inflation rates each month and each year. It also uses the CPI to adjust Social Security benefits and income tax brackets for inflation. The CPI reports the price of a "market basket" of some 300 consumer goods and services that are purchased by a typical urban consumer.

The composition of the market basket for the CPI is based on spending patterns of urban consumers in a specific period, presently 2005–2006. The BLS updates the composition of the market basket every 2 years so that it reflects the most recent

Consumer Price Index (CPI)
An index that compares the price of a market basket of consumer goods and services in one period with the price of the same (or highly similar) market basket in a base period.

patterns of consumer purchases and captures the inflation that consumers are currently experiencing. The BLS arbitrarily sets the CPI equal to 100 for 1982–1984. So the CPI for any particular year is found as follows:

$$CPI = \frac{\text{price of the most recent market basket in the particular year}}{\text{price of the same market basket in 1982–1984}}$$

The rate of inflation for a certain year is found by comparing, in percentage terms, that year's index with the index in the previous year. For example, the CPI rose from 214.5 in 2009 to 218.1 in 2010. So the rate of inflation for 2010 was 1.6 percent.

$$\text{Rate of inflation} = \frac{218.1 - 214.5}{214.5} \times 100 = 1.6\%$$

In rare cases, the CPI declines from one year to the next. For example, the CPI fell from 215.3 in 2008 to 214.5 in 2009. The rate of inflation for 2009 therefore was −0.4 percent. Such price level declines are called **deflation.**

In Chapter 5 we discussed the mathematical approximation called the *rule of 70,* which tells us that we can find the number of years it will take for some measure to double, given its annual percentage increase, by dividing that percentage increase into the number 70. For example, annual rates of inflation of 3 percent will double the price level in about 23 (= 70/3) years.

deflation
A decline in the general level of prices in an economy.

Facts of Inflation

Figure 6.3 shows December-to-December rates of annual inflation in the United States between 1960 and 2010. Observe that inflation reached double-digit rates in the 1970s and early 1980s but has since declined and has been relatively mild recently.

In recent years U.S. inflation has been neither unusually high nor unusually low relative to inflation in several other industrial countries (see Global Snapshot 6.2). Some nations (not shown) have had double-digit or even higher annual rates of inflation in recent years. In 2009, for example, the annual inflation rate in the Democratic Republic of Congo was 46 percent; Eritrea, 35 percent; Afghanistan, 31 percent; and Venezuela, 27 percent. Zimbabwe's inflation rate was 14.9 billion percent in 2008 before Zimbabwe did away with its existing currency.

FIGURE 6.3 Annual inflation rates in the United States, 1960–2010 (December-to-December changes in the CPI). The major periods of inflation in the United States in the past 50 years were in the 1970s and 1980s.
Source: Bureau of Labor Statistics, **www.bls.gov**.

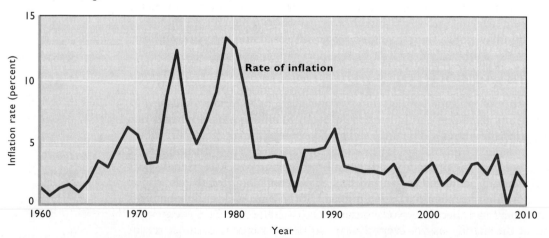

GLOBAL SNAPSHOT 6.2

Inflation Rates in Five Industrial Nations, 2000–2010

Inflation rates in the United States in recent years were neither extraordinarily high nor extraordinarily low relative to rates in other industrial nations.

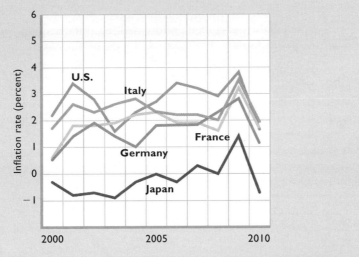

Source: Data from *IMF World Economic Outlook Database,* April 2011. International Monetary Fund, **www.imf.org.**

Types of Inflation

Nearly all prices in the economy are set by supply and demand. Consequently, if the economy is experiencing inflation and the overall level of prices is rising, we need to look for an explanation in terms of supply and demand. Reflecting this, economists distinguish between two types of inflation: *demand-pull inflation* and *cost-push inflation*.

Demand-Pull Inflation Usually, increases in the price level are caused by an excess of total spending beyond the economy's capacity to produce. Where inflation is rapid and sustained, the cause invariably is an overissuance of money by the central bank (the Federal Reserve in the United States). When resources are already fully employed, the business sector cannot respond to excess demand by expanding output. So the excess demand bids up the prices of the limited output, producing **demand-pull inflation.** The essence of this type of inflation is "too much spending chasing too few goods."

demand-pull inflation
Inreases in the price level (inflation) caused by excessive spending.

ILLUSTRATING THE IDEA

Clipping Coins

Some interesting early episodes of demand-pull inflation occurred in Europe during the ninth to the fifteenth centuries under feudalism. In that economic system, *lords* (or *princes*) ruled individual fiefdoms, and their *vassals* (or *peasants*) worked the fields. The peasants initially paid parts of their harvest as taxes to the princes. Later, when the princes began issuing "coins of the realm," peasants began paying their taxes with gold coins.

Some princes soon discovered a way to transfer purchasing power from their vassals to themselves without explicitly increasing taxes. As coins came into the treasury, princes clipped off parts of the gold coins, making them slightly smaller. From the clippings they minted new coins and used them to buy more goods for themselves.

This practice of clipping coins was a subtle form of taxation. The quantity of goods being produced in the fiefdom remained the same, but the number of gold coins increased. With "too much money chasing too few goods," inflation occurred. Each gold coin earned by the peasants therefore had less purchasing power than previously because prices were higher. The increase of the money supply shifted purchasing power away from the peasants and toward the princes just as surely as if the princes had increased taxation of the peasants.

In more recent eras, some dictators have simply printed money to buy more goods for themselves, their relatives, and their key loyalists. These dictators, too, have levied hidden taxes on their population by creating inflation.

The moral of the story is quite simple: A society that values price-level stability should not entrust the control of its money supply to people who benefit from inflation.

QUESTION: Why might a government with a huge foreign debt be tempted to increase its domestic money supply and cause inflation?

Cost-Push Inflation Inflation may also arise on the supply, or cost, side of the economy. During some periods in U.S. economic history, including the mid-1970s, the price level increased even though total spending was not excessive. These were periods when output and employment were both *declining* (evidence that total spending was not excessive) while the general price level was *rising*.

cost-push inflation
Increases in the price level (inflation) caused by sharp rises in the cost of key resources.

The theory of **cost-push inflation** explains rising prices in terms of factors that raise the average cost of a particular level of output. Rising average production costs squeeze profits and reduce the economy's supply of goods and services. In this scenario, costs are *pushing* the price level upward, whereas in demand-pull inflation demand is *pulling* it upward.

The major source of cost-push inflation has been so-called *supply shocks*. Specifically, abrupt increases in the costs of raw materials or energy inputs have on occasion driven up per-unit production costs and thus product prices. The rocketing prices of imported oil in 1973–1974 and again in 1979–1980 are good illustrations. As energy prices surged upward during these periods, the costs of producing and transporting virtually every product in the economy rose. Cost-push inflation ensued.

Redistribution Effects of Inflation

Inflation redistributes real income. This redistribution helps some people and hurts others, while leaving many people largely unaffected. Who gets hurt? Who benefits? Before we can answer, we need some terminology. There is a difference between money (or nominal) income and real income. **Nominal income** is the number of dollars received as wages, rent, interest, or profits. **Real income** is a measure of the amount of goods and services nominal income can buy; it is the purchasing power of nominal income, or income adjusted for inflation. That is,

nominal income
The number of dollars received as wages, rent, interest, and profit.

real income
The purchasing power of nominal income; the amount of goods and services that nominal income can buy.

$$\text{Real income} = \frac{\text{nominal income}}{\text{price index (in hundredths)}}$$

Inflation need not alter an economy's overall real income—its total purchasing power. It is evident from the above equation that real income will remain the same when nominal income and the price index rise at the same percentage rate.

But when inflation occurs, not everyone's nominal income rises at the same pace as the price level. Therein lies the potential for redistribution of real income from some to others. If the change in the price level differs from the change in a person's nominal income, his or her real income will be affected. The following approximation (shown by the $\cong$ sign) tells us roughly how much real income will change:

WORKED PROBLEMS
W 6.2
Nominal and real income

$$\begin{array}{ccc} \text{Percentage} & \text{percentage} & \text{percentage} \\ \text{change in} & \cong \quad \text{change in} & \text{change in} \\ \text{real income} & \text{nominal income} & \text{price level} \end{array}$$

For example, suppose that the price level rises by 6 percent in some period. If Bob's nominal income rises by 6 percent, his real income will *remain unchanged*. But if his nominal income instead rises by 10 percent, his real income will *increase* by about 4 percent. And if Bob's nominal income rises by only 2 percent, his real income will *decline* by about 4 percent.

The redistribution effects of inflation depend on whether or not it is expected. With fully expected or *anticipated inflation*, an income receiver may be able to avoid or lessen the adverse effects of inflation on real income. The generalizations that follow assume *unanticipated inflation*—inflation whose full extent was not expected.

Who Is Hurt by Inflation?

Unanticipated inflation hurts fixed-income recipients, savers, and creditors. It redistributes real income away from them and toward others.

Fixed-Income Receivers People whose incomes are fixed see their real incomes fall when inflation occurs. The classic case is the elderly couple living on a private pension or annuity that provides a fixed amount of nominal income each month. They may have retired on what appeared to be an adequate pension. However, years later they discover that inflation has severely cut the purchasing power of that pension—their real income.

Similarly, landlords who receive lease payments of fixed dollar amounts will be hurt by inflation as they receive dollars of declining value over time. Likewise, public sector workers whose incomes are dictated by fixed pay schedules may suffer from inflation. The fixed "steps" (the upward yearly increases) in their pay schedules may not keep up with inflation. Minimum-wage workers and families living on fixed welfare incomes also will be hurt by inflation.

Savers Unanticipated inflation hurts savers. As prices rise, the real value, or purchasing power, of an accumulation of savings deteriorates. Paper assets such as savings accounts, insurance policies, and annuities, which once were adequate to meet rainy-day contingencies or provide for a comfortable retirement, decline in real value during periods of inflation.

Creditors Unanticipated inflation harms creditors (lenders). Suppose Chase Bank lends Bob $1000, to be repaid in 2 years. If in that time the price level doubles, the $1000 that Bob repays will have only half the purchasing power of the $1000 he borrowed. True, if we ignore interest charges, the same number of dollars will be repaid as was borrowed. But because of inflation, each of those dollars will buy only half as much as it did when the loan was negotiated. As prices go up, the value of the dollar goes down. So the borrower pays back less-valuable dollars than those received from the lender. The owners of Chase Bank suffer a loss of real income.

Who Is Unaffected or Helped by Inflation?

Some people are unaffected by inflation, and others are actually helped by it. For the second group, inflation redistributes real income toward them and away from others.

Flexible-Income Receivers People who have flexible incomes may escape inflation's harm or even benefit from it. For example, individuals who derive their incomes solely from Social Security are largely unaffected by inflation because Social Security payments are *indexed* to the CPI. Benefits automatically increase when the CPI increases, preventing erosion of benefits from inflation. Some union workers also get automatic *cost-of-living adjustments (COLAs)* in their pay when the CPI rises, although such increases rarely equal the full percentage rise in inflation.

Some flexible-income receivers are helped by unanticipated inflation. The strong product demand and labor shortages implied by rapid demand-pull inflation may cause some nominal incomes to spurt ahead of the price level, thereby enhancing real incomes. As an example, property owners faced with an inflation-induced real estate boom may be able to boost rents more rapidly than the rate of inflation. Also, some business owners may benefit from inflation. If their product prices rise faster than their resource prices, business revenues will increase more rapidly than costs. In those cases, the growth rate of profit incomes will outpace the rate of inflation.

Debtors Unanticipated inflation benefits debtors (borrowers). In our earlier example, Chase Bank's loss of real income from inflation is Bob's gain of real income. Debtor Bob borrows "dear" dollars but, because of inflation, pays back the principal and interest with "cheap" dollars whose purchasing power has been eroded by inflation. Real income is redistributed away from the owners of Chase Bank toward borrowers such as Bob.

Anticipated Inflation

The redistribution effects of inflation are less severe or are eliminated altogether if people anticipate inflation and can adjust their nominal incomes to reflect the expected price-level rises. The prolonged inflation that began in the late 1960s prompted many workers in the 1970s to insist on high wage and salary increases that would protect them from expected inflation.

Similarly, if inflation is anticipated, the redistribution of income from lender to borrower may be altered. Suppose a lender (perhaps a bank) and a borrower (a household) both agree that 5 percent is a fair rate of interest on a 1-year loan provided the price level is stable. But assume that inflation has been occurring and is expected to be 6 percent over the next year. The lender will neutralize inflation by charging an *inflation premium* of 6 percent, the amount of the anticipated inflation.

Our example reveals the difference between the real rate of interest and the nominal rate of interest. The **real interest rate** is the percentage increase in *purchasing power* that the borrower pays the lender. In our example, the real interest rate is 5 percent. The **nominal interest rate** is the percentage increase in *money* that the borrower pays the lender, including that resulting from the built-in expectation of inflation, if any. In equation form:

$$\text{Nominal interest rate} = \text{real interest rate} + \text{inflation premium}$$
$$\text{(the expected rate of inflation)}$$

As illustrated in Figure 6.4, the nominal interest rate in our example is 11 percent.

real interest rate
The percentage increase in purchasing power that a borrower pays a lender; the nominal interest rate less the expected rate of inflation.

nominal interest rate
The percentage increase in money that a borrower pays a lender.

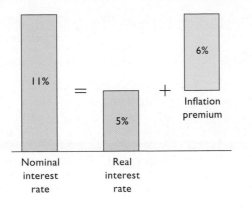

FIGURE 6.4 **The inflation premium and nominal and real interest rates.** The inflation premium—the expected rate of inflation—gets built into the nominal interest rate. Here, the nominal interest rate of 11 percent comprises the real interest rate of 5 percent plus the inflation premium of 6 percent.

Does Inflation Affect Output?

Thus far, our discussion has focused on how inflation redistributes a given level of total real income. But inflation also may affect an economy's level of real output (and thus its level of real income). The direction and significance of this effect on output depends on the type of inflation and its severity.

Cost-Push Inflation and Real Output

Recall that abrupt and unexpected rises in key resource prices such as oil can sufficiently drive up overall production costs to cause cost-push inflation. As prices rise, the quantity of goods and services demanded falls. So firms respond by producing less output, and unemployment goes up. In short, cost-push inflation reduces real output. It redistributes a decreased level of real income.

Demand-Pull Inflation and Real Output

Economists do not fully agree on the effects of mild inflation (less than 3 percent) on real output. One perspective is that even low levels of inflation reduce real output because inflation diverts time and effort toward activities designed to hedge against inflation. For example, businesses must incur the cost of changing thousands of prices on their shelves and in their computers simply to reflect inflation. Also, households and businesses must spend considerable time and effort obtaining the information they need to distinguish between real and nominal values such as prices, wages, and interest rates. Further, to limit the loss of purchasing power from inflation, people try to limit the amount of money they hold in their billfolds and checking accounts at any one time and instead put more money into interest-bearing accounts and stock and bond funds. But cash and checking deposits are needed in even greater amounts to buy the higher-priced goods and services. Therefore, people must make more frequent trips, phone calls, or Internet visits to financial institutions to transfer funds to checking accounts and billfolds, when needed. Bottom line: From this perspective even mild inflation reduces total output.

In contrast, other economists point out that full employment and economic growth depend on strong levels of total spending. Such spending creates high profits, strong demand for labor, and a powerful incentive for firms to expand their plants and equipment. In this view, the mild inflation that is a by-product of strong spending is a small price to pay for full employment and continued economic growth. Defenders of mild inflation say that it is much better for an economy to err on the side of strong spending, full employment, economic growth, and mild inflation than on the side of weak spending, unemployment, recession, and deflation.

Hyperinflation

All economists agree that *hyperinflation*, which is extraordinarily rapid inflation, can have a devastating impact on real output and employment.

As prices shoot up sharply and unevenly during hyperinflation, normal economic relationships are disrupted. Business owners do not know what to charge for their products. Consumers do not know what to pay. Resource suppliers want to be paid with actual output, rather than with rapidly depreciating money. Money eventually becomes almost worthless and ceases to do its job as a medium of exchange. The economy may be thrown into a state of barter, and production and exchange drop dramatically. The net result is economic, social, and possibly political chaos.

Examples of hyperinflation are Germany after the First World War and Japan after the Second World War. In Germany, "prices increased so rapidly that waiters changed the prices on the menu several times during the course of a lunch. Sometimes customers had to pay double the price listed on the menu when they ordered."[*] In postwar Japan, in 1947 "fishermen and farmers…used scales to weigh currency and change, rather than bothering to count it."[†]

There are also more recent examples: Between June 1986 and March 1991 the cumulative inflation in Nicaragua was 11,895,866,143 percent. From November 1993 to December 1994 the cumulative inflation rate in the Democratic Republic of Congo was 69,502 percent. From February 1993 to January 1994 the cumulative inflation rate in Serbia was 156,312,790 percent.[‡]

Such dramatic hyperinflations are always the consequence of highly imprudent expansions of the money supply by government. The rocketing money supply produces frenzied total spending and severe demand-pull inflation. Zimbabwe's 14.9 billion percent in 2008 is just the latest example.

QUESTION: How would you alter your present spending plans if you were quite certain that the prices of everything were going to double in the coming week?

[*]Theodore Morgan, *Income and Employment*, 2d ed. (Englewood Cliffs, N.J.: Prentice-Hall, 1952), p. 361.
[†]Raburn M. Williams, *Inflation! Money, Jobs, and Politicians* (Arlington Heights, Ill.: AHM Publishing, 1980), p. 2.
[‡]Stanley Fischer, Ratna Sahay, and Carlos Végh, "Modern Hyper- and High Inflations," *Journal of Economic Literature*, September 2002, p. 840.

Summary

1. Business cycles are recurring ups and downs in economic activity. Their two primary phases are expansions and recessions.

2. Economists distinguish between frictional, structural, and cyclical unemployment. The rate of unemployment at full employment consists of frictional and structural unemployment and currently is about 5 percent.

3. The economic cost of unemployment, as measured by the negative GDP gap, consists of the goods and services forgone by society when its resources are involuntarily idle.

4. Inflation is a rise in the general price level and is measured in the United States by the Consumer Price Index (CPI). When inflation occurs, each dollar of income will buy fewer goods and services than before. That is, inflation reduces the purchasing power of money. Deflation is a decline in the general price level.

5. Economists discern both demand-pull and cost-push (supply-side) inflation. Demand-pull inflation results from an excess of total spending relative to the economy's capacity

to produce. The main source of cost-push inflation is abrupt and rapid increases in the prices of key resources. These supply shocks push up per-unit production costs and ultimately the prices of consumer goods.

6. Unanticipated inflation arbitrarily redistributes real income at the expense of fixed-income receivers, creditors, and savers. If inflation is anticipated, individuals and businesses may be able to take steps to lessen or eliminate adverse redistribution effects.

7. Cost-push inflation reduces real output and employment. Proponents of zero inflation argue that even mild demand-pull inflation (1 to 3 percent) reduces the economy's real output. Other economists say that mild inflation may be a necessary by-product of the high and growing spending that produces high levels of output, full employment, and economic growth.

8. Hyperinflation, caused by highly imprudent expansions of the money supply, may undermine the monetary system and cause severe declines in real output.

Terms and Concepts

business cycles	unemployment rate	deflation
recession	frictional unemployment	demand-pull inflation
expansion	structural unemployment	cost-push inflation
shocks	cyclical unemployment	nominal income
demand shocks	potential output	real income
supply shocks	GDP gap	real interest rate
sticky prices	inflation	nominal interest rate
labor force	Consumer Price Index (CPI)	

Questions McGraw Hill connect ECONOMICS

1. What are the two primary phases of the business cycle? What tends to happen to real GDP, unemployment, and inflation during these phases? LO1

2. How many recessions has the United States experienced since 1950? Which ones were the longest in duration? Which ones were the most severe in terms of declines in real output? LO1

3. Because the United States has an unemployment compensation program that provides income for those out of work, why should we worry about unemployment? LO3

4. What are the three types of unemployment? Unemployment is seen by some as undesirable. Are all three types of unemployment undesirable? Explain. LO3

5. What is the Consumer Price Index (CPI), and how is it determined each month? What effect does inflation have on the purchasing power of a dollar? How does it explain differences between nominal and real interest rates? How does deflation differ from inflation? LO2

6. Briefly distinguish between demand-pull inflation and cost-push inflation. LO3

7. How does unanticipated inflation hurt creditors and help borrowers? How can anticipating the inflation make these effects less severe? LO3

8. Explain how hyperinflation might lead to a severe decline in total output. LO3

Problems

1. Suppose that a country's annual growth rates were 5, 3, 4, −1, −2, 2, 3, 4, 6, and 3 in yearly sequence over a 10-year period. What was the country's trend rate of growth over this period? Which set of years most clearly demonstrates an expansionary phase of the business cycle? Which set of years best illustrates a recessionary phase of the business cycle? LO1

2. Assume the following data for a country: total population, 500; population under 16 years of age or institutionalized, 120; not in labor force, 150; unemployed, 23; part-time workers looking for full-time jobs, 10. What is the size of the labor force? What is the official unemployment rate? LO2

3. If the CPI was 110 last year and is 121 this year, what is this year's rate of inflation? In contrast, suppose that the CPI was 110 last year and is 108 this year. What is this year's rate of inflation? What term do economists use to describe this second outcome? **LO3**

4. How long would it take for the price level to double if inflation persisted at (a) 2 percent per year, (b) 5 percent per year, and (c) 10 percent per year? **LO3**

5. If your nominal income rose by 5.3 percent and the price level rose by 3.8 percent in some year, by what percentage would your real income (approximately) increase? If your nominal income rose by 2.8 percent and your real income rose by 1.1 percent in some year, what must have been the (approximate) rate of inflation? **LO3**

6. Suppose that the nominal rate of interest is 4 percent and the inflation premium is 2 percent. What is the real interest rate? Alternatively, assume that the real interest rate is 1 percent and the nominal interest rate is 6 percent. What is the inflation premium? **LO3**

FURTHER TEST YOUR KNOWLEDGE AT
www.mcconnellbrief2e.com

At the text's Online Learning Center, **www.mcconnellbrief2e.com**, you will find one or more web-based questions that require information from the Internet to answer. We urge you to check them out, since they will familiarize you with websites that may be helpful in other courses and perhaps even in your career. The OLC also features multiple-choice quizzes that give instant feedback and provides other helpful ways to further test your knowledge of the chapter.

Visit your mobile app store and download the McConnell Brief Edition: Study Econ app *today!*

Aggregate Demand and Aggregate Supply

During the recession of 2007–2009, the economic terms *aggregate demand* and *aggregate supply* moved from the obscurity of economic journals and textbooks to the spotlight of national newspapers, websites, radio, and television.

The media and public asked: Why had *aggregate demand* declined, producing the deepest recession and highest rate of unemployment since 1982? Why hadn't the reductions in interest rates by the Federal Reserve boosted *aggregate demand*? Would the federal government's $787 billion stimulus package increase *aggregate demand* and reduce unemployment, as intended? Would a resurgence of oil prices and other energy prices reduce *aggregate supply,* choking off an economic expansion?

Aggregate demand and aggregate supply are the featured elements of the **aggregate demand–aggregate supply model (AD-AS model),** the focus of this chapter. The AD-AS model enables us to analyze change in real GDP and the price level simultaneously. The model therefore provides keen insights on inflation, recession, unemployment, and economic growth. In later chapters, we will see that the AD-AS model easily depicts fiscal and monetary policies such as those used in 2008 and 2009 to try to halt the downward slide of the economy and promote its recovery.

Aggregate Demand

aggregate demand–aggregate supply (AD-AS) model
The macroeconomic model that uses aggregate demand and aggregate supply to determine and explain the price level and level of real domestic output.

aggregate demand
A schedule or curve that shows the total quantity of goods and services demanded (purchased) at different price levels.

Aggregate demand is a schedule or curve that shows the quantities of a nation's output (real GDP) that buyers collectively want to purchase at each possible price level. These buyers include the nation's households, businesses, and government along with consumers located abroad (households, businesses, and governments in other nations). The relationship between the price level (as measured by the GDP price index) and the amount of real output demanded is inverse or negative: When the price level rises, the quantity of real GDP demanded falls; when the price level falls, the quantity of real GDP demanded rises.

Figure 7.1 shows the inverse relationship between the price level and real GDP. The downward slope of the AD curve reflects the fact that higher U.S. price levels discourage domestic buyers (households and businesses) and foreign buyers from purchasing U.S. real GDP. Lower price levels encourage them to buy more U.S. real output.

Changes in Aggregate Demand

determinants of aggregate demand
Factors that shift the aggregate demand curve when they change.

Other things equal, a change in the price level will change the amount of total spending and therefore change the amount of real GDP demanded by the economy. Movements along a fixed aggregate demand curve represent these changes in real GDP. However, if one or more of those "other things" change, the entire aggregate demand curve will shift. We call these other things **determinants of aggregate demand.** When they change, they shift the AD curve. These AD shifters are listed in the table in Figure 7.2. In that figure, the rightward shift of the curve from AD_1 to AD_2 shows an increase in aggregate demand. The leftward shift from AD_1 to AD_3 shows a decrease in aggregate demand. Notice that the categories of spending are the same as those in the national income and product accounts (Chapter 5). To provide a clear understanding of these AD shifters, we need to elaborate on them.

FIGURE 7.1 The aggregate demand curve. The downsloping aggregate demand curve AD indicates an inverse (or negative) relationship between the price level and the amount of real output purchased.

Price level

Aggregate demand

AD

0   Real domestic output, GDP

FIGURE 7.2 Changes in aggregate demand. A change in one or more of the listed determinants of aggregate demand will shift the aggregate demand curve. The rightward shift from AD_1 to AD_2 represents an increase in aggregate demand; the leftward shift from AD_1 to AD_3 shows a decrease in aggregate demand.

Determinants of Aggregate Demand: Factors That Shift the Aggregate Demand Curve
1. Change in consumer spending
a. Consumer wealth
b. Household borrowing
c. Consumer expectations
d. Personal taxes
2. Change in investment spending
a. Interest rates
b. Expected returns
• Expected future business conditions
• Technology
• Degree of excess capacity
• Business taxes
3. Change in government spending
4. Change in net export spending
a. National income abroad
b. Exchange rates

Consumer Spending

If consumers decide to buy more output at each price level, the aggregate demand curve will shift to the right, as from AD_1 to AD_2 in Figure 7.2. If they decide to buy less output, the aggregate demand curve will shift to the left, as from AD_1 to AD_3.

Several factors can change consumer spending and therefore shift the aggregate demand curve. As the table in Figure 7.2 shows, those factors are real consumer wealth, household borrowing, consumer expectations, and personal taxes.

Consumer Wealth Consumer wealth is the total dollar value of all assets owned by consumers in the economy less the dollar value of their liabilities (debts). Assets include stocks, bonds, and real estate. Liabilities include mortgages, car loans, and credit card balances.

Consumer wealth sometimes changes suddenly and unexpectedly due to surprising changes in asset values. An unforeseen increase in the stock market is a good example. The increase in wealth prompts pleasantly surprised consumers to save less and buy more out of their current incomes than they had previously been planning. The resulting increase in consumer spending—the so-called *wealth effect*—shifts the aggregate demand curve to the right. In contrast, an unexpected decline in asset values will cause an unanticipated reduction in consumer wealth at each price level. As consumers tighten their belts in response to the bad news, a "reverse wealth effect" sets in. Unpleasantly surprised consumers increase savings and reduce consumption, thereby shifting the aggregate demand curve to the left.

Household Borrowing Consumers can increase their consumption spending by borrowing. Doing so shifts the aggregate demand curve to the right. By contrast, a decrease in borrowing for consumption purposes shifts the aggregate demand curve to the left. The aggregate demand curve also will shift to the left if consumers increase their savings rates in order to pay off their debts. With more money flowing to debt repayment, consumption expenditures decline and the AD curve shifts left.

Consumer Expectations Changes in expectations about the future may alter consumer spending. When people expect their future real incomes to rise, they tend to spend more of their current incomes. Thus, current consumption spending increases (current saving falls), and the aggregate demand curve shifts to the right. Similarly, a widely held expectation of surging inflation in the near future may increase aggregate demand today because consumers will want to buy products before their prices escalate. Conversely, expectations of lower future income or lower future prices may reduce current consumption and shift the aggregate demand curve to the left.

Personal Taxes A reduction in personal income tax rates raises take-home income and increases consumer purchases at each possible price level. Tax cuts shift the aggregate demand curve to the right. Tax increases reduce consumption spending and shift the curve to the left.

APPLYING THE ANALYSIS

What Wealth Effect?

The consumption component of aggregate demand is usually relatively stable even during rather extraordinary times. Between March 2000 and July 2002, the U.S. stock market lost a staggering $3.7 trillion of value (yes, trillion). Yet consumption spending was greater at the end of that period than at the beginning. How can that be? Why didn't a negative wealth effect reduce consumption?

There are a number of reasons. Of greatest importance, the amount of consumption spending in the economy depends mainly on the *flow* of income, not the *stock* of wealth. Disposable income (after-tax income) in the United States is nearly $9 trillion annually, and consumers spend a large portion of it. Even though there was a mild recession in 2001, disposable income and consumption spending were both greater in July 2002 than in March 2000. Second, the federal government cut personal income tax rates during this period, and that bolstered consumption spending. Third, household wealth did not fall by the full amount of the $3.7 trillion stock market loss because the value of houses increased dramatically over this period. Finally, lower interest rates during this period enabled many households to refinance their mortgages, reduce monthly loan payments, and increase their current consumption. For all these offsetting reasons, the consumption component of aggregate demand held up in the face of the extraordinary loss of stock market value.

The 2007–2009 recession tells a somewhat different story, with consumption falling but not enough to definitively establish the presence of a wealth effect. Between losses in both the housing and stock markets, U.S. household wealth decreased by about $14 trillion from June 2007 to March 2009, and economic contraction began in December 2007. However, in part because of federal government policies to stimulate spending, household disposable income did not fall until the second half of 2008, reaching a low point in early 2009 and then beginning a slow but steady increase. Consumption spending followed a similar pattern, declining in the latter part of 2008 and bottoming out in the first quarter of 2009. While most economists agree that wealth losses from the housing and financial market crises contributed to lower consumption (or, at the very least, slower growth in consumption spending), the reductions in household expenditures appear to have been far less substantial than one might have anticipated.

QUESTION: Which do you think will decrease consumption more: a 10 percent decrease in after-tax income or a 10 percent decrease in stock market values? Explain.

Investment Spending

Investment spending (the purchase of capital goods) is a second major determinant of aggregate demand. Increases in investment spending at each price level boost aggregate demand, and decreases in investment spending reduce it.

The investment decision is a marginal-benefit–marginal-cost decision. The marginal benefit of the investment is a stream of higher profits that is expected to result from the investment. In percentage terms, economists call these higher profits (net of new operation expenses) the *expected return on the investment*, r. For example, suppose the owner of a small cabinetmaking shop is considering whether to invest in a new sanding machine that costs $1000, expands output, and has a useful life of only 1 year. (Extending the life of the machine beyond 1 year complicates the economic calculation but does not change the fundamental analysis.) Suppose the net expected revenue from the machine (that is, after such operating costs as power, lumber, labor, and certain taxes have been subtracted) is $1100. Then the expected net revenue is sufficient to cover the initial $1000 cost of the machine and leave a profit of $100. Comparing this $100 to the $1000 initial cost of the machine, we find that the expected rate of return, r, on the investment is 10 percent ($= \$100/\$1000$).

It is important to note that the return just discussed is an *expected* rate of return, not a *guaranteed* rate of return. Investment involves risk, so the investment may or may not pay off as anticipated. Moreover, investment faces diminishing returns. As more of it occurs, the best investment projects are completed and the subsequent projects produce lower expected rates of return. So, the expected return, r, tends to fall as firms undertake more and more investment.

The marginal cost of the investment to a firm is reflected in either the explicit costs of borrowing money from others or the implicit cost of using its own retained earnings to make the investment. In percentage terms, and adjusted for expected inflation, this cost is the real interest rate, i.

The business firm compares the real interest rate (marginal cost) with the expected return on investment (marginal benefit). If the expected rate of return (for example, 6 percent) exceeds the interest rate (say, 5 percent), the investment is undertaken. The firm expects the investment to be profitable. But if the interest rate (for example, 7 percent) exceeds the expected rate of return (6 percent), the investment will not be undertaken. The firm expects the investment to be unprofitable. The profit-maximizing firm will undertake all investment that it thinks will be profitable. That means it will invest up to the point where $r = i$ in order to exhaust all investment possibilities for which r exceeds i.

So real interest rates and expected returns are the two main determinants of investment spending.

ORIGIN OF THE IDEA

O 7.1

Interest-rate–investment relationship

Real Interest Rates We will discover that a nation's central bank—the Federal Reserve in the United States—can take monetary actions to increase and decrease interest rates. When it takes those actions, it shifts the nation's aggregate demand curve. Other things equal, increases in real interest rates will raise borrowing costs, lower investment spending, and reduce aggregate demand. Declines in interest rates will have the opposite effects.

Expected Returns Higher expected returns on investment projects will increase the demand for capital goods and shift the aggregate demand curve to the right. Alternatively, declines in expected returns will decrease investment and shift the curve to the left. Expected returns are influenced by several factors:

- *Future business conditions* If firms are generally optimistic about future business conditions, they are more likely to forecast high rates of return on current investment and therefore may invest more today. In contrast, if they think the economy will deteriorate in the future, they will forecast low rates of return and perhaps will invest less today.

- *Technology* New and improved technologies enhance expected returns on investment and thus increase aggregate demand. For example, recent advances in microbiology have motivated pharmaceutical companies to establish new labs and production facilities.
- *Degree of excess capacity* A rise in excess capacity—unused capital—will reduce the expected return on new investment and hence decrease aggregate demand. Other things equal, firms operating factories at well below capacity have little incentive to build new factories. But when firms realize that their excess capacity is dwindling or has completely disappeared, their expected returns on new investment in factories and capital equipment rise. Thus, they increase their investment spending, and the aggregate demand curve shifts to the right.
- *Business taxes* An increase in business taxes will reduce after-tax profits from capital investment and lower expected returns. So investment and aggregate demand will decline. A decrease in business taxes will have the opposite effects.

The variability of interest rates and investment expectations makes investment quite volatile. In contrast to consumption, investment spending rises and falls quite often, independent of changes in total income. Investment, in fact, is the least stable component of aggregate demand.

Global Snapshot 7.1 compares investment spending relative to GDP for several nations in 2010.

GLOBAL SNAPSHOT 7.1

Gross Investment Expenditures as a Percentage of GDP, Selected Nations

As a percentage of GDP, investment varies widely by nation. These differences, of course, can change from year to year.

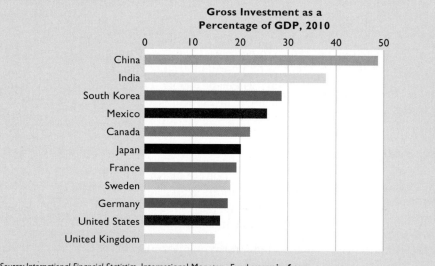

Gross Investment as a
Percentage of GDP, 2010

Source: *International Financial Statistics,* International Monetary Fund, **www.imf.org**.

Government Spending

Government purchases are the third determinant of aggregate demand. An increase in government purchases (for example, more transportation projects) will shift the aggregate demand curve to the right, as long as tax collections and interest rates do not change as a result. In contrast, a reduction in government spending (for example, less military equipment) will shift the curve to the left.

Net Export Spending

The final determinant of aggregate demand is net export spending. Other things equal, higher U.S. *exports* mean an increased foreign demand for U.S. goods. So a rise in net exports (higher exports relative to imports) shifts the aggregate demand curve to the right. In contrast, a decrease in U.S. net exports shifts the aggregate demand curve leftward.

What might cause net exports to change, other than the price level? Two possibilities are changes in national income abroad and changes in exchange rates.

National Income Abroad   Rising national income abroad encourages foreigners to buy more products, some of which are made in the United States. So U.S. net exports rise, and the U.S. aggregate demand curve shifts to the right. Declines in national income abroad do the opposite: They reduce U.S. net exports and shift the U.S. aggregate demand curve to the left.

Exchange Rates   Changes in **exchange rates**—the prices of foreign currencies in terms of one's own currency—may affect U.S. net exports and therefore aggregate demand. When the dollar *depreciates* (declines in value) against foreign currencies, it takes more dollars to buy foreign goods. So foreign goods become more expensive in dollar terms, and Americans reduce their imports. On the opposite side, the depreciation of the dollar means that other currencies *appreciate* (rise in value) relative to the dollar. U.S. exports rise because those foreign currencies can buy more American goods. Conclusion: Dollar depreciation increases net exports (imports go down; exports go up) and therefore increases aggregate demand.

exchange rates
The prices of foreign currencies in terms of one's own currency.

Dollar appreciation has the opposite effects: Net exports fall (imports go up; exports go down) and aggregate demand declines.

As shown in Global Snapshot 7.2, net exports vary greatly among the major industrial nations.

GLOBAL SNAPSHOT 7.2

Net Exports of Goods, Selected Nations, 2009

Some nations, such as Germany and China, have positive net exports; other countries, such as the United States and the United Kingdom, have negative net exports.

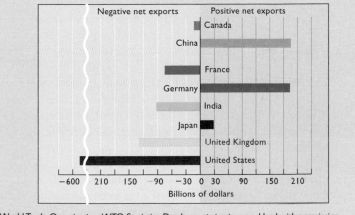

Source: World Trade Organization, WTO Statistics Database, **stat.wto.org**. Used with permission.

Aggregate Supply

aggregate supply
A schedule or curve that shows the total quantity of goods and services supplied (produced) at different price levels.

Aggregate supply is a schedule or curve showing the relationship between a nation's price level and the amount of real domestic output that firms in the economy produce. This relationship varies depending on the time horizon and how quickly output prices and input prices can change. We will define three time horizons.

- In the *immediate short run*, both input prices as well as output prices are fixed.
- In the *short run*, input prices are fixed, but output prices can vary.
- In the *long run*, input prices as well as output prices can vary.

In Chapter 6, we introduced the concept of inflexible (or "sticky") prices. Here we consider different degrees of stickiness in order to discuss how total output varies with the price level in the immediate short run, the short run, and the long run. As you will see, the relationship between the price level and total output is different in each of the three time horizons because input prices are stickier than output prices. While both become more flexible as time passes, output prices usually adjust more rapidly.

✗Aggregate Supply in the Immediate Short Run

Depending on the type of firm, the immediate short run can last anywhere from a few days to a few months. It lasts as long as *both* input prices and output prices stay fixed. Input prices are fixed in both the immediate short run and the short run by contractual agreements. In particular, 75 percent of the average firm's costs are wages and salaries—and these are almost always fixed by labor contracts for months or years at a time. As a result, they are usually fixed for a much longer duration than output prices, which can begin to change within a few days or a few months depending upon the type of firm.

That being said, output prices are also typically fixed in the immediate short run. This is most often caused by firms setting fixed prices for their customers and then agreeing to supply whatever quantity demanded results at those fixed prices. For instance, once an appliance manufacturer sets its annual list prices for refrigerators, stoves, ovens, and microwaves, it is obligated to supply however many or few appliances customers want to buy at those prices. Similarly, a catalogue company is obliged to sell however much customers want to buy of its products at the prices listed in its current catalogue. And it is obligated to supply those quantities demanded until it sends out its next catalogue.

immediate-short-run aggregate supply curve
The aggregate supply curve associated with a period of time in which neither input nor output prices respond to changes in the level of spending or production.

With output prices fixed and firms selling however much customers want to purchase at those fixed prices, the **immediate-short-run aggregate supply curve** AS_{ISR} is a horizontal line, as shown in Figure 7.3. The AS_{ISR} curve is horizontal at the overall price level P_1, which is calculated from all of the individual prices set by the various firms in the economy. Its horizontal shape implies that the total amount of output supplied in the economy depends directly on the volume of spending that results at price level P_1. If total spending is low at price level P_1, firms will supply a small amount to match the low level of spending. If total spending is high at price level P_1, they will supply a high level of output to match the high level of spending. The amount of output that results may be higher than or lower than the economy's full-employment output level Q_f.

Notice, however, that firms will respond in this manner to changes in total spending only as long as output prices remain fixed. As soon as firms are able to change their product prices, they can respond to changes in aggregate spending not only by increasing or decreasing output but also by raising or lowering prices. This is the situation that leads to the upward-sloping short-run aggregate supply curve that we discuss next.

FIGURE 7.3 Aggregate supply in the immediate short run. In the immediate short run, the aggregate supply curve AS_{ISR} is horizontal at the economy's current price level, P_1. With output prices fixed, firms collectively supply the level of output that is demanded at those prices.

Aggregate Supply in the Short Run

The short run begins after the immediate short run ends. As it relates to macroeconomics, the short run is a period of time during which output prices are flexible but input prices are either totally fixed or highly inflexible.

These assumptions about output prices and input prices are general—they relate to the economy in the aggregate. Naturally, some input prices are more flexible than others. Since gasoline prices are quite flexible, a package delivery firm like UPS that uses gasoline as an input will have at least one very flexible input price. On the other hand, wages at UPS are set by five-year labor contracts negotiated with its drivers' union, the Teamsters. Because wages are the firm's largest and most important input cost, it is the case that, overall, UPS faces input prices that are inflexible for several years at a time. Thus, its "short run"—during which it can change the shipping prices that it charges its customers but during which it must deal with substantially fixed input prices—is actually quite long. Keep this in mind as we derive the short-run aggregate supply for the entire economy. Its applicability does not depend on some arbitrary definition of how long the "short run" should be. Instead, the short run for which the model is relevant is any period of time during which output prices are flexible but input prices are fixed or nearly fixed.

As illustrated in Figure 7.4, the **short-run aggregate supply curve** AS slopes upward because, with input prices fixed, changes in the price level will raise or lower real firm profits. To see how this works, consider an economy that has only a single multiproduct firm called Mega Buzzer and in which the firm's owners must receive a real profit of $20 in order to produce the full-employment output of 100 units. Assume the owner's only input (aside from entrepreneurial talent) is 10 units of hired labor at $8 per worker, for a total wage cost of $80. Also, assume that the 100 units of output sell for $1 per unit, so total revenue is $100. Mega Buzzer's nominal profit is $20 (= $100 − $80), and using the $1 price to designate the base-price index of 100, its real profit is also $20 (= $20/1.00). Well and good; the full-employment output is produced.

Next, consider what will happen if the price of Mega Buzzer's output doubles. The doubling of the price level will boost total revenue from $100 to $200, but since we are discussing the short run during which input prices are fixed, the $8 nominal wage for each of the 10 workers will remain unchanged so that total costs stay at $80. Nominal

short-run aggregate supply curve
An aggregate supply curve relevant to a time period in which output prices are flexible, but input prices are sticky.

FIGURE 7.4 The aggregate supply curve (short run). The upsloping aggregate supply curve AS indicates a direct (or positive) relationship between the price level and the amount of real output that firms will offer for sale. The AS curve is relatively flat below the full-employment output because unemployed resources and unused capacity allow firms to respond to price-level rises with large increases in real output. It is relatively steep beyond the full-employment output because resource shortages and capacity limitations make it difficult to expand real output as the price level rises.

profit will rise from \$20 (= \$100 − \$80) to \$120 (= \$200 − \$80). Dividing that \$120 profit by the new price index of 200 (= 2.0 in hundredths), we find that Mega Buzzer's real profit is now \$60. The rise in the real reward from \$20 to \$60 prompts the firm (economy) to produce more output. Conversely, price-level declines reduce real profits and cause the firm (economy) to reduce its output. So, in the short run, there is a direct, or positive, relationship between the price level and real output. When the price level rises, real output rises and when the price level falls, real output falls. The result is an upward-sloping short-run aggregate supply curve.

Notice, however, that the upslope of the short-run aggregate supply curve is not constant. It is flatter at outputs below the full-employment output level Q_f and steeper at outputs above it. This has to do with the fact that per-unit production costs underlie the short-run aggregate supply curve. In equation form,

$$\text{Per-unit production cost} = \frac{\text{total input cost}}{\text{units of output}}$$

The per-unit production cost of any specific level of output establishes that output's price level because the associated price level must cover all the costs of production, including profit "costs."

As the economy expands in the short run, per-unit production costs generally rise because of reduced efficiency. But the extent of that rise depends on where the economy is operating relative to its capacity. When the economy is operating below its full-employment output, it has large amounts of unused machinery and equipment and large numbers of unemployed workers. Firms can put these idle human and property resources back to work with little upward pressure on per-unit production costs. And as output expands, few if any shortages of inputs or production bottlenecks will arise to raise per-unit production costs. That is why the slope of the short-run aggregate supply curve increases only slowly at output levels below the full-employment output level Q_f.

On the other hand, when the economy is operating beyond Q_f, the vast majority of its available resources are already employed. Adding more workers to a relatively fixed number of highly used capital resources such as plant and equipment creates congestion in the workplace and reduces the efficiency (on average) of workers. Adding more capital, given the limited number of available workers, leaves equipment idle and reduces the efficiency of capital. Adding more land resources when capital and labor are highly constrained reduces the efficiency of land resources. Under these circumstances, total input costs rise more rapidly than total output. The result is rapidly rising per-unit production costs that give the short-run aggregate supply curve its rapidly increasing slope at output levels beyond Q_f.

✕Aggregate Supply in the Long Run

In macroeconomics, the long run is the time horizon over which both input prices as well as output prices are flexible. It begins after the short run ends. Depending on the type of firm and industry, this may be from a couple of weeks to several years in the future. But for the economy as a whole, it is the time horizon over which all output and input prices—including wage rates—are fully flexible.

The **long-run aggregate supply curve** AS_{LR} is vertical at the economy's full-employment output Q_f, as shown in Figure 7.5. The vertical curve means that in the long run the economy will produce the full employment output level no matter what the price level is. How can this be? Shouldn't higher prices cause firms to increase output? The explanation lies in the fact that in the long run, when both input prices as well as output prices are flexible, profit levels will always adjust so as to give firms exactly the right profit incentive to produce exactly the full-employment output level, Q_f.

To see why this is true, look back at the short-run aggregate supply curve AS shown in Figure 7.4. Suppose that the economy starts out producing at the full-employment output level Q_f and that the price level at that moment has an index value of $P = 100$. Now suppose that output prices double, so that the price index goes to $P = 200$. We previously demonstrated for our single-firm economy that this doubling of the price level would cause profits to rise in the short run and that the higher profits would motivate the firm to increase output.

This outcome, however, is totally dependent upon the fact that input prices are fixed in the short run. Consider what will happen in the long run when they are free to change. Firms can only produce beyond the full-employment output level by running factories and businesses at extremely high rates. This creates a great deal of demand for the economy's limited supply of productive resources. In particular, labor is in great demand because the only way to produce beyond full employment is if workers are working overtime.

long-run aggregate supply curve
The aggregate supply curve associated with a period of time in which both input and output prices are fully flexible.

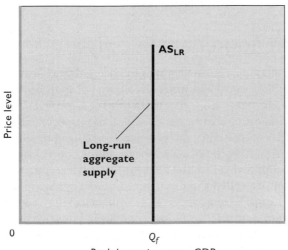

FIGURE 7.5 Aggregate supply in the long run. The long-run aggregate supply curve AS_{LR} is vertical at the full-employment level of real GDP (Q_f) because in the long run wages and other input prices rise and fall to match changes in the price level. So price-level changes do not affect firms' profits, and thus they create no incentive for firms to alter their output.

As time passes and input prices are free to change, the high demand will start to raise input prices. In particular, overworked employees will demand and receive raises as employers scramble to deal with the labor shortages that arise when the economy is producing at above its full-employment output level. As input prices increase, firm profits will begin to fall. And as they decline, so does the motive firms have to produce more than the full-employment output level. This process of rising input prices and falling profits continues until the rise in input prices exactly matches the initial change in output prices (in our example, they both double). When that happens, firm profits in real terms return to their original level so that firms are once again motivated to produce at exactly the full-employment output level. This adjustment process means that in the long run the economy will produce at full employment regardless of the price level (in our example, at either $P = 100$ or $P = 200$). That is why the long-run aggregate supply curve AS_{LR} is vertical above the full-employment output level. Every possible price level on the vertical axis is associated with the economy producing at the full-employment output level in the long run once input prices adjust to exactly match changes in output prices.

Focusing on the Short Run

The immediate-short-run aggregate supply curve, the short-run aggregate supply curve, and the long-run aggregate supply curve are all important. Each curve is appropriate to situations that match their respective assumptions about the flexibility of input and output prices. But our focus in the rest of this chapter and the chapters that immediately follow will be on short-run aggregate supply curves such as the AS curve shown in Figure 7.4. Indeed, unless explicitly stated otherwise, all references to "aggregate supply" will be to aggregate supply in the short run.

Our emphasis on the short-run aggregate supply curve stems from our interest in understanding the business cycle in the simplest possible way. It is a fact that real-world economies typically manifest simultaneous changes in both their price levels and their levels of real output. The upward-sloping short-run AS curve is the only version of aggregate supply that can handle simultaneous movements in both of these variables. By contrast, the price level is assumed fixed in the immediate-short-run version of aggregate supply illustrated in Figure 7.3 and the economy's output is always equal to the full-employment output level in the long-run version of aggregate supply shown in Figure 7.5. This renders these versions of the aggregate supply curve less useful as part of a core model for analyzing business cycles and demonstrating the short-run government policies designed to deal with them.

Changes in Aggregate Supply

An existing aggregate supply curve identifies the relationship between the price level and real output, other things equal. But when other things change, the curve itself shifts. The rightward shift of the curve from AS_1 to AS_2 in Figure 7.6 represents an increase in aggregate supply, indicating that firms are willing to produce and sell more real output at each price level. A decrease in aggregate supply is shown by the leftward shift of the curve from AS_1 to AS_3. At each price level, firms produce less output than before.

determinants of aggregate supply
Factors that shift the aggregate supply curve when they change.

The table in Figure 7.6 lists the factors that collectively position the aggregate supply curve. They are called the **determinants of aggregate supply** and shift the curve when they change. Changes in these determinants raise or lower per-unit production costs *at each price level (or each level of output)*. These changes in per-unit production costs affect profits, thereby leading firms to alter the amount of output they are willing to produce *at each price level*. For example, firms may collectively offer $7 trillion of real output at a price level of 1.0 (= 100 in index-value terms), rather

FIGURE 7.6 Changes in aggregate supply. A change in one or more of the listed determinants of aggregate supply will shift the aggregate supply curve. The rightward shift of the aggregate supply curve from AS₁ to AS₂ represents an increase in aggregate supply; the leftward shift of the curve from AS₁ to AS₃ shows a decrease in aggregate supply.

Determinants of Aggregate Supply: Factors That Shift the Aggregate Supply Curve

1. Change in input prices
   a. Domestic resource prices
   b. Prices of imported resources
2. Change in productivity
3. Change in legal-institutional environment
   a. Business taxes
   b. Government regulations

than $6.8 trillion. Or they may offer $6.5 trillion rather than $7 trillion. The point is that when one of the determinants listed in Figure 7.6 changes, the aggregate supply curve shifts to the right or left. Changes that reduce per-unit production costs shift the aggregate supply curve to the right, as from AS₁ to AS₂; changes that increase per-unit production costs shift it to the left, as from AS₁ to AS₃. *When per-unit production costs change for reasons other than changes in real output, the aggregate supply curve shifts.*

The aggregate supply determinants listed in Figure 7.6 are very important and therefore require more discussion.

Input Prices

Input or resource prices—to be distinguished from the output prices that make up the price level—are a major ingredient of per-unit production costs and therefore a key determinant of aggregate supply. These resources can be either domestic or imported.

Domestic Resource Prices   As stated earlier, wages and salaries make up about 75 percent of all business costs. Other things equal, decreases in wages reduce per-unit production costs. So the aggregate supply curve shifts to the right. Increases in wages shift the curve to the left. Examples:

- Labor supply increases because of substantial immigration. Wages and per-unit production costs fall, shifting the AS curve to the right.
- Labor supply decreases because a rapid increase in pension income causes many older workers to opt for early retirement. Wage rates and per-unit production costs rise, shifting the AS curve to the left.

Similarly, the aggregate supply curve shifts when the prices of land and capital inputs change. Examples:

- The price of machinery and equipment falls because of declines in the prices of steel and electronic components. Per-unit production costs decline, and the AS curve shifts to the right.
- The supply of available land resources expands through discoveries of mineral deposits, irrigation of land, or technical innovations that transform "nonresources" (say, vast desert lands) into valuable resources (productive lands). The price of land declines, per-unit production costs fall, and the AS curve shifts to the right.

Prices of Imported Resources Just as foreign demand for U.S. goods contributes to U.S. aggregate demand, resources imported from abroad (such as oil, tin, and copper) add to U.S. aggregate supply. Added supplies of resources—whether domestic or imported—typically reduce per-unit production costs. A decrease in the price of imported resources increases U.S. aggregate supply, while an increase in their price reduces U.S. aggregate supply.

A good example of the major effect that changing resource prices can have on aggregate supply is the oil price hikes of the 1970s. At that time, a group of oil-producing nations called the Organization of Petroleum Exporting Countries (OPEC) worked in concert to decrease oil production in order to raise the price of oil. The 10-fold increase in the price of oil that OPEC achieved during the 1970s drove up per-unit production costs and jolted the U.S. aggregate supply curve leftward. By contrast, a sharp decline in oil prices in the mid-1980s resulted in a rightward shift of the U.S. aggregate supply curve. In 1999 OPEC again reasserted itself, raising oil prices and therefore per-unit production costs for some U.S. producers including airlines and shipping companies like FedEx and UPS. In 2008 the price of oil shot upward, but this increase was attributed to greater demand rather than to decreases in supply caused by OPEC. But keep in mind that no matter what their cause, increases in the price of oil and other resources raise production costs and decrease aggregate supply.

Exchange-rate fluctuations are another factor that may alter the price of imported resources. Suppose that the dollar appreciates, enabling U.S. firms to obtain more foreign currency with each dollar. This means that domestic producers face a lower *dollar* price of imported resources. U.S. firms will respond by increasing their imports of foreign resources, thereby lowering their per-unit production costs at each level of output. Falling per-unit production costs will shift the U.S. aggregate supply curve to the right.

A depreciation of the dollar will have the opposite set of effects and will shift the aggregate supply curve to the left.

Productivity

productivity
A measure of real output per unit of input.

The second major determinant of aggregate supply is **productivity,** which is a measure of the relationship between a nation's level of real output and the amount of resources used to produce that output. Thus productivity is a measure of average real output, or of real output per unit of input:

$$\text{Productivity} = \frac{\text{total output}}{\text{total inputs}}$$

WORKED PROBLEMS

W 7.1

Productivity and costs

With no change in resource prices, increases in productivity affect aggregate supply by reducing the per-unit production cost of output. Recall that this cost is determined by dividing the total cost of production by the dollar amount of output. For example, if the total cost of production is $20 billion and total output is $40 billion, per-unit production cost is $.50. If productivity rises such that output increases from $40 billion to $60 billion, the per-unit production cost will fall from $.50 (= $20/$40) to $.33 (= $20/$60).

The generalization is this: By reducing per-unit production costs, increases in productivity shift the aggregate supply curve to the right. The main source of productivity advance is improved production technology, often embodied within new plant and equipment that replaces old plant and equipment. Other sources of productivity increases are a better-educated and better-trained workforce, improved forms of business enterprises, and the reallocation of labor resources from lower-productivity to higher-productivity uses.

Much rarer, decreases in productivity increase per-unit production costs and therefore reduce aggregate supply (shift the AS curve to the left).

Legal-Institutional Environment

Changes in the legal-institutional setting in which businesses operate are the final determinant of aggregate supply. Such changes may alter the per-unit costs of output and, if so, shift the aggregate supply curve. Two changes of this type are (1) changes in business taxes and (2) changes in the extent of regulation.

Business Taxes Higher business taxes, such as sales, excise, and payroll taxes, increase per-unit costs and reduce short-run aggregate supply in much the same way as a wage increase does. An increase in such taxes paid by businesses will increase per-unit production costs and shift aggregate supply to the left.

Government Regulation It is usually costly for businesses to comply with government regulations. More regulation therefore tends to increase per-unit production costs and shift the aggregate supply curve to the left. "Supply-side" proponents of deregulation of the economy have argued forcefully that, by increasing efficiency and reducing the paperwork associated with complex regulations, deregulation will reduce per-unit costs and shift the aggregate supply curve to the right. Other economists are less certain. Deregulation that results in accounting manipulations, monopolization, and business failures is likely to shift the AS curve to the left rather than to the right.

Equilibrium Price Level and Real GDP

Of all the possible combinations of price levels and levels of real GDP, which combination will the economy gravitate toward, at least in the short run? Figure 7.7 and its accompanying table provide the answer. Equilibrium occurs at the price level that equalizes the amounts of real output demanded and supplied. The intersection of the aggregate demand curve AD and the aggregate supply curve AS establishes the

FIGURE 7.7 The equilibrium price level and equilibrium real GDP. The intersection of the aggregate demand curve and the aggregate supply curve determines the economy's equilibrium price level. At the equilibrium price level of 100 (in index-value terms), the $510 billion of real output demanded matches the $510 billion of real output supplied. So equilibrium real GDP is $510 billion.

Real Output Demanded (Billions)	Price Level (Index Number)	Real Output Supplied (Billions)
$506	108	$513
508	104	512
510	**100**	**510**
512	96	507
514	92	502

equilibrium price level
The price level at which the aggregate demand curve and the aggregate supply curve intersect.

equilibrium real output
The level of real GDP at which the aggregate demand curve and aggregate supply curve intersect.

INTERACTIVE GRAPHS

G 7.1
Aggregate demand–aggregate supply

---

economy's **equilibrium price level** and **equilibrium real output.** So aggregate demand and aggregate supply jointly establish the price level and level of real GDP.

In Figure 7.7 the equilibrium price level and level of real output are 100 and $510 billion, respectively. To illustrate why, suppose the price level is 92 rather than 100. We see from the table that the lower price level will encourage businesses to produce real output of $502 billion. This is shown by point a on the AS curve in the graph. But, as revealed by the table and point b on the aggregate demand curve, buyers will want to purchase $514 billion of real output at price level 92. Competition among buyers to purchase the lesser available real output of $502 billion will eliminate the $12 billion (= $514 billion − $502 billion) shortage and pull up the price level to 100.

As the table and graph show, the rise in the price level from 92 to 100 encourages producers to increase their real output from $502 billion to $510 billion and causes buyers to scale back their purchases from $514 billion to $510 billion. When equality occurs between the amounts of real output produced and purchased, as it does at price level 100, the economy has achieved equilibrium (here, at $510 billion of real GDP). Note that although the equilibrium price level happens to be 100 in our example, nothing special is implied by that. Any price level can be an equilibrium price level.

Changes in the Price Level and Real GDP

Aggregate demand and aggregate supply typically change from one period to the next. If aggregate demand and aggregate supply increase proportionately over time, real GDP will expand and neither demand-pull inflation nor cyclical unemployment will occur. But we know from our discussion of the business cycle that macroeconomic stability is not always certain. A number of less-desirable situations can confront the economy. Let's apply the model to several such situations. For simplicity we will use P and Q symbols, rather than actual numbers. Remember that these symbols represent price index values and amounts of real GDP.

APPLYING THE ANALYSIS

Demand-Pull Inflation

Suppose the economy is operating at its full-employment output and businesses and government increase their spending—actions that shift the aggregate demand curve to the right. Our list of determinants of aggregate demand (Figure 7.2) provides several reasons why this shift might occur. Perhaps firms boost their investment spending because they anticipate higher future profits from investments in new capital. Those profits are predicated on having new equipment and facilities that incorporate a number of new technologies. And perhaps government increases spending to expand national defense.

As shown by the rise in the price level from P_1 to P_2 in Figure 7.8, the increase in aggregate demand beyond the full-employment level of output moves the economy from a to b and causes inflation. This is *demand-pull inflation* because the price level is being pulled up by the increase in aggregate demand. Also, observe that the increase in demand expands real output from the full-employment level Q_f to Q_1. The distance between Q_1 and Q_f is a positive, or "inflationary," *GDP gap*: Actual GDP exceeds potential GDP.*

A classic American example of demand-pull inflation occurred in the late 1960s. The escalation of the war in Vietnam resulted in a 40 percent increase in defense

---

*This positive GDP gap cannot last forever because eventually the price of labor and other inputs will increase and therefore shift the short-run AS curve leftward. The economy will eventually return to its full-employment output, Q_f, along its vertical long-run aggregate supply curve (not shown) that is located there.

FIGURE 7.8
Demand-pull inflation. The increase of aggregate demand from AD_1 to AD_2 moves the economy from *a* to *b*, causing demand-pull inflation of P_1 to P_2. It also causes a positive GDP gap of Q_1 minus Q_f.

spending between 1965 and 1967 and another 15 percent increase in 1968. The rise in government spending, imposed on an already growing economy, shifted the economy's aggregate demand curve to the right, producing the worst inflation in two decades. Actual GDP exceeded potential GDP, thereby creating an inflationary GDP gap. Inflation jumped from 1.6 percent in 1965 to 5.7 percent by 1970.

A more recent example of demand-pull inflation occurred in the late 1980s. As aggregate demand expanded beyond its full-employment level between 1986 and 1990, the price level rose at an increasing rate. Specifically, the annual rate of inflation increased from 1.9 percent in 1986 to 3.6 percent in 1987 to 4.1 percent in 1988 to 4.8 percent in 1989. In terms of Figure 7.8, the aggregate demand curve moved rightward from year to year, raising the price level and the size of the positive GDP gap. The gap closed and the rate of inflation fell as the expansion gave way to the recession of 1990–1991.

QUESTION: How is the upward slope of the aggregate supply curve important in explaining demand-pull inflation?

Cost-Push Inflation

Inflation also can arise on the aggregate supply side of the economy. Suppose that warfare in the Middle East severely disrupts world oil supplies and drives up oil prices by some huge amount, say, 300 percent. Higher energy prices would spread through the economy, driving up production and distribution costs on a wide variety of goods. The U.S. aggregate supply curve would spring to the left, say, from AS_1 to AS_2 in Figure 7.9. The resulting increase in the price level would be *cost-push inflation*.

The effects of a leftward shift in aggregate supply are doubly bad. When aggregate supply shifts from AS_1 to AS_2, the economy moves from *a* to *b*. The price level rises from P_1 to P_2 and real output declines from Q_f to Q_1. Along with the cost-push inflation, a recession (and negative GDP gap) occurs. That is exactly what happened in the United States in the mid-1970s when the price of oil rocketed upward.

FIGURE 7.9 Cost-push inflation. A leftward shift of aggregate supply from AS$_1$ to AS$_2$ moves the economy from a to b, raises the price level from P_1 to P_2, and produces cost-push inflation. Real output declines and a negative GDP gap (of Q_1 minus Q_f) occurs.

Today, the effect of oil prices on the U.S. economy has weakened relative to earlier periods. In the mid-1970s, oil expenditures were about 10 percent of U.S. GDP, compared to only 3 percent today. So the U.S. economy is now less vulnerable to cost-push inflation arising from oil-related "aggregate supply shocks."

QUESTION: Which is costlier to an economy in terms of lost real output, an equal degree of demand-pull inflation or cost-push inflation?

© Royalty-Free/CORBIS   © Photodisc/Getty Images

PHOTO OP Demand-Pull versus Cost-Push Inflation

A boom in investment spending, such as that for new construction, can cause demand-pull inflation. Soaring prices of key resources, such as oil, can cause cost-push inflation.

Downward Price-Level Inflexibility

We have just seen examples where, despite what we have learned about price "stickiness," the price level is readily flexible upward. But in the U.S. economy, deflation (a decline in the price level) rarely occurs even though the rate of inflation rises and falls. Why is the price level "sticky" or inflexible, particularly on the downside? Economists have offered several possible reasons for this:

- *Fear of price wars*   Some oligopolists may be concerned that if they reduce their prices, rivals not only will match their price cuts but may retaliate by making even deeper cuts. An initial price cut may touch off an unwanted *price war:* successively deeper and deeper rounds of price cuts. In such a situation, all the firms end up with far less profit or higher losses than would be the case if they had simply maintained their prices. For this reason, each firm may resist making the initial price cut, choosing instead to reduce production and lay off workers.

- *Menu costs*   Firms that think a recession will be relatively short-lived may be reluctant to cut their prices. One reason is what economists metaphorically call *menu costs,* named after their most obvious example: the cost of printing new menus when a restaurant decides to reduce its prices. But lowering prices also creates other costs. There are the costs of (1) estimating the magnitude and duration of the shift in demand to determine whether prices should be lowered, (2) repricing items held in inventory, (3) printing and mailing new catalogs, and (4) communicating new prices to customers, perhaps through advertising. When menu costs are present, firms may choose to avoid them by retaining current prices. That is, they may wait to see if the decline in aggregate demand is permanent.

- *Wage contracts*   It usually is not profitable for firms to cut their product prices if they cannot also cut their wage rates. Wages are usually inflexible downward because large parts of the labor force work under contracts prohibiting wage cuts for the duration of the contract. (It is not uncommon for collective bargaining agreements in major industries to run for 3 years.) Similarly, the wages and salaries of nonunion workers are usually adjusted once a year, rather than quarterly or monthly.

- *Morale, effort, and productivity*   Wage inflexibility downward is reinforced by the reluctance of many employers to reduce wage rates. If worker productivity (output per hour of work) remains constant, lower wages *do* reduce labor costs per unit of output. But lower wages might impair worker morale and work effort, thereby reducing productivity. Considered alone, lower productivity raises labor costs per unit of output because less output is produced. If the higher labor costs resulting from reduced productivity exceed the cost savings from the lower wage, then wage cuts will increase rather than reduce labor costs per unit of output. In such situations, firms will resist lowering wages when they are faced with a decline in aggregate demand.

- *Minimum wage*   The minimum wage imposes a legal floor under the wages of the least skilled workers. Firms paying those wages cannot reduce that wage rate when aggregate demand declines.

Conclusion: In the United States, the price level readily rises but only reluctantly falls.

ILLUSTRATING THE IDEA

The Ratchet Effect

A *ratchet analogy* is a good way to think about the asymmetry of price-level changes. A ratchet is a tool or mechanism such as a winch, car jack, or socket wrench that cranks a wheel forward but does not allow it to go backward. Properly set, each allows the operator to move an object (boat, car, or nut) in one direction while preventing it from moving in the opposite direction.

The price level, wage rates, and per-unit production costs readily rise when aggregate demand increases along the aggregate supply curve. In the United States, the price level has increased in every year but one since 1950.

But the price level, wage rates, and per-unit production costs are inflexible downward when aggregate demand declines. The U.S. price level has fallen in only a single year (1955) since 1950, even though aggregate demand and real output have declined in a number of years.

In terms of our analogy, increases in aggregate demand ratchet the U.S. price level upward. Once in place, the higher price level remains until it is ratcheted up again. The higher price level tends to remain even with declines in aggregate demand. Inflation rates *do* rise and fall in the United States, but the price level mainly rises.

QUESTION: Does the ratchet analogy also apply to changes in real GDP? Why or why not?

APPLYING THE ANALYSIS

Recession and Cyclical Unemployment

Decreases in aggregate demand, combined with downward price-level inflexibility, can create recessions. For example, suppose that for some reason investment spending sharply declines. In Figure 7.10 we show the resulting decline in aggregate demand as a leftward shift from AD_1 to AD_2.

With the price level inflexible downward at P_1, the decline in aggregate demand moves the economy from *a* to *b* and reduces real output from Q_f to Q_1. The distance between Q_1 and Q_f measures the negative GDP gap—the amount by which actual output falls short of potential output. Because fewer workers are needed to produce the lower output, *cyclical unemployment* arises.

FIGURE 7.10 **A recession.**
If the price level is downwardly inflexible, a decline of aggregate demand from AD_1 to AD_2 will move the economy from *a* to *b* and reduce real GDP from Q_f to Q_1. Idle production capacity, cyclical unemployment, and a negative GDP gap (of Q_1 minus Q_f) will result.

All recent demand-caused recessions in the United States have mimicked the "GDP gap but no deflation" scenario shown in Figure 7.10. Consider the recession that began in December 2007. In 2008, home foreclosures skyrocketed, several major financial institutions failed, and credit became very tight. New construction and other investment spending plummeted. Because of the resulting decline of aggregate demand, GDP fell short of potential output. The nation's unemployment rate rose from 4.7 percent in December 2007 to 10.1 percent in October 2009. The price level fell in some months and the rate of inflation declined (an outcome called *disinflation*). Considering the full period, however, *deflation* did not occur.

QUESTION: How can a decline in expected investment returns on the construction of new houses, condominiums, and office buildings contribute to a recession?

The Multiplier Effect

Before leaving the topic of aggregate demand and aggregate supply, we need to supply two additional insights. First, shifts in the aggregate demand curves such as those in Figures 7.8 and 7.10 embody an "initial change" in spending, say, an increase in investment, followed by successive rounds of additional spending by businesses and households that are on the receiving end of the prior spending. Our shifts from one AD curve to another AD curve simply show the final results.

Assuming an economy has room to expand, an initial change in investment spending changes aggregate demand and GDP (and thus income) by more than the initial spending change. That surprising result is called the *multiplier effect*. The **multiplier** measures how much larger the final change in GDP will be; it is the ratio of a change in GDP to the initial change in spending (in this case, investment). Stated generally,

multiplier
The ratio of a change in GDP to an initial change in spending.

$$\text{Multiplier} = \frac{\text{change in real GDP}}{\text{initial change in spending}}$$

By rearranging this equation, we can also say that

$$\text{Change in real GDP} = \text{multiplier} \times \text{initial change in spending}$$

So if investment in an economy rises by $30 billion and aggregate demand and real GDP increase by $90 billion as a result, we then know from our first equation that the multiplier is 3 (= $90/30).

Note these two points about the multiplier:

- The initial change in spending is often associated with investment spending because of investment's volatility. But changes in consumption spending (unrelated to change in income), government purchases, and net exports also lead to the multiplier effect.
- The multiplier works in both directions. An increase in initial spending may create a multiple increase in GDP, and a decrease in spending may be multiplied into a larger decrease in GDP.

The multiplier effect follows from the fact that the economy supports repetitive, continuous flows of expenditures and income, as we saw in the circular flow model in Chapter 2. Through this process, dollars spent by Smith are received as income by

Chin, who then spends a portion that is received as income by Gonzales, and so on. Because a portion of new income is saved (not spent), the amount of new spending in each successive round declines, eventually bringing the multiplier process to an end.

Self-Correction?

The second insight is a caution: There is some evidence that the price level and average level of wages are becoming more flexible downward in the United States. Intense international competition and the declining power of unions in the United States seem to be undermining the ability of firms and workers to resist price and wage cuts when faced with falling aggregate demand. This increased flexibility of some prices and wages may be one reason the recession of 2001 was relatively mild. The U.S. auto manufacturers, for example, maintained output in the face of falling demand by offering zero-interest loans on auto purchases. This, in effect, was a disguised price cut.

In theory, fully flexible downward prices and wages would automatically "self-correct" a recession. Reduced aggregate demand, with its accompanying negative GDP gap and greater unemployment, would reduce the price level and level of (nominal) wages. In Figure 7.10, the lower wages would reduce per-unit production costs and shift the AS curve rightward. Eventually the economy would return to its full-employment output, but at a considerably lower price level than before. That is, the economy would move back to its long-run aggregate supply curve, like the one shown in Figure 7.5. (We will demonstrate this adjustment mechanism graphically in Chapter 11: Long-Run Aggregate Supply and Aggregate Demand.)

In reality, the government and monetary authorities have been reluctant to wait for these slow and uncertain "corrections." Instead, they focus on trying to move the aggregate demand curve to its prerecession location. For example, throughout 2001 the Federal Reserve lowered interest rates to try to halt the recession and promote recovery. Those Fed actions, along with large federal tax cuts, increased military spending, and strong demand for new housing, helped increase aggregate demand and spur recovery. The economy haltingly resumed its economic growth in 2002 and 2003, and then expanded rapidly in 2004 and 2005. Robust growth continued in 2006 and for the first three quarters of 2007.

Toward the end of 2007, however, crises in the housing and credit markets precipitated a new recession, prompting the Fed to begin a series of interest rate cuts to try to boost spending. In February 2008, the federal government passed a tax rebate package, which it followed in February 2009 with $787 billion in spending increases and tax cuts, also in an effort to support aggregate demand and deal with the recession. We will examine stabilization policies such as these in the chapters that follow.

Summary

1. The aggregate demand–aggregate supply model (AD-AS model) enables analysis of simultaneous changes of real GDP and the price level.

2. The aggregate demand curve shows the level of real output that the economy will purchase at each price level. It slopes downward because higher price levels dissuade U.S. businesses and households, along with foreign buyers, from purchasing as much output as before.

3. The determinants of aggregate demand consist of spending by domestic consumers, businesses, and government and by foreign buyers. Changes in the factors listed in Figure 7.2 alter the spending by these groups and shift the aggregate demand curve.

4. The aggregate supply curve shows the levels of real output that businesses will produce at various possible price levels. The slope of the aggregate supply curve depends upon the

flexibility of input and output prices. Since these vary over time, aggregate supply curves are categorized into three time horizons, each having different underlying assumptions about the flexibility of input and output prices.

5. The *immediate-short-run aggregate supply curve* assumes that both input prices and output prices are fixed. With output prices fixed, the aggregate supply curve is a horizontal line at the current price level. The *short-run aggregate supply curve* assumes nominal wages and other input prices remain fixed while output prices vary. The aggregate supply curve is generally upsloping because per-unit production costs, and hence the prices that firms must receive, rise as real output expands. The aggregate supply curve is relatively steep to the right of the full-employment output level and relatively flat to the left of it. The *long-run aggregate supply curve* assumes that nominal wages and other input prices fully match any change in the price level. The curve is vertical at the full-employment output level.

6. Because the short-run aggregate supply curve is the only version of aggregate supply that can handle simultaneous changes in the price level and real output, it serves well as the core aggregate supply curve for analyzing the business cycle and economic policy. Unless stated otherwise, all references to "aggregate supply" refer to the short-run aggregate supply curve.

7. Figure 7.6 lists the determinants of aggregate supply: input prices, productivity, and the legal-institutional environment. A change in any one of these factors will change per-unit production costs at each level of output and therefore will shift the aggregate supply curve.

8. The intersection of the aggregate demand and aggregate supply curves determines an economy's equilibrium price level and real GDP. At the intersection, the quantity of real GDP demanded equals the quantity of real GDP supplied.

9. Increases in aggregate demand beyond the full-employment output cause inflation and positive GDP gaps (actual GDP exceeds potential GDP). Such gaps eventually evaporate as wages and other input prices rise to match the increase in the price level.

10. Leftward shifts of the aggregate supply curve reflect increases in per-unit production costs at each level of output and cause cost-push inflation, with accompanying negative GDP gaps.

11. Shifts of the aggregate demand curve to the left of the full-employment output cause recession, negative GDP gaps, and cyclical unemployment. The price level typically does not fall during U.S. recessions because of downwardly inflexible prices and wages. This inflexibility results from fear of price wars, menu costs, wage contracts, morale concerns, and minimum wages.

12. In theory, price and wage flexibility would allow the economy automatically to self-correct from a recession. In reality, downward price and wage flexibility make the process slow and uncertain. Recessions usually prompt the federal government and the Federal Reserve to take actions to try to increase aggregate demand.

13. Changes in spending (consumption, investment, government purchases, and net exports) will lead to larger changes in GDP through the multiplier effect.

Terms and Concepts

aggregate demand–aggregate supply (AD-AS) model

aggregate demand

determinants of aggregate demand

exchange rates

aggregate supply

immediate-short-run aggregate supply curve

short-run aggregate supply curve

long-run aggregate supply curve

determinants of aggregate supply

productivity

equilibrium price level

equilibrium real output

multiplier

Questions ![McGraw-Hill Connect ECONOMICS]

1. What is the general relationship between a country's price level and the quantity of its domestic output (real GDP) demanded? Who are the buyers of U.S. real GDP? LO1

2. What assumptions cause the immediate-short-run aggregate supply curve to be horizontal? Why is the long-run aggregate supply curve vertical? Explain the shape of the short-run aggregate supply curve. Why is the short-run curve relatively flat to the left of the full-employment output and relatively steep to the right? LO2

3. Other things equal, what effects would each of the following have on aggregate demand or aggregate supply? In each

case use a diagram to show the expected effects on the equilibrium price level and the level of real output. LO3

a. A reduction in the economy's real interest rate.

b. A major increase in federal spending for health care (with no increase in taxes).

c. The complete disintegration of OPEC, causing oil prices to fall by one-half.

d. A 10 percent reduction in personal income tax rates (with no change in government spending).

e. A sizable increase in labor productivity (with no change in nominal wages).

f. A 12 percent increase in nominal wages (with no change in productivity).

g. A sizable depreciation in the international value of the dollar.

4. Other things equal, what effect will each of the following have on the equilibrium price level and level of real output? LO3

a. An increase in aggregate demand in the steep portion of the aggregate supply curve.

b. An increase in aggregate supply, with no change in aggregate demand (assume that prices and wages are flexible upward and downward).

c. Equal increases in aggregate demand and aggregate supply.

d. A reduction in aggregate demand in the relatively flat portion of the aggregate supply curve.

e. An increase in aggregate demand and a decrease in aggregate supply.

5. Why does a reduction in aggregate demand tend to reduce real output, rather than the price level? LO4

6. Explain: "Unemployment can be caused by a decrease of aggregate demand or a decrease of aggregate supply." In each case, specify the price-level outcomes. LO4

7. In early 2001 investment spending sharply declined in the United States. In the 2 months following the September 11, 2001, attacks on the United States, consumption also declined. Use AD-AS analysis to show the two impacts on real GDP. LO4

8. Using the concept of the multiplier, explain why mass layoffs by large companies such as Boeing or General Motors are a concern to the citizens and leaders where those firms are located. LO4

Problems

1. Suppose that consumer spending initially rises by $5 billion for every 1 percent rise in household wealth and that investment spending initially rises by $20 billion for every 1 percentage point fall in the real interest rate. Also assume that the economy's multiplier is 4. If household wealth falls by 5 percent because of declining house values, and the real interest rate falls by 2 percentage points, in what direction and by how much will the aggregate demand curve initially shift at each price level? In what direction and by how much will it eventually shift? LO1

2. Answer the following questions on the basis of the three sets of data below for the country of North Vaudeville: LO2

a. Which set of data illustrates aggregate supply in the immediate short-run in North Vaudeville? The short run? The long run?

b. Assuming no change in hours of work, if real output per hour of work increases by 10 percent, what will be the new levels of real GDP in the right column of A? Does the new data reflect an increase in aggregate supply or does it indicate a decrease in aggregate supply?

3. Suppose that the aggregate demand and aggregate supply schedules for a hypothetical economy are as shown in the table to the right. LO3

Amount of Real GDP Demanded, Billions	Price Level (Price Index)	Amount of Real GDP Supplied, Billions
$100	300	$450
200	250	400
300	200	300
400	150	200
500	100	100

a. Use the data above to graph the aggregate demand and aggregate supply curves. What is the equilibrium price level and the equilibrium level of real output in this hypothetical economy? Is the equilibrium real output also necessarily the full-employment real output?

b. If the price level in this economy is 150, will quantity demanded equal, exceed, or fall short of quantity supplied? By what amount? If the price level is 250, will quantity demanded equal, exceed, or fall short of quantity supplied? By what amount?

(A)		(B)		(C)	
Price Level	Real GDP	Price Level	Real GDP	Price Level	Real GDP
110	275	100	200	110	225
100	250	100	225	100	225
95	225	100	250	95	225
90	200	100	275	90	225

c. Suppose that buyers desire to purchase $200 billion of extra real output at each price level. Sketch in the new aggregate demand curve as AD_1. What is the new equilibrium price level and level of real output?

4. Suppose that the following table shows an economy's relationship between real output and the inputs needed to produce that output: **LO3**

Input Quantity	Real GDP
150.0	$400
112.5	300
75.0	200

a. What is productivity in this economy?

b. What is the per-unit cost of production if the price of each input unit is $2?

c. Assume that the input price increases from $2 to $3 with no accompanying change in productivity. What is the new per-unit cost of production? In what direction would the $1 increase in input price push the economy's aggregate supply curve? What effect would this shift of aggregate supply have on the price level and the level of real output?

d. Suppose that the increase in input price does not occur but, instead, that productivity increases by 100 percent. What would be the new per-unit cost of production? What effect would this change in per-unit production cost have on the economy's aggregate supply curve? What effect would this shift of aggregate supply have on the price level and the level of real output?

5. Refer to the data in the table that accompanies problem 2. Suppose that the present equilibrium price level and level of real GDP are 100 and $225, and that data set B represents the relevant aggregate supply schedule for the economy. **LO4**

a. What must be the current amount of real output demanded at the 100 price level?

b. If the amount of output demanded declined by $25 at the 100 price levels shown in B, what would be the new equilibrium real GDP? In business cycle terminology, what would economists call this change in real GDP?

FURTHER TEST YOUR KNOWLEDGE AT
www.mcconnellbrief2e.com

At the text's Online Learning Center, **www.mcconnellbrief2e.com**, you will find one or more web-based questions that require information from the Internet to answer. We urge you to check them out, since they will familiarize you with websites that may be helpful in other courses and perhaps even in your career. The OLC also features multiple-choice quizzes that give instant feedback and provides other helpful ways to further test your knowledge of the chapter.

Visit your mobile app store and download the McConnell Brief Edition: Study Econ app today!

8

After reading this chapter, you should be able to:

1 Identify and explain the purposes, tools, and limitations of fiscal policy.

2 Explain the role of built-in stabilizers in dampening business cycles.

3 Describe how the cyclically adjusted budget reveals the status of U.S. fiscal policy.

4 Discuss the size, composition, and consequences of the U.S. public debt.

5 Explain why there is a long-run fiscal imbalance in the Social Security system.

Fiscal Policy, Deficits, and Debt

ORIGIN OF THE IDEA

O 8.1
Fiscal policy

fiscal policy
Changes in government spending or taxation to promote full employment, price-level stability, and economic growth.

In the previous chapter we saw that an excessive increase in aggregate demand can cause demand-pull inflation and that a significant decline in aggregate demand can cause recession and cyclical unemployment. For those reasons, central governments sometimes use budgetary actions to try to "stimulate the economy" or "rein in inflation." Such countercyclical **fiscal policy** consists of deliberate changes in government spending and tax collections designed to achieve full employment, control inflation, and encourage economic growth. (The adjective "fiscal" simply means "financial.")

We begin this chapter by examining the logic behind fiscal policy, its current status, and its limitations. Then we examine two related topics: the U.S. public debt and the Social Security funding problem.

Our discussion of fiscal policy and public debt is very timely. In 2009, the Congress and the Obama administration began a $787 billion stimulus program designed to help lift the U.S. economy out of a deep recession. This fiscal policy contributed to a $1.4 trillion federal budget deficit in 2009, which increased the size of the U.S. public debt to $11.9 trillion. Continued deficits increased the public debt to over $14.3 trillion in July 2011, and it has become a major political issue.

Fiscal Policy and the AD-AS Model

The fiscal policy that we have been describing is *discretionary* (or "active"). It is often initiated on the advice of the president's **Council of Economic Advisers (CEA),** a group of three economists appointed by the president to provide expertise and assistance on economic matters. Such changes in government spending and taxes are *at the option* of the federal government. They do not occur automatically, independent of congressional action. The latter changes are *nondiscretionary* (or "passive" or "automatic"), and we will examine them later in this chapter.

Council of Economic Advisers (CEA)
A group of three economists appointed by the U.S. president to provide advice and assistance on economic matters.

Expansionary Fiscal Policy

When recession occurs, an **expansionary fiscal policy** may be in order. This policy consists of government spending increases, tax reductions, or both, designed to increase aggregate demand and therefore raise real GDP. Consider Figure 8.1, where we suppose that a sharp decline in investment spending has shifted the economy's aggregate demand curve to the left from AD_1 to AD_2. (Disregard the arrow for now.) The cause of the recession may be that profit expectations on investment projects have dimmed, curtailing investment spending and reducing aggregate demand.

Suppose the economy's potential or full-employment output is $510 billion in Figure 8.1. If the price level is inflexible downward at P_1, the aggregate demand curve slides leftward at that price level and reduces real GDP to $490 billion. A negative GDP gap of $20 billion (= $490 billion − $510 billion) arises. An increase in unemployment accompanies this negative GDP gap because fewer workers are needed to produce the reduced output. In short, the economy depicted is suffering both recession and cyclical unemployment.

expansionary fiscal policy
An increase in government spending, a decrease in taxes, or some combination of the two for the purpose of increasing aggregate demand and real output.

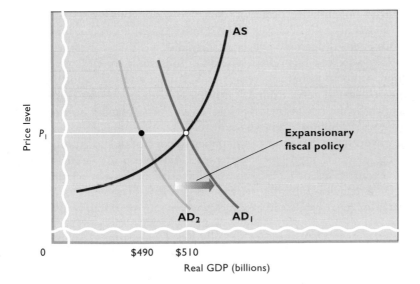

FIGURE 8.1 Expansionary fiscal policy. Expansionary fiscal policy uses increases in government spending, tax cuts, or a combination of both to increase aggregate demand and push the economy out of recession. Here, this policy increases aggregate demand from AD_2 to AD_1, increases real GDP from $490 billion to $510 billion, and restores full employment.

What fiscal policy should the federal government adopt to try to remedy the situation? It has three main options: (1) government-spending increases, (2) tax reductions, or (3) some combination of the two. If the federal budget is balanced at the outset, expansionary fiscal policy will create a government **budget deficit** (government spending in excess of tax revenues).

budget deficit
The amount by which expenditures of the federal government exceed its revenues in any year.

Government Spending Increases To increase aggregate demand, the federal government can increase its spending. For example, it might boost spending on highways, education, and health care. Other things equal, a sufficient increase in government spending will shift an economy's aggregate demand curve to the right, as from AD_2 to AD_1 in Figure 8.1. Observe that real output rises to $510 billion, up $20 billion from its recessionary level of $490 billion. Firms increase their employment to the full-employment level, output increases, and the negative GDP gap disappears.

Tax Reductions Alternatively, the government could reduce taxes to shift the aggregate demand curve rightward, as from AD_2 to AD_1. Suppose the government cuts personal income taxes, which increases disposable income. Households will spend a large part of that income and save the rest. The part spent—the new consumption spending—will increase aggregate demand. In Figure 8.1, this increase in aggregate demand from AD_2 to AD_1 expands real GDP by $20 billion, eliminating the negative GDP gap. Employment increases accordingly, and the unemployment rate falls.

A tax cut must be larger than an increase in government spending to achieve the same rightward shift of the aggregate demand curve. This is because households save part of the higher after-tax income provided by the tax cut. Only the part of the tax cut that increases consumption spending shifts the aggregate demand curve to the right.

Combined Government Spending Increases and Tax Reductions The government may combine spending increases and tax cuts to produce the desired initial increase in spending and the eventual increase in aggregate demand and real GDP. In the economy depicted in Figure 8.1, there is some combination of greater government spending and lower taxes (increased consumption spending) that will shift the aggregate demand curve from AD_2 to AD_1 and remove the negative GDP gap.

Contractionary Fiscal Policy

contractionary fiscal policy
A decrease in government spending, an increase in taxes, or some combination of the two for the purpose of decreasing aggregate demand and halting inflation.

When demand-pull inflation occurs, a restrictive or **contractionary fiscal policy** may help control it. This policy consists of government spending reductions, tax increases, or both, designed to decrease aggregate demand and therefore lower or eliminate inflation. Take a look at Figure 8.2, where the full-employment level of real GDP is $510 billion. Suppose a sharp increase in investment and net export spending shifts the aggregate demand curve from AD_3 to AD_4. The outcomes are demand-pull inflation, as shown by the rise of the price level from P_1 to P_2, and a positive GDP gap of $12 billion (=$522 billion − $510 billion).

If the government decides on fiscal policy to control this inflation, its options are the opposite of those used to combat recession. It can (1) decrease government spending, (2) raise taxes, or (3) use some combination of those two policies. When the economy faces demand-pull inflation, fiscal policy should move toward a government **budget surplus** (tax revenues in excess of government spending).

budget surplus
The amount by which revenues of the federal government exceed its expenditures in any year.

Government Spending Decreases Reduced government spending shifts the aggregate demand curve leftward to control demand-pull inflation. In Figure 8.2, this

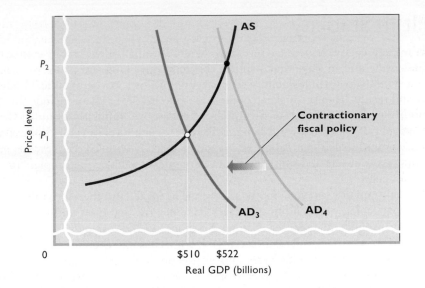

FIGURE 8.2 Contractionary fiscal policy. Contractionary fiscal policy uses decreases in government spending, increases in taxes, or a combination of both to reduce aggregate demand and slow or eliminate demand-pull inflation. Here, this policy shifts the aggregate demand curve from AD_4 to AD_3, removes the upward pressure on the price level, and halts the demand-pull inflation. Note, however, that even though the inflation is stopped, the presence of inflexible ("sticky") prices may prevent the price level from falling to P_1.

spending cut shifts the aggregate demand curve leftward from AD_4 to AD_3. If the price level were downwardly flexible, the price level would return to P_1, where it was before demand-pull inflation occurred. That is, deflation would occur.

Unfortunately, the actual economy is not as simple and tidy as Figure 8.2 suggests. Increases in aggregate demand tend to ratchet the price level upward, but declines in aggregate demand do not seem to push the price level downward. So stopping inflation is a matter of halting the rise of the price level, not trying to lower it to the previous level. Demand-pull inflation usually is experienced as a continual rightward shifting of the aggregate demand curve. Contractionary fiscal policy is designed to stop a further shift, not to restore a lower price level. Successful fiscal policy eliminates a continuing positive (and thus inflationary) GDP gap and prevents the price level from continuing its inflationary rise. Nevertheless, Figure 8.2 displays the basic principle: Reductions in government expenditures can be used as a fiscal policy action to tame demand-pull inflation.

Tax Increases

Just as government can use tax cuts to increase consumption spending, it can use tax increases to reduce consumption spending. In the economy in Figure 8.2, the government must raise taxes sufficiently to reduce consumption such that the aggregate demand curve will shift leftward from AD_4 to AD_3. That way, the demand-pull inflation will have been controlled.

Because part of any tax increase reduces saving rather than consumption, a tax increase must exceed a decrease in government spending to cause the same leftward shift of the aggregate demand curve. Only the part of the tax increase that lowers consumption spending reduces aggregate demand.

Combined Government Spending Decreases and Tax Increases

The government may choose to combine spending decreases and tax increases in order to reduce aggregate demand and check inflation. Some combination of lower government spending and higher taxes will shift the aggregate demand curve from AD_4 to AD_3.

Built-In Stability

To some degree, government tax revenues change automatically over the course of the business cycle and in ways that stabilize the economy. This automatic response, or built-in stability, constitutes nondiscretionary (or "passive" or "automatic") budgetary policy and results from the makeup of most tax systems. We did not include this built-in stability in our discussion of fiscal policy because we implicitly assumed that the same amount of tax revenue was being collected at each level of GDP. But the actual U.S. tax system is such that *net tax revenues* vary directly with GDP. (*Net taxes* are tax revenues less transfers and subsidies. From here on, we will use the simpler "taxes" to mean "net taxes.")

Virtually any tax will yield more tax revenue as GDP (and therefore total income) rises. In particular, personal income taxes have progressive rates and thus generate more-than-proportionate increases in tax revenues as GDP expands. Furthermore, as GDP rises and more goods and services are purchased, revenues from corporate income taxes and from sales taxes and excise taxes also increase. And, similarly, revenues from payroll taxes rise as economic expansion creates more jobs and income. Conversely, when GDP declines, tax receipts from all these sources also decline.

Transfer payments (or "negative taxes") behave in the opposite way from tax revenues. For example, welfare and unemployment compensation payments decline during an economic expansion and increase during an economic contraction.

Automatic or Built-In Stabilizers

built-in stabilizer
Anything that increases the government's budget deficit (or reduces its budget surplus) during a recession and increases its budget surplus (or reduces its budget deficit) during expansion without requiring explicit action by policymakers.

A **built-in stabilizer** is anything that increases the government's budget deficit (or reduces its budget surplus) during a recession and increases its budget surplus (or reduces its budget deficit) during inflation without requiring explicit action by policymakers. As Figure 8.3 reveals, this is precisely what the U.S. tax system does. Government expenditures G are fixed and assumed to be independent of the level of GDP. Congress decides on a particular level of spending, but it does not determine the magnitude of tax revenues. Instead, it establishes tax rates, and the tax revenues then vary directly with the level of GDP that the economy achieves. Line T represents that direct relationship between tax revenues and GDP.

FIGURE 8.3 Built-in stability.
Tax revenues T vary directly with GDP, and government spending G is assumed to be independent of GDP. As GDP falls in a recession, deficits occur automatically and help alleviate the recession. As GDP rises during expansion, surpluses occur automatically and help offset possible inflation.

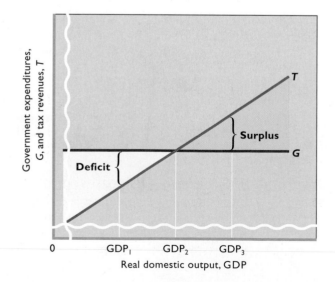

Economic Importance

The economic importance of the direct relationship between tax receipts and GDP becomes apparent when we consider that:

- Taxes reduce spending and aggregate demand.
- Reductions in spending are desirable when the economy is moving toward inflation, whereas increases in spending are desirable when the economy is slumping.

As shown in Figure 8.3, tax revenues automatically increase as GDP rises during prosperity, and since taxes reduce household and business spending, they restrain the economic expansion. That is, as the economy moves toward a higher GDP, tax revenues automatically rise and move the budget from deficit toward surplus. In Figure 8.3, observe that the high and perhaps inflationary income level GDP_3 automatically generates a contractionary budget surplus.

Conversely, as output and income fall during recession, tax revenues automatically decline, increasing spending by households and businesses and thus cushioning the economic contraction. With a falling GDP, tax receipts decline and move the government's budget from surplus toward deficit. In Figure 8.3, the low level of income GDP_1 will automatically yield an expansionary budget deficit.

Built-in stability has reduced the severity of U.S. business fluctuations, perhaps by as much as 8 to 10 percent of the change in GDP that otherwise would have occurred.[1] In recession year 2009, for example, revenues from the individual income tax fell by a staggering 22 percent. This decline helped keep household spending and real GDP from falling even more than they did. But built-in stabilizers can only dampen, not counteract, swings in real GDP. Discretionary fiscal policy (changes in tax rates and expenditures) or monetary policy (central bank-caused changes in interest rates) may be needed to correct recession or inflation of any appreciable magnitude.

Evaluating Fiscal Policy

How can we determine whether a government's discretionary fiscal policy is expansionary, neutral, or contractionary? We cannot simply examine the actual budget deficits or surpluses that take place under the current policy because they will necessarily include the automatic changes in tax revenues that accompany every change in GDP. In addition, the expansionary or contractionary strength of any change in discretionary fiscal policy depends not on its absolute size but on how large it is relative to the size of the economy. So, in evaluating the status of fiscal policy, we must adjust deficits and surpluses to eliminate automatic changes in tax revenues and also compare the sizes of the adjusted budget deficits and surpluses to the level of potential GDP.

Economists use the **cyclically adjusted budget** (or *full-employment budget*) to adjust actual federal budget deficits and surpluses to account for the changes in tax revenues that happen automatically whenever GDP changes. The cyclically adjusted budget measures what the federal budget deficit or surplus would have been under existing tax rates and government spending programs if the economy had achieved its full-employment level of GDP (its potential output). The idea is to compare *actual* government expenditures with the tax revenues *that would have occurred* if the economy had achieved full-employment GDP. That procedure removes budget deficits or surpluses that arise simply because of cyclical changes in GDP and thus tell us nothing

cyclically adjusted budget
A measure of what the federal budget deficit or surplus would be with existing tax rates and government spending programs if the economy had achieved its full-employment GDP in the year.

---

[1]Alan J. Auerbach and Daniel Feenberg, "The Significance of Federal Taxes as Automatic Stabilizers," *Journal of Economic Perspectives*, Summer 2000, p. 54.

FIGURE 8.4 Cyclically adjusted budget deficits. The cyclically adjusted budget deficit is zero at the full-employment output GDP_1. But it is also zero at the recessionary output GDP_2 because the $500 billion of government expenditures at GDP_2 equals the $500 billion of tax revenues that would be forthcoming at the full-employment GDP_1. Here, fiscal policy did not change as the economy slid into recession. The deficit that arose is simply a cyclical deficit.

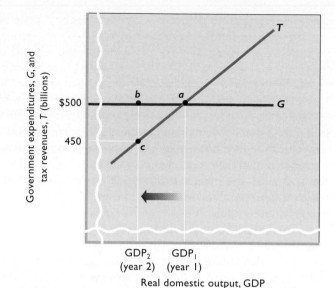

cyclical deficit
A federal budget deficit that is caused by a recession and the consequent decline in tax revenues.

about whether the government's current discretionary fiscal policy is fundamentally expansionary, contractionary, or neutral.

Consider Figure 8.4, where line G represents government expenditures and line T represents tax revenues. In full-employment year 1, government expenditures of $500 billion equal tax revenues of $500 billion, as indicated by the intersection of lines G and T at point a. The actual budget deficit and the cyclically adjusted budget deficit in year 1 are zero—government expenditures equal tax revenues, and government spending equals the tax revenues forthcoming at the full-employment output GDP_1. Obviously, the cyclically adjusted budget deficit *as a percentage of potential GDP* is also zero. The government's fiscal policy is neutral.

Now suppose that a recession occurs and GDP falls from GDP_1 to GDP_2, as shown in Figure 8.4. Let's also assume that the government takes no discretionary action, so lines G and T remain as shown in the figure. Tax revenues automatically fall to $450 billion (point c) at GDP_2, while government spending (we assume) remains unaltered at $500 billion (point b). A $50 billion actual budget deficit (represented by distance bc) arises. But this **cyclical deficit** is simply a by-product of the economy's slide into recession, not the result of discretionary fiscal actions by the government. We would be wrong to conclude from this deficit that the government is engaging in an expansionary fiscal policy. The government's fiscal policy has not changed; it is still neutral.

That fact is highlighted when we consider the cyclically adjusted budget deficit for year 2 in Figure 8.4. The $500 billion of government expenditures in year 2 is shown by b on line G. And, as shown by a on line T, $500 billion of tax revenues would have occurred if the economy had achieved its full-employment GDP. Because both b and a represent $500 billion, the cyclically adjusted budget deficit in year 2 is zero, as is this deficit as a percentage of potential GDP. Since the full-employment deficits are zero in both years, we know that government did not change its discretionary fiscal policy, even though a recession occurred and an actual deficit of $50 billion resulted.

In contrast, if we observed a cyclically adjusted deficit of zero in a specific year, followed by a cyclically adjusted budget deficit in the next, we could conclude that fiscal policy is expansionary. Because the cyclically adjusted budget adjusts for automatic changes in tax revenues, the increase in the cyclically adjusted budget deficit reveals that government either increased its spending (*G*) or decreased tax rates such that tax revenues (*T*) decreased. In Figure 8.4, the government either shifted the line *G* upward or the line *T* downward. These changes in *G* and *T* are precisely the discretionary actions that we have identified as elements of an *expansionary* fiscal policy. Similarly, if we observed a cyclically adjusted deficit of zero in one year, followed by a cyclically adjusted budget surplus in the next, we could conclude that fiscal policy is contractionary. Government either decreased its spending (*G*) or increased tax rates such that tax revenues (*T*) increased. We know that these changes in *G* and *T* are elements of a *contractionary* fiscal policy.

Global Snapshot 8.1 shows the extent of the cyclically adjusted budget deficits or surpluses of a number of countries in a recent year.

GLOBAL SNAPSHOT 8.1

Cyclically Adjusted Budget Deficits or Surpluses as a Percentage of Potential GDP, Selected Nations

Because of the global recession, in 2009 all but a few of the world's major nations had cyclically adjusted budget deficits. These deficits varied as percentages of potential GDP, but they each reflected some degree of expansionary fiscal policy.

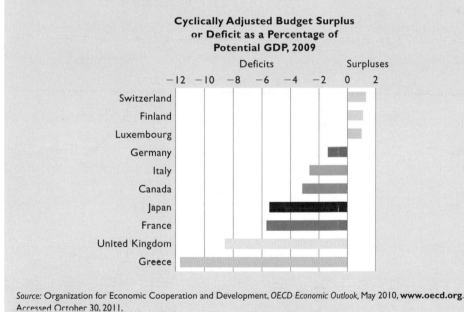

Source: Organization for Economic Cooperation and Development, *OECD Economic Outlook*, May 2010, **www.oecd.org**. Accessed October 30, 2011.

APPLYING THE ANALYSIS

Recent U.S. Fiscal Policy

Table 8.1 lists the actual federal budget deficits and surpluses (column 2) and the cyclically adjusted deficits and surpluses (column 3), as percentages of actual GDP and potential GDP, respectively, between 2000 and 2010. Observe that the cyclically adjusted deficits are generally smaller than the actual deficits. This is because the actual

TABLE 8.1 Federal Deficits (−) and Surpluses (+) as Percentages of GDP, 2000–2010

(1) Year	(2) Actual Deficit − or Surplus +	(3) Cyclically Adjusted Deficit − or Surplus +*
2000	+2.5	+1.0
2001	+1.3	+0.5
2002	−1.5	−1.3
2003	−3.4	−2.8
2004	−3.5	−3.3
2005	−2.6	−2.7
2006	−1.9	−2.2
2007	−1.2	−1.3
2008	−3.2	−2.9
2009	−9.4	−7.3
2010	−8.4	−6.1

*As a percentage of potential GDP.

Source: Congressional Budget Office, **www.cbo.gov**.

deficits include cyclical deficits, whereas the cyclically adjusted deficits eliminate them. Only cyclically adjusted surpluses and deficits as percentages of potential GDP (column 3) provide the information needed to assess discretionary fiscal policy and determine whether it is expansionary, contractionary, or neutral.

Take a look at the data for 2000, for example, which shows that fiscal policy was contractionary that year. Note that the actual budget surplus was 2.5 percent of GDP in 2000 and the cyclically adjusted budget surplus was 1.0 percent of potential GDP. Because the economy was fully employed and corporate profits were strong, tax revenues poured into the federal government and exceeded government expenditures.

But not all was well in 2000. Specifically, the so-called dot-com stock market bubble burst that year, and the U.S. economy noticeably slowed over the latter half of the year. In March 2001 the economy slid into a recession. Congress and the Bush administration responded by cutting taxes by $44 billion in 2001 and scheduling an additional $52 billion of cuts for 2002. These stimulus policies helped boost the economy and offset the recession as well as cushion the economic blow delivered by the September 11, 2001, terrorist attacks. In March 2002 Congress passed further tax cuts totaling $122 billion over two years and extended unemployment benefits.

As Table 8.1 reveals, the cyclically adjusted budget moved from a surplus of 1.0 percent of potential GDP in 2000 to a deficit of −1.3 percent two years later in 2002. Fiscal policy had definitely turned expansionary. Nevertheless, the economy remained sluggish through 2002 and into 2003. In June 2003 Congress again cut taxes, this time by a much larger $350 billion over several years. Specifically, the tax legislation accelerated the reduction of marginal tax rates already scheduled for future years and slashed tax rates on income from dividends and capital gains. It also increased tax breaks for families and small businesses. Note from the table that this tax package increased the cyclically adjusted budget deficit as a percentage of potential GDP to −2.8 percent in 2003. The economy strengthened and both real output and employment grew between 2003 and 2007. By 2007 full employment had been restored, although a −1.3 percent cyclically adjusted budget deficit still remained.

As pointed out in previous chapters, major economic trouble began in 2007. In the summer of 2007, a crisis in the market for mortgage loans flared up. Later in 2007 that crisis spread rapidly to other financial markets, threatened the survival of several major U.S. financial institutions, and severely disrupted the entire financial system. As credit markets began to freeze, general pessimism spread beyond the financial markets to the overall economy. Businesses and households retrenched on their borrowing and spending, and in December 2007 the economy entered a recession. Over the following two years, it became known as the Great Recession—one of the steepest and longest economic downturns since the 1930s.

In 2008 Congress acted rapidly to pass an economic stimulus package. This law provided a total of $152 billion in stimulus, with some of it coming as tax breaks for businesses, but most of it delivered as checks of up to $600 each to taxpayers, veterans, and Social Security recipients.

As a percentage of GDP, the *actual* federal budget deficit jumped from −1.2 percent in 2007 to −3.2 percent in 2008. This increase resulted from an automatic drop-off of tax revenues during the recession, along with the tax rebates (fiscal stimulus checks) paid out in 2008. As shown in Table 8.1, the *cyclically adjusted* budget deficit rose from −1.3 percent of potential GDP in 2007 to −2.9 percent in 2008. This increase in the cyclically adjusted budget reveals that fiscal policy in 2008 was expansionary.

The government hoped that those receiving checks would spend the money and thus boost consumption and aggregate demand. But households instead saved substantial parts of the money from the checks or used some of the money to pay down credit card loans. Although this stimulus plan boosted output somewhat in mid-2008, it was neither as expansionary nor long-lasting as policymakers had hoped. The continuing forces of the Great Recession simply overwhelmed the policy.

With the economy continuing its precipitous slide, the Obama administration and Congress enacted the American Recovery and Reinvestment Act of 2009. This gigantic $787 billion program—coming on top of a $700 billion rescue package for financial institutions—consisted of low- and middle-income tax rebates, plus large increases in expenditures on infrastructure, education, and health care. The idea was to flood the economy with additional spending to try to boost aggregate demand and get people back to work.

The tax cuts in the package were aimed at lower- and middle-income individuals and households, who were thought to be more likely than high-income people to spend (rather than save) the extra income from the tax rebates. Rather than sending out lump-sum stimulus checks as in 2008, the new tax rebates showed up as small increases in workers' monthly payroll checks. With smaller amounts per month rather than a single large check, the government hoped that people would spend the bulk of their enhanced income—rather than save it as they had done with the one-time-only, lump-sum checks received in 2008. The second part of the fiscal policy (60 percent of the funding) consisted of increases in government expenditures on a wide assortment of programs, including transportation, education, and aid to state governments. The highly stimulative fiscal policy for 2009 is fully reflected in column 3 of Table 8.1. The cyclically adjusted budget deficit rose dramatically from −2.9 percent of potential GDP in 2008 to a very high −7.3 percent of potential GDP in 2009.

Figure 8.5 shows the absolute magnitudes of actual (not cyclically adjusted) U.S. budget surpluses and deficits, here from 1994 through 2010. It also shows the projected future deficits through 2014, as estimated by the Congressional Budget Office (CBO). In recession year 2009, the federal budget deficit reached $1413 billion, mainly but not totally due to reduced tax revenues from lower income and record amounts of stimulus spending. The CBO projects high deficits for several years to come. But projected deficits

FIGURE 8.5 **Federal budget deficits and surpluses, actual and projected, fiscal years 1994–2014 (in billions of nominal dollars).** The annual budget deficits of 1992 through 1997 gave way to budget surpluses from 1998 through 2001. Deficits reappeared in 2002 and declined through 2007. They greatly ballooned in recessionary years 2008 and 2009 and are projected to remain high for many years to come.

Source: Congressional Budget Office, **www.cbo.gov**.

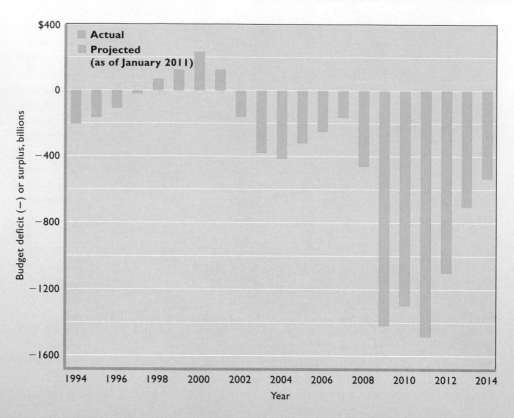

and surpluses are subject to large and frequent changes, as government alters its fiscal policy and GDP growth accelerates or slows. So we suggest that you update this figure by going to the Congressional Budget Office website, **www.cbo.gov**, and selecting Budget and Economic Outlook: Fiscal Years 2011 to 2021 (or more recent) and then Budget Projections. The relevant numbers are in Table 1-1 in the row labeled Total Deficit.

QUESTION: Use Figure 8.5 to demonstrate how each of the following contributed to increased actual budget deficits in recent years: (a) the recession of 2007–2009, (b) the war on terrorism in the United States and abroad, and (c) the Bush administration tax cuts.

✓ Problems, Criticisms, and Complications

Economists recognize that governments may encounter a number of significant problems in enacting and applying fiscal policy.

Problems of Timing

Several problems of timing may arise in connection with fiscal policy:

- *Recognition lag*   The recognition lag is the time between the beginning of recession or inflation and the certain awareness that it is actually happening. This lag arises because the economy does not move smoothly through the business cycle.

Even during good times, the economy has slow months interspersed with months of rapid growth and expansion. This makes recognizing a recession difficult since several slow months will have to happen in succession before people can conclude with any confidence that the good times are over and a recession has begun.

The same is true with inflation. Several high-inflation months must come in sequence before people can confidently conclude that inflation has moved to a higher level.

Efforts to reduce the length of the recognition lag by trying to predict the future course of the economy have also proven to be highly difficult, at best. As a result, the economy is often 4 to 6 months into a recession or inflation before the situation is clearly discernible in the relevant statistics. Due to this recognition lag, the economic downslide or the inflation may become more serious than it would have if the situation had been identified and acted on sooner.

- *Administrative lag* The wheels of democratic government turn slowly. There will typically be a significant lag between the time the need for fiscal action is recognized and the time action is taken. Following the terrorist attacks of September 11, 2001, the U.S. Congress was stalemated for 5 months before passing a compromise economic stimulus law in March 2002. (In contrast, the Federal Reserve began lowering interest rates the week after the attacks.)

- *Operational lag* A lag also occurs between the time fiscal action is taken and the time that action affects output, employment, or the price level. Although changes in tax rates can be put into effect relatively quickly once new laws are passed, government spending on public works—new dams, interstate highways, and so on—requires long planning periods and even longer periods of construction. Such spending is of questionable use in offsetting short (for example, 6- to 12-month) periods of recession. Consequently, discretionary fiscal policy has increasingly relied on tax changes rather than on changes in spending as its main tool.

Political Considerations

Fiscal policy is conducted in a political arena. That reality not only may slow the enactment of fiscal policy but also may create the potential for political considerations swamping economic considerations in its formulation. It is a human trait to rationalize actions and policies that are in one's self-interest. Politicians are very human—they want to get reelected. A strong economy at election time will certainly help them. So they may favor large tax cuts under the guise of expansionary fiscal policy even though that policy is economically inappropriate. Similarly, they may rationalize increased government spending on popular items such as farm subsidies, health care, education, and homeland security.

At the extreme, elected officials and political parties might collectively "hijack" fiscal policy for political purposes, cause inappropriate changes in aggregate demand, and thereby cause (rather than avert) economic fluctuations. For instance, before an election they may try to stimulate the economy to improve their reelection hopes. And then after the election they may try to use contractionary fiscal policy to dampen the excessive aggregate demand that they caused with their pre-election stimulus. Such **political business cycles**—swings in overall economic activity and real GDP resulting from election-motivated fiscal policy, rather than from inherent instability in the private sector—are difficult to document and prove, but there is little doubt that political considerations weigh heavily in the formulation of fiscal policy. The question is how often, if ever, those political considerations run counter to "sound economics."

political business cycle
The alleged tendency of presidential administrations and Congress to create macroeconomic instability by reducing taxes and increasing government spending before elections, and by raising taxes and reducing expenditures after elections.

An example of the interaction of political and economic considerations—and a notable exception to the administrative lag mentioned previously—was the Economic Stimulus Act of 2008. The proposal was unveiled by President Bush on January 28, 2008; passed through both houses of Congress less than two weeks later; and signed into law on February 14, 2008. While there seemed to be strong consensus among lawmakers that the U.S. economy needed a boost, some have also suggested that the looming 2008 elections provided additional motivation to act quickly.

Future Policy Reversals

Fiscal policy may fail to achieve its intended objectives if households expect future reversals of policy. Consider a tax cut, for example. If taxpayers believe the tax reduction is temporary, they may save a large portion of their tax cut, reasoning that rates will return to their previous level in the future. They save more now so that they will be able to draw on this extra savings to maintain their future consumption levels if taxes do indeed rise again in the future. So a tax reduction thought to be temporary may not increase present consumption spending and aggregate demand by as much as our simple model (Figure 8.1) suggests.

The opposite may be true for a tax increase. If taxpayers think it is temporary, they may reduce their saving to pay the tax while maintaining their present consumption. They may reason that they can restore their saving when the tax rate again falls. So the tax increase may not reduce current consumption and aggregate demand by as much as policymakers intended.

To the extent that this so-called *consumption smoothing* occurs over time, fiscal policy will lose some of its strength. The lesson is that tax-rate changes that households view as permanent are more likely to alter consumption and aggregate demand than tax changes they view as temporary.

Offsetting State and Local Finance

The fiscal policies of state and local governments are frequently *pro-cyclical*, meaning that they worsen rather than correct recession or inflation. Unlike the federal government, most state and local governments face constitutional or other legal requirements to balance their budgets. Like households and private businesses, state and local governments increase their expenditures during prosperity and cut them during recession.

During the Great Depression of the 1930s, most of the increase in federal spending was offset by decreases in state and local spending. During and immediately following the recession of 2001, many state and local governments had to offset lower tax revenues resulting from the reduced personal income and spending of their citizens. They offset the decline in revenues by raising tax rates, imposing new taxes, and reducing spending.

In view of these past experiences, the $787 billion fiscal package of 2009 made a special effort to reduce this problem by giving substantial aid dollars to state governments. Because of the sizeable federal aid, the states did not have to increase taxes and reduce expenditures by as much as otherwise. So their collective fiscal actions did not fight as much against the increase in aggregate demand that the federal government wanted to achieve with its tax cuts and expenditure increases.

crowding-out effect
A decrease in private investment caused by higher interest rates that result from the federal government's increased borrowing to finance deficits (or debt).

Crowding-Out Effect

Another potential flaw of fiscal policy is the so-called **crowding-out effect:** An expansionary fiscal policy (deficit spending) may increase the interest rate and reduce investment spending, thereby weakening or canceling the stimulus of the expansionary policy. The rising interest rate might also potentially crowd out interest-sensitive consumption spending (such as purchasing automobiles on credit). But since investment is the most volatile component of GDP, the crowding-out effect focuses its attention on investment and whether the stimulus provided by deficit spending may be partly or even fully neutralized by an offsetting reduction in investment spending.

To see the potential problem, realize that whenever the government borrows money (as it must if it is deficit spending), it increases the overall demand for money. If the monetary authorities are holding the money supply constant, this increase in demand will raise the price paid for borrowing money: the interest rate. Because investment spending varies inversely with the interest rate, some investment will be choked off or "crowded out."

Economists vary in their opinions about the strength of the crowding-out effect. An important thing to keep in mind is that crowding out is likely to be less of a problem when the economy is in recession because investment demand tends to be low. Why? Because the sale of products slows down during recessions, so that most businesses end up with substantial amounts of excess capacity. As a result, they do not have much incentive to add new machinery or build new factories. After all, why should they add capacity when some of the capacity they already have is lying idle?

With investment demand low during a recession, the crowding-out effect is likely to be very small. Simply put, there isn't much investment for the government to crowd out. Even if deficit spending does increase the interest rate, investment spending cannot fall by that much for the simple reason that it is only a small number to begin with.

By contrast, when the economy is operating at or near full capacity, investment demand is likely to be quite high so that crowding out will probably be a much more serious problem. When the economy is booming, factories will be running at or near full capacity and firms will have investment demand for two reasons. First, equipment running at full capacity wears out fast, so that firms will be doing a lot of investment just to replace machinery and equipment that wears out and depreciates. Second, the economy is likely to be growing overall so that firms will be investing to *add* to their production capacity so they can meet anticipated demand.

Current Thinking on Fiscal Policy

Where do these complications leave us as to the advisability and effectiveness of discretionary fiscal policy? In view of the complications and uncertain outcomes of fiscal policy, some economists argue that it is better not to engage in it at all. Those holding that view point to the superiority of monetary policy (changes in interest rates engineered by the Federal Reserve) as a stabilizing device or believe that most economic fluctuations tend to be mild and self-correcting.

But most economists believe that fiscal policy remains an important, useful policy lever in the government's macroeconomic toolkit. The current popular view is that fiscal policy can help "push the economy" in a particular direction but cannot "fine-tune it" to a precise macroeconomic outcome. Mainstream economists generally agree that monetary policy is the best month-to-month stabilization tool for the U.S. economy. If monetary policy is doing its job, the government should maintain a relatively neutral fiscal policy, with a cyclically adjusted budget deficit or surplus of no more than 2 percent of potential GDP. It should hold major discretionary fiscal policy in reserve to help counter situations where recession threatens to be deep and long-lasting (as in 2008 and 2009) or where a substantial reduction in aggregate demand might help the Federal Reserve to quell a major bout of inflation.

Finally, there is general agreement that proposed fiscal policy should be evaluated for its potential positive and negative impacts on long-run productivity growth. The

INTERACTIVE GRAPHS

G 8.1

Crowding out

ORIGIN OF THE IDEA

O 8.2

Crowding out

short-run policy tools used for conducting active fiscal policy often have long-run impacts. Countercyclical fiscal policy should be shaped to strengthen, or at least not impede, the growth of long-run aggregate supply (shown as a rightward shift of the long-run aggregate supply curve in Figure 7.5). For example, a tax cut might be structured to enhance work effort, strengthen investment, and encourage innovation. Or an increase in government spending might center on preplanned projects for "public capital" (highways, mass transit, ports, airports) that are complementary to private investment and thus conducive to long-term economic growth.

The U.S. Public Debt

public debt
The total amount of money owed by the federal government to the owners of government securities; equal to the sum of past government budget deficits less government budget surpluses.

The U.S. national debt, or **public debt,** is essentially the accumulation of all past federal deficits and surpluses. The deficits have greatly exceeded the surpluses and have emerged mainly from war financing, recessions, and fiscal policy. In 2010 the total public debt was $13.6 trillion—$9 trillion held by the public, excluding the Federal Reserve; and $4.5 trillion held by federal agencies and the Federal Reserve. Between 2007 and 2009, the public debt expanded by a huge $2.9 trillion. During the Great Recession, federal tax revenues plummeted because incomes and profit fell, and federal expenditures jumped because of huge spending to rescue failing financial institutions and to stimulate the shrinking economy.

You can find the current size of the public debt at the website of the Department of Treasury, Bureau of the Public Debt, at **www.treasurydirect.gov/NP/BPDLogin? application=np.** At this site, you will see that the U.S. Treasury defines "the public" to include the Federal Reserve. But because the Federal Reserve is the nation's central bank, economists view it as essentially part of the federal government and not part of the public. Economists typically focus on the part of the debt that is not owned by the federal government and the Federal Reserve.

Ownership

U.S. securities
Treasury bills, Treasury notes, Treasury bonds, and U.S. savings bonds issued by the federal government to finance expenditures that exceed tax revenues.

The total public debt of $13.6 trillion represents the total amount of money owed by the federal government to the holders of **U.S. securities:** financial instruments issued by the federal government to borrow money to finance expenditures that exceed tax revenues. These U.S. securities (loan instruments) are of four types: *Treasury bills* (short-term securities), *Treasury notes* (medium-term securities), *Treasury bonds* (long-term securities), and *U.S. savings bonds* (long-term, nonmarketable bonds).

Figure 8.6 shows that the public, sans the Federal Reserve, held 61 percent of the federal debt in 2010 and that federal government agencies and the Federal Reserve held the remaining 39 percent. Observe that "the public" in the pie chart consists of individuals here and abroad, state and local governments, and U.S. financial institutions. Foreigners held about 32 percent of the total U.S. public debt in 2010, meaning that most of the U.S. public debt is held internally and not externally. Americans owed 68 percent of the public debt to Americans.

Debt and GDP

A simple statement of the absolute size of the debt ignores the fact that the wealth and productive ability of the U.S. economy is also vast. A wealthy, highly productive nation can incur and carry a large public debt much more easily than a poor nation can. A more meaningful measure of the public debt relates it to an economy's GDP. Figure 8.7 shows the yearly relative sizes of the U.S. public debt held outside the Federal Reserve and federal agencies. In 2010 the percentage was 57 percent. Most noticeably, the percentage

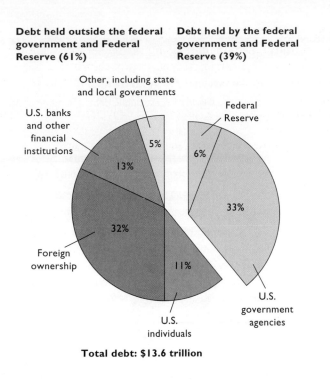

Debt held outside the federal government and Federal Reserve (61%)

Debt held by the federal government and Federal Reserve (39%)

Other, including state and local governments

U.S. banks and other financial institutions

Federal Reserve

5%

6%

13%

33%

32%

11%

Foreign ownership

U.S. individuals

U.S. government agencies

Total debt: $13.6 trillion

FIGURE 8.6 Ownership of the total public debt, 2010. The $13.6 trillion public debt can be divided into the proportion held by the public, excluding the Federal Reserve (61 percent), and the proportion held by federal agencies and the Federal Reserve System (39 percent). Of the total debt, 31 percent is foreign-owned.

Source: Economic Report of the President, 2011, **www.gpoaccess.gov/eop;** authors' derivation from Table B-89, September 2010 data. Federal Reserve percentage is from the U.S. Treasury, **www.fms.treas.gov/bulletin.**

rose dramatically in 2008 through 2010 because of huge budget deficits together with declining real GDP in 2008 and 2009.

International Comparisons

It is not uncommon for countries to have sizable public debts. As shown in Global Snapshot 8.2, the public debt as a percentage of real GDP in the United States is neither particularly high nor low relative to such debt percentages in other advanced industrial nations.

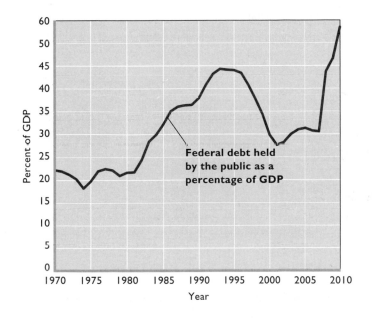

Federal debt held by the public as a percentage of GDP

FIGURE 8.7 Federal debt held by the public, excluding the Federal Reserve, as a percentage of GDP, 1970–2010. As a percentage of GDP, the federal debt held by the public (held outside the Federal Reserve and federal government agencies) increased sharply over the 1980–1995 period and declined significantly between 1995 and 2001. Since 2001, the percentage has gone up again, and jumped abruptly and sharply from 2008 through 2010.

Source: Derived by the authors by subtracting Fed-held debt (**www.fms.treas.gov/bulletin**) from debt held by the public (**www.gpoaccess.gov/eop**).

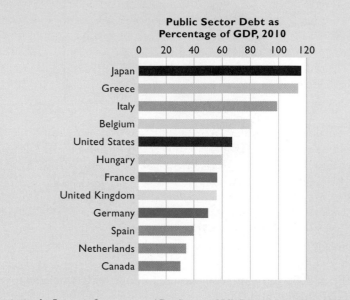

GLOBAL SNAPSHOT 8.2

Publicly Held Debt: International Comparisons

Although the United States has the world's largest public debt, a number of other nations have larger debts as percentages of their GDPs.

Public Sector Debt as Percentage of GDP, 2010

Japan
Greece
Italy
Belgium
United States
Hungary
France
United Kingdom
Germany
Spain
Netherlands
Canada

Source: Organization for Economic Cooperation and Development, *OECD Economic Outlook,* May 2010, **www.oecd.org**. Accessed October 30, 2011. These debt calculations encompass federal, state, and local debt, including the debt of government-owned enterprises (not just federal debt as in Figure 8.7).

Interest Charges

Many economists conclude that the primary burden of the debt is the annual interest charge accruing on the bonds sold to finance the debt. In 2010 interest on the total public debt was $196 billion. Although this amount is sizable in absolute terms, it was only 1.4 percent of GDP for 2010. So, the federal government had to collect taxes equal to 1.4 percent of GDP to service the total public debt. This percentage was down from 3.2 percent in 1990 and 2.3 percent in 2000, mainly because interest rates in 2010 were extremely low.

False Concerns?

You may wonder if the large public debt might bankrupt the United States or at least place a tremendous burden on your children and grandchildren. Fortunately, these are largely false concerns. People were wondering the same things 50 years ago!

Bankruptcy

The large U.S. public debt does not threaten to bankrupt the federal government, leaving it unable to meet its financial obligations. There are two main reasons: refinancing and taxation.

Refinancing As long as the U.S. public debt is viewed by lenders as manageable and sustainable, the public debt is easily refinanced. As portions of the debt come due on maturing Treasury bills, notes, and bonds each month, the government does not cut expenditures or raise taxes to provide the funds required. Rather, it refinances the debt by selling new bonds and using the proceeds to pay holders of the maturing bonds. The new bonds are in strong demand because lenders can obtain a market-determined interest return with no risk of default by the federal government.

Of course, refinancing could become an issue with a high enough debt-to-GDP ratio. Some countries such as Greece have run into this problem. High and rising ratios in the United States might raise fears that the U.S. government might be unable to pay back loans as they come due. But, with the present U.S. debt-to-GDP ratio and the prospects of long-term economic growth, this is a false concern for the United States.

Taxation The federal government has the constitutional authority to levy and collect taxes. A tax increase is a government option for gaining sufficient revenue to pay interest and principal on the public debt. Financially distressed private households and corporations cannot extract themselves from their financial difficulties by taxing the public. If their incomes or sales revenues fall short of their expenses, they can indeed go bankrupt. But the federal government does have the option to impose new taxes or increase existing tax rates if necessary to finance its debt. Such tax hikes may be politically unpopular and may weaken incentives to work and invest, but they *are* a means of raising funds to finance the debt.

Burdening Future Generations

In 2010 public debt per capita was $43,931. Was each child born in 2010 handed a $43,931 bill from the federal government? Not really. The public debt does not impose as much of a burden on future generations as commonly thought.

The United States owes a substantial portion of the public debt to itself. U.S. citizens and institutions (banks, businesses, insurance companies, governmental agencies, and trust funds) own about 68 percent of the U.S. government securities. Although that part of the public debt is a liability to Americans (as taxpayers), it is simultaneously an asset to Americans (as holders of Treasury bills, Treasury notes, Treasury bonds, and U.S. savings bonds).

To eliminate the American-owned part of the public debt would require a gigantic transfer payment from Americans to Americans. Taxpayers would pay higher taxes, and holders of the debt would receive an equal amount for their U.S. securities. Purchasing power in the United States would not change. Only the repayment of the 32 percent of the public debt owned by foreigners would negatively impact U.S. purchasing power.

The public debt increased sharply during the Second World War. But the decision to finance military purchases through the sale of government bonds did not shift the economic burden of the war to future generations. The economic cost of the Second World War consisted of the civilian goods society had to forgo in shifting scarce resources to war goods production (recall production possibilities analysis). Regardless of whether society financed this reallocation through higher taxes or through borrowing, the real economic burden of the war would have been the same. That burden was borne almost entirely by those who lived during the war. They were the ones who did without a multitude of consumer goods to enable the United States to arm itself and its allies.

The next generation inherited the debt from the war but also an equal amount of government bonds that would pay them cash in future years. It also inherited the enormous benefits from the victory—namely, preserved political and economic systems at home and the "export" of those systems to Germany, Italy, and Japan. Those outcomes enhanced postwar U.S. economic growth and helped raise the standard of living of future generations of Americans.

Substantive Issues

Although the preceding issues relating to the public debt are false concerns, a number of substantive issues are not. Economists, however, attach varying degrees of importance to them.

Income Distribution

The distribution of ownership of government securities is highly uneven. Some people own much more than the $43,931-per-person portion of government securities; other people own less or none at all. In general, the ownership of the public debt is concentrated among wealthier groups, who own a large percentage of all stocks and bonds. Because the overall federal tax system is only slightly progressive, payment of interest on the public debt mildly increases income inequality. Income is transferred from people who, on average, have lower incomes to the higher-income bondholders. If greater income equality is one of society's goals, then this redistribution is undesirable.

Incentives

The current public debt necessitates annual interest payments of $196 billion. With no increase in the size of the debt, that interest charge must be paid out of tax revenues. Higher taxes may dampen incentives to bear risk, to innovate, to invest, and to work. So, in this indirect way, a large public debt may impair economic growth and therefore impose a burden of reduced output (and income) on future generations.

Foreign-Owned Public Debt

external public debt
The part of the public debt owed to foreign citizens, firms, and institutions.

The 32 percent of the U.S. debt held by citizens and institutions of foreign countries *is* an economic burden to Americans. Because we do not owe that portion of the debt "to ourselves," the payment of interest and principal on this **external public debt** enables foreigners to buy some of our output. In return for the benefits derived from the borrowed funds, the United States transfers goods and services to foreign lenders. Of course, Americans also own debt issued by foreign governments, so payment of principal and interest by those governments transfers some of their goods and services to Americans.

Crowding-Out Effect Revisited

A potentially more serious problem is the financing (and continual refinancing) of the large public debt, which can transfer a real economic burden to future generations by passing on to them a smaller stock of capital goods. This possibility involves the previously discussed crowding-out effect: the idea that public borrowing drives up real interest rates, which reduces private investment spending. If public borrowing only happened during recessions, crowding out would not likely be much of a problem. Because private investment demand tends to be weak during recessions, any increase in interest rates caused by public borrowing will at most cause a small reduction in investment spending.

In contrast, the need to continuously finance a large public debt may be more troublesome. At times, that financing requires borrowing large amounts of money when the economy is near or at its full-employment output. Because this usually is when private demand is strong, any increase in interest rates caused by the borrowing necessary to refinance the debt may result in a substantial decline in investment spending. If the amount of current investment crowded out is extensive, future generations will inherit an economy with a smaller production capacity and, other things equal, a lower standard of living.

A Graphical Look at Crowding Out We know from Chapter 7 that the amount of investment spending is inversely related to the real interest rate. When graphed, that relationship is shown as a downsloping **investment demand curve,** such as either ID_1 or ID_2 in Figure 8.8. Let's first consider curve ID_1. (Ignore curve ID_2 for now.) Suppose that government borrowing increases the real interest rate from 6 percent to 10 percent. Investment spending will then fall from $25 billion to $15 billion, as shown by the economy's move from *a* to *b*. That is, the financing of the debt will compete with the financing of private investment projects and crowd out $10 billion of private investment. So the stock of private capital handed down to future generations will be $10 billion less than it would have been without the need to finance the public debt.

Public Investments and Public-Private Complementarities But even with crowding out, two factors could partly or fully offset the net economic burden shifted to future generations. First, just as private expenditures may involve either consumption or investment, so it is with public goods. Part of the government spending enabled by the public debt is for public investment outlays (for example, highways, mass transit systems, and electric power facilities) and "human capital" (for example, investments in education, job training, and health). Like private expenditures on machinery and equipment, those **public investments** increase the economy's future production

investment demand curve
A curve that shows the amount of investment forthcoming in an economy at each real interest rate in a series of such rates.

public investments
Government expenditures on public capital (such as highways, bridges, mass-transit systems, and electric power facilities) and on human capital (such as education, training, and health).

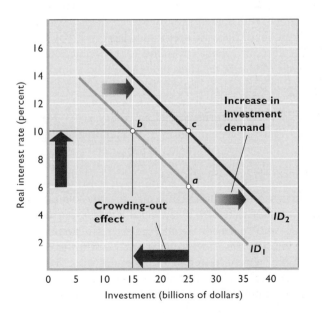

FIGURE 8.8 The investment demand curve and the crowding-out effect. If the investment demand curve (ID_1) is fixed, the increase in the interest rate from 6 percent to 10 percent caused by financing a large public debt will move the economy from *a* to *b*, crowding out $10 billion of private investment and decreasing the size of the capital stock inherited by future generations. However, if the public goods enabled by the debt improve the investment prospects of businesses, the private investment demand curve will shift rightward, as from ID_1 to ID_2. That shift may offset the crowding-out effect wholly or in part. In this case, it moves the economy from *a* to *c*.

capacity. Because of the financing through debt, the stock of public capital passed on to future generations may be higher than otherwise. That greater stock of public capital may offset the diminished stock of private capital resulting from the crowding-out effect, leaving overall production capacity unimpaired.

So-called public-private complementarities are a second factor that could reduce the crowding out effect. Some public and private investments are complementary. Thus, the public investment financed through debt could spur some private-sector investment by increasing its expected rate of return. For example, a federal building in a city may encourage private investment in the form of nearby office buildings, shops, and restaurants. Through its complementary effect, the spending on public capital may shift the private investment demand curve to the right, as from ID_1 to ID_2 in Figure 8.8. Even though the government borrowing boosts the interest rate from 6 percent to 10 percent, total private investment need not fall. In the case shown as the move from a to c in Figure 8.8, it remains at $25 billion. Of course, the increase in investment demand might be smaller than that shown. If it were smaller, the crowding-out effect would not be fully offset. But the point is that an increase in investment demand may counter the decline in investment that would otherwise result from the higher interest rate.

The Long-Run Fiscal Imbalance: Social Security

The most significant fiscal issue in the United States is not the budget deficit or the public debt but, rather, the long-term funding imbalance in the Social Security and Medicare programs. Over the next 75 years, benefits to Social Security and Medicare beneficiaries are expected to exceed program revenues by trillions of dollars. We will focus our attention on Social Security.

The Future Funding Shortfall

The Social Security program (excluding Medicare) has grown from less than one-half of 1 percent of U.S. GDP in 1950 to 4.2 percent of GDP in 2007. That percentage is projected to grow to 6.2 percent of GDP in 2035 and level off at around 6.0 percent of GDP by 2050. There is a severe long-run shortfall in Social Security funding because of growing payments to retiring baby boomers.

The $615 billion Social Security program is largely a "pay-as-you-go" plan, meaning that most of the current revenues from the 12.4 percent Social Security tax (the rate when the 2.9 percent Medicare tax is excluded) are paid out to current Social Security retirees. In anticipation of the large benefits owed to the baby boomers when they retire, however, the Social Security Administration has been placing an excess of current revenues over current payouts into the **Social Security trust fund,** consisting of U.S. Treasury securities. But the accumulation of money in the trust fund will be greatly inadequate for paying the retirement benefits promised to all future retirees.

Social Security trust fund
A federal fund that saves excessive Social Security tax revenues received in one year to meet Social Security benefit obligations that exceed Social Security tax revenues in some subsequent year.

In 2010, because of the weakened economy, payroll tax revenues fell $49 billion short of program expenditures. Interest earnings on trust fund assets were sufficient to overcome this deficit, so the trust fund continued to grow, but at a slower pace than during more robust economic times. In 2022, Social Security retirement revenues (including interest earnings) will fall below Social Security retirement benefits, and the system will begin dipping into the trust fund to make up the difference. The trust fund will be exhausted in 2036, after which the annual tax revenues will cover only 75 percent of the promised benefits. The federal government faces a several-trillion-dollar shortfall of long-run revenues for funding Social Security.

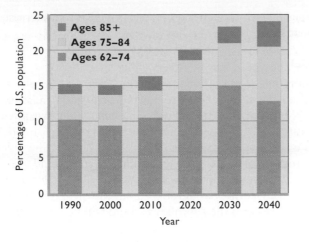

FIGURE 8.9 The aging U.S. population. The percentage of the U.S. population that is age 62 or older is rapidly rising. Depending on policy responses, this could result in a severe funding shortfall for Social Security in the decades ahead.

As shown in Figure 8.9, the problem is one of demographics. The percentage of the American population age 62 or older will rise substantially over the next several decades, with the greatest increases for people who are age 75 and older. High fertility rates during the "baby boom" (1946–1964), declining birthrates thereafter, and rising life expectancies have combined to produce an aging population. In the future, more people will be receiving Social Security benefits for longer periods, and fewer workers will pay for each person's benefits. The number of workers per Social Security beneficiary was 5:1 in 1960. Today it is 3:1, and by 2040 it will be only 2:1.

There is no easy way to restore long-run balance to Social Security funding. Either benefits must be reduced or revenues must be increased. The Social Security Administration concludes that bringing projected Social Security revenues and payments into balance over the next 75 years would require a 14 percent permanent

© Purestock/PunchStock

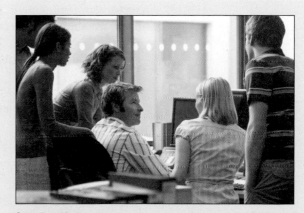

© moodboard/Corbis

PHOTO OP Will Social Security Be There for You?

Social Security is largely a "pay-as-you-go" plan, in which current retirement benefits are paid out of current payroll taxes. But the number of retirees in the United States is growing faster than the number of workers, foretelling a future funding shortfall.

reduction in Social Security benefits, a 17 percent permanent increase in tax revenues, or some combination of the two.[2]

Policy Options

Several suggestions have been offered to help make Social Security financially sound. These ideas include increasing the retirement age, subjecting a larger portion of total earnings to the Social Security tax, and reducing benefits for wealthy retirees.

Other ideas are more novel. For example, one suggestion is to boost the trust fund by investing all or part of it in corporate stocks and bonds. The federal government would own the stock investments, and an appointed panel would oversee the direction of those investments. The presumed higher returns on the investments relative to the lower returns on U.S. securities would stretch out the life of the trust fund. Nevertheless, a substantial increase in the payroll tax would still be needed to cover the shortfalls after the trust fund is exhausted.

Another option is to increase the payroll tax immediately—perhaps by as much as 1.5 percentage points—and allocate the new revenues to individual accounts. Government would own the accumulations in the accounts, but individuals could direct their investments to a restricted list of broad stock or bond funds. When they retire, recipients could convert these individual account balances to annuities—securities paying monthly payments for life. That annuity income would supplement reduced monthly benefits from the pay-as-you-go system when the trust fund is exhausted.

A different route is to place half the payroll tax into accounts that individuals, not the government, would own, maintain, and bequeath. Individuals could invest these funds in bank certificates of deposit or in approved stock and bond funds and draw upon the accounts when they reach retirement age. A flat monthly benefit would supplement the accumulations in the private accounts. The personal security accounts would be phased in over time, so people now receiving or about to receive Social Security benefits would continue to receive benefits.

These general ideas do not exhaust the possible reforms, since the variations on each plan are nearly endless. Reaching consensus on Social Security reform will be difficult because every citizen has a direct economic stake in the outcome and little agreement is present among them on the proper magnitude of the benefits, how the program should be structured, and how we should pay for the projected funding shortfall. Nevertheless, Americans will eventually need to confront the problem of trillions of dollars of unfunded Social Security liabilities.

---

[2]Social Security Board of Trustees, "Status of the Social Security and Medicare Programs: A Summary of the 2011 Annual Reports," **www.ssa.gov.**

Summary

1. Fiscal policy consists of deliberate changes in government spending, taxes, or some combination of both to promote full employment, price-level stability, and economic growth. Fiscal policy requires increases in government spending, decreases in taxes, or both—a budget deficit—to increase aggregate demand and push an economy from a recession. Decreases in government spending, increases in taxes, or both—a budget surplus—are appropriate fiscal policy for dealing with demand-pull inflation.

2. Built-in stability arises from net tax revenues, which vary directly with the level of GDP. During recession, the federal budget automatically moves toward a stabilizing deficit; during expansion, the budget automatically moves toward an anti-inflationary surplus. Built-in stability lessens, but does not fully correct, undesired changes in real GDP.

3. Actual federal budget deficits can go up or down because of changes in GDP, changes in fiscal policy, or both. Deficits

caused by changes in GDP are called cyclical deficits. The cyclically adjusted budget removes cyclical deficits from the budget and therefore measures the budget deficit or surplus (if either) that would occur if the economy operated at its full-employment output throughout the year. Changes in the cyclical budget deficit or surplus provide meaningful information as to whether the government's fiscal policy is expansionary, neutral, or contractionary. Changes in the actual budget deficit or surplus do not, since such deficits or surpluses can include cyclical deficits or surpluses.

4. In 2001 the Bush administration and Congress chose to reduce marginal tax rates and phase out the federal estate tax. A recession occurred in 2001, the stock market crashed, and federal spending for the war on terrorism rocketed. The federal budget swung from a surplus of $127 billion in 2001 to a deficit of $158 billion in 2002. In 2003 the Bush administration and Congress accelerated the tax reductions scheduled under the 2001 tax law and cut tax rates on capital gains and dividends. The purposes were to stimulate a sluggish economy. By 2007 the economy had reached its full-employment level of output.

5. The federal government responded to the deep recession of 2007–2009 by implementing highly expansionary fiscal policy. In 2008 the federal government passed a tax rebate program that sent $600 checks to qualified individuals. Later that year, it created a $700 billion emergency fund to keep key financial institutions from failing. These and other programs increased the cyclically adjusted budget deficit from −1.3 percent of potential GDP in 2007 to −2.9 percent in 2008. When the economy continued to plunge, the Obama administration and Congress enacted a massive $787 billion stimulus program to be implemented over $2\frac{1}{2}$ years. The cyclically adjusted budget deficit shot up from −2.9 percent of potential GDP in 2008 to −7.3 percent in 2009.

6. Certain problems complicate the enactment and implementation of fiscal policy. They include (a) timing problems associated with recognition, administrative, and operational lags; (b) the potential for misuse of fiscal policy for political rather than economic purposes; (c) the fact that state and local finances tend to be pro-cyclical; (d) potential ineffectiveness if households expect future policy reversals; and (e) the possibility of fiscal policy crowding out private investment.

7. Most economists believe that fiscal policy can help move the economy in a desired direction but cannot reliably be used to fine-tune the economy to a position of price stability and full employment. Nevertheless, fiscal policy is a valuable backup tool for aiding monetary policy in fighting significant recession or inflation.

8. The public debt is the total accumulation of the government's deficits (minus surpluses) over time and consists of Treasury bills, Treasury notes, Treasury bonds, and U.S. savings bonds. In 2010 the U.S. public debt was $13.6 trillion, or $43,931 per person. The public (which here includes banks and state and local governments) holds 61 percent of that federal debt; the Federal Reserve and federal agencies hold the other 39 percent. Foreigners hold 32 percent of the federal debt. Interest payments as a percentage of GDP were about 1.4 percent in 2010. This is down from 3.2 percent in 1990.

9. The concern that a large public debt may bankrupt the government is a false worry because (a) the debt need only be refinanced rather than refunded and (b) the federal government has the power to increase taxes to make interest payments on the debt.

10. In general, the public debt is not a vehicle for shifting economic burdens to future generations. Americans inherit not only most of the public debt (a liability) but also most of the U.S. securities (an asset) that finance the debt.

11. More substantive problems associated with public debt include the following: (a) Payment of interest on the debt may increase income inequality. (b) Interest payments on the debt require higher taxes, which may impair incentives. (c) Paying interest or principal on the portion of the debt held by foreigners means a transfer of real output to abroad. (d) Government borrowing to refinance or pay interest on the debt may increase interest rates and crowd out private investment spending, leaving future generations with a smaller stock of capital than they would have otherwise.

12. The increase in investment in public capital that may result from debt financing may partly or wholly offset the crowding-out effect of the public debt on private investment. Also, the added public investment may stimulate private investment, where the two are complements.

13. The Social Security system has a significant long-run funding problem. The number of Social Security beneficiaries is projected to significantly rise in future years, and those retirees, on average, are expected to live longer than current retirees. Meanwhile, the number of workers paying Social Security taxes will increase relatively slowly. So a large gap between Social Security revenues and payments will eventually arise. This problem has created calls for various kinds of Social Security reform.

Terms and Concepts

fiscal policy	built-in stabilizer	U.S. securities
Council of Economic Advisers (CEA)	cyclically adjusted budget	external public debt
expansionary fiscal policy	cyclical deficit	investment demand curve
budget deficit	political business cycle	public investments
contractionary fiscal policy	crowding-out effect	Social Security trust fund
budget surplus	public debt	

Questions ![McGraw Hill] connect™ | ECONOMICS

1. The federal government establishes its budget to decide what programs to provide and how to pay for them. How does fiscal policy differ from this ordinary fiscal activity of budgeting? LO1

2. What are government's fiscal policy options for moving the economy out of a recession? Speculate on which of these fiscal options might be favored by (a) a person who wants to preserve the size of government and (b) a person who thinks the public sector is too large. How does the "ratchet effect" affect anti-inflationary fiscal policy? LO1

3. Explain how built-in (or automatic) stabilizers work. What are the differences between proportional, progressive, and regressive tax systems as they relate to an economy's built-in stability? LO2

4. Briefly state and evaluate the problem of time lags in enacting and applying fiscal policy. How might "politics" complicate fiscal policy? How might expectations of a near-term policy reversal weaken fiscal policy based on changes in tax rates? What is the crowding-out effect, and why might it be relevant to fiscal policy? LO1

5. Define the cyclically adjusted budget, explain its significance, and state why it may differ from the actual budget. Suppose the full-employment, noninflationary level of real output is GDP_3 (not GDP_2) in the economy depicted in Figure 8.3. If the economy is operating at GDP_2, instead of GDP_3, what is the status of its cyclically adjusted budget? The status of its current fiscal policy? What change in fiscal policy would you recommend? How would you accomplish that in terms of the G and T lines in the figure? LO3

6. Use Figure 8.4 to explain why the deliberate increase of the cyclically adjusted budget deficit (resulting from the tax cut) will reduce the size of the actual budget deficit if the fiscal policy succeeds in pushing the economy to its full-employment output of GDP_1. In requesting a tax cut in the early 1960s, President Kennedy said, "It is a paradoxical truth that tax rates are too high today and tax revenues are too low and the soundest way to raise tax revenues in the long run is to cut tax rates now." Relate this quotation to your previous answer in this question. LO3

7. Why did the budget surpluses in 2000 and 2001 give way to a series of budget deficits beginning in 2002? Why did those deficits increase substantially beginning in 2008? LO3

8. Distinguish between the total U.S. debt and the debt held by the public. Why is the debt as a percentage of GDP more relevant than the total debt? Contrast the effects of paying off an internally held debt and paying off an externally held debt. LO4

9. True or false? If the statement is false, explain why: LO4
   a. An internally held public debt is like a debt of the left hand owed to the right hand.
   b. The Federal Reserve and federal government agencies hold more than half the public debt.
   c. As a percentage of GDP, the federal debt held by the public was smaller in 2010 than it was in 1990.
   d. As a percentage of GDP, the total U.S. public debt is the highest such debt among the world's advanced industrial nations.

10. Why might economists be quite concerned if the annual interest payments on the debt sharply increased as a percentage of GDP? LO4

11. Trace the cause-and-effect chain through which financing and refinancing of the public debt might affect real interest rates, private investment, the stock of capital, and economic growth. How might investment in public capital and complementarities between public capital and private capital alter the outcome of the cause-effect chain? LO4

12. What do economists mean when they refer to Social Security as a pay-as-you-go plan? What is the Social Security trust fund? What is the nature of the long-run fiscal imbalance in the Social Security retirement system? What are the broad options for fixing the long-run problem? LO5

Problems

1. Refer back to the table in Figure 7.7 in the previous chapter. Suppose that aggregate demand increases such that the amount of real output demanded rises by $7 billion at each price level. By what percentage will the price level increase? Will this inflation be demand-pull inflation or will it be cost-push inflation? If potential real GDP (that is, full-employment GDP) is $510 billion, what will be the size of the positive GDP gap after the change in aggregate demand? If government wants to use fiscal policy to counter the resulting inflation without changing tax rates, would it increase government spending or decrease it? LO1

2. Refer to the accompanying table for Waxwania: LO2, LO3

Government Expenditures, G	Tax Revenues, T	Real GDP
$160	$100	$500
160	120	600
160	140	700
160	160	800
160	180	900

a. What is the marginal tax rate in Waxwania? The average tax rate? Which of the following describes the tax system: proportional, progressive, regressive?

b. Suppose Waxwania is producing $600 of real GDP, whereas the potential real GDP (or full-employment real GDP) is $700. How large is its budget deficit? Its cyclically adjusted budget deficit? Its cyclically adjusted budget deficit as a percentage of potential real GDP? Is Waxwania's fiscal policy expansionary or is it contractionary?

3. Suppose that a country has no public debt in year 1 but experiences a budget deficit of $40 billion in year 2, a budget deficit of $20 billion in year 3, a budget surplus of $10 billion in year 4, and a budget deficit of $2 billion in year 5. What is the absolute size of its public debt in year 5? If its real GDP in year 5 is $104 billion, what is this country's public debt as a percentage of real GDP in year 5? **LO4**

4. Suppose that the investment demand curve in a certain economy is such that investment declines by $100 billion for every 1 percentage point increase in the real interest rate. Also, suppose that the investment demand curve shifts rightward by $150 billion at each real interest rate for every 1 percentage point increase in the expected rate of return from investment. If stimulus spending (an expansionary fiscal policy) by government increases the real interest rate by 2 percentage points, but also raises the expected rate of return on investment by 1 percentage point, how much investment, if any, will be crowded out? **LO4**

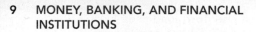

MONEY, BANKING, AND MONETARY POLICY

9

After reading this chapter, you should be able to:

1 **Identify and explain the functions of money and the components of the U.S. money supply.**

2 **Describe what "backs" the money supply, making us willing to accept it as payment.**

3 **Discuss the makeup of the Federal Reserve and the U.S. banking system.**

4 **Identify the functions and responsibilities of the Federal Reserve.**

5 **Identify and explain the main factors that contributed to the financial crisis of 2007–2008.**

6 **Discuss the actions of the U.S. Treasury that helped keep the banking and financial crisis of 2007–2008 from worsening.**

7 **Identify the main subsets of the financial services industry in the United States and provide examples of some firms in each category.**

8 **Describe how banks create money in a "fractional reserve" banking system.**

Money, Banking, and Financial Institutions

Money is a fascinating aspect of the economy:

> Money bewitches people. They fret for it, and they sweat for it. They devise most ingenious ways to get it, and most ingenious ways to get rid of it. Money is the only commodity that is good for nothing but to be gotten rid of. It will not feed you, clothe you, shelter you, or amuse you unless you spend it or invest it. It imparts value only in parting. People will do almost anything for money, and money will do almost anything for people. Money is a captivating, circulating, masquerading puzzle.[1]

---

[1]Federal Reserve Bank of Philadelphia, "Creeping Inflation," *Business Review,* August 1957, p. 3. Used with permission.

In this chapter and the next we want to unmask the critical role of money and the monetary system in the economy. When the monetary system is working properly, it provides the lifeblood of the circular flows of income and expenditure. A well-operating monetary system helps the economy achieve both full employment and the efficient use of resources. A malfunctioning monetary system distorts the allocation of resources and creates severe fluctuations in the economy's levels of output, employment, and prices.

The Functions of Money

There is an old saying that "money *is* what money *does*." In a conceptual sense, anything that performs the functions of money *is* money. Here are those functions:

medium of exchange
An item that sellers generally accept and buyers generally use to pay for goods and services.

- *Medium of exchange* First and foremost, money is a **medium of exchange** that is usable for buying and selling goods and services. A bakery worker does not want to be paid 200 bagels per week. Nor does the bakery owner want to receive, say, halibut in exchange for bagels. Money, however, is readily acceptable as payment. As we saw in Chapter 2, money is a social invention with which resource suppliers and producers can be paid and that can be used to buy any of the full range of items available in the marketplace. As a medium of exchange, money allows society to escape the complications of barter. And because it provides a convenient way of exchanging goods, money enables society to gain the advantages of geographic and human specialization.

unit of account
A standard measurement unit in terms of which prices can be stated and the relative value of goods and services compared.

- *Unit of account* Money is also a **unit of account.** Society uses monetary units—dollars, in the United States—as a yardstick for measuring the relative worth of a wide variety of goods, services, and resources. Just as we measure distance in miles or kilometers, we gauge the value of goods in dollars. With money as an acceptable unit of account, the price of each item need be stated only in terms of the monetary unit. We need not state the price of cows in terms of corn, crayons, and cranberries. Money aids rational decision making by enabling buyers and sellers to easily compare the prices of various goods, services, and resources. It also permits us to define debt obligations, determine taxes owed, and calculate the nation's GDP.

store of value
An asset set aside to purchase items in the future.

- *Store of value* Money also serves as a **store of value** that allows people to transfer purchasing power from the present to the future. People normally do not spend all their incomes on the day they receive them. In order to buy things later, they store some of their wealth as money. The money you place in a safe or a checking account will still be available to you a few weeks or months from now. When inflation is nonexistent or mild, holding money is a relatively risk-free way to store wealth for later use.

People can, of course, choose to hold some or all of their wealth in a wide variety of assets besides money. These include real estate, stocks, bonds, precious metals such as gold, and even collectible items like fine art or comic books. But a key advantage that money has over all other assets is that it has the most *liquidity*, or spendability.

liquidity
The ease with which an asset can be converted into cash.

An asset's **liquidity** is the ease with which it can be converted quickly into the most widely accepted and easily spent form of money, cash, with little or no loss of purchasing power. The more liquid an asset is, the more quickly it can be converted into cash and used for either purchases of goods and services or purchases of other assets.

Levels of liquidity vary radically. By definition, cash is perfectly liquid. By contrast, a house is highly illiquid for two reasons. First, it may take several months before a willing buyer can be found and a sale negotiated so that its value can be converted into cash.

Second, there is a loss of purchasing power when the house is sold because numerous fees have to be paid to real estate agents and other individuals in order to complete the sale.

As we are about to discuss, our economy uses several different types of money including cash, coins, checking account deposits, savings account deposits, and even more exotic things like deposits in money market mutual funds. As we describe the various forms of money in detail, take the time to compare their relative levels of liquidity—both with each other and with other assets like stocks, bonds, and real estate. Cash is perfectly liquid. Other forms of money are highly liquid, but less liquid than cash.

The Components of the Money Supply

Money is a "stock" of some item or group of items (unlike income, for example, which is a "flow"). Societies have used many items as money, including whales' teeth, circular stones, elephant-tail bristles, gold coins, furs, and pieces of paper. Anything that is widely accepted as a medium of exchange can serve as money. In the United States, currency is not the only form of money. As you will see, certain debts of government and financial institutions are also used as money.

Money Definition: *M*1

The narrowest definition of the U.S. money supply is called **M1.** It consists of:

- Currency (coins and paper money) in the hands of the nonbank public.
- All checkable deposits (all deposits in commercial banks and "thrift" or savings institutions on which checks of any size can be drawn).[2]

Government and government agencies supply coins and paper money. Commercial banks and savings institutions provide checkable deposits.

Currency: Coins + Paper Money The currency of the United States consists of metal coins and paper money. The coins are issued by the U.S. Treasury while the paper money consists of **Federal Reserve Notes** issued by the Federal Reserve System (the U.S. central bank). Coins are minted by the U.S. Mint while the paper money is printed by the Bureau of Engraving and Printing. Both the U.S. Mint and the Bureau of Engraving and Printing are part of the U.S. Department of the Treasury.

As with the currencies of other countries, the currency of the United States is **token money**. This means that the face value of any piece of currency is unrelated to its *intrinsic value*—the value of the physical material (metal or paper and ink) out of which that currency is constructed. Governments make sure that face values exceed intrinsic values in order to discourage people from destroying coins and bills in order to resell the material that they are made out of. For instance, if 50-cent pieces each contained 75 cents' worth of metal, then it would be profitable to melt them down and sell the metal. Fifty-cent pieces would disappear from circulation very quickly!

Figure 9.1 shows that coins and paper money (currency) constitute half of the U.S. economy's *M*1 money supply.

Checkable Deposits The safety and convenience of checks has made checkable deposits a large component of the *M*1 money supply. You would not think of stuffing $4896 in bills in an envelope and dropping it in a mailbox to pay a debt. But writing

M1
The most narrowly defined money supply, equal to currency (outside banks) plus the checkable deposits of commercial bank and thrift institutions.

Federal Reserve Notes
Paper bills issued by the Federal Reserve Banks.

token money
Currency that has a face value greater than the materials used to produce it.

---

[2]In order to avoid a maze of details in the ensuing discussion, we do not discuss several of the quantitatively less significant components of the definitions of money. For example, traveler's checks are included in the *M*1 money supply. The statistical appendix of any recent *Federal Reserve Bulletin* provides more comprehensive definitions.

FIGURE 9.1 Components of money supply *M*1 and money supply *M*2, in the United States. *M*1 is a narrow definition of the money supply that includes currency (in circulation) and checkable deposits. *M*2 is a broader definition that includes *M*1 along with several other relatively liquid account balances. * These categories include other, quantitatively smaller components such as traveler's checks.
Source: Federal Reserve System, **www.federalreserve.gov**. Data are for May 2011.

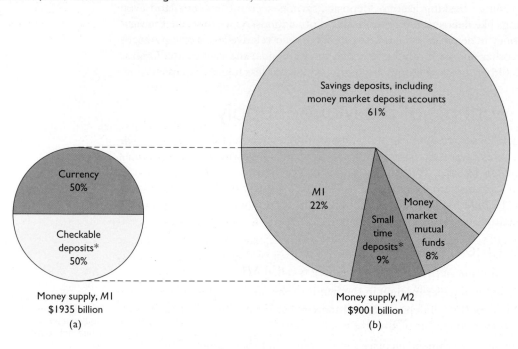

and mailing a check for a large sum is commonplace. The person cashing a check must endorse it (sign it on the reverse side); the writer of the check subsequently receives a record of the cashed check as a receipt attesting to the fulfillment of the obligation. Similarly, because the writing of a check requires a signature, the theft or loss of your checkbook is not nearly as calamitous as losing an identical amount of currency. Finally, it is more convenient to write a check than to transport and count out a large sum of currency. For all these reasons, **checkable deposits** (checkbook money) are a large component of the stock of money in the United States. About half of *M*1 is in the form of checkable deposits, on which checks can be drawn.

It might seem strange that checking account balances are regarded as part of the money supply. But the reason is clear: Checks are nothing more than a way to transfer the ownership of deposits in banks and other financial institutions and are generally acceptable as a medium of exchange. Although checks are less generally accepted than currency for small purchases, for major purchases most sellers willingly accept checks as payment. Moreover, people can convert checkable deposits into paper money and coins on demand; checks drawn on those deposits are thus the equivalent of currency.

To summarize:

$$\text{Money, } M1 = \text{Curency} + \text{Checkable Deposits}$$

Institutions That Offer Checkable Deposits In the United States, a variety of financial institutions allow customers to write checks in any amount on the funds they have deposited. **Commercial banks** are the primary depository institutions. They accept the deposits of households and businesses, keep the money safe until it is demanded via checks, and in the meantime use it to make available a wide variety of loans. Commercial bank loans provide short-term financial capital to businesses, and they finance consumer purchases of automobiles and other durable goods.

checkable deposits
Deposits in banks or thrifts against which checks may be written.

commercial banks
Firms that engage in the business of banking (accepting deposits, offering checking accounts, and making loans).

Savings and loan associations (S&Ls), mutual savings banks, and credit unions supplement the commercial banks and are known collectively as savings or **thrift institutions,** or simply "thrifts." *Savings and loan associations* and *mutual savings banks* accept the deposits of households and businesses and then use the funds to finance housing mortgages and to provide other loans. *Credit unions* accept deposits from and lend to "members," who usually are a group of people who work for the same company.

The checkable deposits of banks and thrifts are known variously as demand deposits, NOW (negotiable order of withdrawal) accounts, ATS (automatic transfer service) accounts, and share draft accounts. Their commonality is that depositors can write checks on them whenever, and in whatever amount, they choose.

Two Qualifications We must qualify our discussion in two important ways. First, currency held by the U.S. Treasury, the Federal Reserve Banks, commercial banks, and thrift institutions is *excluded* from M1 and other measures of the money supply. A paper dollar or four quarters in the billfold of, say, Emma Buck obviously constitutes just $1 of the money supply. But if we counted currency held by banks as part of the money supply, the same $1 would count for $2 of money supply when Emma deposited the currency into her checkable deposit in her bank. It would count for $1 of checkable deposit owned by Buck and also $1 of currency in the bank's cash drawer or vault. By excluding currency held by banks when determining the total supply of money, we avoid this problem of double counting.

Also *excluded* from the money supply are any checkable deposits of the government (specifically, the U.S. Treasury) or the Federal Reserve that are held by commercial banks or thrift institutions. This exclusion is designed to enable a better assessment of the amount of money available *to the private sector* for potential spending. The amount of money available to households and businesses is of keen interest to the Federal Reserve in conducting its monetary policy (a topic we cover in the next chapter).

thrift institutions
Savings and loan associations, mutual savings banks, or credit unions that offer savings and checking accounts.

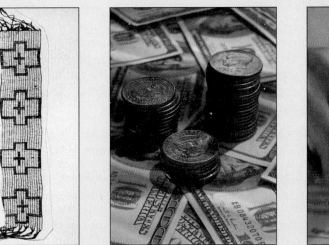

© Getty Images   © Getty Images/Stockbyte   © Getty Images

PHOTO OP Money: Then and Now

Items such as wampum belts were once used as money. Today, bills and coins, along with checkable deposits, constitute the M1 money supply.

Money Definition: *M2*

A second and broader definition of money includes *M*1 plus several near-monies. **Near-monies** are certain highly liquid financial assets that do not function directly or fully as a medium of exchange but can be readily converted into currency or checkable deposits. Three categories of near-monies owned by individuals are included in the *M*2 definition of money:

- *Savings deposits, including money market deposit accounts* A depositor can withdraw funds from an interest-earning **savings account** at a bank or thrift or simply request that the funds be transferred to a checkable account. A person can also withdraw funds from a **money market deposit account (MMDA),** which is an interest-earning account containing interest-earning short-term securities. MMDAs, however, have a minimum-balance requirement and a limit on how often a person can withdraw funds.

- *Small-denominated (less than $100,000) time deposits* Funds from **time deposits** become available at their maturity. For example, a person can convert a 6-month time deposit ("certificate of deposit" or simply "CD") to currency without penalty 6 months or more after it has been deposited. In return for this withdrawal limitation, the financial institution pays a higher interest rate on such deposits than it does on its MMDAs. Also, a person can "cash in" a CD before its maturity but must pay a severe penalty.

- *Money market mutual funds* By making a telephone call, using the Internet, or writing a check for $500 or more, a depositor can redeem shares in a **money market mutual fund (MMMF)** offered by a mutual fund company. Such companies combine the funds of individual shareholders to buy interest-bearing short-term credit instruments such as certificates of deposit and U.S. government securities. Then they can offer interest on the MMMF accounts of the shareholders (depositors) who jointly own those financial assets.

All three categories of near-monies imply substantial liquidity. In summary, *M*2 includes the immediate medium-of-exchange items (currency and checkable deposits) that constitute *M*1 plus certain near-monies that can be easily converted into currency and checkable deposits. In Figure 9.1 we see that the addition of all these items yields an *M*2 money supply that is about five times larger than the narrower *M*1 money supply. Thus, to summarize in equation form,

$$\text{Money, } M2 = M1 + \text{savings deposits, including MMDAs} + \text{small-denominated} \\ \text{(less than \$100,000) time deposits} + \text{MMMFs}$$

Actually, there is an entire spectrum of assets that vary slightly in terms of their liquidity or "moneyness" that are not included in *M*1 or *M*2. Because the simple *M*1 definition includes only items directly and immediately usable as a medium of exchange, it is often cited in discussions of the money supply. But, for some purposes, economists prefer the broader *M*2 definition. For example, *M*2 is used as one of the 10 trend variables in the index of leading indicators (an economic forecasting tool). Still broader definitions of money are so inclusive that they have limited usefulness.

We will use the narrow *M*1 definition of the money supply in our discussion and analysis, unless stated otherwise. The important principles we will develop relating to *M*1 also apply to *M*2 because *M*1 is included in *M*2.

---

near-monies
Financial assets that do not directly serve as a medium of exchange but readily can be converted into narrowly defined money (currency + checkable deposits).

M2
A more broadly defined money supply, equal to M1 plus noncheckable savings accounts (including money market deposit accounts), time deposits of less than $100,000, and individual money market mutual fund balances.

savings account
An interest-earning account (at a bank or thrift) from which funds normally can be withdrawn at any time.

money market deposit account (MMDA)
An interest-earning account (at a bank or thrift) consisting of short-term securities and on which a limited number of checks can be written each year.

time deposits
Interest-earning deposits (at a bank or thrift) such as certificates of deposit (CDs) that depositors can withdraw without penalty after the end of a specified period.

money market mutual fund (MMMF)
An interest-earning account at an investment company, which pools the funds of depositors to purchase short-term securities.

What "Backs" the Money Supply?

The money supply in the United States essentially is "backed" (guaranteed) by government's ability to keep the value of money relatively stable. Nothing more! Paper currency and checkable deposits have no intrinsic value. A $5 bill is just an inscribed piece of paper. A checkable deposit is merely a bookkeeping entry. And coins, we know, have less intrinsic value than their face value. Nor will government redeem the paper money you hold for anything tangible, such as gold.

To many people, the fact that the government does not back the currency with anything tangible seems implausible and insecure. But the decision not to back the currency with anything tangible was made for a very good reason. If the government backed the currency with something tangible like gold, then the supply of money would vary with how much gold was available. By not backing the currency, the government avoids this constraint and indeed receives a key freedom—the ability to provide as much or as little money as needed to maintain the value of money and to best suit the economic needs of the country. In effect, by choosing not to back the currency, the government has chosen to give itself the ability to freely "manage" the nation's money supply. Its monetary authorities attempt to provide the amount of money needed for the particular volume of business activity that will promote full employment, price-level stability, and economic growth.

Nearly all today's economists agree that managing the money supply is more sensible than linking it to gold or to some other commodity whose supply might change arbitrarily and capriciously. For instance, if we used gold to back the money supply so that gold was redeemable for money, and *vice versa*, then a large increase in the nation's gold stock as the result of a new gold discovery might increase the money supply too rapidly and thereby trigger rapid inflation. Or a long-lasting decline in gold production might reduce the money supply to the point where recession and unemployment resulted.

In short, people cannot convert paper money into a fixed amount of gold or any other precious commodity. Money is exchangeable only for paper money. If you ask the government to redeem $5 of your paper money, it will swap one paper $5 bill for another bearing a different serial number. That is all you can get. Similarly, checkable deposits can be redeemed not for gold but only for paper money, which, as we have just seen, the government will not redeem for anything tangible.

Value of Money

So why are currency and checkable deposits money, whereas, say, Monopoly (the game) money is not? What gives a $20 bill or a $100 checking account entry its value? The answer to these questions has three parts.

Acceptability Currency and checkable deposits are money because people accept them as money. By virtue of long-standing business practice, currency and checkable deposits perform the basic function of money: They are acceptable as a medium of exchange. We accept paper money in exchange because we are confident it will be exchangeable for real goods, services, and resources when we spend it.

Legal Tender Our confidence in the acceptability of paper money undoubtedly is strengthened because government has designated currency as **legal tender.** Specifically, each bill contains the statement "This note is legal tender for all debts, public and private." That means paper money is a valid and legal means of payment of any debt that was contracted in dollars. (But private firms and government are not

legal tender
A legal designation of a nation's official currency (bills and coins).

mandated to accept cash. It is not illegal for them to specify payment in noncash forms such as checks, cashier's checks, money orders, or credit cards.)

The general acceptance of paper currency as money is more important than the government's decree that money is legal tender, however. The government has never decreed checks to be legal tender, and yet they serve as such in many of the economy's exchanges of goods, services, and resources. But it is true that government agencies—the Federal Deposit Insurance Corporation (FDIC) and the National Credit Union Administration (NCUA)—insure individual deposits of up to $250,000 at commercial banks and thrifts. That fact enhances our willingness to store money in checkable accounts and write checks on those accounts to buy goods, services, and resources.

ILLUSTRATING THE IDEA

Are Credit Cards Money?

You may wonder why we have ignored credit cards such as Visa and MasterCard in our discussion of the money supply. After all, credit cards are a convenient way to buy things and account for about 25 percent of the dollar value of all transactions in the United States. The answer is that a credit card is not money. Rather, it is a convenient means of obtaining a short-term loan from the financial institution that issued the card.

What happens when you purchase an item with a credit card? The bank that issued the card will reimburse the seller by making a money payment, charging the establishment a transaction fee, and later you will reimburse the bank for its loan to you by also making a money payment. Rather than reduce your cash or checking account with each purchase, you bunch your payments once a month. You may have to pay an annual fee for the services provided, and if you pay the bank in installments, you will pay a sizable interest charge on the loan. Credit cards are merely a means of deferring or postponing payment for a short period. Your checking account balance used to pay your monthly credit card bill *is* money; the credit card is *not* money.*

Although credit cards are not money, they allow individuals and businesses to "economize" in the use of money. Credit cards enable people to hold less currency in their billfolds and have smaller checkable deposit balances (prior to the due date for paying the credit card bill) in their bank accounts. Credit cards also help people coordinate the timing of their expenditures with their receipt of income.

QUESTION: If credit cards are not money, why are they so popular?

*A bank debit card, however, is very similar to a blank check in your checkbook. Unlike a purchase with a credit card, a purchase with a debit card creates a direct "debit" (a subtraction) from your checking account balance. That checking account balance *is* money—it is part of $M1$.

Relative Scarcity The value of money, like the economic value of anything else, depends on its supply and demand. Money derives its value from its scarcity relative to its utility (its want-satisfying power). The utility of money lies in its capacity to be exchanged for goods and services, now or in the future. The economy's demand for money thus depends on the total dollar volume of transactions in any period plus the amount of money individuals and businesses want to hold for future transactions. With a reasonably constant demand for money, the supply of money provided by the monetary authorities will determine the value or "purchasing power" of the monetary unit (dollar, yen, peso, or whatever).

Money and Prices

The purchasing power of money is the amount of goods and services a unit of money will buy. When money rapidly loses its purchasing power, it loses its role as money.

The Purchasing Power of the Dollar The amount a dollar will buy varies inversely with the price level, meaning a reciprocal relationship exists between the general price level and the purchasing power of the dollar. When the Consumer Price Index or "cost-of-living" index goes up, the purchasing power of the dollar goes down, and vice versa. Higher prices lower the purchasing power of the dollar because more dollars are needed to buy a particular amount of goods, services, or resources. For example, if the price level doubles, the purchasing power of the dollar declines by one-half, or 50 percent.

Conversely, lower prices increase the purchasing power of the dollar because fewer dollars are needed to obtain a specific quantity of goods and services. If the price level falls by, say, one-half, or 50 percent, the purchasing power of the dollar doubles.

Inflation and Acceptability In Chapter 6 we noted situations in which a nation's currency became worthless and unacceptable in exchange. These instances of runaway inflation, or *hyperinflation*, happened when the government issued so many pieces of paper currency that the purchasing power of each of those units of money was almost totally undermined. The infamous post–World War I hyperinflation in Germany is an example. In December 1919 there were about 50 billion marks in circulation. Four years later there were 496,585,345,900 billion marks in circulation! The result? The German mark in 1923 was worth an infinitesimal fraction of its 1919 value.[3]

Runaway inflation may significantly depreciate the purchasing power of money between the time it is received and the time it is spent. Rapid declines in the purchasing power of a currency may cause it to cease being used as a medium of exchange. Businesses and households may refuse to accept paper money in exchange because they do not want to bear the loss in its value that will occur while it is in their possession. (All this despite the fact that the government says that paper currency is legal tender!) Without an acceptable domestic medium of exchange, the economy may simply revert to barter. Alternatively, more internally stable currencies such as the U.S. dollar may come into widespread use.

Similarly, people will use money as a store of value only as long as there is no sizable deterioration in the value of that money because of inflation. And an economy can effectively employ money as a unit of account only when its purchasing power is relatively stable. A monetary yardstick that no longer measures a yard (in terms of purchasing power) does not permit buyers and sellers to establish the terms of trade clearly. When the value of the dollar is declining rapidly, sellers do not know what to charge and buyers do not know what to pay.

The Federal Reserve and the Banking System

A key element of the U.S. banking system is the **Federal Reserve System** (the "Fed"). As shown in Figure 9.2, a Board of Governors directs the activities of 12 Federal Reserve Banks, which in turn control the lending activity of the nation's banks and thrift institutions. The Fed's major goal is to control the money supply. But since checkable deposits in banks are such a large part of the money supply, an important part of its duties involves assuring the stability of the banking system.

Federal Reserve System
A central component of the U.S. banking system, consisting of the Board of Governors of the Federal Reserve and 12 regional Federal Reserve Banks.

---

[3]Frank G. Graham, *Exchange, Prices and Production in Hyperinflation Germany, 1920–1923* (Princeton, N.J.: Princeton University Press, 1930), p. 13.

FIGURE 9.2 The framework of the Federal Reserve System and its relationship to the nonbank public. The Board of Governors makes the basic policy decisions that provide monetary control of the U.S. money and banking system. The 12 Federal Reserve Banks implement these decisions. Both the Board of Governors and the 12 Federal Reserve Banks are aided by the Federal Open Market Committee (FOMC).

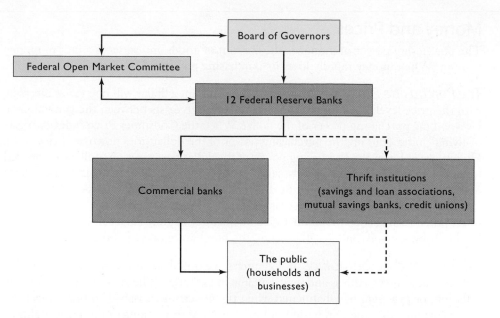

Board of Governors

Board of Governors
The seven-member group that supervises and controls the money and banking system of the United States; the Board of Governors of the Federal Reserve System; the Federal Reserve Board.

The central authority of the U.S. money and banking system is the **Board of Governors** of the Federal Reserve System. The U.S. president, with the confirmation of the Senate, appoints the seven Board members. Terms are 14 years and staggered so that one member is replaced every 2 years. In addition, new members are appointed when resignations occur. The president selects the chairperson and vice-chairperson of the Board from among the members. Those officers serve 4-year terms and can be reappointed to new 4-year terms by the president. The long-term appointments provide the Board with continuity, experienced membership, and independence from political pressures that could result in inflation.

The 12 Federal Reserve Banks

Federal Reserve Banks
The 12 banks chartered by the U.S. government to control the money supply and perform other functions. (See central bank, quasi-public bank, and bankers' bank.)

The 12 **Federal Reserve Banks,** which blend private and public control, collectively serve as the nation's "central bank." These banks also serve as bankers' banks.

Central Banks Most nations have a single central bank—for example, Britain's Bank of England or Japan's Bank of Japan. The United States' central bank consists of 12 banks whose policies are coordinated by the Fed's Board of Governors. The 12 Federal Reserve Banks accommodate the geographic size and economic diversity of the United States and the nation's large number of commercial banks and thrifts.

Figure 9.3 locates the 12 Federal Reserve Banks and indicates the district that each serves. These banks implement the basic policy of the Board of Governors.

Quasi-Public Banks The 12 Federal Reserve Banks are quasi-public banks, which blend private ownership and public control. Each Federal Reserve Bank is owned by the private commercial banks in its district. (Federally chartered commercial banks are required to purchase shares of stock in the Federal Reserve Bank in their district.) But the Board of Governors is an independent, quasi-government body that sets the basic policies that the Federal Reserve Banks pursue.

Despite their private ownership, the Federal Reserve Banks are in practice public institutions. Unlike private firms, they are not motivated by profit. The policies they

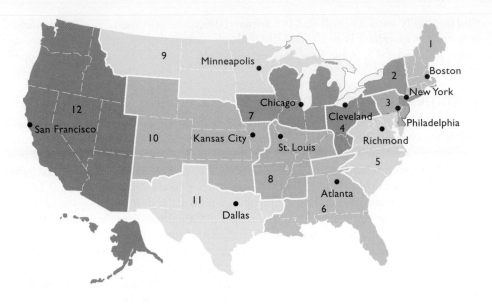

FIGURE 9.3 **The 12 Federal Reserve Districts.** The Federal Reserve System divides the United States into 12 districts, each having one central bank and in some instances one or more branches of the central bank. Hawaii and Alaska are included in the 12th district.
Source: Federal Reserve Bulletin, **www.federalreserve.gov/pubs/bulletin.**

follow are designed by the Board of Governors to promote the well-being of the economy as a whole. Also, the Federal Reserve Banks do not compete with commercial banks. In general, they do not deal with the public; rather, they interact with the government and commercial banks and thrifts.

Bankers' Banks The Federal Reserve Banks are "bankers' banks." They perform essentially the same functions for banks and thrifts as those institutions perform for the public. Just as banks and thrifts accept the deposits of and make loans to the public, so the central banks accept the deposits of and make loans to banks and thrifts. Normally, these loans average only about $150 million a day. But in emergency circumstances the Federal Reserve Banks become the "lender of last resort" to the banking system and can lend out as much as needed to ensure that banks and thrifts can meet their cash obligations. During the mortgage debt crisis of 2007–2008, the Fed loaned billions of dollars to banks and thrifts and also loaned funds to other financial institutions that were in severe financial distress. We discuss that crisis and the Fed's emergency response to the crisis later in this chapter.

But the Federal Reserve Banks have a third function, which banks and thrifts do not perform: They issue currency. Congress has authorized the Federal Reserve Banks to put into circulation Federal Reserve Notes, which constitute the economy's paper money supply.

FOMC

The **Federal Open Market Committee (FOMC)** aids the Board of Governors in conducting monetary policy. The FOMC is made up of 12 individuals:

- The seven members of the Board of Governors.
- The president of the New York Federal Reserve Bank.
- Four of the remaining presidents of Federal Reserve Banks on a 1-year rotating basis.

The FOMC meets regularly to direct the purchase and sale of government securities (bills, notes, bonds) in the open market in which such securities are bought and

Federal Open Market Committee (FOMC)
The 12-member Federal Reserve group that determines the purchase and sale policies of the Federal Reserve Banks in the market for U.S. government securities.

sold on a daily basis. We will find in Chapter 10 that the purpose of these aptly named *open-market operations* is to control the nation's money supply and influence interest rates. The Federal Reserve Bank in New York City conducts most of the Fed's open-market operations.

Commercial Banks and Thrifts

There are about 6800 commercial banks. Roughly three-fourths are *state banks*, which are chartered (authorized) by individual states to operate within those states. The other one-fourth of all banks are *national banks*, chartered by the federal government to operate nationally. Some of the U.S. national banks are very large, ranking among the world's largest financial institutions (see Global Snapshot 9.1). The 8700 thrift institutions—the vast majority of which are credit unions—are regulated by agencies separate and apart from the Board of Governors and the Federal Reserve Banks. For example, the operations of savings and loan associations are regulated and monitored by the Treasury Department's Office of Thrift Supervision. But the thrifts *are* subject to monetary control by the Federal Reserve System. In particular, like the banks, thrifts are required to keep a certain percentage of their checkable deposits as reserves. In Figure 9.2 we use dashed arrows to indicate that the thrift institutions are partially subject to the control of the Board of Governors and the central banks. Decisions concerning monetary policy affect the thrifts along with the commercial banks.

GLOBAL SNAPSHOT 9.1

The World's 12 Largest Financial Institutions

The world's 12 largest private sector financial institutions are headquartered in Europe, Japan, and the United States (2011 data).

	Assets (billions of U.S. dollars)
BNP Paribas (France)	2,681
Deutsche Bank (Germany)	2,557
HSBC Holdings (U.K.)	2,468
Barclays (U.K.)	2,328
Royal Bank of Scotland (U.K.)	2,266
Bank of America (U.S.)	2,265
Mitsubishi UFJ (Japan)	2,177
Crédit Agricole (France)	2,131
JP Morgan Chase (U.S.)	2,118
Citigroup (U.S.)	1,914
ICBC (China)	1,724
Mizuho Financial (Japan)	1,667

Source: Forbes Global 2000, **www.forbes.com**. Used with permission of Forbes Media LLC © 2011.

Fed Functions and Responsibilities

The Fed performs several functions, some of which we have already mentioned. They and other functions are worth summarizing:

- *Issuing currency*   The Federal Reserve Banks issue Federal Reserve Notes, the paper currency used in the U.S. monetary system. (The Federal Reserve Bank that issued a particular bill is identified in black in the upper left of the front of the newly designed bills. "A1," for example, identifies the Boston bank; "B2," the New York bank; and so on.)

- *Setting reserve requirements and holding reserves*   The Fed sets legal reserve ratios, which are the fractions of checking account balances that banks must maintain as currency reserves. The central banks accept as deposits from the banks and thrifts any portion of their mandated reserves not held as vault cash.

- *Lending money to financial institutions*   The Fed routinely lends money to banks and thrifts. Additionally, in times of national emergency, the Fed serves as a *lender of last resort* not only to banks and thrifts but also to other critical firms in the financial industry.

- *Providing for check collection*   The Fed provides the banking system with a means for collecting checks. If Sue writes a check on her Miami bank or thrift to Joe, who deposits it in his Dallas bank or thrift, how does the Dallas bank collect the money represented by the check drawn against the Miami bank? Answer: The Fed handles it in 2 or 3 days by adjusting the reserves (deposits) of the two banks.

- *Acting as fiscal agent*   The Fed acts as the fiscal agent (provider of financial services) for the federal government. The government collects huge sums through taxation, spends equally large amounts, and sells and redeems bonds. To carry out these activities, the government uses the Fed's facilities as its bank.

- *Supervising banks*   The Fed supervises the operations of banks. It makes periodic examinations to assess bank profitability, to ascertain that banks perform in accordance with the many regulations to which they are subject, and to uncover questionable practices or fraud.[4]

- *Controlling the money supply*   Finally, the major task of the Fed is to manage the nation's money supply, and thus indirectly set interest rates, according to the needs of the economy. This involves making an amount of money available that is consistent with high and rising levels of output and employment *and* a relatively constant price level. While all the other functions of the Fed are routine activities or have a service nature, managing the nation's money supply requires making basic, but unique, policy decisions. (We discuss those decisions in detail in Chapter 10.)

Federal Reserve Independence

Congress purposely established the Fed as an independent agency of government. The objective was to protect the Fed from political pressures so that it could effectively control the money supply and interest rates in order to maintain price-level stability. Political pressures on Congress and the executive branch may at times result in inflationary fiscal policies, including tax cuts and special-interest spending. If Congress and the executive branch also controlled the nation's monetary policy, citizens and lobbying

---

[4]The Fed is not alone in this task of supervision. The individual states supervise the banks that they charter. The Comptroller of the Currency supervises the national banks, and the Office of Thrift Supervision supervises the thrifts. Also, the Federal Deposit Insurance Corporation supervises the banks and thrifts whose deposits it insures.

groups undoubtedly would pressure elected officials to keep interest rates low even though at times high interest rates are necessary to reduce aggregate demand and thus control inflation. An independent monetary authority (the Fed) can take actions to increase interest rates when higher rates are needed to stem inflation. Studies show that countries that have independent central banks like the Fed have lower rates of inflation, on average, than countries that have little or no central bank independence.

The Financial Crisis of 2007 and 2008

A properly functioning monetary system supports the continuous circular flows of income and expenditures in the economy. In contrast, a malfunctioning monetary system causes major problems in credit markets and can cause severe fluctuations in the economy's levels of output, employment, and prices.

"Malfunctioning" is too gentle an adjective to describe the monetary system in late 2007 and 2008. In that period, the U.S. financial system faced its most serious crisis since the Great Depression of the 1930s. The financial crisis soon spread to the entire economy, culminating in the severe recession of 2007–2009. We discussed the recession in detail in previous chapters, and we now want to examine the financial crisis that led up to it. What was the nature of the financial crisis? What caused it? How has it changed the structure of the U.S. financial services industry?

The Mortgage Default Crisis

In 2007 a major wave of defaults on home mortgage loans threatened the health of not only the original mortgage lenders but of any financial institution that had made such loans or invested in such loans either directly or indirectly. A majority of these mortgage defaults were on **subprime mortgage loans**—high-interest-rate loans to home buyers with higher-than-average credit risk. Several of the biggest indirect investors in these subprime loans had been banks. The banks had lent money to investment companies that had purchased many of the mortgages from mortgage lenders. When the mortgages started to go bad, many investment funds "blew up" and could not repay the loans they had taken out from the banks. The banks thus had to "write off" (declare unrecoverable) the loans they had made to the investment companies, but doing that meant reducing their banks' reserves and limiting their ability to generate new loans. This greatly threatened the economy because both consumers and businesses rely on loans to finance consumption and investment expenditures.

A strange thing about the crisis was that before it happened, banks and government regulators had mistakenly believed that an innovation known as the "mortgage-backed security" had eliminated most of the bank exposure to mortgage defaults. **Mortgage-backed securities** are bonds backed by mortgage payments. To create them, banks and other mortgage lenders first made mortgage loans. But then instead of holding all of those loans as assets on their balance sheets and collecting the monthly mortgage payments, the banks and other mortgage lenders bundled hundreds or thousands of them together and sold them off as bonds—in essence selling the right to collect all the future mortgage payments. The banks obtained a single, upfront cash payment for the bond and the bond buyer started to collect the mortgage payments as the return on the investment.

From the banks' perspective, this seemed like a smart business decision because it transferred any future default risk on those mortgages to the buyer of the bond. The banks thought that they were off the hook for these mortgages. Unfortunately for them, however, they lent a substantial portion of the money they received from selling

subprime mortgage loans
High-interest rate loans to home buyers with above-average credit risk.

mortgage-backed securities
Bonds that represent claims to all or part of the monthly mortgage payments from the pools of mortgage loans made by lenders to borrowers to help them purchase residential property.

the bonds to investment funds that invested in mortgage-backed bonds. They also purchased large amounts of mortgage-backed securities as financial investments to help meet bank capital requirements set by bank regulators. So while the banks were no longer directly exposed to major portions of the mortgage default risk, they were still indirectly exposed to it. When many homebuyers started to default on their mortgages, the banks lost money on the mortgages they still held. The banks also lost money on the loans they had made to the investors who had purchased mortgage-backed securities, and also on the mortgage-backed securities the banks had purchased from investment firms.

But what caused the skyrocketing mortgage default rates in the first place? There were many causes, including certain government programs that greatly encouraged and subsidized home ownership for former renters. Also contributing were declining real estate values that arrived at the end of a long housing boom during which house prices had greatly increased. But an equally important factor was the bad incentives provided by the previously discussed mortgage-backed bonds. Because the banks and other mortgage lenders thought that they were no longer exposed to large portions of their mortgage default risk, they became lax in their lending practices—so much so that people were granted subprime mortgage loans that they were unlikely to be able to repay. Some mortgage companies were so eager to sign up new homebuyers (in order to bundle their loans together to sell bonds) that they stopped running credit checks and even allowed applicants to claim higher incomes than they were actually earning in order to qualify them for big loans. The natural result was that many people took on "too much mortgage" and were soon failing to make their monthly payments.

Securitization

The problems just described relate to **securitization**—the process of slicing up and bundling groups of loans, mortgages, corporate bonds, or other financial debts into distinct new securities. This process was not new and was viewed favorably by government regulators, who thought securitization made the banking system safer by allowing banks to shed risk. As noted in our discussion of mortgages, these securities were sold to financial investors, who purchased them to obtain the interest payments and the eventual return of principal generated by the underlying securities. For example, the mortgage loans provided to the subprime borrowers were bundled together as mortgage-backed securities and sold to private investors, mutual fund firms, and pension funds. These securities were attractive to many private investors and financial institutions alike because they offered higher-interest returns than securities backed by less-risky mortgages or other safer investments.

Once created, loan-backed securities are bought and sold in financial markets just like other securities such as stocks and bonds. These sorts of securities can therefore end up worldwide in the investment portfolios of banks, thrifts, insurance companies, and pensions, as well as in personal accounts.

To reduce the risk for holders of these securities, a few large insurance companies developed other securities that the holders of loan-backed securities could purchase to insure against losses from defaults. American International Group (AIG), in particular, issued billions of dollars of *collateralized default swaps*—essentially insurance policies—that were designed to compensate the holders of loan-backed securities if the loans underlying these investments went into default and did not pay off. Thus, collateralized default swaps became yet another category of investment security that was highly exposed to mortgage-loan risk.

securitization
The process of aggregating many individual financial debts into a pool and then issuing new securities (financial instruments) backed by the pool. The holders of the new securities are entitled to receive debt payments made on the individual financial debts in the pool.

Securitization is so widespread and so critical to the modern financial system that economists sometimes refer to it as the *shadow banking system*. All sorts of securities backed by loans or other securities are issued, bought, sold, and resold each day in a process that helps to keep credit flowing to the households and firms that rely on it for their personal and business needs. In general, securitization therefore is a positive financial innovation. But mortgage-backed securities, in particular, turned out to contain much more risk than most people thought.

Investors and government regulators failed to ask three related questions about mortgage-backed securities: What would happen if the value of one of the types of loans (say, mortgages) that underlies part of the securitization process unexpectedly plunged? And what then would happen if some of the largest holders of the securities based on these mortgages were major U.S. financial institutions that are vitally important to the day-to-day financing of the credit needed to keep the American economy running smoothly? And what would happen after that if the main insurer of these securities not only was the largest insurance company in the United States but in the world?

All three seemingly improbable "what ifs?" occurred! As previously explained, interest rates on adjustable-rate mortgages increased and house prices fell. Borrowers who had made relatively small down payments on home purchases or had previously cashed out home equity through refinancing discovered that they owed more on their mortgages than their properties were worth. Their loans were said to be "underwater." As interest rates adjusted upward and the economy slowed, borrowers began falling behind on their monthly mortgage payments. Lenders began to foreclose on many houses, while other borrowers literally handed in their house keys and walked away from their houses *and* their mortgages.

Failures and Near-Failures of Financial Firms

When the mortgage loan "card" underpinning mortgage-based securitization fell, the securitization layers above it collapsed like a house of cards. First, the big mortgage lenders faced demise because they still held large amounts of the bad debt. Three huge mortgage lenders collapsed or nearly collapsed. Countrywide, the second largest mortgage lender, was saved from bankruptcy by Bank of America. Regulators also seized Washington Mutual bank, the nation's largest mortgage lender, and arranged a quick takeover by JPMorgan Chase. Wachovia bank's heavy exposure to mortgages through its Golden West subsidiary resulted in near bankruptcy, and it was rescued through acquisition by Wells Fargo.

The exposure to the growing problem of loan defaults quickly jumped from direct mortgage lenders to other financial institutions. Securities firms and investment banks that held large amounts of loan-backed securities began to suffer huge losses. Merrill Lynch lost more in two years than it made in the prior decade and was acquired at a fire-sale price by Bank of America. Lehman Brothers, a major holder of mortgage-backed securities, declared bankruptcy. Goldman Sachs, Morgan Stanley, and other financial firms that had heavy exposures to mortgage-backed securities and collateralized default swaps rushed to become bank holding companies so they could qualify for the massive emergency loans that the Federal Reserve was making available to banks and bank holding companies. Citibank survived through infusions of federal government loans. Insurance company AIG suffered enormous losses because it had not set aside sufficient reserves to pay off the unexpectedly large losses that accrued on the insurance policies that it had sold to holders of mortgage-backed securities. The nightmarish thought of a total collapse of the U.S. financial system suddenly became a realistic possibility.

The Treasury Bailout: TARP

In late 2008 Congress passed the **Troubled Asset Relief Program (TARP),** which allocated $700 billion to the U.S. Treasury to make emergency loans to critical financial and other U.S. firms. Of that $700 billion, $411 billion was distributed before lending from TARP ended in October 2010. As of July 2011, approximately $255 billion had been repaid, and the U.S. Treasury estimates that the final cost of the program will be less than $50 billion (and may even generate a positive return). The federal government and Federal Reserve spent $182 billion just keeping insurer AIG afloat. Other major recipients of TARP funds included Citibank, Bank of America, JPMorgan Chase, and Goldman Sachs. Later, nonfinancial firms such as General Motors and Chrysler also received several billion dollars of TARP loans.

TARP indeed saved several financial institutions whose bankruptcy would have caused a tsunami of secondary effects that probably would have brought down other financial firms and frozen credit throughout the economy. But this very fact demonstrates the problem of **moral hazard**—a situation where individuals or institutions may change their behavior as the result of a contract or agreement. As it relates to financial investment, moral hazard is the tendency for financial investors and financial services firms to take on greater risks because they assume they are at least partially insured against losses. Without TARP, several firms would have gone bankrupt and their stockholders, bondholders, and executives all would have suffered large personal losses. With TARP, those outcomes were at least partially avoided. TARP and similar government bailouts were essentially government-provided insurance payouts to financial firms that never had to pay a single cent in insurance premiums for the massive bailouts that kept them afloat.

The correct assumption by large firms that they were simply too big for government to let them fail may have given them an incentive to make riskier investments than if no government bailouts were likely to be forthcoming.

The Postcrisis U.S. Financial Services Industry

Table 9.1 lists the major categories of firms within the U.S. financial services industry and gives examples of firms in each category. Note that the main categories of the **financial services industry** are commercial banks, thrifts, insurance companies, mutual fund companies, pension funds, security firms, and investment banks. Even before the financial crisis of 2007–2008, the financial services industry was consolidating into fewer, larger firms, each offering a wider spectrum of services. In 1999 Congress ended the Depression-era prohibition against banks selling stocks, bonds, and mutual funds. Thus, the lines between the subsets of the financial industry began to blur. Many banks acquired stock brokerage firms and, in a few cases, insurance companies. For example, Citigroup, which was once only into banking, now owns Smith Barney, a large securities firm. Many large banks (for example, Wells Fargo) and pension funds (for example, TIAA-CREF) now provide mutual funds, including money market mutual funds that pay relatively high interest and on which checks of $500 or more can be written.

The upheaval in the financial markets caused by the financial crisis of 2007–2008 further consolidated the industry and further blurred the lines between its segments. Between September 2007 and July 2011, the FDIC shut down more than 370 U.S. banks and transferred their bank deposits to other, usually larger, banks. In 2010 the three largest U.S. banks (JPMorgan Chase, Bank of America, and Wells Fargo) held roughly $3 of every $10 on deposit in the United States.

Troubled Asset Relief Program (TARP)
A 2008 federal government program that authorized the U.S. Treasury to loan up to $700 billion to critical financial institutions and other U.S. firms that were in extreme financial trouble and therefore at high risk of failure.

moral hazard
The possibility that individuals or institutions will change their behavior as the result of a contract or agreement.

financial services industry
The broad category of firms that provide financial products and services to help households and businesses earn *interest*, receive *dividends*, obtain *capital gains*, insure against *losses*, and plan for retirement.

TABLE 9.1 Major Categories of Financial Institutions within the U.S. Financial Services Industry

Institution	Description	Examples
Commercial banks	State and national banks that provide checking and savings accounts, sell certificates of deposit, and make loans. The Federal Deposit Insurance Corporation (FDIC) insures checking and savings accounts up to $250,000.	JPMorgan Chase, Bank of America, Citibank, Wells Fargo
Thrifts	Savings and loan associations (S&Ls), mutual saving banks, and credit unions that offer checking and savings accounts and make loans. Historically, S&Ls made mortgage loans for houses while mutual savings banks and credit unions made small personal loans, such as automobile loans. Today, major thrifts offer the same range of banking services as commercial banks. The Federal Deposit Insurance Corporation and the National Credit Union Administration insure checking and savings deposits up to $250,000.	Charter One, New York Community Bank, Pentagon Federal Credit Union, Boeing Employees Credit Union (BECU)
Insurance companies	Firms that offer policies (contracts) through which individuals pay premiums to insure against some loss, say, disability or death. In some life insurance policies and annuities, the funds are invested for the client in stocks and bonds and paid back after a specified number of years. Thus, insurance sometimes has a saving or financial-investment element.	Prudential, New York Life, Northwestern Mutual, Hartford, MetLife
Mutual fund companies	Firms that pool deposits by customers to purchase stocks or bonds (or both). Customers thus indirectly own a part of a particular set of stocks or bonds, say stocks in companies expected to grow rapidly (a growth fund) or bonds issued by state governments (a municipal bond fund).	Fidelity, Vanguard, Putnam, Janus, T. Rowe Price
Pension funds	For-profit or nonprofit institutions that collect savings from workers (or from employers on their behalf) throughout their working years and then buy stocks and bonds with the proceeds and make monthly retirement payments.	TIAA-CREF, Teamsters' Union, CalPERS
Securities firms	Firms that offer security advice and buy and sell stocks and bonds for clients. More generally known as *stock brokerage firms*.	Merrill Lynch, Smith Barney, Charles Schwab
Investment banks	Firms that help corporations and governments raise money by selling stocks and bonds. They also typically offer advisory services for corporate mergers and acquisitions as well as brokerage services and advice.	Goldman Sachs, Morgan Stanley, Deutsche Bank, Nomura Securities

Wall Street Reform and Consumer Protection Act of 2010
A law that gave authority to the Federal Reserve to regulate all large financial institutions, created an oversight council to look for growing risk to the financial system, established a process for the federal government to sell off the assets of large failing financial institutions, provided federal regulatory oversight of asset-backed securities, and created a financial consumer protection bureau within the Fed.

Also, during the financial crisis of 2007–2008, major investment banks Goldman Sachs and Morgan Stanley opted to become commercial banks to gain access to emergency Federal Reserve loans (we will discuss these emergency loans in Chapter 10). The nation's largest thrift—Washington Mutual—was absorbed by commercial bank JPMorgan Chase. But even with all this blending, the categories in Table 9.1 remain helpful. The main lines of a firm's businesses often are in one category or another. For example, even though Goldman Sachs is licensed and regulated as a bank, it is first and foremost an investment company. And the insurance companies and pension funds do most of their business as such.

The financial crisis of 2007–2008 generated much introspection about what went wrong and how to prevent anything like it from happening again. Politicians and financial regulators tightened lending rules to offset the "pass the buck" incentives created by mortgage-backed securities and prevent loans from being issued to people who are unlikely to be able to make the required monthly payments. They also passed legislation to help homeowners who were "underwater" on mortgage loans remain in their homes.

In mid-2010 Congress passed and the president signed the **Wall Street Reform and Consumer Protection Act.** This sweeping law includes provisions that

- eliminate the Office of Thrift Supervision and give broader authority to the Federal Reserve to regulate all large financial institutions;

- create a Financial Stability Oversight Council to be on the lookout for risks to the financial system;
- establish a process for the federal government to liquidate (sell off) the assets of large failing financial institutions, much like the FDIC does with failing banks;
- provide federal regulatory oversight of mortgage-backed securities and other derivatives and require that they be traded on public exchanges;
- require companies selling asset-backed securities to retain a portion of those securities so the sellers share part of the risk; and
- establish a stronger consumer financial protection role for the Fed through creation of the Bureau of Consumer Financial Protection.

Proponents of the new law say that it will help prevent many of the practices that led up to the financial crisis of 2007–2008. They also contend that the law will send a strong message to stockholders, bondholders, and executives of large financial firms that they will suffer unavoidable and extremely high personal financial losses if they allow their firms to ever again get into serious financial trouble.

Skeptics of the new law say that regulators already had all the tools they needed to prevent the financial crisis. They also point out that the government's own efforts to promote home ownership, via quasi-government institutions that purchased mortgage-backed securities, greatly contributed to the financial crisis. Critics of the new law say that it will simply impose heavy new regulatory costs on the financial industry while doing little to prevent future government bailouts.

The Fractional Reserve System

We have seen that the $M1$ money supply consists of currency (coins and Federal Reserve Notes) and checkable deposits. The U.S. Mint creates the coins and the U.S. Bureau of Engraving creates the Federal Reserve Notes. So who creates the checkable deposits that make up about half the nation's $M1$ money supply? Surprisingly, it is loan officers at banks and thrifts!

The United States, like most other countries today, has a **fractional reserve banking system** in which only a portion (fraction) of the total money supply is held in reserve as currency. Our goal is to explain how commercial banks and thrifts can create checkable deposits by issuing loans. Our examples will involve commercial banks, but remember that thrift institutions also provide checkable deposits. So the analysis applies to banks and thrifts alike.

fractional reserve banking system
A banking system in which banks and thrifts are required to hold less than 100 percent of their checkable-deposit liabilities as reserves.

ILLUSTRATING THE IDEA

The Goldsmiths

Here is the history behind the idea of the fractional reserve system.

When early traders began to use gold in making transactions, they soon realized that it was both unsafe and inconvenient to carry gold and to have it weighed and assayed (judged for purity) every time they negotiated a transaction. So by the 16th century they had begun to deposit their gold with goldsmiths, who would store it in vaults for a fee. On receiving a gold deposit, the goldsmith would issue a receipt to the depositor. Soon people were paying for goods with goldsmiths' receipts, which served as one of the first types of paper money.

At this point the goldsmiths—embryonic bankers—used a 100 percent reserve system; they backed their circulating paper money receipts fully with the gold that they held "in reserve" in their vaults. But because of the public's acceptance of the goldsmiths' receipts as paper money, the goldsmiths soon realized that owners rarely redeemed the gold they had in storage. In fact, the goldsmiths observed that the amount of gold being deposited with them in any week or month was likely to exceed the amount that was being withdrawn.

Then some clever goldsmith hit on the idea that paper "receipts" could be issued in excess of the amount of gold held. Goldsmiths would put these receipts, which were redeemable in gold, into circulation by making interest-earning loans to merchants, producers, and consumers. A borrower might, for instance, borrow $10,000 worth of gold receipts today with the promise to repay $10,500 worth of gold receipts in one year (a five percent interest rate). Borrowers were willing to accept loans in the form of gold receipts because the receipts were accepted as a medium of exchange in the marketplace.

This was the beginning of the fractional reserve system of banking, in which reserves in bank vaults are a fraction of the total money supply. If, for example, the goldsmith issued $1 million in receipts for actual gold in storage and another $1 million in receipts as loans, then the total value of paper money in circulation would be $2 million—twice the value of the gold. Gold reserves would be a fraction (one-half) of outstanding paper money.

QUESTION: Explain how the gold receipts issued by goldsmiths performed the three major functions of money.

The goldsmith story highlights two significant characteristics of fractional reserve banking. First, banks can create money through lending. In fact, goldsmiths created money when they made loans by giving borrowers paper money that was not fully backed by gold reserves. The quantity of such money goldsmiths could create depended on the amount of reserves they deemed prudent to have available. The smaller the amount of reserves thought necessary, the larger the amount of paper money the goldsmiths could create. Today, gold is no longer used as bank reserves. Instead, currency itself serves as bank reserves so that the creation of checkable-deposit money by banks (via their lending) is limited by the amount of *currency reserves* that the banks feel obligated, or are required by law, to keep.

A second reality is that banks operating on the basis of fractional reserves are vulnerable to "panics" or "runs." A goldsmith who issued paper money equal to twice the value of his gold reserves would be unable to convert all that paper money into gold in the event that all the holders of that money appeared at his door at the same time demanding their gold. In fact, many European and U.S. banks were once ruined by this unfortunate circumstance. However, a bank panic is highly unlikely if the banker's reserve and lending policies are prudent. Indeed, one reason why banking systems are highly regulated industries is to prevent runs on banks. This is also the reason why the United States has a system of deposit insurance.

A Single Commercial Bank

To illustrate the workings of the modern fractional reserve banking system, we need to examine a commercial bank's balance sheet.

The **balance sheet** of a commercial bank (or thrift) is a statement of assets— things owned by the bank or owed to the bank—and claims on those assets. A bank balance sheet summarizes the financial position of the bank at a certain time. Every balance sheet must balance; this means that the value of *assets* must equal the amount of claims against those assets. The claims shown on a balance sheet are divided into two groups: the claims of nonowners of the bank against the firm's assets, called *liabilities*, and the claims of the owners of the firm against the firm's assets, called *net worth*. Liabilities are things owed by the bank to depositors or others. A balance sheet is balanced because

$$\text{Assets} = \text{liabilities} + \text{net worth}$$

For every $1 change in assets, there must be an offsetting $1 change in liabilities + net worth. For every $1 change in liabilities + net worth, there must be an offsetting $1 change in assets.

Now let's work through a series of bank transactions involving balance sheets to establish how individual banks can create money.

balance sheet
A statement of the assets, liabilities, and net worth of a firm, individual, or institution at some time.

Transaction 1: Creating a Bank

Suppose some farsighted citizens of the town of Somewhere decide their town needs a new commercial bank to provide banking services for that growing community. Once they have secured a state or national charter for their bank, they turn to the task of selling, say, $250,000 worth of stock certificates (equity shares) to buyers, both in and out of the community. Their efforts meet with success and the Bank of Somewhere comes into existence—at least on paper. What does its balance sheet look like at this stage?

The founders of the bank have sold $250,000 worth of shares of stock in the bank—some to themselves, some to other people. As a result, the bank now has $250,000 in cash on hand and $250,000 worth of stock certificates outstanding. The cash is an asset to the bank. Cash held by a bank is sometimes called *vault cash* or *till money*. The shares of stock outstanding constitute an equal amount of claims that the owners have against the bank's assets. Those shares of stock constitute the net worth of the bank. The bank's balance sheet reads:

Creating a Bank		
Balance Sheet 1: Somewhere Bank		
Assets	Liabilities and net worth	
Cash $250,000	Stock shares	$250,000

Each item listed in a balance sheet such as this is called an *account*.

Transaction 2: Acquiring Property and Equipment

The board of directors (who represent the bank's owners) must now get the new bank off the drawing board and make it a reality. First, property and equipment must be acquired. Suppose the directors, confident of the success of their venture, purchase a building for $220,000 and pay $20,000 for office equipment. This simple transaction changes the composition of the bank's assets. The bank now has $240,000 less in cash and $240,000 of new property assets. Using blue to denote accounts affected by each transaction, we show that the bank's balance sheet at the end of transaction 2 appears as follows:

Acquiring Property and Equipment Balance Sheet 2: Somewhere Bank			
Assets		Liabilities and net worth	
Cash	$ 10,000	Stock shares	$250,000
Property	240,000		

Note that the balance sheet still balances, as it must.

Transaction 3: Accepting Deposits

Commercial banks have two basic functions: to accept deposits of money and to make loans. Now that the bank is operating, suppose that the citizens and businesses of Somewhere decide to deposit $100,000 in the Somewhere bank. What happens to the bank's balance sheet?

The bank receives cash, which is an asset to the bank. Suppose this money is deposited in the bank as checkable deposits (checking account entries), rather than as savings accounts or time deposits. These newly created *checkable deposits* constitute claims that the depositors have against the assets of the Somewhere bank and thus are a new liability account. The bank's balance sheet now looks like this:

Accepting Deposits Balance Sheet 3: Somewhere Bank			
Assets		Liabilities and net worth	
Cash	$110,000	Checkable deposits	$100,000
Property	240,000	Stock shares	250,000

There has been no change in the economy's total supply of money as a result of transaction 3, but a change has occurred in the composition of the money supply. Bank money, or checkable deposits, has increased by $100,000, and currency held by the public has decreased by $100,000. Currency held by a bank, you will recall, is not part of the economy's money supply.

A withdrawal of cash will reduce the bank's checkable-deposit liabilities and its holdings of cash by the amount of the withdrawal. This, too, changes the composition, but not the total supply, of money in the economy.

Transaction 4: Depositing Reserves in a Federal Reserve Bank

required reserves
The funds that banks and thrifts must deposit with the Federal Reserve Bank (or hold as vault cash) to meet the Fed's reserve requirement.

reserve ratio
The legally required percentage of reserves for every $1 of a bank or thrift's checkable deposits.

All commercial banks and thrift institutions that provide checkable deposits must by law keep **required reserves.** Required reserves are an amount of funds equal to a specified percentage of the bank's own deposit liabilities. A bank must keep these reserves on deposit with the Federal Reserve Bank in its district or as cash in the bank's vault. To simplify, we suppose the Bank of Somewhere keeps its required reserves entirely as deposits in the Federal Reserve Bank of its district. But remember that vault cash is counted as reserves and real-world banks keep a significant portion of their own reserves in their vaults.

The "specified percentage" of checkable-deposit liabilities that a commercial bank must keep as reserves is known as the **reserve ratio**—the ratio of the required reserves the commercial bank must keep to the bank's own outstanding checkable-deposit liabilities:

$$\text{Reserve ratio} = \frac{\text{commercial bank's required reserves}}{\text{commercial bank's checkable-deposit liabilities}}$$

If the reserve ratio is $\frac{1}{10}$, or 10 percent, the Somewhere bank, having accepted $100,000 in deposits from the public, would have to keep $10,000 as reserves. If the ratio is $\frac{1}{5}$, or 20 percent, $20,000 of reserves would be required. If $\frac{1}{2}$, or 50 percent, $50,000 would be required.

The Fed has the authority to establish and vary the reserve ratio within limits legislated by Congress. A 10 percent reserve is required on checkable deposits over $55.2 million, although the Fed can vary that percentage between 8 and 14 percent. Also, after consultation with appropriate congressional committees, the Fed for 180 days may impose reserve requirements outside the 8–14 percent range. Beginning in late 2008, the Fed began paying banks interest on their required reserves and on their excess reserves held at the Federal Reserve Banks.

In order to simplify, we will suppose that the reserve ratio for checkable deposits in commercial banks is $\frac{1}{5}$, or 20 percent. Although 20 percent obviously is higher than the requirement really is, the figure is convenient for calculations. The main point is that reserve requirements are fractional, meaning that they are less than 100 percent.

By depositing $20,000 in the Federal Reserve Bank, the Somewhere bank will just be meeting the required 20 percent ratio between its reserves and its own deposit liabilities. We will use "reserves" to mean the funds commercial banks deposit in the Federal Reserve Banks, to distinguish those funds from the public's deposits in commercial banks.

But suppose the Somewhere bank anticipates that its holdings of checkable deposits will grow in the future. Then, instead of sending just the minimum amount, $20,000, it sends an extra $90,000, for a total of $110,000. In so doing, the bank will avoid the inconvenience of sending additional reserves to the Federal Reserve Bank each time its own checkable-deposit liabilities increase. And, as you will see, it is these extra reserves that enable banks to lend money and earn interest income.

Actually, a real-world bank would not deposit *all* its cash in the Federal Reserve Bank. However, because (1) banks as a rule hold vault cash only in the amount of $1\frac{1}{2}$ or 2 percent of their total assets and (2) vault cash can be counted as reserves, we will assume for simplicity that all of Somewhere's cash is deposited in the Federal Reserve Bank and therefore constitutes the commercial bank's actual reserves. By making this simplifying assumption, we do not need to bother adding two assets—"cash" and "deposits in the Federal Reserve Bank"—to determine reserves.

After the Somewhere bank deposits $110,000 of reserves at the Fed, its balance sheet becomes:

Depositing Reserves at the Fed			
Balance Sheet 4: Somewhere Bank			
Assets		Liabilities and net worth	
Cash	$ 0	Checkable deposits	$100,000
Reserves	110,000		
Property	240,000	Stock shares	250,000

There are three things to note about this latest transaction.

excess reserves
Actual bank or thrift
reserves minus legally
required reserves.

actual reserves
The funds that a bank or
thrift has on deposit at a
Federal Reserve Bank or
is holding as vault cash.

Excess Reserves A bank's **excess reserves** are found by subtracting its *required reserves* (or legally required reserves) from its **actual reserves:**

$$\text{Excess reserves} = \text{actual reserves} - \text{required reserves}$$

In this case,

Actual reserves	$110,000
Required reserves	−20,000
Excess reserves	$ 90,000

The only reliable way of computing excess reserves is to multiply the bank's checkable-deposit liabilities by the reserve ratio to obtain required reserves ($100,000 × 20 percent = $20,000) and then to subtract the required reserves from the actual reserves listed on the asset side of the bank's balance sheet.

To test your understanding, compute the bank's excess reserves from balance sheet 4, assuming that the reserve ratio is (1) 10 percent, (2) $33\frac{1}{3}$ percent, and (3) 50 percent.

We will soon demonstrate that the ability of a commercial bank to make loans depends on the existence of excess reserves. Understanding this concept is crucial in seeing how the banking system creates money.

Control You might think the basic purpose of reserves is to enhance the liquidity of a bank and protect commercial bank depositors from losses. Reserves would constitute a ready source of funds from which commercial banks could meet large, unexpected cash withdrawals by depositors.

But this reasoning breaks down under scrutiny. Although historically reserves have been seen as a source of liquidity and therefore as protection for depositors, a bank's required reserves are not great enough to meet sudden, massive cash withdrawals. If the banker's nightmare should materialize—everyone with checkable deposits appearing at once to demand those deposits in cash—the legal reserves held as vault cash or at the Federal Reserve Bank would be insufficient. The banker simply could not meet this "bank panic." Because reserves are fractional, checkable deposits are usually much greater than a bank's required reserves.

So commercial bank deposits must be protected by other means. Periodic bank examinations are one way of promoting prudent commercial banking practices. Furthermore, as we have mentioned, government-sponsored deposit insurance funds insure individual deposits in banks and thrifts up to $250,000.

If it is not the purpose of reserves to provide for commercial bank liquidity, then what is their function? *Control* is the answer. Required reserves help the Fed control the lending ability of commercial banks. The Fed can take certain actions that either increase or decrease commercial bank reserves and affect the ability of banks to grant credit. The objective is to prevent banks from overextending or underextending bank credit. To the degree that these policies successfully influence the volume of commercial bank credit, the Fed can help the economy avoid business fluctuations. Another function of reserves is to facilitate the collection or "clearing" of checks.

Transaction 5: Clearing a Check Drawn against the Bank

Assume that Fred Bradshaw, a Somewhere farmer, deposited a substantial portion of the $100,000 in checkable deposits that the Somewhere bank received in transaction 3. Now suppose that Bradshaw buys $50,000 of farm machinery from the Ajax Farm Implement Company of Elsewhere. Bradshaw pays for this machinery by writing a

$50,000 check against his deposit in the Somewhere bank. He gives the check to the Ajax Company. What are the results?

Ajax deposits the check in its account with the Elsewhere bank. The Elsewhere bank increases Ajax's checkable deposits by $50,000 when Ajax deposits the check. Ajax is now paid in full. Bradshaw is pleased with his new machinery.

Now the Elsewhere bank has Bradshaw's check. This check is simply a claim against the assets of the Somewhere bank. The Elsewhere bank will collect this claim by sending the check (along with checks drawn on other banks) to the regional Federal Reserve Bank. Here a clerk will clear, or collect, the check for the Elsewhere bank by increasing Elsewhere's reserve in the Federal Reserve Bank by $50,000 and decreasing the Somewhere bank's reserve by that same amount. The check is "collected" merely by making bookkeeping notations to the effect that Somewhere's claim against the Federal Reserve Bank is reduced by $50,000 and Elsewhere's claim is increased by $50,000.

Finally, the Federal Reserve Bank sends the cleared check back to the Somewhere bank, and for the first time the Somewhere bank discovers that one of its depositors has drawn a check for $50,000 against his checkable deposit. Accordingly, the Somewhere bank reduces Bradshaw's checkable deposit by $50,000 and notes that the collection of this check has caused a $50,000 decline in its reserves at the Federal Reserve Bank. All the balance sheets balance: The Somewhere bank has reduced both its assets (reserves) and its liabilities (checkable deposits) by $50,000. The Elsewhere bank has $50,000 more both assets (reserves) and liabilities (checkable deposits). Ownership of reserves at the Federal Reserve Bank has changed—with Somewhere owning $50,000 less and Elsewhere owning $50,000 more—but total reserves stay the same.

Whenever a check is drawn against one bank and deposited in another bank, collection of that check will reduce both the reserves and the checkable deposits of the bank on which the check is drawn. Conversely, if a bank receives a check drawn on another bank, the bank receiving the check will, in the process of collecting it, have its reserves and deposits increased by the amount of the check. In our example, the Somewhere bank loses $50,000 in both reserves and deposits to the Elsewhere bank. But there is no loss of reserves or deposits for the banking system as a whole. What one bank loses, another bank gains.

If we bring all the other assets and liabilities back into the picture, the Somewhere bank's balance sheet looks like this at the end of transaction 5:

Clearing a Check

Balance Sheet 5: Somewhere Bank

Assets		Liabilities and net worth	
Reserves	$ 60,000	Checkable deposits	$ 50,000
Property	240,000	Stock shares	250,000

Verify that with a 20 percent reserve requirement, the bank's excess reserves now stand at $50,000.

Transaction 6: Granting a Loan (Creating Money)

In addition to accepting deposits, commercial banks grant loans to borrowers. What effect does lending by a commercial bank have on its balance sheet?

Suppose the Gristly Meat Packing Company of Somewhere decides it is time to expand its facilities. Suppose, too, that the company needs exactly $50,000—which just happens to be equal to the Somewhere bank's excess reserves—to finance this project.

Gristly goes to the Somewhere bank and requests a loan for this amount. The Somewhere bank knows the Gristly Company's fine reputation and financial soundness and is convinced of its ability to repay the loan. So the loan is granted. In return, the president of Gristly hands a promissory note—a fancy IOU—to the Somewhere bank. Gristly wants the convenience and safety of paying its obligations by check. So, instead of receiving a bushel basket full of currency from the bank, Gristly gets a $50,000 increase in its checkable-deposit account in the Somewhere bank.

The Somewhere bank has acquired an interest-earning asset (the promissory note, which it files under "Loans") and has created checkable deposits (a liability) to "pay" for this asset. Gristly has swapped an IOU for the right to draw an additional $50,000 worth of checks against its checkable deposit in the Somewhere bank. Both parties are pleased.

At the moment the loan is completed, the Somewhere bank's position is shown by balance sheet 6a:

When a Loan Is Negotiated
Balance Sheet 6a: Somewhere Bank

Assets		Liabilities and net worth	
Reserves	$ 60,000	Checkable deposits	$100,000
Loans	50,000		
Property	240,000	Stock shares	250,000

All this looks simple enough. But a close examination of the Somewhere bank's balance statement reveals a startling fact: *When a bank makes loans, it creates money.* The president of Gristly went to the bank with something that is *not* money—her IOU—and walked out with something that *is* money—a checkable deposit.

Contrast transaction 6a with transaction 3, in which checkable deposits were created but only as a result of currency having been taken out of circulation. There was a change in the *composition* of the money supply in that situation but no change in the *total supply* of money. But when banks lend, they create checkable deposits that *are* money. By extending credit, the Somewhere bank has "monetized" an IOU. Gristly and the Somewhere bank have created and then swapped claims. The claim created by Gristly and given to the bank is not money; an individual's IOU is not acceptable as a medium of exchange. But the claim created by the bank and given to Gristly *is* money; checks drawn against a checkable deposit are acceptable as a medium of exchange. Checkable deposit money like this constitutes about one-half the quantity of $M1$ money in the United States and about 10 percent of $M2$.

Much of the money used in the United States, therefore, is created through the extension of credit by commercial banks. This checkable-deposit money may be thought of as "debts" of commercial banks and thrift institutions. Checkable deposits are bank debts in the sense that they are claims that banks and thrifts promise to pay "on demand."

But there are factors limiting the ability of a commercial bank to create checkable deposits ("bank money") by lending. The Somewhere bank can expect the newly created checkable deposit of $50,000 to be a very active account. Gristly would not borrow $50,000 at, say, 7, 10, or 12 percent interest for the sheer joy of knowing that funds were available if needed.

Assume that Gristly awards a $50,000 building contract to the Quickbuck Construction Company. Quickbuck, true to its name, completes the expansion promptly and is paid with a check for $50,000 drawn by Gristly against its checkable deposit in the Somewhere bank. Quickbuck does not deposit this check in the Somewhere bank but instead deposits it in the Elsewhere bank. Elsewhere now has a $50,000 claim against the Somewhere bank. The check is collected in the manner described in transaction 5. As a result, the Somewhere bank loses both reserves and deposits equal to the amount of the check; Elsewhere acquires $50,000 of reserves and deposits.

In summary, assuming a check is drawn by the borrower for the entire amount of the loan ($50,000) and is given to a firm that deposits it in some other bank, the Somewhere bank's balance sheet will read as follows *after the check has been cleared against it:*

After a Check Is Drawn on the Loan			
Balance Sheet 6b: Somewhere Bank			
Assets		Liabilities and net worth	
Reserves	$ 10,000	Checkable	
Loans	50,000	deposits	$ 50,000
Property	240,000	Stock shares	250,000

After the check has been collected, the Somewhere bank just meets the required reserve ratio of 20 percent (= $10,000/$50,000). The bank has *no* excess reserves. This poses a question: Could the Somewhere bank have lent more than $50,000—an amount greater than its excess reserves—and still have met the 20 percent reserve requirement when a check for the full amount of the loan was cleared against it? The answer is no; the bank is "fully loaned up."

Here is why: Suppose the Somewhere bank had lent $55,000 to the Gristly company and that the Gristly company had spent all of that money by writing a $55,000 check to Quickbuck Construction. Collection of the check against the Somewhere bank would have lowered its reserves to $5000 (= $60,000 − $55,000), and checkable deposits would once again stand at $50,000 (= $105,000 − $55,000). The ratio of actual reserves to checkable deposits would then be $5000/$50,000, or 10 percent, not the 20 percent required. So the Somewhere bank could not have lent $55,000.

By experimenting with other amounts over $50,000, you will find that the maximum amount the Somewhere bank could lend at the outset of transaction 6 is $50,000. This amount is identical to the amount of excess reserves the bank had available when the loan was negotiated. *A single commercial bank in a multibank banking system can lend only an amount equal to its initial preloan excess reserves.* When it lends, the lending bank faces the possibility that checks for the entire amount of the loan will be drawn and cleared against it. If that happens, the lending bank will lose (to other banks) reserves equal to the amount it lends. So, to be safe, it limits its lending to the amount of its excess reserves.

Bank creation of money raises an interesting question: If banks create checkable deposit money when they lend their excess reserves, is money destroyed when borrowers pay off their loans? The answer is yes. When loans are paid off, the process just described works in reverse. Checkable deposits decline by the amount of the loan payment.

WORKED PROBLEMS

W 9.1

Single bank accounting

The Banking System: Multiple-Deposit Expansion

Thus far we have seen that a single bank in a banking system can lend one dollar for each dollar of its excess reserves. The situation is different for all commercial banks as a group. We will find that the commercial banking system can lend—that is, can create money—by a multiple of its excess reserves. This multiple lending is accomplished even though each bank in the system can lend only "dollar for dollar" with its excess reserves.

How do these seemingly paradoxical results come about? To answer this question succinctly, we will make three simplifying assumptions:

- The reserve ratio for all commercial banks is 20 percent.
- Initially all banks are meeting this 20 percent reserve requirement exactly. No excess reserves exist; or, in the parlance of banking, they are "loaned up" (or "loaned out") fully in terms of the reserve requirement.
- If any bank can increase its loans as a result of acquiring excess reserves, an amount equal to those excess reserves will be lent to one borrower, who will write a check for the entire amount of the loan and give it to someone else, who will deposit the check in another bank. This third assumption means that the worst thing possible happens to every lending bank—a check for the entire amount of the loan is drawn and cleared against it in favor of another bank.

The Banking System's Lending Potential

Suppose a junkyard owner finds a $100 bill while dismantling a car that has been on the lot for years. He deposits the $100 in bank A, which adds the $100 to its reserves. We will record only changes in the balance sheets of the various commercial banks. The deposit changes bank A's balance sheet as shown by entries (a_1):

Multiple-Deposit Expansion Process			
Balance Sheet: Commercial Bank A			
Assets		Liabilities and net worth	
Reserves	$+100 ($a_1$)	Checkable	
	− 80 (a_3)	deposits	$+100 ($a_1$)
Loans	+ 80 (a_2)		+ 80 (a_2)
			− 80 (a_3)

Recall from transaction 3 that this $100 deposit of currency does not alter the money supply. While $100 of checkable-deposit money comes into being, it is offset by the $100 of currency no longer in the hands of the nonbank public (the junkyard owner). But bank A *has* acquired excess reserves of $80. Of the newly acquired $100 in currency, 20 percent, or $20, must be earmarked for the required reserves on the new $100 checkable deposit, and the remaining $80 goes to excess reserves. Remembering that a single commercial bank can lend only an amount equal to its excess reserves, we conclude that bank A can lend a maximum of $80. When a loan for this amount is made, bank A's loans increase by $80 and the borrower gets an $80 checkable deposit. We add these figures—entries (a_2)—to bank A's balance sheet.

But now we employ our third assumption: The borrower uses the full amount of the loan ($80) to write a check ($80) to someone else, and that person deposits the amount in bank B, a different bank. As we saw in transaction 6, bank A loses both reserves and deposits equal to the amount of the loan, as indicated in entries (a_3). The net result of these transactions is that bank A's reserves now stand at + $20 (= $100 − $80), loans at +$80, and checkable deposits at + $100 (= $100 + $80 − $80). When the dust has settled, bank A is just meeting the 20 percent reserve ratio.

Recalling our previous discussion, we know that bank B acquires both the reserves and the deposits that bank A has lost. Bank B's balance sheet is changed as shown in the entries (b_1) that follow.

Multiple-Deposit Expansion Process
Balance Sheet: Commercial Bank B

Assets		Liabilities and net worth	
Reserves	$+80 ($b_1$)	Checkable deposits	$+80 ($b_1$)
	−64 (b_3)		+64 (b_2)
Loans	+64 (b_2)		−64 (b_3)

When the borrower's check is drawn and cleared, bank A loses $80 in reserves and deposits and bank B gains $80 in reserves and deposits. But 20 percent, or $16, of bank B's new reserves must be kept as required reserves against the new $80 in checkable deposits. This means that bank B has $64 (= $80 − $16) in excess reserves. It can therefore lend $64 [entries ($b_2$)]. When the new borrower writes a check for $64 to buy a product, and the seller deposits the check in bank C, the reserves and deposits of bank B both fall by $64 [entries ($b_3$)]. As a result of these transactions, bank B's reserves now stand at +$16 (= $80 − $64), loans at +$64, and checkable deposits at + $80 (= $80 + $64 − $64). After all this, bank B is just meeting the 20 percent reserve requirement.

We could go ahead with this procedure by bringing banks C, D, E, ... , N and so on into the picture. In fact, the process will go on almost indefinitely, just as long as banks further down the line receive at least one penny in new reserves that they can use to back another round of lending and money creation. But that might be annoying! Instead, we summarize the entire analysis in Table 9.2. Our conclusion is startling: On the basis of only $80 in excess reserves (acquired by the banking system when someone deposited $100 of currency in bank A), the entire commercial banking system is able to lend $400, the sum of the amounts in column 4. The banking system can

TABLE 9.2 Expansion of the Money Supply by the Commercial Banking System

Bank	(1) Acquired Reserves and Deposits	(2) Required Reserves (Reserve Ratio = .2)	(3) Excess Reserves, (1) − (2)	(4) Amount Bank Can Lend; New Money Created = (3)
Bank A	$100.00 ($a_1$)	$20.00	$80.00	$80.00 ($a_2$)
Bank B	80.00 (a_3, b_1)	16.00	64.00	64.00 (b_2)
Bank C	64.00	12.80	51.20	51.20
Bank D	51.20	10.24	40.96	40.96
Bank E	40.96	8.19	32.77	32.77
Bank F	32.77	6.55	26.21	26.21
Bank G	26.21	5.24	20.97	20.97
Bank H	20.97	4.20	16.78	16.78
Bank I	16.78	3.36	13.42	13.42
Bank J	13.42	2.68	10.74	10.74
Bank K	10.74	2.15	8.59	8.59
Bank L	8.59	1.72	6.87	6.87
Bank M	6.87	1.37	5.50	5.50
Bank N	5.50	1.10	4.40	4.40
Other banks	21.99	4.40	17.59	17.59
Total amount of money created (sum of the amounts in column 4)				**$400.00**

lend excess reserves by a multiple of 5 (= \$400/\$80) when the reserve ratio is 20 percent. Yet each single bank in the banking system is lending only an amount equal to its own excess reserves. How do we explain this? How can the banking system as a whole lend by a multiple of its excess reserves, when each individual bank can lend only dollar for dollar with its excess reserves?

The answer is that reserves lost by a single bank are not lost to the banking system as a whole. The reserves lost by bank A are acquired by bank B. Those lost by B are gained by C. C loses to D, D to E, E to F, and so forth. Although reserves can be, and are, lost by individual banks in the banking system, there is no loss of reserves for the banking system as a whole.

An individual bank can safely lend only an amount equal to its excess reserves, *but the commercial banking system can lend by a multiple of its collective excess reserves.* Commercial banks as a group can create money by lending in a manner very different from that of the individual banks in the group.

The Monetary Multiplier

monetary multiplier
The multiple of its excess reserves by which the banking system can expand checkable deposits and thus the money supply by making new loans.

The **monetary multiplier** (or, less commonly, the *checkable deposit multiplier*) defines the relationship between any new excess reserves in the banking system and the magnified creation of new checkable-deposit money by banks as a group. The monetary multiplier exists because the reserves and deposits lost by one bank become reserves of another bank. It magnifies excess reserves into a larger creation of checkable-deposit money. The monetary multiplier m is the reciprocal of the required reserve ratio R (the leakage into required reserves that occurs at each step in the lending process). In short,

$$\text{Monetary multiplier} = \frac{1}{\text{required reserve ratio}}$$

or, in symbols,

$$m = \frac{1}{R}$$

WORKED PROBLEMS

W 9.2

Money creation

In this formula, m represents the maximum amount of new checkable-deposit money that can be created by a single dollar of excess reserves, given the value of R. By multiplying the excess reserves E by m, we can find the maximum amount of new checkable-deposit money, D, that can be created by the banking system. That is,

Maximum checkable-deposit creation = excess reserves × monetary multiplier or, more simply,

$$D = E \times m$$

In our example in Table 9.2, R is .20, so m is 5 (=1/.20). Then

$$D = \$80 \times 5 = \$400$$

Reversibility: The Multiple Destruction of Money

The process we have described is reversible. Just as money is created when banks make loans, money is destroyed when loans are paid off. Loan repayment, in effect, sets off a process of multiple destruction of money akin to the multiple creation process. Because loans are both made and paid off in any period, the direction of the money supply in a given period will depend on the net effect of the two processes. If the dollar amount of loans made in some period exceeds the dollar amount of loans paid off, checkable deposits will expand and the money supply will increase. In contrast, if the dollar amount of loans made in some period is less than the dollar amount of loans paid off, checkable deposits will contract and the money supply will decline.

The Bank Panics of 1930 to 1933

In the early months of the Great Depression, before there was deposit insurance, several financially weak banks went out of business. As word spread that customers of those banks had lost their deposits, a general concern arose that something similar could happen at other banks. Depositors became frightened that their banks did not, in fact, still have all the money they had deposited. And, of course, that is a reality in a fractional reserve banking system. Acting on their fears, people en masse tried to "cash out" their bank accounts by withdrawing their money before it was all gone. This "run on the banks" caused many previously financially sound banks to declare bankruptcy. More than 9000 banks failed within 3 years.

The massive conversion of checkable deposits to currency during 1930 to 1933 reduced the nation's money supply. This might seem strange, since a check written for "cash" reduces checkable-deposit money and increases currency in the hands of the public by the same amount. So how does the money supply decline? Our discussion of the money-creation process provides the answer, but now the story becomes one of money destruction.

Suppose that people collectively cash out $10 billion from their checking accounts. As an immediate result, checkable-deposit money declines by $10 billion, while currency held by the public increases by $10 billion. But here is the catch: Assuming a reserve ratio of 20 percent, the $10 billion of currency in the banks had been supporting $50 billion of deposit money, the $10 billion of deposits plus $40 billion created through loans. The $10 billion withdrawal of currency forces banks to reduce loans (and thus checkable-deposit money) by $40 billion to continue to meet their reserve requirement. In short, a $40 billion destruction of deposit money occurs. This is the scenario that occurred in the early years of the 1930s.

Accompanying this multiple contraction of checkable deposits was the banks' "scramble for liquidity" to try to meet further withdrawals of currency. To obtain more currency, they sold many of their holdings of government securities to the public. A bank's sale of government securities to the public, like a reduction in loans, reduces the money supply. People write checks for the securities, reducing their checkable deposits, and the bank uses the currency it obtains to meet the ongoing bank run. In short, the loss of reserves from the banking system, in conjunction with the scramble for security, reduced the amount of checkable-deposit money by far more than the increase in currency in the hands of the public. Thus, the money supply collapsed.

In 1933, President Franklin Roosevelt ended the bank panic by declaring a "national bank holiday," during which all national banks were shut down for 1 week so that government inspectors could have time to go over each bank's accounting records. Only healthy banks with plenty of reserves were allowed to reopen. This meant that when the holiday was over, people could trust in any bank that had been allowed to reopen. This identification of healthy banks, along with the initiation of the federal deposit insurance program, reassured depositors and ended the bank panics.

But before these policies could begin to turn things around, the nation's money supply had plummeted by 25–33 percent, depending on how narrowly or broadly the money supply is defined. This was the largest drop in the money supply in U.S. history. This decline contributed substantially to the nation's deepest and longest depression. Simply put, less money meant less spending on goods and services as well as fewer loans for businesses. Both effects exacerbated the Great Depression.

Today, a multiple contraction of the money supply of the 1930–1933 magnitude is unthinkable. FDIC deposit insurance has kept individual bank failures from becoming general panics. For example, during the financial crisis of 2007–2008, the FDIC increased deposit insurance from $100,000 to $250,000 per account, and the federal government guaranteed the safety of all balances in money market mutual fund accounts. Also, while the Fed stood idly by during the bank panics of 1930 to 1933, in 2007–2008 it took immediate and dramatic actions to maintain the banking system's reserves and the nation's money supply. We discussed these lender-of-last-resort actions earlier. In Chapter 10 we will discuss the interest rate policies that the Fed undertook during the crisis.

QUESTION: Why do fractional reserve banking and deposit insurance closely accompany one another in modern banking systems?

Summary

1. Conceptually, money is any item that society accepts as (a) a medium of exchange, (b) a unit of monetary account, and (c) a store of value.

2. In the United States, two "official" definitions of money are *M*1, consisting of currency (outside banks) and checkable deposits, and *M*2, consisting of *M*1 plus savings deposits, including money market deposit accounts, small-denominated (less than $100,000) time deposits, and money market mutual fund balances.

3. Money has value because of the goods, services, and resources it will command in the market. Maintaining the purchasing power of money depends largely on the government's effectiveness in managing the money supply to prevent inflation.

4. The U.S. banking system consists of (a) the Board of Governors of the Federal Reserve System, (b) the 12 Federal Reserve Banks, and (c) some 6800 commercial banks and 8700 thrift institutions (mainly credit unions). The Board of Governors is the basic policymaking body for the entire banking system. The directives of the Board and the Federal Open Market Committee (FOMC) are made effective through the 12 Federal Reserve Banks, which are simultaneously (a) central banks, (b) quasi-public banks, and (c) bankers' banks.

5. The major functions of the Fed are to (a) issue Federal Reserve Notes, (b) set reserve requirements and hold reserves deposited by banks and thrifts, (c) lend money to financial institutions and serve as a lender of last resort in national financial emergencies, (d) provide for the rapid collection of checks, (e) act as the fiscal agent for the federal government, (f) supervise the operations of the banks, and (g) control the supply of money in the best interests of the economy.

6. The Fed is essentially an independent institution, controlled neither by the president of the United States nor by Congress. This independence shields the Fed from political pressure and allows it to raise and lower interest rates (via changes in the money supply) as needed to promote full employment, price stability, and economic growth.

7. The financial crisis of 2007–2008 consisted of an unprecedented rise in mortgage loan defaults, the collapse or near-collapse of several major financial institutions, and the generalized freezing up of credit availability. The crisis resulted from bad mortgage loans together with declining real estate prices. It also resulted from underestimation of risk by holders of mortgage-backed securities and faulty insurance securities designed to protect holders of mortgage-backed securities from the risk of default.

8. In 2008 Congress passed the Troubled Asset Relief Program (TARP), which authorized the U.S. Treasury to spend up to $700 billion to make emergency loans and guarantees to failing financial firms.

9. The TARP loans intensified the moral hazard problem. This is the tendency of financial investors and financial firms to take on greater risk when they assume they are at least partially insured against loss.

10. The main categories of the U.S. financial services industry are commercial banks, thrifts, insurance companies, mutual fund companies, pension funds, securities firms, and investment banks. The reassembly of the wreckage from the financial crisis of 2007–2008 has further consolidated the already consolidating financial services industry and has further blurred some of the lines between the subsets of the industry.

11. In response to the financial crisis, Congress passed the Wall Street Reform and Consumer Financial Protection Act of 2010.

12. Modern banking systems are fractional reserve systems: Only a fraction of checkable deposits is backed by currency. Commercial banks keep required reserves on deposit in a Federal Reserve Bank or as vault cash. These required

reserves are equal to a specified percentage of the commercial bank's checkable-deposit liabilities. Excess reserves are equal to actual reserves minus required reserves.

13. Commercial banks create money—checkable deposits, or checkable-deposit money—when they make loans. The ability of a single commercial bank to create money by lending depends on the size of its excess reserves. Generally, a commercial bank can lend only an amount equal to its excess reserves. Money creation is thus limited because, in all likelihood, checks drawn by borrowers will be deposited in other banks, causing a loss of reserves and deposits to the lending bank equal to the amount of money lent.

14. The commercial banking system as a whole can lend by a multiple of its excess reserves because the system as a whole cannot lose reserves. Individual banks, however, can lose reserves to other banks in the system. The multiple by which the banking system can lend on the basis of each dollar of excess reserves is the reciprocal of the reserve ratio.

15. The bank panics of 1930–1933 resulted in a significant contraction of the U.S. money supply, contributed to the Great Depression, and gave rise to federal deposit insurance.

Terms and Concepts

medium of exchange

unit of account

store of value

liquidity

M1

Federal Reserve Notes

token money

checkable deposits

commercial banks

thrift institutions

near-monies

M2

savings account

money market deposit account (MMDA)

time deposits

money market mutual fund (MMMF)

legal tender

Federal Reserve System

Board of Governors

Federal Reserve Banks

Federal Open Market Committee (FOMC)

subprime mortgage loans

mortgage-backed securities

securitization

Troubled Asset Relief Program (TARP)

moral hazard

financial services industry

Wall Street Reform and Consumer Protection Act

fractional reserve banking system

balance sheet

required reserves

reserve ratio

excess reserves

actual reserves

monetary multiplier

Questions   McGraw Hill connect™ ECONOMICS

1. What are the three basic functions of money? Describe how rapid inflation can undermine money's ability to perform each of the three functions. **LO1**

2. Which two of the following financial institutions offer checkable deposits included within the M1 money supply: mutual fund companies; insurance companies; commercial banks; securities firms; thrift institutions? Which of the following is *not* included in either M1 or M2: currency held by the public; checkable deposits; money market mutual fund balances; small-denominated (less than $100,000) time deposits; currency held by banks; savings deposits? **LO1**

3. What are the components of the M1 money supply? What is the largest component? Which of the components of M1 is *legal tender*? Why is the face value of a coin greater than its intrinsic value? What near-monies are included in the M2 money supply? **LO1**

4. How does the purchasing power of the dollar relate to the nation's price level? **LO2**

5. Who selects the chairperson of the Federal Reserve System? Describe the relationship between the Board of Governors of the Federal Reserve System and the 12 Federal Reserve Banks. What is the composition and purpose of the Federal Open Market Committee (FOMC)? **LO3**

6. What is meant when economists say that the Federal Reserve Banks are central banks, quasi-public banks, and bankers' banks? What are the seven basic functions of the Federal Reserve System? **LO4**

7. How do each of the following relate to the financial crisis of 2007–2008: declines in real estate values, subprime mortgage loans, mortgage-backed securities, AIG. **LO5**

8. What is TARP and how was it funded? How do government loans relate to the concept of moral hazard? **LO6**

9. What are the major categories of firms that make up the U.S. financial services industry? Are there more or fewer banks today than before the start of the financial crisis of 2007–2008? Why are the lines between the categories of

financial firms even more blurred than they were before the crisis? How did the Wall Street Reform and Consumer Protection Act of 2010 try to address some of the problems that helped cause the crisis? LO7

10. What is the difference between an asset and a liability on a bank's balance sheet? How does net worth relate to each? Why must a balance sheet always balance? What are the major assets and claims on a commercial bank's balance sheet? LO8

11. Why does the Federal Reserve require that commercial banks have reserves? What are excess reserves? How do you calculate the amount of excess reserves held by a bank? What is the significance of excess reserves? LO8

12. "Whenever currency is deposited in a commercial bank, cash goes out of circulation and, as a result, the $M1$ supply of money is reduced." Do you agree? Explain why or why not. LO8

13. Explain why a single commercial bank can safely lend only an amount equal to its excess reserves but the commercial banking system as a whole can lend by a multiple of its excess reserves. What is the monetary multiplier, and how does it relate to the reserve ratio? LO8

Problems

1. Assume that the following asset values (in millions of dollars) exist in Ironmania: Federal Reserve Notes in circulation = $700; Money market mutual funds (MMMFs) held by individuals = $400; Corporate bonds = $300; Iron ore deposits = $50; Currency in commercial banks = $100; Savings deposits, including money market deposit accounts (MMDAs) = $140; Checkable deposits = $1500; Small-denominated (less than $100,000) time deposits = $100; Coins in circulation = $40. LO1
   a. What is $M1$ in Ironmania?
   b. What is $M2$ in Ironmania?

2. Assume that Jimmy Cash has $2000 in his checking account at Folsom Bank and uses his checking account card to withdraw $200 of cash from the bank's ATM machine. By what dollar amount did the $M1$ money supply change as a result of this single, isolated transaction? LO1

3. Suppose the price level and value of the U.S. dollar in year 1 are 1 and $1, respectively. If the price level rises to 1.25 in year 2, what is the new value of the dollar? If, instead, the price level falls to .50, what is the value of the dollar? LO2

4. Suppose that Lady Gaga goes to Las Vegas to play poker and at the last minute her record company says it will reimburse her for 50 percent of any gambling losses that she incurs. Will Lady Gaga wager more or less as a result of the reimbursement offer? What economic concept does your answer illustrate? LO5

5. Assume that securitization combined with borrowing and irrational exuberance in Hyperville have driven up the value of existing financial securities at a geometric rate, specifically from $2 to $4 to $8 to $16 to $32 to $64 over a six-year time period. Over the same period, the value of the assets underlying the securities rose at an arithmetic rate from $2 to $3 to $4 to $5 to $6 to $7. If these patterns hold for decreases as well as for increases, by how much would the value of the financial securities decline if the value of the underlying asset suddenly and unexpectedly fell by $5? LO5

6. Suppose the assets of the Silver Lode Bank are $100,000 higher than on the previous day and its net worth is up $20,000. By how much and in what direction must its liabilities have changed from the day before? LO8

7. Suppose that Serendipity Bank has excess reserves of $8000 and checkable deposits of $150,000. If the reserve ratio is 20 percent, what is the size of the bank's actual reserves? LO8

8. Third National Bank has reserves of $20,000 and checkable deposits of $100,000. The reserve ratio is 20 percent. Households deposit $5000 in currency into the bank and that currency is added to reserves. What level of excess reserves does the bank now have? LO8

9. The balance sheet below is for Big Bucks Bank. The reserve ratio is 20 percent. LO8
   a. What is the maximum amount of new loans that Big Bucks Bank can make? Show in columns 1 and 1′ how the bank's balance sheet will appear after the bank has lent this additional amount.
   b. By how much has the supply of money changed?
   c. How will the bank's balance sheet appear after checks drawn for the entire amount of the new loans have been cleared against the bank? Show the new balance sheet in columns 2 and 2′.
   d. Answer questions a, b, and c on the assumption that the reserve ratio is 15 percent.

Assets		(1)	(2)	Liabilities and net worth		(1′)	(2′)
Reserves	$22,000	___	___	Checkable deposits	$100,000	___	___
Securities	38,000	___	___				
Loans	40,000	___	___				

10. Suppose the simplified consolidated balance sheet shown in the right column is for the entire commercial banking system and that all figures are in billions of dollars. The reserve ratio is 25 percent. **LO8**

   a. What is the amount of excess reserves in this commercial banking system? What is the maximum amount the banking system might lend? Show in columns 1 and 1′ how the consolidated balance sheet would look after this amount has been lent. What is the size of the monetary multiplier?

   b. Answer the questions in part *a* assuming the reserve ratio is 20 percent. What is the resulting difference in the amount that the commercial banking system can lend?

Assets		(1)	Liabilities and net worth		(1′)
Reserves	$ 52	___	Checkable deposits	$200	___
Securities	48	___			
Loans	100	___			

11. If the required reserve ratio is 10 percent, what is the monetary multiplier? If the monetary multiplier is 4, what is the required reserve ratio? **LO8**

FURTHER TEST YOUR KNOWLEDGE AT
www.mcconnellbrief2e.com

At the text's Online Learning Center, **www.mcconnellbrief2e.com**, you will find one or more web-based questions that require information from the Internet to answer. We urge you to check them out, since they will familiarize you with websites that may be helpful in other courses and perhaps even in your career. The OLC also features multiple-choice quizzes that give instant feedback and provides other helpful ways to further test your knowledge of the chapter.

Visit your mobile app store and download the McConnell Brief Edition: Study Econ app *today*!

10

After reading this chapter, you should be able to:

1 Discuss how the equilibrium interest rate is determined in the market for money.

2 List and explain the goals and tools of monetary policy.

3 Describe the mechanisms by which monetary policy affects GDP and the price level.

4 Discuss the effectiveness of monetary policy and its shortcomings.

5 Describe how the Fed has used monetary policy in recent years to promote macroeconomic stability.

Interest Rates and Monetary Policy

Some newspaper commentators have stated that the chairperson of the Federal Reserve Board (currently Ben Bernanke) is the second most powerful person in the United States, after the U.S. president.

monetary policy
A central bank's changing of the money supply to influence interest rates and assist the economy in achieving price-level stability, full employment, and economic growth.

That is undoubtedly an exaggeration because the chair has only a single vote on the 7-person Federal Reserve Board and 12-person Federal Open Market Committee. But there can be no doubt about the chair's influence, the overall importance of the Federal Reserve, and the **monetary policy** that it conducts. Such policy consists of deliberate changes in the money supply to influence interest rates and thus the total level of spending in the economy. The goal of monetary policy is to achieve and maintain price-level stability, full employment, and economic growth.

Interest Rates

Before we examine how the Federal Reserve can influence the money supply and interest rates, we need to better understand the market in which interest rates are established. As indicated in Table 10.1, there are many different interest rates that vary by purpose, size, risk, maturity, and taxability. (Global Snapshot 10.1 compares one interest rate—the percentage rate on 3-month loans—for several countries in a recent year.) But for simplicity economists often speak of a single interest rate. As we will see, the interest rate in the economy results from the interaction of money demand and money supply.

The Demand for Money

Why does the public want to hold some of its wealth as *money?* There are two main reasons: to make purchases with it and to hold it as an asset.

Transactions Demand, D_t People hold money because it is convenient for purchasing goods and services. Households usually are paid once a week, every 2 weeks, or monthly, whereas their expenditures are less predictable and typically more frequent. So households must have enough money on hand to buy groceries and pay mortgage and utility bills. Nor are businesses' revenues and expenditures simultaneous. Businesses need to have money available to pay for labor, materials, power, and other inputs. The demand for money as a medium of exchange is called the **transactions demand** for money.

transactions demand
The amount of money people want to hold for use as a medium of exchange.

The level of nominal GDP is the main determinant of the amount of money demanded for transactions. The larger the total money value of all goods and services exchanged in the economy, the larger the amount of money needed to negotiate those transactions. The transactions demand for money varies directly with nominal GDP. We specify *nominal* GDP because households and firms will want more money for transactions if prices rise or if real output increases. In both instances there will be a need for a larger dollar volume to accomplish the desired transactions.

TABLE 10.1 **Selected U.S. Interest Rates, July 2011**

Type of Interest Rate	Annual Percentage
20-year Treasury bond rate (interest rate on federal government security used to finance the public debt)	4.05%
90-day Treasury bill rate (interest rate on federal government security used to finance the public debt)	0.02
Prime interest rate (interest rate used as a reference point for a wide range of bank loans)	3.25
30-year mortgage rate (fixed interest rate on loans for houses)	4.60
4-year automobile loan rate (interest rate for new autos by automobile finance companies)	4.05
Tax-exempt state and municipal bond rate (interest rate paid on a low-risk bond issued by a state or local government)	4.65
Federal funds rate (interest rate on overnight loans between banks)	0.08
Consumer credit card rate (interest rate charged for credit card purchases)	14.42

Source: Federal Reserve, **www.federalreserve.gov,** and Bankrate.com, **www.bankrate.com.**

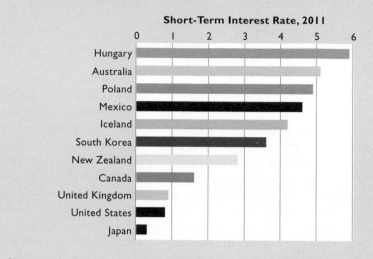

GLOBAL SNAPSHOT 10.1

Short-Term Nominal Interest Rates, Selected Nations

These data show the short-term nominal interest rates (percentage rates on 3-month loans) in various countries in 2011. Because these are nominal rates, much of the variation reflects differences in rates of inflation. But differences in central bank monetary policies and in risk of default also explain the variations.

Short-Term Interest Rate, 2011

Source: Organization for Economic Cooperation and Development, *OECD Economic Outlook,* May 2010. **www.oecd.org.** Accessed October 30, 2011.

In Figure 10.1a we graph the quantity of money demanded for transactions against the interest rate. For simplicity, let's assume that the amount demanded depends exclusively on the level of nominal GDP and is independent of the real interest rate. (In reality, higher interest rates are associated with slightly lower volumes of money demanded for transactions.) Our simplifying assumption allows us to graph the transactions demand, D_t, as a vertical line. This demand curve is positioned at $100 billion, on the assumption that each dollar held for transactions purposes is spent an average of three times per year and that nominal GDP is $300 billion. Thus the public needs $100 billion (= $300 billion/3) to purchase that GDP.

Asset Demand, D_a The second reason for holding money derives from money's function as a store of value. People may hold their financial assets in many forms, including corporate stocks, corporate or government bonds, or money. To the extent they want to hold money as an asset, there is an **asset demand** for money.

People like to hold some of their financial assets as money (apart from using it to buy goods and services) because money is the most liquid of all financial assets; it is immediately usable for purchasing other assets when opportunities arise. Money is also an attractive asset to hold when the prices of other assets such as bonds are expected to decline. For example, when the price of a bond falls, the bondholder who sells the bond prior to the payback date of the full principal will suffer a loss (called a *capital loss*). That loss will partially or fully offset the interest received on the bond. Holding money presents no such risk of capital loss from changes in interest rates.

asset demand
The amount of money people want to hold as a store of value.

ORIGIN OF THE IDEA

O 10.1

Liquidity preference

FIGURE 10.1 The demand for money, supply of money, and equilibrium interest rate. The total demand for money, D_m, is determined by horizontally adding the asset demand for money, D_a, to the transactions demand, D_t. The transactions demand is vertical because it is assumed to depend solely on nominal GDP rather than on the interest rate. The asset demand varies inversely with the interest rate because of the opportunity cost involved in holding currency and checkable deposits that pay no interest or very low interest. Combining the money supply, S_m, with the total money demand, D_m, portrays the money market and determines the equilibrium interest rate, i_e.

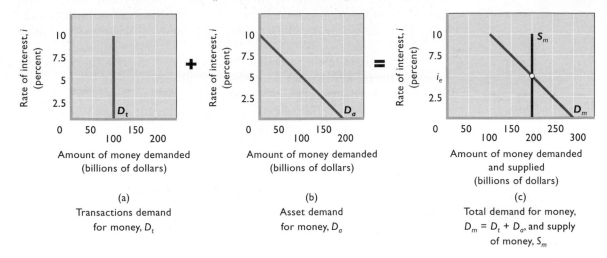

(a)
Transactions demand
for money, D_t

(b)
Asset demand
for money, D_a

(c)
Total demand for money,
$D_m = D_t + D_a$, and supply
of money, S_m

The disadvantage of holding money as an asset is that it earns no or very little interest. Checkable deposits pay either no interest or lower interest rates than bonds. Currency itself earns no interest at all.

Knowing these advantages and disadvantages, the public must decide how much of its financial assets to hold as money, rather than other assets such as bonds. The answer depends primarily on the rate of interest. A household or a business incurs an opportunity cost when it holds money; in both cases, interest income is forgone or sacrificed. If a bond pays 6 percent interest, for example, it costs $6 per year of forgone income to hold $100 as cash or in a noninterest checkable account.

The amount of money demanded as an asset therefore varies inversely with the rate of interest (which is the opportunity cost of holding money as an asset). When the interest rate rises, it becomes more costly to be liquid and to avoid capital losses. The public reacts by reducing its holdings of money as an asset. When the interest rate falls, the cost of being liquid and avoiding capital losses also declines. The public therefore increases the amount of financial assets that it wants to hold as money. This inverse relationship just described is shown by D_a in Figure 10.1b.

Total Money Demand, D_m As shown in Figure 10.1, we find the **total demand for money,** D_m, by horizontally adding the asset demand to the transactions demand. The resulting downward-sloping line in Figure 10.1c represents the total amount of money the public wants to hold, both for transactions and as an asset, at each possible interest rate.

Recall that the transactions demand for money depends on the nominal GDP. A change in the nominal GDP—working through the transactions demand for money—will shift the total money demand curve. Specifically, an increase in nominal GDP means that the public wants to hold a larger amount of money for transactions, and that extra demand will shift the total money demand curve to the right. In contrast, a decline in the nominal GDP will shift the total money demand curve to the left. As an example, suppose nominal GDP increases from $300 billion to $450 billion and the average dollar held for transactions is still spent three times per year. Then the transactions demand curve will shift from $100 billion (= $300 billion/3) to $150 billion (= $450 billion/3). The total money demand curve will then lay $50 billion farther to the right at each possible interest rate.

total demand for money
The sum of the transactions demand and asset demand for money.

WORKED PROBLEMS

W 10.1

The demand for money

money market
The market in which the demand for and the supply of money determine the interest rate (or series of interest rates) in the economy.

The Equilibrium Interest Rate

We can combine the demand for money with the supply of money to determine the equilibrium rate of interest. In Figure 10.1c the vertical line, S_m, represents the money supply. It is a vertical line because the monetary authorities and financial institutions have provided the economy with some particular stock of money. Here it is $200 billion.

Just as in a product market or a resource market, the intersection of demand and supply in the **money market** determines equilibrium price. In Figure 10.1, this equilibrium price is the equilibrium interest rate, i_e. At this interest rate, the quantity of money demanded (= $200 billion) equals the quantity of money supplied (= $200 billion). The equilibrium interest rate can be thought of as the market-determined price that borrowers must pay for using someone else's money over some period of time.

ILLUSTRATING THE IDEA

That Is Interest

Interest is needed to entice individuals to give up liquidity or sacrifice their present consumption, that is, to let someone else use their money for a period of time. The following story told by economist Irving Fisher (1867–1947) helps illustrate the idea of the "time value of money." The irony is that it was Fisher who had earlier formalized this exact idea in his theory of interest.

> In the process of a massage, a masseur informed Fisher that he was a socialist who believed that "interest is the basis of capitalism and is robbery." Following the massage, Fisher asked, "How much do l owe you?"
>
> The masseur replied, "Thirty dollars."
>
> "Very well," said Fisher, "I will give you a note payable a hundred years hence. I suppose you have no objections to taking this note without any interest. At the end of that time, you, or perhaps your grandchildren, can redeem it."
>
> "But I cannot afford to wait that long," said the masseur.
>
> "I thought you said that interest was robbery. If interest is robbery, you ought to be willing to wait indefinitely for the money. If you are willing to wait ten years, how much would you require?"
>
> "Well, I would have to get more than thirty dollars. "
>
> His point now made, Fisher replied, "That is interest."*

QUESTION: Who benefits most from lending at interest: the lender or the borrower?

*Irving Fisher, as quoted in Irving Norton Fisher, *My Father Irving Fisher* (New York: Comet, 1956), p. 77.

Tools of Monetary Policy

We can now explore how the Federal Reserve (the "Fed") can change the supply of money in the economy and therefore alter the interest rate. The Fed has three main tools of monetary control that it can use to alter the money supply: open-market operations, the reserve ratio, and the discount rate..

Open-Market Operations

Bond markets are "open" to all buyers and sellers of corporate and government bonds (securities). The Federal Reserve is the largest single holder of U.S. government securities. The U.S. government, not the Fed, issued these Treasury bills (short-term securities), Treasury notes (mid-term securities), and Treasury bonds (long-term securities) to finance past budget deficits. Over the decades, the Fed has purchased these securities from major financial institutions that buy and sell government and corporate securities for themselves or their customers.

The Fed's **open-market operations** consist of the buying of government bonds (U.S. securities) from, or the selling of government bonds to, commercial banks and the general public. The conduit for the Fed's open-market operations is the New York Federal Reserve Bank and a group of 16 or so large financial firms called "primary dealers." These financial institutions, in turn, buy the bonds from, and sell the bonds to, commercial banks and the general public. Open-market operations are the Fed's most important day-to-day instrument for influencing the money supply.

open-market operations
The buying and selling of U.S. government securities by the Fed for purposes of carrying out monetary policy.

Buying Securities Suppose the Federal Open Market Committee (FOMC) directs the Federal Reserve Bank of New York to buy $100 million of government bonds. The Federal Reserve Bank indirectly purchases these bonds from commercial banks (or thrifts) or the public. In both cases the reserves of the commercial banks will increase.

When a Federal Reserve Bank buys government bonds from *commercial banks*, those banks send some of their holdings of securities to the Federal Reserve Bank. In paying for the securities, the Federal Reserve Bank in essence writes checks for $100 million to the commercial banks. The banks deposit the $100 million of checks in their own accounts. When the checks clear against the Federal Reserve Bank, $100 million of reserves flow to the commercial banks. Because there are no new checkable deposits, the entire $100 million of new reserves in the banking system are excess reserves.

We know from Chapter 9 that excess reserves allow the banking system to make loans (expand the money supply) by a multiple of excess reserves. Suppose the reserve requirement is 20 percent, so the monetary multiplier is 5. Then commercial banks can expand the $100 million of excess reserves to $500 million of new checkable-deposit money.

The effect on commercial bank reserves is much the same when a Federal Reserve Bank purchases securities from the *general public* rather than directly from banks. The Federal Reserve Bank buys the $100 million of securities by issuing checks to the sellers, who deposit the checks in their checkable-deposit accounts at their commercial banks. When the checks clear, $100 million of new reserves flow from the Federal Reserve Bank to the commercial banks. Because the banks need only 20 percent of the new reserves for the $100 million of new checkable deposits, the commercial banks have excess reserves of $80 million (= $100 million of actual reserves − $20 million of required reserves). They lend out the excess reserves, expanding checkable deposits by $400 million (= 5 × $80 million). When added to the original checkable deposits of $100 million, the $400 million of loan-created checkable deposits result in a total of $500 million of new money in the economy.

WORKED PROBLEMS

W 10.2

Open-market operations

Selling Securities As you may suspect, when a Federal Reserve Bank sells government bonds, the reserves of commercial banks are reduced. Let's see why, this time dispensing with the math because it is the exact reverse of the prior examples.

When a Federal Reserve Bank sells securities in the open market to commercial banks, the Federal Reserve Bank gives up securities that the commercial banks acquire. To pay for those securities, the commercial banks in essence write checks payable to the Federal Reserve Bank. When the checks clear, reserves flow from the commercial banks to the Federal Reserve Bank. If all excess reserves are already lent out, this decline in commercial bank reserves produces a multiple decline in money created through lending. That is, the nation's money supply declines. This multiple decline in money will equal the decline in reserves times the monetary multiplier.

The outcome is the same when a Federal Reserve Bank sells securities to the public rather than directly to banks. The public pays for the securities with checks drawn on individuals' banks. When the checks clear, the commercial banks send reserves to the Federal Reserve Bank and reduce accordingly the checkable deposits of customers who wrote the checks. The lower reserves mean a multiple contraction of the money supply.

The Reserve Ratio

The Fed can also manipulate the reserve ratio in order to influence the ability of commercial banks to lend. Suppose a commercial bank's balance sheet shows that reserves are $5000 and checkable deposits are $20,000. If the reserve ratio is 20 percent (row 2, Table 10.2), the bank's required reserves are $4000. Since actual reserves are $5000, the excess reserves of this bank are $1000. On the basis of $1000 of excess reserves, this one bank can lend $1000; however, the banking system as a whole can create a maximum of $5000 of new checkable-deposit money by lending (column 7).

Raising the Reserve Ratio Now, what if the Fed raised the reserve ratio from 20 to 25 percent? (See row 3.) Required reserves would jump from $4000 to $5000, shrinking excess reserves from $1000 to zero. Raising the reserve ratio increases the amount of required reserves banks must keep. As a consequence, either the banks lose excess reserves, diminishing their ability to create money by lending, or they find their reserves deficient and are forced to contract checkable deposits and therefore the money supply. In the example in Table 10.2, excess reserves are transformed into required reserves, and the money-creating potential of our single bank is reduced from $1000 to zero (column 6). Moreover, the banking system's money-creating capacity declines from $5000 to zero (column 7).

What if the Fed increases the reserve requirement to 30 percent? (See row 4.) The commercial bank, to protect itself against the prospect of failing to meet this requirement, would be forced to lower its checkable deposits and at the same time increase its reserves. To reduce its checkable deposits, the bank could let outstanding loans mature and be repaid without extending new credit. This action would reduce the supply of money.

Lowering the Reserve Ratio What would happen if the Fed lowered the reserve ratio from the original 20 percent to 10 percent? (See row 1.) In this case, required reserves would decline from $4000 to $2000, and excess reserves would jump from

TABLE 10.2 The Effects of Changes in the Reserve Ratio on the Lending Ability of Commercial Banks

(1) Reserve Ratio, %	(2) Checkable Deposits	(3) Actual Reserves	(4) Required Reserves	(5) Excess Reserves, (3) − (4)	(6) Money-Creating Potential of Single Bank, = (5)	(7) Money-Creating Potential of Banking System
(1) 10	$20,000	$5000	$2000	$ 3000	$ 3000	$30,000
(2) 20	20,000	5000	4000	1000	1000	5,000
(3) 25	20,000	5000	5000	0	0	0
(4) 30	20,000	5000	6000	−1000	−1000	−3,333

$1000 to $3000. The single bank's lending (money-creating) ability would increase from $1000 to $3000 (column 6), and the banking system's money-creating potential would expand from $5000 to $30,000 (column 7). Lowering the reserve ratio transforms required reserves into excess reserves and enhances the ability of banks to create new money by lending.

The examples in Table 10.2 show that a change in the reserve ratio affects the money-creating ability of the *banking system* in two ways:

- It changes the amount of excess reserves.
- It changes the size of the monetary multiplier.

For example, when the legal reserve ratio is raised from 10 to 20 percent, excess reserves are reduced from $3000 to $1000 and the monetary multiplier is reduced from 10 to 5. The money-creating potential of the banking system declines from $30,000 (= $3000 × 10) to $5000 (= $1000 × 5). Raising the reserve ratio forces banks to reduce the amount of checkable deposits they create through lending.

The Discount Rate

One of the functions of a central bank is to be a "lender of last resort." Occasionally, commercial banks have unexpected and immediate needs for additional funds. In such cases, each Federal Reserve Bank will make short-term loans to commercial banks in its district.

When a commercial bank borrows, it gives the Federal Reserve Bank a promissory note (IOU) drawn against itself and secured by acceptable collateral—typically U.S. government securities. Just as commercial banks charge interest on the loans they make to their clients, so too Federal Reserve Banks charge interest on loans they grant to commercial banks. The interest rate they charge is called the **discount rate.**

In providing the loan, the Federal Reserve Bank increases the reserves of the borrowing commercial bank. Since no required reserves need be kept against loans from Federal Reserve Banks, all new reserves acquired by borrowing from Federal Reserve Banks are excess reserves. In short, borrowing from the Federal Reserve Banks by commercial banks increases the reserves of the commercial banks and enhances their ability to extend credit.

The Fed has the power to set the discount rate at which commercial banks borrow from Federal Reserve Banks. From the commercial banks' point of view, the discount rate is a cost of acquiring reserves. A lowering of the discount rate entices commercial banks to obtain additional reserves, if needed, by borrowing from Federal Reserve Banks. When the commercial banks lend new reserves to bank customers, the money supply increases.

An increase in the discount rate discourages commercial banks from obtaining additional reserves through borrowing from the Federal Reserve Banks. So the Fed may raise the discount rate when it wants to restrict the money supply.

discount rate
The interest rate the Federal Reserve Banks charge on the loans they make to commercial banks and thrifts.

Relative Importance

All three of the Fed's primary instruments of monetary control are useful in particular economic circumstances, but open-market operations are clearly the most important of the three main tools over the course of the business cycle. The buying and selling of securities in the open market has the advantage of flexibility—government securities can be purchased or sold daily in large or small amounts—and the impact on bank reserves is prompt. And, compared with reserve-requirement changes, open-market operations work subtly and less directly. Furthermore, the ability of the Federal Reserve Banks to affect commercial bank reserves through the purchase and sale of bonds is virtually unquestionable. The Federal Reserve Banks have very large holdings of government securities ($1624 billion in July 2011, for example). The sale of those securities could theoretically reduce commercial bank reserves to zero.

Changing the reserve requirement is a potentially powerful instrument of monetary control, but the Fed has used this technique only sparingly. Normally, it can accomplish its monetary goals more easily through open-market operations. The last change in the reserve requirement was in 1992, when the Fed reduced the requirement from 12 percent to 10 percent. The main purpose was to shore up the profitability of banks and thrifts in the aftermath of the 1990–91 recession rather than to reduce interest rates by increasing reserves and expanding the money supply.

Until recently, the discount rate was mainly a passive tool of monetary control, with the Fed raising and lowering the rate simply to keep it in line with other interest rates. However, during the financial crisis of 2007–2008, the Fed aggressively lowered the discount rate independently of other interest rates in order to provide a cheap and plentiful source of reserves to banks whose reserves were being sharply reduced by unexpectedly high default rates on home mortgage loans. Banks borrowed billions at the lower discount rate. This allowed them to meet reserve requirements and thereby preserved their ability to keep extending loans.

Easy Money and Tight Money

Suppose the economy faces recession and unemployment. The Fed decides that an increase in the supply of money is needed to increase aggregate demand so as to employ idle resources. To increase the supply of money, the Fed must increase the excess reserves of commercial banks. How can it do that?

- *Buy securities*   By purchasing securities in the open market, the Fed can increase commercial bank reserves. When the Fed's checks for the securities are cleared against it, the commercial banks discover that they have more reserves.
- *Lower the reserve ratio*   By lowering the reserve ratio, the Fed changes required reserves into excess reserves and increases the size of the monetary multiplier.
- *Lower the discount rate*   By lowering the discount rate, the Fed may entice commercial banks to borrow more reserves from the Fed.

easy money policy
Fed actions designed to increase the money supply, lower interest rates, and expand real GDP.

These actions are called an **easy money policy** (or *expansionary monetary policy*). Its purpose is to make bank loans less expensive and more available and thereby increase aggregate demand, output, and employment.

Suppose, on the other hand, excessive spending is pushing the economy into an inflationary spiral. Then the Fed should try to reduce aggregate demand by limiting or contracting the supply of money. That means reducing the reserves of commercial banks. How is that done?

- *Sell securities*   By selling government bonds in the open market, the Federal Reserve Banks can reduce commercial bank reserves.
- *Increase the reserve ratio*   An increase in the reserve ratio will automatically strip commercial banks of their excess reserves and decrease the size of the monetary multiplier.
- *Raise the discount rate*   A boost in the discount rate will discourage commercial banks from borrowing from Federal Reserve Banks in order to build up their reserves.

tight money policy
Fed actions to reduce (or restrict) the growth of the nation's money supply, increase interest rates, and restrain inflation.

These actions are called a **tight money policy** (or *restrictive monetary policy*). The objective is to tighten the supply of money in order to reduce spending and control inflation.

Monetary Policy, Real GDP, and the Price Level

So far we have explained only how the Fed can change the money supply. Now we need to link up the money supply, the interest rate, investment spending, and aggregate demand to see how monetary policy affects the economy. How does monetary policy work?

INTERACTIVE GRAPHS

G 10.2

Monetary policy

Cause-Effect Chain

The three diagrams in Figure 10.2 will help you understand how monetary policy works toward achieving its goals.

Market for Money Figure 10.2a represents the market for money, in which the demand curve for money and the supply curve of money are brought together. Recall that the total demand for money is made up of the transactions and asset demands. The transactions demand is directly related to the nominal GDP. The asset demand is inversely related to the interest rate. The interest rate is the opportunity cost of holding money as an asset; the higher that cost, the smaller the amount of money the public wants to hold. The total demand for money, D_m, is thus inversely related to the interest rate, as is indicated in Figure 10.2a. Also, recall that an increase in nominal GDP will shift D_m to the right and a decline in nominal GDP will shift D_m to the left.

This figure also shows three potential money supply curves, S_{m1}, S_{m2}, and S_{m3}. In each case the money supply is shown as a vertical line representing some fixed amount of money determined by the Fed. While monetary policy (specifically, the supply of money) helps determine the interest rate, the interest rate does not determine the location of the money supply curve.

The equilibrium interest rate is the rate at which the amount of money demanded and the amount supplied are equal. With money demand D_m in Figure 10.2a, if the supply of money is $125 billion ($S_{m1}$), the equilibrium interest rate is 10 percent. With a money supply of $150 billion ($S_{m2}$), the equilibrium interest rate is 8 percent; with a money supply of $175 billion ($S_{m3}$), it is 6 percent.

Investment These 10, 8, and 6 percent real interest rates are carried rightward to the investment demand curve in Figure 10.2b. This curve shows the inverse relationship between the interest rate—the cost of borrowing to invest—and the amount of investment spending. At the 10 percent interest rate it will be profitable for the nation's businesses to invest $15 billion; at 8 percent, $20 billion; at 6 percent, $25 billion.

Changes in the interest rate mainly affect the investment component of total spending, although they also affect spending on durable consumer goods (such as autos) that are purchased on credit. The impact of changing interest rates on investment spending is great because of the large cost and long-term nature of capital purchases. Manufacturing equipment, factory buildings, and warehouses are tremendously expensive. In absolute terms, interest charges on funds borrowed for these purchases are considerable.

Similarly, the interest cost on a house purchased on a long-term contract is very large: A percentage-point change in the interest rate would amount to thousands of dollars in the total cost of a typical home.

Also, changes in the interest rate may affect investment spending by changing the relative attractiveness of purchases of capital equipment versus purchases of bonds. In purchasing capital goods, the interest rate is the cost of borrowing the funds to make the investment. In purchasing bonds, the interest rate is the return on the financial investment. If the interest rate increases, the cost of buying capital goods increases while the return on bonds increases. Businesses are then more inclined to use business

FIGURE 10.2 Monetary policy and equilibrium GDP. An easy money policy that shifts the money supply curve rightward from S_{m1} to S_{m2} lowers the interest rate from 10 percent to 8 percent. As a result, investment spending increases from $15 billion to $20 billion, shifting the aggregate demand curve rightward from AD_1 to AD_2, and real output rises from the recessionary level Q_1 to the full-employment level Q_f. A tight money policy that shifts the money supply curve leftward from S_{m3} to S_{m2} increases the interest rate from 6 percent to 8 percent. Investment spending thus falls from $25 billion to $20 billion, and the aggregate demand curve shifts leftward from AD_3 to AD_2, curtailing inflation.

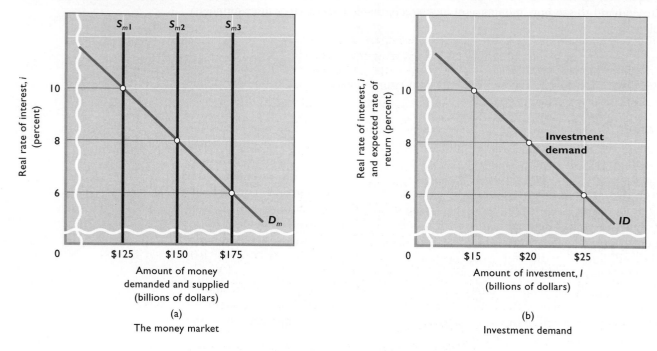

(a)
The money market

(b)
Investment demand

(c)
Equilibrium real
GDP and the price
level

savings to buy securities than to buy equipment. Conversely, a drop in the interest rate makes purchases of capital goods relatively more attractive than bond ownership.

In brief, the impact of changing interest rates is mainly on investment (and, through that, on aggregate demand, output, employment, and the price level). Moreover, as Figure 10.2b shows, investment spending varies inversely with the interest rate.

Equilibrium GDP Figure 10.2c shows the impact of our three interest rates and corresponding levels of investment spending on aggregate demand. As noted, aggregate demand curve AD_1 is associated with the $15 billion level of investment, AD_2 with investment of $20 billion, and AD_3 with investment of $25 billion. That is, investment spending is one of the determinants of aggregate demand. Other things equal, the greater the investment spending, the farther to the right lies the aggregate demand curve.

Suppose the money supply in Figure 10.2a is $150 billion ($S_{m2}$), producing an equilibrium interest rate of 8 percent. In Figure 10.2b we see that this 8 percent interest rate will bring forth $20 billion of investment spending. This $20 billion of investment spending joins with consumption spending, net exports, and government spending to yield aggregate demand curve AD_2 in Figure 10.2c. The equilibrium levels of real output and prices are Q_f and P_2, as determined by the intersection of AD_2 and the aggregate supply curve AS.

To test your understanding of these relationships, explain why each of the other two levels of money supply in Figure 10.2a results in a different interest rate, level of investment, aggregate demand curve, and equilibrium real output.

Effects of an Easy Money Policy

Next, suppose that the money supply is $125 billion ($S_{m1}$) in Figure 10.2a. Because the resulting real output Q_1 in Figure 10.2c is far below the full-employment output, Q_f, the economy must be experiencing recession and substantial unemployment. The Fed therefore should institute an easy money policy.

To increase the money supply, the Federal Reserve Banks will take some combination of the following actions: (1) Buy government securities from banks and the public in the open market, (2) lower the legal reserve ratio, and (3) lower the discount rate. The intended outcome will be an increase in excess reserves in the commercial banking system. Because excess reserves are the basis on which commercial banks and thrifts can earn profit by lending and thus creating checkable-deposit money, the nation's money supply probably will rise. An increase in the money supply will lower the interest rate, increasing investment, aggregate demand, and equilibrium GDP.

For example, an increase in the money supply from $125 billion to $150 billion ($S_{m1}$ to S_{m2}) will reduce the interest rate from 10 to 8 percent, as indicated in Figure 10.2a, and will boost investment from $15 billion to $20 billion, as shown in Figure 10.2b. This $5 billion increase in investment will shift the aggregate demand curve rightward, as shown by the shift from AD_1 to AD_2 in Figure 10.2c. This rightward shift in the aggregate demand curve will eliminate the negative GDP gap by increasing GDP from Q_1 to the full-employment GDP of Q_f.[1]

Column 1 in Table 10.3 summarizes the chain of events associated with an easy money policy.

---

[1]For simplicity we assume that the increase in real GDP does not increase the demand for money. In reality, the transactions demand for money would rise, slightly dampening the decline in the interest rate shown in Figure 10.2a. We also assume that the price level was inflexible downward at P_2 when the economy entered the recession. So the easy money policy expands real GDP from Q_1 to Q_f without causing inflation.

TABLE 10.3 Monetary Policies for Recession and Inflation

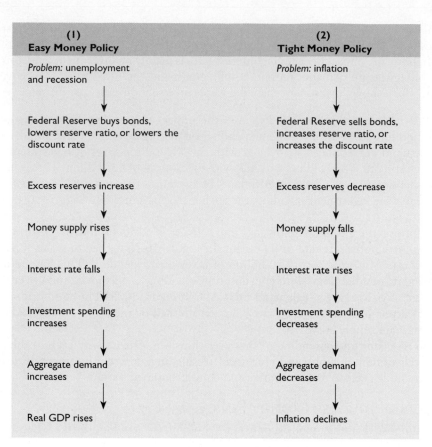

(1) Easy Money Policy	(2) Tight Money Policy
Problem: unemployment and recession	*Problem:* inflation
↓	↓
Federal Reserve buys bonds, lowers reserve ratio, or lowers the discount rate	Federal Reserve sells bonds, increases reserve ratio, or increases the discount rate
↓	↓
Excess reserves increase	Excess reserves decrease
↓	↓
Money supply rises	Money supply falls
↓	↓
Interest rate falls	Interest rate rises
↓	↓
Investment spending increases	Investment spending decreases
↓	↓
Aggregate demand increases	Aggregate demand decreases
↓	↓
Real GDP rises	Inflation declines

Effects of a Tight Money Policy

Now let's assume that the money supply is $175 billion ($S_{m3}$) in Figure 10.2a. This results in an interest rate of 6 percent, investment spending of $25 billion, and aggregate demand AD_3. As you can see in Figure 10.2c, we have depicted a positive GDP gap of $Q_3 - Q_f$ and demand-pull inflation. Aggregate demand AD_3 is excessive relative to the economy's full-employment level of real output Q_f. To rein in spending, the Fed will institute a tight money policy.

The Federal Reserve Board will direct Federal Reserve Banks to undertake some combination of the following actions: (1) Sell government securities to banks and the public in the open market, (2) increase the legal reserve ratio, and (3) increase the discount rate. Banks then will discover that their reserves are below those required. So they will need to reduce their checkable deposits by refraining from issuing new loans as old loans are paid back. This will shrink the money supply and increase the interest rate. The higher interest rate will discourage investment, lowering aggregate demand and restraining demand-pull inflation.

If the Fed reduces the money supply from $175 billion to $150 billion ($S_{m3}$ to S_{m2} in Figure 10.2a), the interest rate will rise from 6 to 8 percent and investment will decline from $25 billion to $20 billion (Figure 10.2b). This $5 billion decrease in investment will shift the aggregate demand curve leftward from AD_3 to AD_2 (Figure 10.2c). This leftward shift of the aggregate demand curve will eliminate the excessive spending and halt the demand-pull inflation. In the real world, of course, the goal will be to stop inflation—that is, to halt further increases in the price level—rather than to actually drive down the price level, which tends to be inflexible downward.[2] Given the downward inflexibility of prices, reducing the money supply to $150 billion would push the equilibrium GDP below its full employment level. To stop the inflation and restore output to its full employment level without causing a recession, a smaller monetary contraction would be necessary.

Column 2 in Table 10.3 summarizes the cause-effect chain of a tight money policy.

Monetary Policy in Action

We now turn from monetary policy in theory to monetary policy in action. Monetary policy has become the dominant component of U.S. national stabilization policy. It has two key advantages over fiscal policy:

- Speed and flexibility.
- Isolation from political pressure.

Compared with fiscal policy, monetary policy can be quickly altered. Recall that congressional deliberations may delay the application of fiscal policy for months. In contrast, the Fed can buy or sell securities from day to day and thus affect the money supply and interest rates almost immediately.

Also, because members of the Fed's Board of Governors are appointed and serve 14-year terms, they are relatively isolated from lobbying and need not worry about retaining their popularity with voters. Thus, the Board, more readily than Congress, can engage in politically unpopular policies (higher interest rates) that may be necessary for the long-term health of the economy. Moreover, monetary policy is a subtler and more politically neutral measure than fiscal policy. Changes in government spending directly affect the allocation of resources, and changes in taxes can have extensive political ramifications. Because monetary policy works more subtly, it is more politically palatable.

The Focus on the Federal Funds Rate

The Fed currently focuses monetary policy on altering the **Federal funds rate** as needed to stabilize the economy. Normal day-to-day flows of funds to banks rarely leave all banks with their exact levels of legally required reserves. Also, funds held at the Federal Reserve Banks are highly liquid, but they earn less interest than commercial banks can obtain from other sources. Banks therefore prefer to lend these excess reserves to other banks on an overnight basis to earn interest without sacrificing long-term liquidity. Banks that borrow in this Federal funds market—the market for immediately available reserve balances at the Federal Reserve—do so because they are temporarily short of required reserves. The interest rate paid on these overnight loans is called the *Federal funds rate*.

Because the Federal Reserve can control the supply of Federal funds—the supply of reserves in the banking system—it can control the Federal funds interest rate. The Fed is a monopoly supplier of reserves. When it wants to increase the Federal funds

Federal funds rate
The interest rate banks and thrifts charge one another on overnight loans made out of their excess reserves.

---

[2]Again, we assume for simplicity that the decrease in nominal GDP does not feed back to reduce the demand for money and thus the interest rate. In reality, this would occur, slightly dampening the increase in the interest rate shown in Figure 10.2a.

FIGURE 10.3 The prime interest rate and the Federal funds rate in the United States, 1998–2010. The prime interest rate rises and falls with changes in the Federal funds rate. *Source: Federal Reserve Statistical Release,* Historical Data, H.15, **www.federalreserve.gov.**

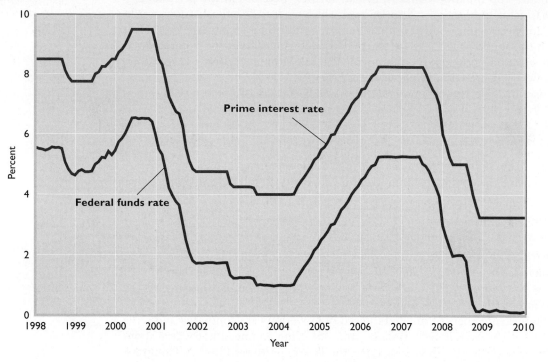

rate, it sells securities in the open market to reduce (or withdraw) bank reserves. This is a "tighter" or "more restrictive" monetary policy. When it wants to reduce the Federal funds rate, it buys securities in the open market to increase (or inject) reserves. This is an "easier" or "more accommodating" monetary policy.

The Fed can target the Federal funds rate because it knows that interest rates in general typically rise and fall with that rate. For example, in Figure 10.3 observe that the **prime interest rate** generally parallels the Federal funds rate. The prime interest rate is the benchmark rate that banks use as a reference point for a wide range of interest rates on loans to businesses and individuals. By changing the Federal funds rate, the Fed in effect alters the economy's prime interest rate along with a wide array of other short-term interest rates.

Why the lockstep pattern between the Federal funds rate and the prime interest rate? Sales of securities by the Fed in the open market reduce excess reserves in the banking system, lessening the supply of excess reserves available for overnight loans in the Federal funds market. The decreased supply of excess reserves in that market increases the Federal funds rate. In addition, reduced excess reserves decrease the amount of bank lending and hence the amount of checkable-deposit money. Declines in the supply of money produce higher interest rates in general, including the prime interest rate.

Purchases of securities by the Fed in the open market increase the supply of reserves in the Federal funds market, reducing the Federal funds rate. The money supply rises because the increased supply of excess reserves leads to more lending and thus greater creation of checkable-deposit money. As a result, interest rates in general fall, including the prime interest rate.

prime interest rate
The benchmark interest rate that banks and thrifts use as a reference point for a wide range of loans to businesses and individuals.

Recent U.S. Monetary Policy

The Fed has been highly active in its use of monetary policy in recent decades. To demonstrate this fact, let's begin with the year 2000, when the economy abruptly slowed after a long period of full employment and strong economic growth. The Fed responded to the slowdown by cutting the Federal funds interest rate by a full percentage point in two increments in January 2001. Despite those rate cuts, the economy entered a recession in March 2001. Between March 20, 2001, and August 21, 2001, the Fed reduced the Federal funds rate from 5 percent to 3.5 percent in a series of steps. In the 3 months following the terrorist attacks of September 11, 2001, it lowered the Federal funds rate from 3.5 percent to 1.75 percent, and it left the rate there until it lowered it to 1.25 percent in November 2002. Partly because of the Fed's actions, the prime interest rate dropped from 9.5 percent at the end of 2000 to 4.25 percent in December 2002.

Economists generally give the Fed high marks for helping to keep the recession of 2001 relatively mild, particularly in view of the adverse economic impacts of the terrorist attacks of September 11, 2001, and the steep stock-market decline in 2001–2002.

The Fed left the Federal funds rate at historic lows in 2003. But as the economy began to expand robustly in 2004, the Fed engineered a gradual series of rate hikes designed to boost the prime interest rate and other interest rates to make sure that aggregate demand continued to grow at a pace consistent with low inflation. By the summer of 2006, the target for the Federal funds rate had risen to 5.25 percent and the prime rate was 8.25 percent. With the economy enjoying sustainable, noninflationary growth, the Fed left the Federal funds rate at 5.25 percent for over a year.

The mortgage default crisis (discussed in Chapter 9) began during the late summer of 2007 and posed a grave threat to the financial system and the economy. In response, the Fed took several actions. In August it lowered the discount rate by half a percentage point. Then, between September 2007 and April 2008, it lowered the target for the Federal funds rate from 5.25 percent to 2 percent. As discussed below, the Fed also took a series of extraordinary actions to prevent the failure of key financial firms.

In October 2008, the Fed first reduced the Federal funds target rate to 1.5 percent and then later that same month to 1 percent. In December 2008, the Fed lowered it further to a targeted range of 0 percent to 0.25 percent. The Federal funds rate remained in that range through September 2009. The Fed aggressively increased the supply of Federal funds to lower the actual Federal funds rate to its target level. All these monetary actions and lender-of-last resort functions described below helped to stabilize the banking sector and keep credit flowing—thereby offsetting at least some of the damage done by the financial crisis.

The decline in the Federal funds rate to near zero during the financial and economic crisis dropped the prime interest rate (review Figure 10.3). In December 2007, the prime interest rate stood at 7.3 percent. By January 2009, it had declined to 3.25 percent, where it remained well into 2011.

In addition to lowering interest rates, the Fed engaged heavily in open-market operations, albeit with a twist. In what has come to be known as *quantitative easing*, the Fed purchased both government and private securities in an effort to expand bank reserves. However, with the economy slow to recover and with no further room to lower short-term interest rates, in November 2010 the Fed initiated a second round of quantitative easing, often termed *QE2*. QE2 differed from traditional open-market operations in that it focused on purchasing longer-term U.S. Treasury securities in an effort to lower longer-term interest rates that influence business investment and larger consumer purchases. From November 2010 until QE2's completion in June 2011, the Fed purchased $600 billion in longer-term Treasury securities. In July 2011, with the economy still sluggish, the Fed announced that it was considering a third round of quantitative easing.

The Federal Reserve is lauded by many observers for its quick and innovative actions during the financial crisis and severe recession. Nevertheless, some economists contend that the Fed contributed to the financial crisis by holding the Federal funds interest rate too low for too long during the recovery from the 2001 recession. These critics say that the artificially low interest rates made mortgage and other loans too inexpensive and therefore contributed to the borrowing frenzy by homeowners and other financial investors. Other economists counter that the low mortgage interest rates resulted from huge inflows of savings from abroad to a wide variety of U.S. financial markets.

QUESTION: What is the current monetary policy stance of the Fed? Has it been increasing interest rates, decreasing them, or leaving them unchanged in recent months? (Answer this question by going to the Federal Reserve's website, www.federalreserve.gov.)

APPLYING THE ANALYSIS

The Financial Crisis: The Fed Responds

As noted in Chapter 9's list of Fed functions, one of the roles of the Federal Reserve is to serve as the lender of last resort to financial institutions in times of financial emergencies. The Fed performed this vital function well following the 9/11 terrorist attacks. The financial crisis of 2007–2008 presented another, broader-based financial emergency. Under Fed Chair Ben Bernanke, the Fed designed and implemented several highly creative new lender-of-last-resort facilities to pump liquidity into the financial system. These facilities, procedures, and capabilities were in addition to both the TARP efforts by the U.S. Treasury and the Fed's use of standard tools of monetary policy designed to reduce interest rates. All the new Fed facilities had the single purpose and desired outcome of keeping credit flowing.

Total Fed assets rose from $885 billion in February 2008 to $2854 billion in July 2011. This increase reflected a huge rise in the amount of securities (U.S. securities, mortgage-backed securities, and others) owned by the Fed. In undertaking its lender-of-last-resort functions, the Fed bought these securities from financial institutions. The purpose was to increase liquidity in the financial system by exchanging illiquid bonds (that the firms could not easily sell during the crisis) for cash, the most liquid of all assets.

Many economists believe that TARP and the Fed's actions helped avert a second Great Depression. The following list of new Fed credit facilities underscores the extraordinary extent of the Fed's lender-of-last-resort response to the crisis. Most of these programs terminated in 2010, but the Fed could reestablish them in the event of another financial crisis.

- *Term Auction Facility (TAF)* Provided short-term loans of reserves to commercial banks through a secret bidding process. With auctions conducted twice monthly, the Fed received written bids from commercial banks, indicating the quantity of reserves desired and the maximum interest rate the commercial bank was willing to pay. Starting with the highest interest rate bidder, commercial banks received desired reserves until the total reserves available through the auction were exhausted. (Final auction held March 8, 2010)

- *Primary Dealer Credit Facility (PDCF)* Provided overnight loans to primary dealers who were willing to post loan-backed securities as collateral. (The Fed kept the collateral on any loan not repaid on time.) Primary dealers are the 16 major financial institutions that the Fed uses to buy and sell U.S. securities. (Closed February 1, 2010)

- *Term Securities Lending Facility (TSLF)* Lent U.S. securities to primary dealers for one-month terms to promote liquidity in the markets for those U.S. securities. The financial institutions obtained the securities from the Fed through participating in competitive single-bid auctions. (Closed February 1, 2010)

- *Asset-Backed Commercial Paper Money Market Mutual Fund Liquidity Facility (AMLF)* Provided loans to U.S. banks and thrifts to finance their purchases of *commercial paper* from money market mutual funds. Commercial paper consists of asset-backed, short-term IOUs that are mainly issued by corporations. These short-term loans were vital for financing the day-to-day operations of businesses. (Closed February 1, 2010)

- *Commercial Paper Funding Facility (CPFF)* Purchased commercial paper to support the commercial paper market and therefore the short-term credit needs of businesses. (Closed February 1, 2010)

- *Money Market Investor Funding Facility (MMIFF)* Provided funding support to a private-sector initiative designed to ensure the liquidity of U.S. money market mutual funds. Many Americans rely on money market mutual funds as low-risk investments. (Expired October 30, 2009)

- *Term Asset-Backed Securities Loan Facility (TALF)* Helped households and business with their credit needs by providing funding support for asset-backed securities collateralized by student loans, auto loans, credit card loans, and loans guaranteed by the Small Business Administration (SBA). (Closed June 30, 2010)

- *Interest Payments on Reserves* Bolsters the profitability of banks by paying interest on the reserves they hold in their vaults or in the Federal Reserve Banks.

These extraordinary efforts, like those of the Treasury, helped prevent total disarray in the credit markets. But like TARP, the Fed efforts intensified the moral hazard problem by greatly limiting the losses that otherwise would have resulted from bad financial assumptions and decisions.

QUESTION: Did the Fed's action (along with fiscal policies enacted during the same period) succeed in preventing recession or promoting a strong recovery?

Problems and Complications

Despite its recent successes in the United States, monetary policy has certain limitations and faces real-world complications.

Lags Recall that fiscal policy is hindered by three delays, or lags—a recognition lag, an administrative lag, and an operational lag. Monetary policy also faces a recognition lag and an operational lag, but because the Fed can decide and implement policy changes within days, it avoids the long administrative lag that hinders fiscal policy.

A recognition lag affects monetary policy because normal monthly variations in economic activity and the price level mean that the Fed may not be able to quickly recognize when the economy is truly starting to recede or when inflation is really starting to rise. Once the Fed acts, an operational lag of 3 to 6 months or more affects monetary policy because that much time is typically required for interest-rate changes to have their full impacts on investment, aggregate demand, real GDP, and the price level.

Cyclical Asymmetry and the Liquidity Trap

cyclical asymmetry
The potential problem of monetary policy successfully controlling inflation during the expansionary phase of the business cycle but failing to expand spending and real GDP during the recessionary phase of the cycle.

Monetary policy may be highly effective in slowing expansions and controlling inflation but may be much less reliable in pushing the economy from a severe recession. Economists say that monetary policy may suffer from **cyclical asymmetry.** The metaphor of "pushing on a string" is often invoked to capture this problem. Imagine the Fed standing on the left-hand side of Figure 10.2c, holding one end of a "monetary-policy string." And imagine that the other end of the monetary-policy string is tied to the AD curve. Because the string would go taut if pulled on, monetary policy may be useful in *pulling* aggregate demand to the left. But because the string would go limp if pushed on, monetary policy will be rather ineffective at *pushing* aggregate demand to the right.

The reason for this asymmetry has to do with the asymmetric way in which people may act in response to changes in bank reserves. If pursued vigorously, a restrictive monetary policy can deplete commercial banking reserves to the point where banks are forced to reduce the volume of loans. That means a contraction of the money supply, higher interest rates, and reduced aggregate demand. The Fed can absorb sufficient reserves and eventually achieve its goal.

liquidity trap
A situation in a severe recession in which the Fed's injection of additional reserves into the banking system has little or no additional positive impact on lending, borrowing, investment, or aggregate demand.

But the Fed cannot be certain of achieving its goal when it adds reserves to the banking system because of the so-called **liquidity trap,** in which adding more liquidity to banks has little or no additional positive effect on lending, borrowing, investment, or aggregate demand. For example, during the recent recession, the Fed created billions of dollars of excess reserves that drove down the Federal funds rate to as low as 0.2 percent. The prime interest rate fell from 7.3 percent (December 2007) to 3.25 percent (March 2009). Nevertheless, lending by banks stalled throughout the first 15 months of the recession. The banks were fearful that the loans they would make to households, businesses, and other financial institutions would not be paid back. Consequently, they were content to hold reserves at the Federal Reserve Banks.

To switch analogies, an expansionary monetary policy suffers from a "you can lead a horse to water, but you can't make it drink" problem. The Fed can create excess reserves, but it cannot guarantee that the banks will actually make additional loans and thus promote spending. If commercial banks seek liquidity and are unwilling to lend, the efforts of the Fed will be of little avail. Similarly, households and businesses can frustrate the intentions of the Fed by not borrowing excess reserves being made available as loans. And when the Fed buys securities from the public, people may choose to pay off existing loans with the money received, rather than increasing their spending on goods and services.

Furthermore, a severe recession may so undermine business confidence that the investment demand curve shifts to the left and overwhelms the lower interest rates associated with an expansionary monetary policy. That is what happened in the most recent recession. Although the Fed drove the real interest rate down to zero percent, investment spending remained low and the economy remained mired in recession. The recent U.S. experience reminds us that active monetary policy certainly is not a cure-all for the business cycle. Under some circumstances, monetary policy may be like "pushing on a string."

The liquidity trap that occurred during the severe recession was a primary reason why public policy in the United States turned so significantly and forcefully toward fiscal policy in 2009. Recall our discussion of the American Recovery and Redevelopment Act of 2009, which authorized the infusion of $787 billion of new tax cuts and government spending in 2009 and 2010.

Up, Up, and Away

The consolidated balance sheet of the 12 Federal Reserve Banks changed markedly during the severe recession of 2007–2009. Total Fed assets increased from $885 billion in February 2008 to $2831 billion in June 2011. This increase reflected an enormous rise in the number of U.S. securities, mortgage-backed securities, and other financial assets purchased by the Federal Reserve. In undertaking its monetary policy and its lender-of-last-resort functions, the Fed bought these securities from financial institutions—purposely increasing the liquidity of the financial system. The Fed also increased its loans to financial institutions, particularly through the term auction facility. Because term auction loans are "owed to" the Fed, the accounting credits for them are assets on the Fed's balance sheet.

On the liability side, the reserves of commercial banks rose from $43 billion in February 2008 to $1706 billion in June 2011. To make sure they were liquid and the funds were safe, banks placed much of the proceeds from selling securities to the Fed into their respective reserve accounts at the Fed. This flow was strengthened because the Fed began paying interest on the reserves that banks were holding at the Fed.

In June 2011 total bank reserves held at the Fed exceeded total checkable deposits held by the banks. The severe distress in the financial system had voluntarily turned the fractional reserve system into a 100-percent-plus reserve system! The banks had enormous excess reserves from which to increase lending once the banks became more certain of their own financial viability and the likelihood that newly issued loans would be paid back.

The Fed therefore faces a challenging task of using monetary policy to absorb large portions of this overstock of excess reserves as the economy recovers and picks up momentum. It does not want the banks to lend out the full amount of these excess reserves because that would flood the economy with bank-created money and excessively expand the money supply. During a vigorous economic expansion, the excessive money and resulting very low interest rates could produce such large expansions of aggregate demand that rapid inflation would occur.

QUESTION: What does a 100-percent-plus reserve system imply for the monetary multiplier?

Summary

1. There is a set of interest rates that vary by loan purpose, size, risk, maturity, and taxability. Nevertheless, economists often speak of a single interest rate in order to simplify their analysis.

2. The total demand for money consists of the transactions demand and asset demand for money. The amount of money demanded for transactions varies directly with the nominal GDP; the amount of money demanded as an asset varies inversely with the interest rate. The money market combines the total demand for money with the money supply to determine equilibrium interest rates.

3. The goal of monetary policy is to help the economy achieve price stability, full employment, and economic growth.

4. The three main instruments of monetary policy are (a) open-market operations, (b) the reserve ratio, and (c) the discount rate.

5. The Fed's most often used monetary policy tool is its open-market operations. The Fed injects reserves into the banking system (and reduces interest rates) by buying securities from commercial banks and the general public. The Fed withdraws reserves from the banking system (and increases

interest rates) by selling securities to commercial banks and the general public.

6. Monetary policy affects the economy through a complex cause-effect chain: (a) Policy decisions affect commercial bank reserves; (b) changes in reserves affect the money supply; (c) changes in the money supply alter the interest rate; (d) changes in the interest rate affect investment; (e) changes in investment affect aggregate demand; and (f) changes in aggregate demand affect the equilibrium real GDP and the price level. Table 10.3 draws together all the basic ideas relevant to the use of monetary policy.

7. The advantages of monetary policy include its flexibility and political acceptability. Recently, the Fed has targeted changes in the Federal funds rate as the immediate focus of its monetary policy. When it deems it necessary, the Fed uses open-market operations to change that rate, which is the interest rate banks charge one another on overnight loans of excess reserves. Interest rates in general, including the prime interest rate, rise and fall with the Federal funds rate. The prime interest rate is the benchmark rate that banks use as a reference rate for a wide range of interest rates on short-term loans to businesses and individuals.

8. In recent years, the Fed has used monetary policy to keep inflation low while helping to limit the depth of the recession of 2001, boost the economy as it recovered from that recession, help stabilize the banking sector in the wake of the mortgage debt crisis, and promote recovery from the severe recession of 2007–2009.

9. In response to the financial crisis, the Federal Reserve provided lender-of-last-resort loans to financial institutions through a series of newly established Fed facilities. Most of these facilities closed in 2010 but could be reestablished in the event of another financial crisis.

10. Monetary policy has two major limitations and potential problems: (a) Recognition and operation lags complicate the timing of monetary policy. (b) In a severe recession, the reluctance of banks to lend excess reserves and firms to borrow money to spend on capital goods may contribute to a liquidity trap that limits the effectiveness of an expansionary monetary policy.

Terms and Concepts

monetary policy
transactions demand
asset demand
total demand for money
money market

open-market operations
discount rate
easy money policy
tight money policy
Federal funds rate

prime interest rate
cyclical asymmetry
liquidity trap

Questions

1. What is the basic determinant of (a) the strength of the transactions demand for money (the location of the transactions demand for money curve) and (b) the amount of money demanded for assets, given a particular asset demand for money curve? How is the equilibrium interest rate in the market for money determined? Use a graph to show the impact of an increase in the total demand for money on the equilibrium interest rate (no change in money supply). Use your general knowledge of equilibrium prices to explain why the previous interest rate is no longer sustainable. LO1

2. What is the basic objective of monetary policy? State the cause-effect chain through which monetary policy is made effective. What are the major strengths of monetary policy? Why is monetary policy easier to undertake than fiscal policy? LO2, LO4

3. What is the impact of each of the following transactions on commercial bank reserves? LO2

   a. The New York Federal Reserve Bank purchases government securities from private businesses and consumers.

   b. Commercial banks borrow from Federal Reserve Banks at the discount rate.

   c. The Fed reduces the reserve ratio.

4. Why do changes in bank reserves resulting from open-market operations by the Fed produce *multiple* changes in checkable deposits (and therefore money) in the economy? LO3

5. Suppose that you are a member of the Board of Governors of the Federal Reserve System. The economy is experiencing a sharp and prolonged inflationary trend. What changes in (a) the reserve ratio, (b) the discount rate, and (c) open-market operations would you recommend? Explain in each case how the change you advocate would affect commercial bank reserves, the money supply, interest rates, and aggregate demand. LO3

6. What do economists mean when they say that monetary policy can exhibit cyclical asymmetry? How does the idea of a liquidity trap relate to cyclical asymmetry? Why is this possibility of a liquidity trap significant to policymakers? LO4

7. Distinguish between the Federal funds rate and the prime interest rate. Which of these two rates does the Fed explicitly target in undertaking its monetary policy? **LO5**
8. How did the Fed use the main tools of monetary policy to respond to the financial crisis that began in 2007? What additional programs did the Fed create and implement to facilitate its role as lender of last resort? What was the primary purpose of these new programs? **LO5**

Problems

1. Assume that the following data characterize the hypothetical economy of Trance: money supply = $200 billion; quantity of money demanded for transactions = $150 billion; quantity of money demanded as an asset = $10 billion at 12 percent interest, increasing by $10 billion for each 2-percentage-point fall in the interest rate. **LO1**
   a. What is the equilibrium interest rate in Trance?
   b. At the equilibrium interest rate, what are the quantity of money supplied, the total quantity of money demanded, the amount of money demanded for transactions, and the amount of money demanded as an asset in Trance?
2. Refer to Table 10.2 and assume that the Fed's reserve ratio is 10 percent and the economy is in a severe recession. Also suppose that the commercial banks are hoarding all excess reserves (not lending them out) because of their fear of loan defaults. Finally, suppose that the Fed is highly concerned that the banks will suddenly lend out these excess reserves and possibly contribute to inflation once the economy begins to recover and confidence is restored. By how many percentage points would the Fed need to increase the reserve ratio to eliminate one-third of the excess reserves? What would be the size of the monetary multiplier before and after the change in the reserve ratio? By how much would the lending potential of the banks decline as a result of the increase in the reserve ratio? **LO2**
3. Refer to the table for Moola at the bottom of this page to answer the following questions. What is the equilibrium interest rate in Moola? What is the level of investment at the equilibrium interest rate? Is there either a recessionary output gap (negative GDP gap) or an inflationary output gap (positive GDP gap) at the equilibrium interest rate and, if either, what is the amount? Given money demand, by how much would the Moola central bank need to change the money supply to close the output gap? What is the expenditure multiplier in Moola? **LO4**

Money Supply	Money Demand	Interest Rate	Investment at Interest (Rate Shown)	Potential Real GDP	Actual Real GDP at Interest (Rate Shown)
$500	$800	2%	$50	$350	$390
500	700	3	40	350	370
500	600	4	30	350	350
500	500	5	20	350	330
500	400	6	10	350	310

FURTHER TEST YOUR KNOWLEDGE AT
www.mcconnellbrief2e.com

At the text's Online Learning Center, **www.mcconnellbrief2e.com**, you will find one or more web-based questions that require information from the Internet to answer. We urge you to check them out, since they will familiarize you with websites that may be helpful in other courses and perhaps even in your career. The OLC also features multiple-choice quizzes that give instant feedback and provides other helpful ways to further test your knowledge of the chapter.

Visit your mobile app store and download the McConnell Brief Edition: Study Econ app *today*!

LONG-RUN CONSIDERATIONS
AND INTERNATIONAL ECONOMICS

After reading this chapter, you should be able to:

1 **Explain the relationship between short-run aggregate supply and long-run aggregate supply.**

2 **Discuss how to apply the long-run AD-AS model to inflation, recessions, and economic growth.**

3 **Explain the short-run trade-off between inflation and unemployment (the Phillips Curve).**

4 **Discuss why there is no long-run trade-off between inflation and unemployment.**

5 **Explain the relationship between tax rates, tax revenues, and long-run aggregate supply.**

Long-Run Aggregate Supply and Aggregate Demand

During the early years of the Great Depression, many economists suggested that the economy would correct itself in the long run without government intervention. To this line of thinking, economist John Maynard Keynes remarked, "In the long run we are all dead!"

For several decades following the Great Depression, macroeconomic economists understandably focused on refining fiscal and monetary policy to smooth business cycles and address the problems of unemployment and inflation. The main emphasis was on the short-run problems and policies associated with the business cycle.

But over people's lifetimes, and from generation to generation, the long run is tremendously important for economic well-being. For that reason, macroeconomists have refocused attention on long-run macroeconomic adjustments, processes, and outcomes. The renewed emphasis on the long run has produced significant insights about aggregate supply and economic growth.

In Chapter 5 we discussed economic growth. Our goals in this chapter are to develop the long-run model of aggregate supply and aggregate demand, examine the inflation-unemployment relationship, and evaluate the effect of taxes on aggregate supply. The latter is a key concern of so-called *supply-side economics.*

From Short Run to Long Run

short run
A period in which prices of output are flexible, but wages and other input prices are inflexible.

long run
A period in which output prices, wages, and other input prices are all flexible.

In Chapter 7, we noted that in macroeconomics the difference between the **short run** and the **long run** has to do with the flexibility of input prices, particularly wages and salaries. Input prices are inflexible or even totally fixed in the short run but fully flexible in the long run. By contrast, output prices are assumed under these definitions to be flexible in both the short run and the long run. (They are fixed only in the immediate short run.)

The assumption that input prices are flexible only in the long run leads to large differences in the shape and position of the short-run aggregate supply curve and the long-run aggregate supply curve. As explained in Chapter 7, the short-run aggregate supply curve is an upward-sloping line, whereas the long-run aggregate supply curve is a vertical line situated directly above the economy's full-employment output level, Q_f.

Short-Run Aggregate Supply

Our first objective is to demonstrate the *relationship* between short-run aggregate supply and long-run aggregate supply. We begin by briefly reviewing short-run aggregate supply.

Consider the short-run aggregate supply curve AS_1 in Figure 11.1a. This curve is based on three assumptions: (1) The initial price level is P_1, (2) firms and workers have established nominal wages on the expectation that this price level will persist, and (3) the price level is flexible both upward and downward. Observe from point a_1 that at price level P_1 the economy is operating at its full-employment output Q_f. This output is the real production forthcoming when the economy is operating at its natural rate of unemployment (or potential output).

Now let's review the short-run effects of changes in the price level, say, from P_1 to P_2 in Figure 11.1a. The higher prices associated with price level P_2 increase firms' revenues, and because their nominal wages and other input prices remain unchanged, their profits rise. Those higher profits lead firms to increase their output from Q_f to Q_2, and the economy moves from a_1 to a_2 on aggregate supply AS_1. At output Q_2 the economy is operating beyond its full-employment output. The firms make this possible by extending the work hours of part-time and full-time workers, enticing new workers such as homemakers and retirees into the labor force, and hiring and training the structurally unemployed. Thus, the nation's unemployment rate declines below its natural rate.

How will the firms respond when the price level *falls*, say, from P_1 to P_3 in Figure 11.1a? Because the prices they receive for their products are lower while the nominal wages they pay workers remain unchanged, firms discover that their revenues and profits have diminished or disappeared. So they reduce their production and employment, and, as shown by the movement from a_1 to a_3, real output falls to Q_3. Increased unemployment and a higher unemployment rate accompany the decline in real output. At output Q_3 the unemployment rate is greater than the natural rate of unemployment associated with output Q_f.

FIGURE 11.1 Short-run and long-run aggregate supply. (a) In the short run, nominal wages and other input prices are unresponsive to price-level changes and based on the expectation that price level P_1 will continue. An increase in the price level from P_1 to P_2 increases profits and output, moving the economy from a_1 to a_2; a decrease in the price level from P_1 to P_3 reduces profits and real output, moving the economy from a_1 to a_3. The short-run aggregate supply curve therefore slopes upward. (b) In the long run, a rise in the price level results in higher nominal wages and other input prices and thus shifts the short-run aggregate supply curve to the left. Conversely, a decrease in the price level reduces nominal wages and shifts the short-run aggregate supply curve to the right. After such adjustments, the economy obtains equilibrium at points such as b_1 and c_1. Thus, the long-run aggregate supply curve is vertical at the full-employment output.

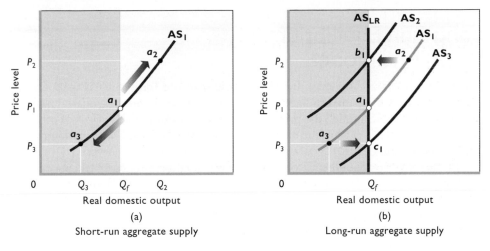

Long-Run Aggregate Supply

The outcomes are different in the long run. To see why, we need to extend the analysis of aggregate supply to account for changes in nominal wages that occur *in response to changes in the price level.* That will enable us to derive the economy's long-run aggregate supply curve.

We illustrate the implications for aggregate supply in Figure 11.1b. Again, suppose that the economy is initially at point a_1 (P_1 and Q_f). As we just demonstrated, an increase in the price level from P_1 to P_2 will move the economy from point a_1 to a_2 along the short-run aggregate supply curve AS_1. At a_2, the economy is producing at more than its potential output. This implies very high demand for productive inputs, so input prices will begin to rise. In particular this high demand for labor will drive up nominal wages, which will increase per-unit production costs. As a result, the short-run supply curve then shifts leftward from AS_1 to AS_2, which now reflects the higher price level P_2 and the new expectation that P_2, not P_1, will continue. The leftward shift in the short-run aggregate supply curve to AS_2 moves the economy from a_2 to b_1. Real output falls to its full-employment level Q_f, and the unemployment rate rises to its natural rate.

What is the long-run outcome of a *decrease* in the price level? *Assuming eventual downward wage flexibility,* a decline in the price level, as from P_1 to P_3 in Figure 11.1b, works in the opposite way from a price-level increase. At first the economy moves from point a_1 to a_3 on AS_1. Profits are squeezed or eliminated because prices have fallen and nominal wages have not. But this movement along AS_1 is the short-run supply response that results only while input prices remain constant. As time passes, input prices will begin to fall because the economy is producing less than its full-employment output. With so little output being produced, the demand for inputs will be weak and their product prices will begin to decline. In particular, the low demand for labor will drive down nominal wages and reduce per-unit production costs. Lower nominal wages therefore shift the short-run aggregate supply curve rightward from AS_1 to AS_3, and real output returns to its full-employment level of Q_f at point c_1.

By tracing a line between the long-run equilibrium points b_1, a_1, and c_1, we obtain a long-run aggregate supply curve. Observe that it is vertical at the full-employment level of real GDP. After long-run adjustments in nominal wages and other input prices, real output is Q_f regardless of the specific price level.

Long-Run Equilibrium in the AD-AS Model

long-run AD-AS model
A model in which the equilibrium price level and level of real GDP are determined by the intersection of the AD curve and the vertical long-run AS curve.

Figure 11.2 helps us understand the equilibrium in the **long-run AD-AS model**, which includes the distinction between short-run and long-run aggregate supply. In the long-run AD-AS model, the price level, the wage rate, and the prices of other inputs are all flexible. The equilibrium price level and level of real GDP are determined by the intersection of the AD curve and the vertical long-run AS curve.

In the short run, equilibrium occurs wherever the downsloping aggregate demand curve and upsloping short-run aggregate supply curve intersect. This can be at any level of output, not simply the full-employment level. Either a negative GDP gap or a positive GDP gap is possible in the short run.

But in the long run, the short-run aggregate supply curve adjusts as we have just described. After those adjustments, long-run equilibrium occurs where the aggregate demand curve, vertical long-run aggregate supply curve, and short-run aggregate supply curve all intersect. Figure 11.2 shows the long-run outcome. Equilibrium occurs at point a, where AD_1 intersects both AS_{LR} and AS_1, and the economy achieves its full-employment (or potential) output, Q_f. At long-run equilibrium price level P_1 and output level Q_f, there is neither a negative GDP gap nor a positive GDP gap. The economy's *natural rate of unemployment* prevails, meaning that the economy achieves full employment.

INTERACTIVE GRAPHS
G 11.1
Long-run AD-AS model

In the United States, output Q_f in Figure 11.2 implies a 4 to 5 percent unemployment rate. The natural rate of unemployment can vary from one time period to another and can differ between countries. But whatever the rate happens to be, it defines the level of potential output and establishes the location of the long-run AS curve.

FIGURE 11.2 The long-run AD-AS model. The equilibrium price level P_1 and level of real output Q_f occur at the intersection of the aggregate demand curve AD_1, the long-run aggregate supply curve AS_{LR}, and the short-run aggregate supply curve AS_1. At this equilibrium price-output combination, neither a positive GDP gap nor a negative GDP gap occurs. The economy achieves it full-employment level of real GDP.

Demand-Pull Inflation in the Long-Run AD-AS Model

The long-run AD-AS model provides added understanding of demand-pull inflation. Recall that demand-pull inflation occurs when an increase in aggregate demand pulls up the price level. Previously, we depicted this inflation by shifting an aggregate demand curve rightward along a stable aggregate supply curve (Figure 7.8)—and that was the end of the matter.

In our more complex version of aggregate supply, however, an increase in the price level will eventually lead to a "catch-up" increase in nominal wages and thus a leftward shift of the short-run aggregate supply curve. This is shown in Figure 11.3, where we initially suppose the price level is P_1 at the intersection of aggregate demand curve AD_1, short-run supply curve AS_1, and long-run aggregate supply curve AS_{LR}. Observe that the economy is achieving its full-employment real output Q_f at point a.

Now consider the effects of an unexpected increase in aggregate demand as represented by the rightward shift from AD_1 to AD_2. This shift might result from any one of a number of factors, including an increase in investment spending or a rise in net exports. Whatever its cause, the increase in aggregate demand boosts the price level from P_1 to P_2 and expands real output from Q_f to Q_2 at point b. There, a positive GDP gap of $Q_2 - Q_f$ occurs.

So far, none of this is new to you. But now the distinction between short-run aggregate supply and long-run aggregate supply becomes important. With the economy producing above potential output, inputs will be in high demand. Input prices, including nominal wages, therefore will rise. As they do, the short-run aggregate supply curve will ultimately shift leftward such that it intersects long-run aggregate supply at point c. There, the economy has reestablished long-run equilibrium, with the price level and real output now P_3 and Q_f, respectively. Only at point c does the new aggregate demand curve AD_2 intersect both the short-run aggregate supply curve AS_2 and the long-run aggregate supply curve AS_{LR}.

In the short run, demand-pull inflation drives up the price level and increases real output; in the long run, only the price level rises. In the long run, the initial increase in aggregate demand moves the economy along its vertical aggregate supply curve AS_{LR}. For a while, an economy can operate beyond its full-employment level of output. But the demand-pull inflation eventually causes adjustments of nominal wages that return the economy to its full-employment output Q_f.

FIGURE 11.3 Demand-pull inflation in the long-run AD-AS model. An increase in aggregate demand from AD_1 to AD_2 drives up the price level and increases real output in the short run. But in the long run, nominal wages rise and the short-run aggregate supply curve shifts leftward, as from AS_1 to AS_2. Real output then returns to its prior level, and the price level rises even more. In this scenario, the economy moves from a to b and then eventually to c.

The analysis provides a major insight: What sometimes appears to be cost-push inflation because nominal wages, natural resource prices, and other input prices are rising rapidly is often simply a facet of demand-pull inflation. Higher product prices caused by increasing aggregate demand eventually pull up input prices through the adjustment process that we have just described.

QUESTION: How do long-term contracts between resource suppliers and resource buyers affect the length of the time it takes for the economy to move from *b* to *c* in Figure 11.3?

APPLYING THE ANALYSIS

Cost-Push Inflation in the Long-Run AD-AS Model

The long-run model also clarifies a policy dilemma relating to cost-push inflation. Recall that this kind of inflation arises from factors that increase the cost of production at each price level, shifting the aggregate supply curve leftward and raising the equilibrium price level. Previously (Figure 7.9), we considered cost-push inflation using only the short-run aggregate supply curve. Now we want to analyze that type of inflation in its long-run context.

Look at Figure 11.4, in which we again assume that the economy is initially operating at price level P_1 and output level Q_f (point *a*). Suppose that an unanticipated international crisis causes a boost in the price of oil by, for example, 100 percent in a very short period of time. As a result, the per-unit production cost of producing and transporting goods and services rises substantially in the economy represented by Figure 11.4. This increase in per-unit production costs shifts the short-run aggregate supply curve to the left, as from AS_1 to AS_2, and the price level rises from P_1 to P_2 (as seen by comparing points *a* and *b*). In this case, the leftward shift of the short-run aggregate supply curve is *not a response* to a price-level increase, as it was in our previous discussions of demand-pull inflation; it is the *initiating cause* of the price-level increase.

Cost-push inflation creates a dilemma for policymakers. Without some expansionary stabilization policy, aggregate demand in Figure 11.4 remains in place at AD_1

FIGURE 11.4 Cost-push inflation in the long-run AD-AS model. Cost-push inflation occurs when the short-run aggregate supply curve shifts leftward, as from AS_1 to AS_2. If government counters the decline in real output by increasing aggregate demand to the broken line, the price level rises even more. That is, the economy moves in steps from *a* to *b* to *c*. In contrast, if government allows a recession to occur, nominal wages eventually fall and the aggregate supply curve shifts back rightward to its original location. The economy moves from *a* to *b* and eventually back to *a*.

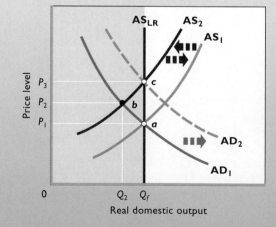

and real output declines from Q_f to Q_2. Government can counter this recession, negative GDP gap, and the attendant high unemployment by using fiscal policy and monetary policy to increase aggregate demand to AD_2. But there is a potential policy trap here: An increase in aggregate demand to AD_2 will further raise inflation by increasing the price level from P_2 to P_3 (a move from point b to point c).

Suppose the government recognizes this policy trap and decides not to increase aggregate demand from AD_1 to AD_2 (you can now disregard the dashed AD_2 curve) and instead decides to allow a cost-push-caused recession to run its course. How will that happen? Widespread layoffs, plant shutdowns, and business failures eventually occur. At some point the demand for oil, labor, and other inputs will decline so much that oil prices and nominal wages will decline. When that happens, the initial leftward shift of the short-run aggregate supply curve will reverse itself. That is, the declining per-unit production costs caused by the recession will shift the short-run aggregate supply curve rightward from AS_2 to AS_1. The price level will return to P_1, and the full-employment level of output will be restored at Q_f (point a on the long-run aggregate supply curve AS_{LR}).

This analysis yields two generalizations:

- If the government attempts to maintain full employment when cost-push inflation occurs, even more inflation will occur.
- If the government takes a hands-off approach to cost-push inflation, the recession will linger. Although falling input prices will eventually undo the initial rise in per-unit production costs, the economy in the meantime will experience high unemployment and a loss of real output.

QUESTION: Why do you think it is so difficult politically for Congress or even the Federal Reserve to let cost-push inflation burn itself out for lack of aggregate demand fuel?

APPLYING THE ANALYSIS

Recession in the Long-Run AD-AS Model

What does the long-run AD-AS model inform us about recession (or depression)? Will recessions caused by decreases in aggregate demand eventually self-correct?

Suppose in Figure 11.5 that aggregate demand initially is AD_1 and that the short-run and long-run aggregate supply curves are AS_1 and AS_{LR}, respectively. Therefore, as shown by point a, the price level is P_1 and output is Q_f. Now suppose that investment spending declines dramatically, reducing aggregate demand to AD_2. Observe that real output declines from Q_f to Q_1, indicating that a recession has occurred. But if we make the controversial assumption that prices and wages are flexible downward, the price level falls from P_1 to P_2. With the economy producing below potential output at point b, demand for inputs will be weak. Eventually, nominal wages themselves fall to restore the previous real wage; when that happens, the short-run aggregate supply curve shifts rightward from AS_1 to AS_2. The negative GDP gap evaporates without the need for expansionary fiscal or monetary policy, since real output expands from Q_1 (point b) back to full-employment real output Q_f (point c). The economy is again located on its long-run aggregate supply curve AS_{LR}, but now at the lower price level P_3.

FIGURE 11.5 Recession in the long-run AD-AS model. A recession occurs when aggregate demand shifts leftward, as from AD₁ to AD₂. If prices and wages are downwardly flexible, the price level falls from P₁ to P₂ as the economy moves from point a to point b. With the economy in recession at point b, wages eventually fall, shifting the short-run aggregate supply curve from AS₁ to AS₂. The price level declines to P₃, and real output returns to Q_f. The economy moves in steps from point a to b to c.

There is considerable disagreement as to whether this hypothetical scenario bears any resemblance to reality. The key point of dispute resolves around the degree to which both input and output prices are downwardly flexible and how long it would take in the actual economy for the necessary downward price and wage adjustments to occur to regain the full-employment level of output. Most economists believe that if such adjustments are forthcoming, they will occur only after the economy has experienced a relatively long-lasting recession with its accompanying high unemployment and large loss of output. The severity and length of the major recession of 2007–2009 has strengthened this view. Also, they point out that it is better to use fiscal and monetary policy to try to halt the decline in real GDP and increase in unemployment than simply to wait and hope that the hypothesized adjustments in the long-run AD-AS model are actually forthcoming. Following such advice, the federal government and Federal Reserve used aggressive fiscal and monetary policy to try to halt and reverse the decline in aggregate demand occurring during the recessionary year 2008. A second, more massive dose of fiscal policy was prescribed for 2009, as the recession continued.

QUESTION: Why are wages so sticky downward, even during recessions?

Economic Growth and Ongoing Inflation

In our analysis so far, we have demonstrated how demand and supply shocks can cause, respectively, demand-pull inflation and cost-push inflation. But in these previous cases, the extent of the inflation was *finite* because the size of the initial movement in either the AD curve or the AS curve was *limited*. For instance, in Figure 11.3, the aggregate demand curve shifts right by a limited amount, from AD₁ to AD₂. As the economy's equilibrium moves from *a* to *b* to *c*, the price level rises from P₁ to P₂ to P₃. During this transition, inflation obviously occurs because the price level is rising. But once the economy reaches its new equilibrium at point *c*, the price level remains constant at P₃ and there is no further inflation. That is, the limited movement in aggregate demand causes a limited amount of inflation that ends when the economy returns to full employment.

But the modern economy almost always experiences continuous, but usually mild, positive rates of inflation. That can only happen with ongoing shifts in either the

FIGURE 11.6 Production possibilities and long-run aggregate supply. (a) Economic growth driven by supply factors (such as improved technologies or the use of more or better resources) shifts an economy's production possibilities outward, as from *AB* to *CD*. (b) The same factors shift the economy's long-run aggregate supply curve to the right, as from AS_{LR1} to AS_{LR2}.

(a)

Increase in

production possibilities

(b)

Increase in long-run

aggregate supply

aggregate demand or long-run aggregate supply curves because any single, finite shift will only cause inflation of limited duration. This insight is crucial to understanding why modern economies usually experience ongoing inflation while achieving economic growth. Both aggregate demand and long-run aggregate supply increase over time in the actual economy, and inflation occurs because the increases in aggregate demand generally exceed the increases in long-run aggregate supply. It will be helpful to examine this point graphically.

As discussed in Chapter 5, economic growth is driven by supply factors such as improved technologies and access to more or better resources. We can illustrate economic growth either as an outward shift of the economy's production possibilities curve or as a rightward shift of its long-run aggregate supply curve. Observe Figure 11.6, in which the outward shift of the production possibilities curve from *AB* to *CD* in graph (a) is equivalent to the rightward shift of the economy's long-run aggregate supply curve from AS_{LR1} to AS_{LR2} in graph (b). Keeping this shift in long-run aggregate supply clearly in mind, let's quickly move our attention to Figure 11.7. There, we show how the long-run aggregate demand–aggregate supply model can depict the economic growth process.

Suppose that an economy's aggregate demand curve, long-run aggregate supply curve, and short-run aggregate supply curve initially are AD_1, AS_{LR1}, and AS_1, as shown. The equilibrium price level and level of real output are P_1 and Q_1.

Now let's assume that economic growth driven by the changes in the supply factors (quantity and quality of resources and technology) shifts the long-run aggregate supply curve rightward from AS_{LR1} to AS_{LR2}. The economy's potential output has increased, as reflected by the expansion of available real output from Q_1 to Q_2.

With no change in aggregate demand, the increase in long-run aggregate supply from AS_{LR1} to AS_{LR2} in Figure 11.7 would expand real GDP and lower the price level. Put plainly, economic growth is deflationary, other things equal. But declines in the price level are not a part of the U.S. growth experience. Why not? The Federal Reserve has expanded the nation's money supply over the years such that increases in

FIGURE 11.7 Depicting U.S. growth via the long-run AD-AS model. Long-run aggregate supply and short-run aggregate supply have increased over time, as from AS_{LR1} to AS_{LR2} and AS_1 to AS_2. Simultaneously, aggregate demand has shifted rightward, as from AD_1 to AD_2. The actual outcome of these combined shifts in the United States has been economic growth, shown as the increase in real GDP from Q_1 to Q_2, accompanied by mild inflation, shown as the rise in the price level from P_1 to P_2.

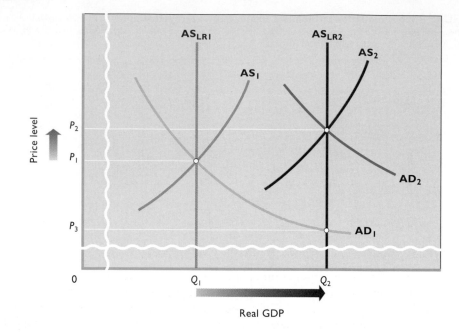

aggregate demand have more than matched the increases in aggregate supply. We depict this increase of aggregate demand as the rightward shift from AD_1 to AD_2.

The increases of aggregate supply and aggregate demand in Figure 11.7 have increased real output from Q_1 to Q_2 and have boosted the price level from P_1 to P_2. At the higher price level P_2, the economy confronts a new short-run aggregate supply curve AS_2. The changes shown in Figure 11.7 describe the actual U.S. experience: economic growth, accompanied by mild inflation.

In brief, economic growth causes increases in aggregate supply and aggregate demand. Whether zero, mild, or rapid inflation accompanies economic growth depends on the extent to which aggregate demand increases relative to aggregate supply. Over long periods, any inflation that occurs is the result of the growth of aggregate demand. It is not the result of the growth of real GDP.

The Inflation-Unemployment Relationship

We have just seen that the Fed can determine how much inflation occurs in the economy by how much it causes aggregate demand to shift relative to long-run aggregate supply. Given that low inflation and low unemployment rates are the Fed's major goals, its ability to control inflation brings up at least two interesting policy questions: Are low unemployment and low inflation compatible goals or conflicting goals? What explains situations in which high unemployment and high inflation coexist?

The long-run AD-AS model supports three significant generalizations relating to these questions:

- Under normal circumstances, a short-run trade-off exists between the rate of inflation and the rate of unemployment.
- Aggregate supply shocks can cause both higher rates of inflation and higher rates of unemployment.
- No significant trade-off exists between inflation and unemployment over long periods of time.

Let's examine each of these three important points.

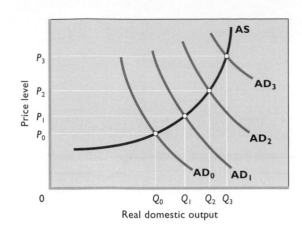

FIGURE 11.8 The effect of changes in aggregate demand on real output and the price level. Comparing the effects of various possible increases in aggregate demand leads to the conclusion that the larger the increase in aggregate demand, the higher the rate of inflation and the greater the increase in real output. Because real output and the unemployment rate move in opposite directions, we can generalize that, given short-run aggregate supply, high rates of inflation should be accompanied by low rates of unemployment.

Short-Run Trade-Off: The Phillips Curve

Let's view the short-run aggregate supply curve in Figure 11.8 and perform a simple mental experiment. Suppose that in some period aggregate demand expands from AD_0 to AD_2, either because firms decided to buy more capital goods or the government decided to increase its expenditures. Whatever the cause, in the short run the price level rises from P_0 to P_2 and real output rises from Q_0 to Q_2. As real output rises, the unemployment rate falls.

Now let's compare what would have happened if the increase in aggregate demand had been larger, say, from AD_0 to AD_3. The new equilibrium tells us that the amount of inflation and the growth of real output would both have been greater (and the unemployment rate would have been lower). Similarly, suppose aggregate demand during the year had increased only modestly, from AD_0 to AD_1.

Compared with our shift from AD_0 to AD_2, the amount of inflation and the growth of real output would have been smaller (and the unemployment rate higher).

The generalization we draw from this mental experiment is this: *Assuming a constant short-run aggregate supply curve*, high rates of inflation are accompanied by low rates of unemployment, and low rates of inflation are accompanied by high rates of unemployment.

We can demonstrate this short-run trade-off between the rate of inflation and the rate of unemployment through the **Phillips Curve.** This curve is named after economist A. W. Phillips, who developed the idea by plotting data points for inflation rates and unemployment rates for each year on a graph. Generalized in Figure 11.9, the Phillips Curve suggests an inverse relationship between the rate of inflation and the rate of unemployment. Lower unemployment rates (measured as leftward movements on the horizontal axis) are associated with higher rates of inflation (measured as upward movements on the vertical axis).

The facts for the United States in the 1960s nicely fit the theory and approximate the Phillips Curve drawn in Figure 11.9. Unemployment rates above 4 percent were associated with inflation rates below 2 percent; unemployment rates below 4 percent were associated with inflation rates from 2 to 6 percent. On the basis of that evidence and evidence from other countries, most economists at that time concluded that a stable, predictable trade-off existed between unemployment and inflation.

Moreover, U.S. economic policy was built on that supposed trade-off. According to this thinking, it was impossible to achieve "full employment without inflation." Manipulation of aggregate demand through fiscal and monetary measures would simply move the economy along the Phillips Curve. An expansionary fiscal and monetary policy that boosted aggregate demand and lowered the unemployment rate

Phillips Curve
A curve showing the relationship between the unemployment rate and the rate of inflation.

ORIGIN OF THE IDEA

O 11.1

Phillips Curve

FIGURE 11.9 The Phillips Curve. The Phillips Curve (here, stylized) relates annual rates of inflation and annual rates of unemployment for a series of years. Because this is an inverse relationship, a trade-off presumably exists between unemployment and inflation.

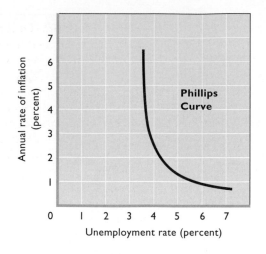

would simultaneously increase inflation. A restrictive fiscal and monetary policy could be used to reduce the rate of inflation but only at the cost of a higher unemployment rate and more forgone production. Society had to choose between the incompatible goals of price stability and full employment; it had to decide where to locate on its Phillips Curve.

For reasons we will soon see, today's economists reject the idea of a stable, predictable Phillips Curve. Nevertheless, they agree there is a short-run trade-off between unemployment and inflation. Given aggregate supply, increases in aggregate demand increase real output and reduce the unemployment rate. As the unemployment rate falls and dips below the natural rate, the excessive spending produces demand-pull inflation. Conversely, when a recession sets in and the unemployment rate jumps, the weak aggregate demand that caused the recession also leads to lower inflation rates.

Aggregate Supply Shocks and Shifts of the Phillips Curve

The unemployment-inflation experience of the 1970s and early 1980s demolished the idea of an always-stable Phillips Curve. In most of the years of the 1970s and early 1980s, the economy experienced both higher inflation rates *and* higher unemployment rates than it did in the 1960s. For example, in 1975 the unemployment rate was 8.5 percent and the inflation rate (December-to-December) was 6.9 percent. In 1981, the unemployment rate was 7.6 percent and the inflation rate was 8.9 percent.

stagflation
Simultaneous increases in the price level and the unemployment rate.

In fact, inflation and unemployment rose simultaneously in some years. This condition is called **stagflation**—a media term that combines the words "stagnation" and "inflation." If any such thing as a Phillips Curve still existed, it had clearly shifted outward. We would show such changes, in a generalized way, as upward and outward shifts of curve PC in Figure 11.9. The shifts in the 1970s and early 1980s would place the curve at some location off the graph!

aggregate supply shocks
Sudden unanticipated large changes in resource costs that shift an economy's aggregate supply curve.

The unemployment rates and inflation rates in the 1970s and early 1980s support our second generalization: Aggregate supply shocks can cause both higher rates of inflation and higher rates of unemployment. A series of adverse **aggregate supply shocks**—sudden, large increases in resource costs that jolt an economy's short-run aggregate supply curve leftward—hit the economy in the 1970s and early 1980s. The most significant of these shocks was a quadrupling of oil prices by the Organization of Petroleum Exporting Countries (OPEC). Consequently, the cost of producing and distributing virtually every product and service rose rapidly. (Other factors working to increase U.S. costs during this period included major agricultural shortfalls, a greatly depreciated dollar, wage hikes previously held down by wage-price controls, and slower rates of productivity growth.)

These shocks shifted the short-run aggregate supply curve to the left and distorted the usual inflation-unemployment relationship. Remember that we derived the inverse relationship between the rate of inflation and the unemployment rate shown in Figure 11.9 by shifting the aggregate demand curve along a stable short-run aggregate supply curve (Figure 11.8). But the cost-push inflation model shown in Figure 11.4 tells us that a *leftward shift* of the short-run aggregate supply curve increases the price level and reduces real output (and increases the unemployment rate). This, say most economists, is what happened in two periods in the 1970s. The U.S. unemployment rate shot up from 4.9 percent in 1973 to 8.5 percent in 1975, contributing to a significant decline in real GDP. In the same period, the U.S. price level rose by 21 percent. The stagflation scenario recurred in 1978, when OPEC increased oil prices by more than 100 percent. The U.S. price level rose by 26 percent between 1978 and 1980, while unemployment increased from 6.1 to 7.1 percent.

The stagflation of the 1970s and early 1980s ended in the 1980s, and by 1989 the lingering effects of the early period had subsided. One precursor to this favorable trend was the deep recession of 1981–1982, largely caused by a tight money policy aimed at reducing double-digit inflation. The recession upped the unemployment rate to 9.5 percent in 1982. With so many workers unemployed, those who were working accepted smaller increases in their nominal wages—or, in some cases, wage reductions— in order to preserve their jobs. Firms, in turn, restrained their price increases to try to retain their relative shares of a greatly diminished market.

Other factors were at work. Foreign competition throughout this period held down wage and price hikes in several basic industries such as automobiles and steel. Deregulation of the airline and trucking industries also resulted in wage reductions or so-called wage givebacks. A significant decline in OPEC's monopoly power and a greatly reduced reliance on oil in the production process produced a stunning fall in the price of oil and its derivative products, such as gasoline.

All these factors combined to reduce per-unit production costs and shift the short-run aggregate supply curve rightward. Employment and output expanded, and the unemployment rate fell from 9.6 percent in 1983 to 5.3 percent in 1989. Since 1990 inflation-unemployment points have settled back to closer to the points associated with the Phillips Curve of the 1960s. Even the recession of 2007–2009 did not greatly alter the recent inflation rate–unemployment rate pattern. In 2008, the unemployment rate was 5.8 percent, but the inflation rate was near zero at just 0.1 percent. The inflation-unemployment point for 2009 and 2010, however, moved up and to the right relative to the point for 2008. This was driven primarily by unemployment rates that exceeded 9 percent in those years.

The media sometimes express the sum of the unemployment rate and the inflation rate as a rough gauge of the economic discomfort that inflation and unemployment jointly impose on an economy in a particular year. The sum of the two rates is used to compute the *misery index*. For example, a nation with a 5 percent unemployment rate and a 5 percent inflation rate has a misery index number of 10, as does a nation with an 8 percent unemployment rate and a 2 percent inflation rate.

Global Snapshot 11.1 shows the misery index for several nations between 2000 and 2010. The U.S. misery index number has been neither exceptionally low nor exceptionally high relative to the misery index numbers for the other major economies shown. But bear in mind that economists do not put much stock in the misery index

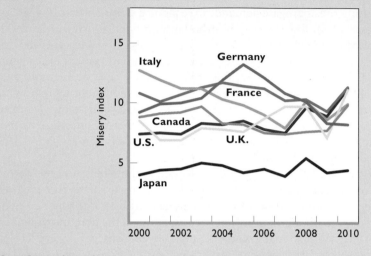

GLOBAL SNAPSHOT 11.1

The Misery Index, Selected Nations, 2000–2010

The U.S. misery index number (the sum of its unemployment rate and inflation rate) has generally been in the midrange of such numbers relative to other major economies in recent years.

Source: Bureau of Labor Statistics, **stats.bls.gov.** Inflation rates and unemployment rates in this calculation are both on an average-annual basis.

because they do not view the national discomfort associated with a 1 percent change in inflation and a 1 percent change in unemployment as necessarily equivalent. In particular, the misery index can greatly disguise the extent of hardship during a recession. The rise in the unemployment rate in these circumstances causes a huge loss of national output and income (and misery!), even if the higher unemployment rate is partially or fully offset with a decline in the rate of inflation.

No Long-Run Inflation-Unemployment Trade-Off

The historical record supports our third generalization relating to the inflation-unemployment relationship: No apparent *long-run* trade-off exists between inflation and unemployment. Economists point out that when decades as opposed to a few years are considered, any rate of inflation is consistent with the natural rate of unemployment prevailing at that time. We know from Chapter 6 that the natural rate of unemployment is the unemployment rate that occurs when cyclical unemployment is zero; it is the full-employment rate of unemployment or the rate of unemployment when the economy achieves it potential output.

How can there be a short-run inflation-unemployment trade-off but not a long-run trade-off? Figure 11.10 provides the answer. Consider Phillips Curve PC_1. Suppose that the economy initially is experiencing a 3 percent rate of inflation and a 5 percent natural rate of unemployment. Such short-term curves as PC_1, PC_2, and PC_3 (drawn as straight lines for simplicity) exist because the actual rate of inflation is not always the same as the expected rate.

Establishing an additional point on Phillips Curve PC_1 will clarify this. We begin at a_1, where we assume nominal wages are set on the assumption that the 3 percent

FIGURE 11.10 The long-run vertical Phillips Curve. Increases in aggregate demand beyond those consistent with full-employment output may temporarily boost profits, output, and employment (as from a_1 to b_1). But nominal wages eventually will catch up so as to sustain real wages. When they do, profits will fall, negating the previous short-run stimulus to production and employment (the economy now moves from b_1 to a_2). Consequently, there is no trade-off between the rates of inflation and unemployment in the long run; that is, the long-run Phillips Curve is roughly a vertical line at the economy's natural rate of unemployment.

rate of inflation will continue. That is, because workers expect output prices to rise by 3 percent per year, they agreed to wage contracts that feature 3 percent per year increases in nominal wages so that these nominal wage increases will exactly offset the expected rises in prices and thereby keep their real wages the same.

But suppose that the rate of inflation rises to 6 percent, perhaps because the Fed has decided to increase aggregate demand even faster than it had before. With a nominal wage rate set on the expectation that the 3 percent rate of inflation will continue, the higher product prices raise business profits. Firms respond to the higher profits by hiring more workers and increasing output. In the short run, the economy moves to b_1, which, in contrast to a_1, involves a lower rate of unemployment (4 percent) and a higher rate of inflation (6 percent). The move from a_1 to b_1 is consistent both with an upsloping aggregate supply curve and with the inflation-unemployment trade-off implied by the Phillips Curve analysis. But this short-run Phillips Curve simply is a manifestation of the following principle: *When the actual rate of inflation is higher than expected, profits temporarily rise and the unemployment rate temporarily falls.*

But point b_1 is not a stable equilibrium. Workers will recognize that their nominal wages have not increased as fast as inflation and will therefore obtain nominal wage increases to restore their lost purchasing power. But as nominal wages rise to restore the level of real wages that previously existed at a_1, business profits will fall to their prior level. The reduction in profits means that the original motivation to employ more workers and increase output has disappeared.

Unemployment then returns to its natural level at point a_2. Note, however, that the economy now faces a higher actual and expected rate of inflation—6 percent rather than 3 percent. This happens because the new labor contracts feature 6 percent per year increases in wage rates to make up for the 6 percent per year inflation rate. Because wages are a production cost, this faster increase in wages will imply faster future increases in output prices as firms are forced to raise prices more rapidly to make up for the faster future rate of wage growth. Stated a bit differently, the initial increase in inflation will become persistent because it leads to renegotiated labor contracts that will perpetuate the higher rate of inflation. In addition, because the new labor contracts are public, it will also be the case that the higher rates of inflation that they will cause will be expected by everyone rather than being a surprise.

In view of the higher 6 percent expected rate of inflation, the short-run Phillips Curve shifts upward from PC_1 to PC_2 in Figure 11.10. An "along-the-Phillips-Curve" kind of move from a_1 to b_1 on PC_1 is merely a short-run or transient occurrence. In the long run, after nominal wage contracts catch up with increases in the inflation rate, unemployment returns to its natural rate at a_2, and there is a new short-run Phillips Curve PC_2 at the higher expected rate of inflation.

The scenario repeats if aggregate demand continues to increase. Prices rise momentarily ahead of nominal wages, profits expand, and employment and output increase (as implied by the move from a_2 to b_2). But, in time, nominal wages increase so as to restore real wages. Profits then fall to their original level, pushing employment back to the normal rate at a_3. The economy's "reward" for lowering the unemployment rate below the natural rate is a still higher (9 percent) rate of inflation.

Movements along the short-run Phillips curve (a_1 to b_1 on PC_1) cause the curve to shift to a less favorable position (PC_2, then PC_3, and so on). A stable Phillips Curve with the dependable series of unemployment-rate–inflation-rate trade-offs simply does not exist in the long run. The economy is characterized by a **long-run vertical Phillips Curve.**

long-run vertical Phillips Curve
A Phillips Curve showing that over long periods of time there is no trade-off between inflation rates and the unemployment rates.

The vertical line through a_1, a_2, and a_3 shows the long-run relationship between unemployment and inflation. Any rate of inflation is consistent with the 5 percent natural rate of unemployment. So, society ought to choose a low rate of inflation rather than a high one.

The distinction between the short-run Phillips Curve and the long-run Phillips Curve also helps explain **disinflation**—reductions in the inflation rate from year to year. Suppose in Figure 11.10 that the economy is at a_3, where the inflation rate is 9 percent. And suppose that the pace of the nation's economic activity slows (as happened during the 1981–1982 recession), such that inflation falls below the 9 percent expected rate to, say, 6 percent. Business profits fall because prices are rising less rapidly than wages. The nominal wage increases, remember, were set on the assumption that the 9 percent rate of inflation would continue. In response to the decline in profits, firms reduce their employment and consequently the unemployment rate rises. The economy temporarily slides downward from point a_3 to c_3 along the short-run Phillips Curve PC_3. *When the actual rate of inflation is lower than the expected rate, profits temporarily fall and the unemployment rate temporarily rises.*

disinflation
A decline in the annual rate of inflation from the previous year.

Firms and workers eventually adjust their expectations to the new 6 percent rate of inflation, and thus newly negotiated wage increases decline. Profits are restored, employment rises, and the unemployment rate falls back to its natural rate of 5 percent at a_2. Because the expected rate of inflation is now 6 percent, the short-run Phillips Curve PC_3 shifts leftward to PC_2.

If there is a further decline in the rate at which aggregate demand shifts to the right faster than aggregate supply, the scenario will continue. Inflation declines from 6 percent to, say, 3 percent, moving the economy from a_2 to c_2 along PC_2. The lower-than-expected rate of inflation (lower prices) squeezes profits and reduces employment. But, in the long run, firms respond to the lower profits by reducing their nominal wage increases. Profits are restored and unemployment returns to its natural rate at a_1 as the short-run Phillips Curve moves from PC_2 to PC_1. Once again, the long-run Phillips Curve is vertical at the 5 percent natural rate of unemployment.

ORIGIN OF THE IDEA

O 11.2

Long-run vertical Phillips Curve

Taxation and Aggregate Supply

A final topic in our discussion of aggregate supply is taxation, a key aspect of **supply-side economics.** "Supply-side economists" or "supply-siders" stress that changes in aggregate supply are an active force in determining the levels of inflation, unemployment, and economic growth. Government policies can either impede or promote rightward shifts of long-run aggregate supply curves such as those shown in Figure 11.7. One such policy is taxation.

These economists say that the enlargement of the U.S. tax system has impaired incentives to work, save, and invest. In this view, high tax rates impede productivity growth and hence slow the expansion of long-run aggregate supply. By reducing the after-tax rewards of workers and producers, high tax rates reduce the financial attractiveness of working, saving, and investing.

Supply-siders focus their attention on *marginal tax rates*—the rates on extra dollars of income—because those rates affect the benefits from working, saving, or investing more. In 2010 the marginal tax rates varied from 10 to 35 percent in the United States.

Supply-siders believe that how long and how hard people work depends on the amounts of additional after-tax earnings they derive from their efforts. They say that lower marginal tax rates on earned incomes induce more work, and therefore increase aggregate inputs of labor. Lower marginal tax rates increase the after-tax wage rate and make leisure more expensive and work more attractive. The higher opportunity cost of leisure encourages people to substitute work for leisure. This increase in productive effort is achieved in many ways: by increasing the number of hours worked per day or week, by encouraging workers to postpone retirement, by inducing more people to enter the labor force, by motivating people to work harder, and by avoiding long periods of unemployment.

High marginal tax rates also reduce the rewards for saving and investing. For example, suppose that Tony saves $10,000 at 8 percent interest, bringing him $800 of interest per year. If his marginal tax rate is 40 percent, his after-tax interest earnings will be $480, not $800, and his after-tax interest rate will fall to 4.8 percent. While Tony might be willing to save (forgo current consumption) for an 8 percent return on his saving, he might rather consume when the return is only 4.8 percent.

Saving, remember, is the prerequisite of investment. Thus, supply-side economists recommend lower marginal tax rates on interest earned from saving. They also call for lower taxes on income from capital to ensure that there are ready investment outlets for the economy's enhanced pool of saving. A critical determinant of investment spending is the expected *after-tax* return on that spending.

To summarize: Lower marginal tax rates encourage saving and investing. Workers therefore find themselves equipped with more and technologically superior machinery and equipment. Labor productivity rises, and that expands long-run aggregate supply and economic growth, which in turn helps keeps unemployment rates and inflation low.

The Laffer Curve

In the supply-side view, reductions in marginal tax rates increase the nation's aggregate supply and can leave the nation's tax revenues unchanged or even enlarge them. Thus, supply-side tax cuts need not produce federal budget deficits.

This idea is based on the **Laffer Curve,** named after Arthur Laffer, who popularized it. As Figure 11.11 shows, the Laffer Curve depicts the relationship between tax rates and tax revenues. As tax rates increase from 0 to 100 percent, tax revenues increase from zero to some maximum level (at *m*) and then fall to zero. Tax revenues

supply-side economics
A view of macroeconomics that emphasizes the role of marginal tax rates and other factors that affect long-run aggregate supply and therefore affect inflation, unemployment, and economic growth.

Laffer Curve
A curve relating tax rates and tax revenues.

FIGURE 11.11 **The Laffer Curve.** The Laffer Curve suggests that up to point *m* higher tax rates will result in larger tax revenues. But higher tax rates will adversely affect incentives to work and produce, reducing the size of the tax base (output and income) to the extent that tax revenues will decline. It follows that if tax rates are above *m*, reductions in tax rates will produce increases in tax revenues.

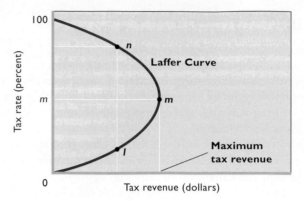

decline beyond some point because higher tax rates discourage economic activity, thereby shrinking the tax base (domestic output and income). This is easiest to see at the extreme, where the tax rate is 100 percent. Tax revenues here are, in theory, reduced to zero because the 100 percent confiscatory tax rate has halted production. A 100 percent tax rate applied to a tax base of zero yields no revenue.

In the early 1980s Laffer suggested that the United States was at a point such as *n* on the curve in Figure 11.11. There, tax rates are so high that production is discouraged to the extent that tax revenues are below the maximum at *m*. If the economy is at *n*, then lower tax rates can either increase tax revenues or leave them unchanged. For example, lowering the tax rate from point *n* to point *l* would bolster the economy such that the government would bring in the same total amount of tax revenue as before.

Laffer's reasoning was that lower tax rates stimulate incentives to work, save and invest, innovate, and accept business risks, thus triggering an expansion of real output and income. That enlarged tax base sustains tax revenues even though tax rates are lowered. Indeed, between *n* and *m* lower tax rates result in *increased* tax revenue.

Also, when taxes are lowered, tax avoidance (which is legal) and tax evasion (which is not) decline. High marginal tax rates prompt taxpayers to avoid taxes through various tax shelters, such as buying municipal bonds, on which the interest earned is tax-free. High rates also encourage some taxpayers to conceal income from the Internal Revenue Service. Lower tax rates reduce the inclination to engage in either tax avoidance or tax evasion.

ILLUSTRATING THE IDEA

Sherwood Forest

The popularization of the idea that tax-rate reductions will increase tax revenues owed much to Arthur Laffer's ability to present his ideas simply. In explaining his thoughts to a *Wall Street Journal* editor over lunch, Laffer reportedly took out his pen and drew the curve on a napkin. The editor retained the napkin and later reproduced the curve in an editorial in *The Wall Street Journal*. The Laffer Curve was born. The idea it portrayed became the centerpiece of economic policy under the Reagan administration (1981–1989), which cut tax rates on personal income by 25 percent over a 3-year period.

Laffer illustrated his supply-side views with a story relating to Robin Hood, who, you may recall, stole from the rich to give to the poor. Laffer likened people traveling through Sherwood Forest to taxpayers, whereas Robin Hood and his band of merry men were government. As taxpayers passed through the forest, Robin Hood and his men intercepted them and forced them to hand over a large portion of their money. Laffer asked audiences, "Do you think that travelers continued to go through Sherwood Forest?"

The answer he sought and got, of course, was "no." Taxpayers will avoid Sherwood Forest to the greatest extent possible. They will lower their taxable income by reducing work hours, retiring earlier, saving less, and engaging in tax avoidance and tax evasion activities. Robin Hood and his men may end up with less revenue than if they collected a relatively small "tax" from each traveler for passage through the forest.

QUESTION: Have you ever changed some buying behavior because the price of some product got too high? If so, relate your change in behavior to how people might respond to increases in marginal tax rates.

Criticisms, Rebuttals, and Assessment

The Laffer Curve and its supply-side implications have been subject to major criticism. A fundamental criticism relates to the degree to which economic incentives are sensitive to changes in tax rates. Skeptics say there is ample empirical evidence showing that the impact of a tax cut on incentives is small, of uncertain direction, and relatively slow to emerge. For example, with respect to work incentives, studies indicate that decreases in tax rates lead some people to work more but others to work less. Those who work more are enticed by the higher after-tax pay; they substitute work for leisure because the opportunity cost of leisure has increased. But other people work less because the higher after-tax pay enables them to "buy more leisure." With the tax cut, they can earn the same level of after-tax income as before with fewer work hours.

Most economists think that the demand-side effects of a tax cut are more immediate and certain than the supply-side effects. Thus, tax cuts undertaken when the economy is at or near full employment may produce increases in aggregate demand that overwhelm any increase in aggregate supply. The likely result is inflation or a tight monetary policy to prevent it. If the latter, real interest rates will rise and investment will decline.

Skeptics say that the Laffer Curve is merely a logical proposition and assert that there must be some level of tax rates between 0 and 100 percent at which tax revenues will be at their maximum. Economists of all persuasions can agree with this. But the issue of where a particular economy is located on its Laffer Curve is an empirical question. If we assume that we are at point n in Figure 11.11, then tax cuts will increase tax revenues. But if the economy is at any point below m on the curve, tax-rate reductions will reduce tax revenues.

Supply-side advocates respond to the skeptics by contending that the Reagan tax cuts in the 1980s worked as Laffer predicted. Although the top marginal income tax rates on earned income were cut from 50 to 28 percent in that decade, real GDP and tax revenues were substantially higher at the end of the 1990s than at the beginning.

But the general view among economists is that the Reagan tax cuts, coming at a time of severe recession, helped boost aggregate demand and return real GDP to its full-employment output and trend-line growth path. As the economy expanded, so did tax revenues, despite the lower tax rates. The rise in tax revenues caused by economic growth swamped the declines in revenues from lower tax rates. That is, the Laffer Curve stretched rightward, increasing net tax revenues. But the tax-rate cuts did not produce extraordinary rightward shifts of the long-run aggregate supply curve. Indeed, saving fell as a percentage of personal income during the period and productivity growth was sluggish. Real GDP sprang back vigorously from recessionary levels, but the economic growth rate soon reverted back to its longer-term average.

Because government expenditures rose more rapidly than tax revenues in the 1980s, large budget deficits occurred. In 1993 the Clinton administration increased the top marginal tax rates from 31 to 39.6 percent to address these deficits. The economy boomed in the last half of the 1990s, and by the end of the decade, tax revenues were so high relative to government expenditures that budget surpluses emerged. In 2001, the Bush administration reduced marginal tax rates over a series of years "to return excess revenues to taxpayers." In 2003 the top marginal tax rate fell to 35 percent. Also, the income tax rates on capital gains and dividends were reduced to 15 percent. Economists generally agree that the Bush tax cuts, along with highly expansionary monetary policy, helped revive and expand the economy following the recession of 2001. Strong growth of income in 2004 and 2005 produced large increases in tax revenues, although large deficits remained because federal spending also increased rapidly. The 2004 deficit was $413 billion, and the 2005 deficit was $318 billion. The deficit fell over the next two years to $162 billion in 2007. But the previously discussed financial crisis plunged the economy into a severe recession beginning in December 2007 and lasting into 2009. That caused income to fall and tax revenues to plummet. Also, the government implemented highly expansionary fiscal policy. Budget deficits increased to $459 billion in 2008, $1.4 trillion in 2009, and $1.3 trillion in 2010.

Today, there is general agreement that the U.S. economy is operating at a point below *m*—rather than above *m*—on the Laffer Curve in Figure 11.11. In this zone, the overall effect is that personal tax-rate increases expand tax revenues while personal tax-rate decreases reduce tax revenues. But at the same time, economists recognize that, other things equal, cuts in tax rates reduce tax revenues in percentage terms by less than the tax-rate reductions. Similarly, tax-rate increases do not raise tax revenues by as much in percentage terms as the tax-rate increases. This is true because changes in marginal tax rates *do* alter taxpayer behavior and thus affect taxable income. Although these effects are relatively modest, they need to be considered in designing tax policy—and, in fact, the federal government's Office of Tax Policy created a special division in 2007 devoted to estimating the magnitude of such effects when it comes to proposed changes in U.S. tax laws. Thus, supply-side economics has contributed to how economists and policymakers design and implement fiscal policy.

Summary

1. In macroeconomics, the short run is a period in which nominal wages do not change in response to changes in the price level. In contrast, the long run is a period in which nominal wages are fully responsive to changes in the price level.

2. The short-run aggregate supply curve is upward-sloping. Because nominal wages are unresponsive to price-level changes, increases in the price level (prices received by firms) increase profits and real output. Conversely, decreases in the price level reduce profits and real output. However, the long-run aggregate supply curve is vertical. With sufficient time for adjustment, nominal wages rise and fall with the price level, moving the economy along a vertical aggregate supply curve at the economy's full-employment output.

3. In the short run, demand-pull inflation raises the price level and real output. Once nominal wages rise to match the increase in the price level, the temporary increase in real output is reversed.

4. In the short run, cost-push inflation raises the price level and lowers real output. Unless the government expands aggregate demand, nominal wages eventually will decline under conditions of recession, and the short-run aggregate supply curve will shift back to its initial location. Prices and real output will eventually return to their original levels.

5. If prices and wages are flexible downward, a decline in aggregate demand will lower output and the price level. The decline in the price level will eventually lower nominal wages and shift the short-run aggregate supply curve rightward. Full-employment output will thus be restored.

6. One-time shifts in the AD and AS curves can only cause limited bouts of inflation. Ongoing inflation, of the kind experienced in the United States, is caused by the Fed purposely shifting AD to the right slightly faster than the AS curve shifts to the right (due to economic growth).

7. Assuming a stable, upsloping aggregate supply curve, rightward shifts of the aggregate demand curve of various sizes yield the generalization that high rates of inflation are associated with low rates of unemployment, and vice versa. This inverse relationship is known as the Phillips Curve, and empirical data for the 1960s seemed to be consistent with it.

8. In the 1970s and early 1980s the Phillips Curve apparently shifted rightward, reflecting stagflation—simultaneously rising inflation rates and unemployment rates. The higher unemployment rates and inflation rates resulted mainly from huge oil price increases that caused large leftward shifts in the short-run aggregate supply curve (so-called aggregate supply shocks). The Phillips Curve shifted inward toward its original position in the 1980s. By 1989 stagflation had subsided, and the data points for the late 1990s and early 2000s were similar to those of the 1960s. The new pattern continued until 2009, when the unemployment rate jumped to over 9 percent in both 2009 and 2010.

9. Although a short-run trade-off exists between inflation and unemployment, there is no long-run trade-off. Workers will adapt their expectations to new inflation realities, and when they do, the unemployment rate will return to the natural rate. So the long-run Phillips Curve is vertical at the natural rate, meaning that higher rates of inflation do not permanently "buy" the economy less unemployment.

10. Supply-side economists focus attention on government policies such as high taxation that impede the expansion of aggregate supply. The Laffer Curve relates tax rates to levels of tax revenue and suggests that, under some circumstances, cuts in tax rates will expand the tax base (output and income) and increase tax revenues. Most economists, however, believe that the United States is currently operating in the range of the Laffer Curve where tax rates and tax revenues move in the same, not opposite, directions.

11. Today's economists recognize the importance of considering supply-side effects of taxes in designing optimal tax structures and fiscal policy.

Terms and Concepts

short run

long run

long-run AD-AS model

Phillips Curve

stagflation

aggregate supply shocks

long-run vertical Phillips Curve

disinflation

supply-side economics

Laffer Curve

Questions   McGraw-Hill connect ECONOMICS

1. Distinguish between the short run and the long run as they relate to macroeconomics. Why is the distinction important? LO1

2. Which of the following statements are true? Which are false? Explain why the false statements are untrue. LO1
   a. Short-run aggregate supply curves reflect an inverse relationship between the price level and the level of real output.
   b. The long-run aggregate supply curve assumes that nominal wages are fixed.
   c. In the long run, an increase in the price level will result in an increase in nominal wages.

3. Suppose the full-employment level of real output (Q) for a hypothetical economy is $250 and the price level (P) initially is 100. Use the short-run aggregate supply schedules to the right to answer the questions that follow: LO1

AS (P_{100})		AS (P_{125})		AS (P_{75})	
P	Q	P	Q	P	Q
125	$280	125	$250	125	$310
100	250	100	220	100	280
75	220	75	190	75	250

   a. What will be the level of real output in the short run if the price level unexpectedly rises from 100 to 125 because of an increase in aggregate demand? What if the price level unexpectedly falls from 100 to 75 because of a decrease in aggregate demand? Explain each situation, using figures from the table.
   b. What will be the level of real output in the long run when the price level rises from 100 to 125? When it falls from 100 to 75? Explain each situation.

c. Show the circumstances described in parts a and b on graph paper, and derive the long-run aggregate supply curve.

4. Use graphical analysis to show how each of the following would affect the economy first in the short run and then in the long run. Assume that the United States is initially operating at its full-employment level of output, that prices and wages are eventually flexible both upward and downward, and that there is no counteracting fiscal or monetary policy. LO2

   a. Because of a war abroad, the oil supply to the United States is disrupted, sending oil prices rocketing upward.

   b. Construction spending on new homes rises dramatically, greatly increasing total U.S. investment spending.

   c. Economic recession occurs abroad, significantly reducing U.S. exports.

5. Between 1990 and 2010, the GDP price level rose by about 65 percent while real GDP increased by about 65 percent. Use the long-run aggregate demand–aggregate supply model to illustrate these outcomes graphically. LO2

6. Assume there is a particular short-run aggregate supply curve for an economy and the curve is relevant for several years. Use the AD-AS analysis to show graphically why higher rates of inflation over this period would be associated with lower rates of unemployment, and vice versa. What is this inverse relationship called? LO3

7. Suppose that the U.S. inflation rate and unemployment rate both increased relative to previous years for several

years in a row. What might explain this, and what could you conclude about the location of the short-run Phillips Curve? LO3

8. Suppose the government misjudges the natural rate of unemployment to be much lower than it actually is and thus undertakes expansionary fiscal and monetary policies to try to achieve the lower rate. Use the concept of the short-run Phillips Curve to explain why these policies might at first succeed. Use the concept of the long-run Phillips Curve to explain the long-run outcome of these policies. LO4

9. What do the distinctions between short-run aggregate supply and long-run aggregate supply have in common with the distinction between the short-run Phillips Curve and the long-run Phillips Curve? Explain. LO4

10. What is the Laffer Curve, and how does it relate to supply-side economics? Why is determining the economy's location on the curve so important in assessing tax policy? LO5

11. Why might one person work more, earn more, and pay more income tax when his or her tax rate is cut, while another person will work less, earn less, and pay less income tax under the same circumstance? LO5

12. The capital gains tax is the tax on the income realized when someone sells an asset for more than its purchase price. Why might tax revenues from this tax source actually decline for awhile if the tax rate on capital gains increases? LO5

Problems

1. Use the figure below to answer the following questions. Assume that the economy initially is operating at price level 120 and real output level $870. This output level is the economy's potential (or full-employment) level of output. Next, suppose that the price level rises from 120

to 130. By how much will real output increase in the short run? In the long run? Instead, now assume that the price level dropped from 120 to 110. Assuming flexible product and resource prices, by how much will real output fall in the short run? In the long run? What is the long-run level of output at each of the three price levels shown? LO1

2. **ADVANCED ANALYSIS** Suppose that the equation for a particular short-run AS curve is $P = 20 + .5Q$, where P is the price level and Q is real output in dollar terms. What is Q if the price level is 120? Suppose that the Q in your answer is the full-employment level of output. By how much will Q increase *in the short run* if the price level unexpectedly rises from 120 to 132? By how much will Q increase *in the long run* due to the price level increase? LO1

3. Suppose that over a 30-year period Buskerville's price level increased from 72 to 138, while its real GDP rose from $1.2 trillion to $2.1 trillion. Did economic growth occur in Buskerville? If so, by what average yearly rate in percentage terms (rounded to one decimal place)? Did Buskerville

experience inflation? If so, by what average yearly rate in percentage terms (rounded to one decimal place)? Which shifted rightward faster in Buskerville: its long-run aggregate supply curve (AS_{LR}) or its aggregate demand curve (AD)? **LO2**

4. Suppose that for years East Confetti's short-run Phillips Curve was such that each 1 percentage point increase in its unemployment rate was associated with a 2 percentage point decline in its inflation rate. Then, during several recent years, the short-run pattern changed such that its inflation rate rose by 3 percentage points for every 1 percentage point drop in its unemployment rate. Graphically, did East Confetti's Phillips Curve shift upward or did it shift downward? **LO3**

FURTHER TEST YOUR KNOWLEDGE AT
www.mcconnellbrief2e.com

At the text's Online Learning Center, **www.mcconnellbrief2e.com**, you will find one or more web-based questions that require information from the Internet to answer. We urge you to check them out, since they will familiarize you with websites that may be helpful in other courses and perhaps even in your career. The OLC also features multiple-choice quizzes that give instant feedback and provides other helpful ways to further test your knowledge of the chapter.

Visit your mobile app store and download the McConnell Brief Edition: Study Econ app *today*!

12

After reading this chapter, you should be able to:

1 List and discuss several key facts about U.S. international trade.

2 Define comparative advantage and demonstrate how specialization and trade add to a nation's output.

3 Explain how exchange rates are determined in currency markets.

4 Analyze the validity of the most frequently presented arguments for protectionism.

5 Discuss the role played by free-trade zones and the World Trade Organization (WTO) in promoting international trade.

International Trade and Exchange Rates

Backpackers in the wilderness like to think they are "leaving the world behind," but, like Atlas, they carry the world on their shoulders. Much of their equipment is imported—knives from Switzerland, rain gear from South Korea, cameras from Japan, aluminum pots from England, sleeping bags from China, and compasses from Finland. Moreover, they may have driven to the trailheads in Japanese-made Toyotas or German-made BMWs, sipping coffee from Brazil or snacking on bananas from Honduras.

International trade and the global economy affect all of us daily, whether we are hiking in the wilderness, driving our cars, listening to music, or working at our jobs. We cannot "leave the world behind." We are enmeshed in a global web of economic relationships—trading of goods and services, multinational corporations, cooperative ventures among the world's firms, and ties among the world's financial markets.

Trade Facts

The following facts provide an "executive summary" of U.S. international trade:

- A *trade deficit* occurs when imports exceed exports. The United States has a trade deficit in goods. In 2010, U.S. imports of goods exceeded U.S. exports of goods by $646 billion.
- A *trade surplus* occurs when exports exceed imports. The United States has a trade surplus in services (such as air transportation services and financial services). In 2010, U.S. exports of services exceeded U.S. imports of services by $146 billion.
- Principal U.S. exports include chemicals, agricultural products, consumer durables, semiconductors, and aircraft; principal imports include petroleum, automobiles, metals, household appliances, and computers.
- Canada is the United States' most important trading partner quantitatively. In 2010, 19 percent of U.S. exported goods were sold to Canadians, who in turn provided 14 percent of the U.S. imports of goods.
- The United States has a sizable trade deficit with China. In 2010, U.S. imports of goods from China exceeded exports of goods to China by $273 billion.
- The U.S. dependence on foreign oil is reflected in its trade with members of OPEC. In 2010, the United States imported $150 billion of goods (mainly oil) from OPEC members, while exporting $54 billion of goods to those countries.
- The United States leads the world in the combined volume of exports and imports, as measured in dollars. China, Germany, the United States, Japan, and the Netherlands were the top five exporters by dollar in 2009. Currently, the United States provides about 8.5 percent of the world's exports. (See Global Snapshot 12.1.)

GLOBAL SNAPSHOT 12.1

Shares of World Exports, Selected Nations

China has the largest share of world exports, followed by Germany and the United States. The eight largest export nations account for about 46 percent of world exports.

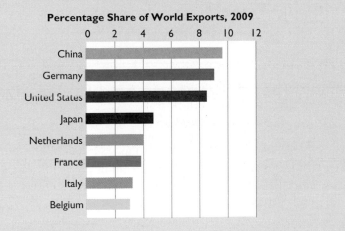

Percentage Share of World Exports, 2009

Source: *International Trade Statistics*, WTO Publications. Used with permission of the World Trade Organization, **www.wto.org**.

GLOBAL SNAPSHOT 12.2

Exports of Goods and Services as a Percentage of GDP, Selected Countries

Although the United States is the world's third-largest exporter, it ranks relatively low among trading nations in terms of exports as a percentage of GDP.

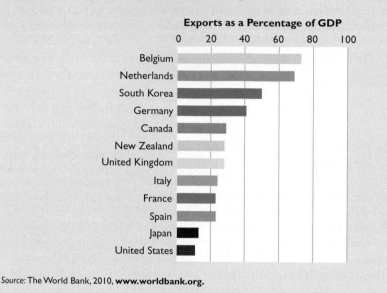

Source: The World Bank, 2010, **www.worldbank.org.**

- Exports of goods and services make up about 14 percent of total U.S. output. That percentage is much lower than the percentage in many other nations, including Canada, Italy, France, and the United Kingdom (see Global Snapshot 12.2).
- China has become a major international trader, with an estimated $1.2 trillion of exports in 2009. Other Asian economies—including South Korea, Taiwan, and Singapore—are also active in international trade. Their combined exports exceed those of France, Britain, or Italy.
- International trade and finance are often at the center of economic policy.

With this information in mind, let's look more closely at the economics of international trade.

Comparative Advantage and Specialization

Given the presence of an *open economy*—one that includes the international sector—the United States produces more of certain goods (exports) and fewer of other goods (imports) than it would otherwise. Thus, U.S. labor and other resources are shifted toward export industries and away from import industries. For example, the United States uses more resources to make computers and to grow wheat and less to make sporting goods and clothing. So we ask: "Do shifts of resources like these make economic sense? Do they enhance U.S. total output and thus the U.S. standard of living?"

The answers are affirmative. Specialization and international trade increase the productivity of a nation's resources and allow for greater total output than would otherwise be possible. This idea is not new. Adam Smith had this to say in 1776:

> It is the maxim of every prudent master of a family, never to attempt to make at home what it will cost him more to make than to buy. The taylor does not attempt to make his own shoes, but buys them of the shoemaker. The shoemaker does not attempt to make his own clothes, but employs a taylor. The farmer attempts to make neither the one nor the other, but employs those different artificers. . . .
>
> What is prudence in the conduct of every private family, can scarce be folly in that of a great kingdom. If a foreign country can supply us with a commodity cheaper than we can make it, better buy it of them with some part of the produce of our own industry, employed in a way in which we have some advantage.[1]

Nations specialize and trade for the same reasons that individuals do: Specialization and exchange result in greater overall output and income. In the early 1800s British economist David Ricardo expanded on Smith's idea by observing that it pays for a person or a country to specialize and trade even if a nation is more productive than a potential trading partner in *all* economic activities. We demonstrate Ricardo's principle in the examples that follow.

ILLUSTRATING THE IDEA

A CPA and a House Painter

Consider the certified public accountant (CPA) who is also a skilled house painter. Suppose the CPA is a swifter painter than the professional painter she is thinking of hiring. Also suppose that she can earn $50 per hour as an accountant but would have to pay the painter $15 per hour. And say it would take the accountant 30 hours to paint her house but the painter would take 40 hours.

Should the CPA take time from her accounting to paint her own house, or should she hire the painter? The CPA's opportunity cost of painting her house is $1500 (= 30 hours of sacrificed CPA time × $50 per CPA hour). The cost of hiring the painter is only $600 (= 40 hours of painting × $15 per hour of painting). Although the CPA is better at both accounting and painting, she will get her house painted at lower cost by specializing in accounting and using some of her earnings from accounting to hire a house painter.

Similarly, the house painter can reduce his cost of obtaining accounting services by specializing in painting and using some of his income to hire the CPA to prepare his income tax forms. Suppose it would take the painter 10 hours to prepare his tax return, while the CPA could handle the task in 2 hours. The house painter would sacrifice $150 of income (= 10 hours of painting time × $15 per hour) to do something he could hire the CPA to do for $100 (= 2 hours of CPA time × $50 per CPA hour). By specializing in painting and hiring the CPA to prepare his tax return, the painter lowers the cost of getting his tax return prepared.

We will see that what is true for our CPA and house painter is also true for nations. Specializing on the basis of comparative advantage enables nations to reduce the cost of obtaining the goods and services they desire.

QUESTION: How might the specialization described above change once the CPA retires? What generalization about the permanency of a particular pattern of specialization can you draw from your answer?

---

[1]Adam Smith, *The Wealth of Nations* (New York: Modern Library, 1937), p. 424. (Originally published in 1776.)

Comparative Advantage: Production Possibilities Analysis

Our simple example shows that the reason specialization is economically desirable is that it results in more efficient production. Now let's put specialization into the context of trading nations and use the familiar concept of the production possibilities table for our analysis.

Assumptions and Comparative Costs

Suppose the production possibilities for one product in Mexico and for one product in the United States are as shown in Tables 12.1 and 12.2. Both tables reflect constant costs. Each country must give up a constant amount of one product to secure a certain increment of the other product. (This assumption simplifies our discussion without impairing the validity of our conclusions. Later we will allow for increasing costs.)

Also for simplicity, suppose that the labor forces in the United States and Mexico are of equal size. The data then tell us that the United States has an *absolute advantage* in producing both products. If the United States and Mexico use their entire (equal-size) labor forces to produce avocados, the United States can produce 90 tons compared with Mexico's 60 tons. Similarly, the United States can produce 30 tons of soybeans compared to Mexico's 15 tons. There are greater production possibilities in the United States, using the same number of workers as in Mexico. So labor productivity (output per worker) in the United States exceeds that in Mexico in producing both products.

Although the United States has an absolute advantage in producing both goods, gains from specialization and trade are possible. Specialization and trade are mutually beneficial or "profitable" to the two nations if the *comparative* costs of producing the two products within the two nations differ. What are the comparative costs of avocados and soybeans in Mexico? By comparing production alternatives A and B in Table 12.1, we see that Mexico must sacrifice 5 tons of soybeans (= 15 − 10) to produce 20 tons of avocados (= 20 − 0). Or, more simply, in Mexico it costs 1 ton of soybeans (S) to produce 4 tons of avocados (A); that is, $1S \equiv 4A$. (The "$\equiv$" sign simply means "equivalent to.") Because we assumed constant costs, this domestic opportunity cost will not change as Mexico expands the output of either product. This is evident from production possibilities B and C, where we see that 4 more tons of avocados (= 24 − 20) cost 1 unit of soybeans (= 10 − 9).

TABLE 12.1 Mexico's Production Possibilities Table (in Tons)

Product	Production Alternatives				
	A	B	C	D	E
Avocados	0	20	24	40	60
Soybeans	15	10	9	5	0

TABLE 12.2 U.S. Production Possibilities Table (in Tons)

Product	Production Alternatives				
	R	S	T	U	V
Avocados	0	30	33	60	90
Soybeans	30	20	19	10	0

Similarly, in Table 12.2, comparing U.S. production alternatives R and S reveals that in the United States it costs 10 tons of soybeans (= 30 − 20) to obtain 30 tons of avocados (= 30 − 0). That is, the domestic (internal) comparative-cost ratio for the two products in the United States is 1S ≡ 3A. Comparing production alternatives S and T reinforces this conclusion: an extra 3 tons of avocados (= 33 − 30) comes at the sacrifice of 1 ton of soybeans (= 20 − 19).

The comparative costs of the two products within the two nations are obviously different. Economists say that the United States has a **comparative advantage** over Mexico in soybeans. The United States must forgo only 3 tons of avocados to get 1 ton of soybeans, but Mexico must forgo 4 tons of avocados to get 1 ton of soybeans. In terms of opportunity costs, soybeans are relatively cheaper in the United States. *A nation has a comparative advantage in some product when it can produce that product at a lower opportunity cost than can a potential trading partner.* Mexico, in contrast, has a comparative advantage in avocados. While 1 ton of avocados costs $\frac{1}{3}$ ton of soybeans in the United States, it costs only $\frac{1}{4}$ ton of soybeans in Mexico. Comparatively speaking, avocados are cheaper in Mexico. We summarize the situation in Table 12.3. Be sure to give it a close look.

Because of these differences in comparative costs, Mexico should produce avocados and the United States should produce soybeans. If both nations specialize according to their comparative advantages, each can achieve a larger total output with the same total input of resources. Together they will be using their scarce resources more efficiently.

Terms of Trade The United States can shift production between soybeans and avocados at the rate of 1S for 3A. Thus, the United States would specialize in soybeans only if it could obtain *more than* 3 tons of avocados for 1 ton of soybeans by trading with Mexico. Similarly, Mexico can shift production at the rate of 4A for 1S. So it would be advantageous to Mexico to specialize in avocados if it could get 1 ton of soybeans for *less than* 4 tons of avocados.

Suppose that through negotiation the two nations agree on an exchange rate of 1 ton of soybeans for $3\frac{1}{2}$ tons of avocados. These **terms of trade** are mutually beneficial to both countries, since each can "do better" through such trade than through domestic production alone. The United States can get $3\frac{1}{2}$ tons of avocados by sending 1 ton of soybeans to Mexico, while it can get only 3 tons of avocados by shifting its own resources domestically from soybeans to avocados. Mexico can obtain 1 ton of soybeans at a lower cost of $3\frac{1}{2}$ tons of avocados through trade with the United States, compared to the cost of 4 tons if Mexico produced the 1 ton of soybeans itself.

comparative advantage
A lower relative or comparative opportunity cost than that of another person, producer, or country.

ORIGIN OF THE IDEA
O 12.1
Absolute and comparative advantage

terms of trade
The rate at which units of one product can be exchanged for units of another product.

Soybeans	Avocados
Mexico: Must give up 4 tons of avocados to get 1 ton of soybeans	**Mexico:** Must give up $\frac{1}{4}$ ton of soybeans to get 1 ton of avocados
United States: Must give up 3 tons of avocados to get 1 ton of soybeans	**United States:** Must give up $\frac{1}{3}$ ton of soybeans to get 1 ton of avocados
Comparative advantage: United States	**Comparative advantage:** Mexico

TABLE 12.3 Comparative-Advantage Example: A Summary

Gains from Specialization and Trade Let's pinpoint the gains in total output from specialization and trade. Suppose that, before specialization and trade, production alternative C in Table 12.1 and alternative T in Table 12.2 were the optimal product mixes for the two countries. That is, Mexico preferred 24 tons of avocados and 9 tons of soybeans (Table 12.1) and the United States preferred 33 tons of avocados and 19 tons of soybeans (Table 12.2) to all other available domestic alternatives. These outputs are shown in column 1 in Table 12.4.

Now assume that both nations specialize according to their comparative advantages, with Mexico producing 60 tons of avocados and no soybeans (alternative E) and the United States producing no avocados and 30 tons of soybeans (alternative R). These outputs are shown in column 2 in Table 12.4. Using our $1S \equiv 3\frac{1}{2} A$ terms of trade, assume that Mexico exchanges 35 tons of avocados for 10 tons of U.S. soybeans. Column 3 in Table 12.4 shows the quantities exchanged in this trade, with a minus sign indicating exports and a plus sign indicating imports. As shown in column 4, after the trade Mexico has 25 tons of avocados and 10 tons of soybeans, while the United States has 35 tons of avocados and 20 tons of soybeans. Compared with their optimal product mixes before specialization and trade (column 1), *both* nations now enjoy more avocados and more soybeans! Specifically, Mexico has gained 1 ton of avocados and 1 ton of soybeans. The United States has gained 2 tons of avocados and 1 ton of soybeans. These gains are shown in column 5.

Specialization based on comparative advantage improves global resource allocation. The same total inputs of world resources and technology result in a larger global output. If Mexico and the United States allocate all their resources to avocados and soybeans, respectively, the same total inputs of resources can produce more output between them, indicating that resources are being allocated more efficiently.

Through specialization and international trade a nation can overcome the production constraints imposed by its domestic production possibilities table and curve. Our discussion of Tables 12.1, 12.2, and 12.4 has shown just how this is done. The domestic production possibilities data (Tables 12.1 and 12.2) of the two countries have not changed, meaning that neither nation's production possibilities curve has shifted. But specialization and trade mean that citizens of both countries can enjoy increased consumption (column 5 of Table 12.4).

Trade with Increasing Costs

To explain the basic principles underlying international trade, we simplified our analysis in several ways. For example, we limited discussion to two products and two nations. But multiproduct and multinational analysis yields the same conclusions.

WORKED PROBLEMS
W 12.1
Gains from specialization

TABLE 12.4 Specialization According to Comparative Advantage and the Gains from Trade (in Tons)

Country	(1) Outputs before Specialization	(2) Outputs after Specialization	(3) Amounts Traded	(4) Outputs Available after Trade	(5) Gains from Specialization and Trade (4) − (1)
Mexico	24 avocados	60 avocados	−35 avocados	25 avocados	1 avocados
	9 soybeans	0 soybeans	+10 soybeans	10 soybeans	1 soybeans
United States	33 avocados	0 avocados	+35 avocados	35 avocados	2 avocados
	19 soybeans	30 soybeans	−10 soybeans	20 soybeans	1 soybeans

We also assumed constant opportunity costs, which is a more substantive simplification. Let's consider the effect of allowing increasing opportunity costs to enter the picture.

As before, suppose that comparative advantage indicates that the United States should specialize in soybeans and Mexico in avocados. But now, as the United States begins to expand soybean production, its cost of soybeans will rise. It will eventually have to sacrifice more than 3 tons of avocados to get 1 additional ton of soybeans. Resources are no longer perfectly substitutable between alternative uses, as our constant-cost assumption implied. Resources less and less suitable to soybean production must be allocated to the U.S. soybean industry in expanding soybean output, and that means increasing costs—the sacrifice of larger and larger amounts of avocados for each additional ton of soybeans.

© Getty Images   © Photolink/Getty Images

PHOTO OP The Fruits of Free Trade*

Because of specialization and exchange, fruits and vegetables from all over the world appear in our grocery stores. For example, apples may be from New Zealand; bananas, from Ecuador; coconuts, from the Philippines; pineapples, from Costa Rica; avocados, from Mexico; plums, from Chile; and potatoes, from Peru.

*This example is from "The Fruits of Free Trade," 2002 Annual Report, by W. Michael Cox and Richard Alm, p. 3, Federal Reserve Bank of Dallas.

Similarly, Mexico will find that its cost of producing an additional ton of avocados will rise beyond 4 tons of soybeans as it produces more avocados. Resources transferred from soybean to avocado production will eventually be less suitable to avocado production.

At some point the differing domestic cost ratios that underlie comparative advantage will disappear, and further specialization will become uneconomical. And, most importantly, this point of equal cost ratios may be reached while the United States is still producing some avocados along with its soybeans and Mexico is producing some soybeans along with its avocados. The primary effect of increasing opportunity costs is less-than-complete specialization. For this reason we often find domestically produced products competing directly against identical or similar imported products within a particular economy.

The Foreign Exchange Market

Buyers and sellers (whether individuals, firms, or nations) use money to buy products or to pay for the use of resources. Within the domestic economy, prices are stated in terms of the domestic currency and buyers use that currency to purchase domestic products. In Mexico, for example, buyers have pesos, and that is what sellers want.

International markets are different. Sellers set their prices in terms of their domestic currencies, but buyers often possess entirely different currencies. How many dollars does it take to buy a truckload of Mexican avocados selling for 3000 pesos, a German automobile selling for 50,000 euros, or a Japanese motorcycle priced at 300,000 yen? Producers in Mexico, Germany, and Japan want payment in pesos, euros, and yen, respectively, so that they can pay their wages, rent, interest, dividends, and taxes.

A **foreign exchange market,** a market in which various national currencies are exchanged for one another, serves this need. The equilibrium prices in such currency markets are called **exchange rates.** An exchange rate is the rate at which the currency of one nation can be exchanged for the currency of another nation. (See Global Snapshot 12.3.)

The market price or exchange rate of a nation's currency is an unusual price; it links all domestic prices with all foreign prices. Exchange rates enable consumers in one country to translate prices of foreign goods into units of their own currency: They need only multiply the foreign product price by the exchange rate. If the U.S. dollar–yen exchange rate is $.01 (1 cent) per yen, a Sony television set priced at ¥20,000 will cost $200 (= 20,000 × $.01) in the United States. If the exchange rate rises to $.02 (2 cents) per yen, the television will cost $400 (= 20,000 × $.02) in the United States. Similarly, all other Japanese products would double in price to U.S. buyers in response to the altered exchange rate.

foreign exchange market
A market in which foreign currencies are exchanged and relative currency prices are established.

exchange rates
The rates at which national currencies trade for one another.

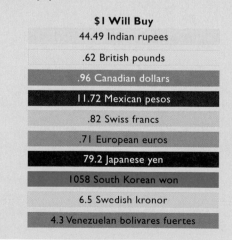

GLOBAL SNAPSHOT 12.3

Exchange Rates: Foreign Currency per U.S. Dollar

The amount of foreign currency that a dollar will buy varies greatly from nation to nation and fluctuates in response to supply and demand changes in the foreign exchange market. The amounts shown here are for July 2011.

$1 Will Buy

44.49 Indian rupees
.62 British pounds
.96 Canadian dollars
11.72 Mexican pesos
.82 Swiss francs
.71 European euros
79.2 Japanese yen
1058 South Korean won
6.5 Swedish kronor
4.3 Venezuelan bolivares fuertes

© PhotoLink/Getty Images/DIL

© Photodisc/Getty Images

PHOTO OP Foreign Currencies

The world is awash with hundreds of national currencies. Currency markets determine the rates of exchange between them.

Exchange Rates

Let's examine the rate, or price, at which U.S. dollars might be exchanged for British pounds. In Figure 12.1 we show the dollar price of 1 pound on the vertical axis and the quantity of pounds on the horizontal axis. The demand for pounds is D_1 and the supply of pounds is S_1 in this market for British pounds.

The *demand-for-pounds curve* is downward-sloping because all British goods and services will be cheaper to the United States if pounds become less expensive to the United States. That is, at lower dollar prices for pounds, the United States can obtain more pounds for each dollar and therefore buy more British goods and services per dollar. To buy those cheaper British goods, U.S. consumers will increase the quantity of pounds they demand.

INTERACTIVE GRAPHS

G 12.1

Exchange rates

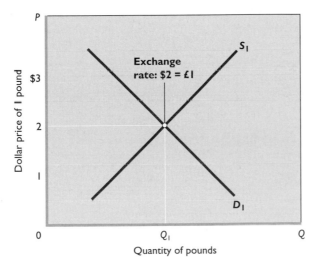

FIGURE 12.1 The market for foreign currency (pounds) The intersection of the demand-for-pounds curve D_1 and the supply-of-pounds curve S_1 determines the equilibrium dollar price of pounds, here, $2. That means that the exchange rate is $2 = £1. Not shown, an increase in demand for pounds or a decrease in the supply of pounds will increase the dollar price of pounds and thus cause the pound to appreciate. Also not shown, a decrease in demand for pounds or an increase in the supply of pounds will reduce the dollar price of pounds, meaning that the pound has depreciated.

The *supply-of-pounds curve* is upsloping because the British will purchase more U.S. goods when the dollar price of pounds rises (that is, as the pound price of dollars falls). When the British buy more U.S. goods, they supply a greater quantity of pounds to the foreign exchange market. In other words, they must exchange pounds for dollars to purchase U.S. goods. So, when the dollar price of pounds rises, the quantity of pounds supplied goes up.

The intersection of the supply curve and the demand curve will determine the dollar price of pounds. In Figure 12.1, that price (exchange rate) is $2 for £1. At this exchange rate, the quantity of pounds supplied and demanded are equal; neither a shortage nor a surplus of pounds occurs.

Depreciation and Appreciation

depreciation (of a currency)
A decrease in the value of a currency relative to another currency.

appreciation (of a currency)
An increase in the value of a currency relative to another currency.

An exchange rate determined by market forces can, and often does, change daily like stock and bond prices. These price changes result from changes in the supply of, or demand for, a particular currency. When the dollar price of pounds *rises*, for example, from $2 = £1 to $3 = £1, the dollar has *depreciated* relative to the pound (and the pound has appreciated relative to the dollar). A **depreciation** of a currency means that more units of it (dollars) are needed to buy a single unit of some other currency (a pound).

When the dollar price of pounds *falls*, for example, from $2 = £1 to $1 = £1, the dollar has *appreciated* relative to the pound. An **appreciation** of a currency means that it takes fewer units of it (dollars) to buy a single unit of some other currency (a pound). For example, the dollar price of pounds might decline from $2 to $1. Each British product becomes less expensive in terms of dollars, so people in the United States purchase more British goods. In general, U.S. imports from the United Kingdom rise. Meanwhile, because it takes more pounds to get a dollar, U.S. exports to the United Kingdom fall.

The central point is this: When the dollar depreciates (dollar price of foreign currencies rises), U.S. exports rise and U.S. imports fall; when the dollar appreciates (dollar price of foreign currencies falls), U.S. exports fall and U.S. imports rise.

In our U.S.-Britain illustrations, depreciation of the dollar means an appreciation of the pound, and vice versa. When the dollar price of a pound jumps from $2 = £1 to $3 = £1, the pound has appreciated relative to the dollar because it takes fewer pounds to buy $1. At $2 = £1, it took £1/2 to buy $1; at $3 = £1, it takes only £1/3 to buy $1. Conversely, when the dollar appreciates relative to the pound, the pound depreciates relative to the dollar. More pounds are needed to buy a U.S. dollar.

In general, the relevant terminology and relationships between the U.S. dollar and another currency are as follows.

- Dollar price of foreign currency increases ≡ dollar depreciates relative to the foreign currency ≡ foreign currency price of dollar decreases ≡ foreign currency appreciates relative to the dollar.

- Dollar price of foreign currency decreases ≡ dollar appreciates relative to the foreign currency ≡ foreign currency price of dollar increases ≡ foreign currency depreciates relative to the dollar.

Determinants of Exchange Rates

What factors would cause a nation's currency to appreciate or depreciate in the market for foreign exchange? Here are three generalizations (other things equal):

- If the demand for a nation's currency increases, that currency will appreciate; if the demand declines, that currency will depreciate.

- If the supply of a nation's currency increases, that currency will depreciate; if the supply decreases, that currency will appreciate.

- If a nation's currency appreciates, some foreign currency depreciates relative to it.

With these generalizations in mind, let's examine the determinants of exchange rates—the factors that shift the demand or supply curve for a certain currency. As we do so, keep in mind that the other-things-equal assumption is always in force. Also note that we are discussing factors *that change the exchange rate*, not things that change *as a result of* a change in the exchange rate.

Tastes Any change in consumer tastes or preferences for the products of a foreign country may alter the demand for that nation's currency and change its exchange rate. If technological advances in U.S. MP3 players make them more attractive to British consumers and businesses, then the British will supply more pounds in the exchange market in order to purchase more U.S. MP3 players. The supply-of-pounds curve will shift to the right, causing the pound to depreciate and the dollar to appreciate.

In contrast, the U.S. demand-for-pounds curve will shift to the right if British woolen apparel becomes more fashionable in the United States. So the pound will appreciate and the dollar will depreciate.

Relative Income A nation's currency is likely to depreciate if its growth of national income is more rapid than that of other countries. Here's why: A country's imports vary directly with its income level. As total income rises in the United States, people there buy both more domestic goods and more foreign goods. If the U.S. economy is expanding rapidly and the British economy is stagnant, U.S. imports of British goods, and therefore U.S. demands for pounds, will increase. The dollar price of pounds will rise, so the dollar will depreciate.

Relative Inflation Rate Changes Other things equal, changes in the relative rates of inflation of two nations change their relative price levels and alter the exchange rate between their currencies. The currency of the nation with the higher inflation rate—the more rapidly rising price level—tends to depreciate. Suppose, for example, that inflation is zero percent in Great Britain and 5 percent in the United States so that prices, on average, are rising by 5 percent per year in the United States while, on average, remaining unchanged in Great Britain. U.S. consumers will seek out more of the now relatively lower-priced British goods, increasing the demand for pounds. British consumers will purchase less of the now relatively higher-priced U.S. goods, reducing the supply of pounds. This combination of increased demand for pounds and reduced supply of pounds will cause the pound to appreciate and the dollar to depreciate.

Relative Interest Rates Changes in relative interest rates between two countries may alter their exchange rate. Suppose that real interest rates rise in the United States but stay constant in Great Britain. British citizens will then find the United States a more attractive place in which to loan money directly or loan money indirectly by buying bonds. To make these loans, they will have to supply pounds in the foreign exchange market to obtain dollars. The increase in the supply of pounds results in depreciation of the pound and appreciation of the dollar.

Changes in Relative Expected Returns on Stocks, Real Estate, and Production Facilities International investing extends beyond buying foreign bonds. It includes international investments in stocks and real estate as well as foreign purchases of factories and production facilities. Other things equal, the extent of this foreign investment depends on relative expected returns. To make the investments, investors in one country must sell their currencies to purchase the foreign currencies needed for the foreign investments.

For instance, suppose that investing in England suddenly becomes more popular due to a more positive outlook regarding expected returns on stocks, real estate, and production facilities there. U.S. investors therefore will sell U.S. assets to buy more assets in England. The U.S. assets will be sold for dollars, which will then be brought to the foreign exchange market and exchanged for pounds, which will in turn be used to purchase British assets. The increased demand for pounds in the foreign exchange market will cause the pound to appreciate and the dollar to depreciate.

Speculation Currency speculators are people who buy and sell currencies with an eye toward reselling or repurchasing them at a profit. Suppose that, as a group, speculators anticipate that the pound will appreciate and the dollar will depreciate. Speculators holding dollars will therefore try to convert them into pounds. This effort will increase the demand for pounds and cause the dollar price of pounds to rise (that is, cause the dollar to depreciate). A self-fulfilling prophecy occurs: The pound appreciates and the dollar depreciates because speculators act on the belief that these changes will in fact take place. In this way, speculation can cause changes in exchange rates.

Government and Trade

If people and nations benefit from specialization and international exchange, why do governments sometimes try to restrict the free flow of imports or encourage exports? What kinds of world trade barriers can governments erect, and why would they do so?

Trade Protections and Subsidies

tariffs
Taxes imposed by a nation on imported goods.

import quotas
Limits imposed by nations on the quantities (or total values) of goods that may be imported during some period of time.

nontariff barriers (NTBs)
All impediments other than protective tariffs that nations establish to impede imports, including import quotas, licensing requirements, unreasonable product-quality standards, and unnecessary bureaucratic detail in customs procedures.

voluntary export restriction (VER)
An agreement by countries or foreign firms to limit their exports to a certain foreign nation to avoid enactment of formal trade barriers by that nation.

Trade interventions by government take several forms. Excise taxes on imported goods are called **tariffs.** A *protective tariff* is implemented to shield domestic producers from foreign competition. These tariffs impede free trade by increasing the prices of imported goods and therefore shifting sales toward domestic producers. Although protective tariffs are usually not high enough to stop the importation of foreign goods, they put foreign producers at a competitive disadvantage. A tariff on imported shoes, for example, would make domestically produced shoes more attractive to consumers.

Import quotas are limits on the quantities or total value of specific items that may be imported in some period. Once a quota is "filled," further imports of that product are choked off. Import quotas are more effective than tariffs in impeding international trade. With a tariff, a product can go on being imported in large quantities; with an import quota, however, all imports are prohibited once the quota is filled.

Nontariff barriers (NTBs) include onerous licensing requirements, unreasonable standards pertaining to product quality, or excessive bureaucratic hurdles and delays in customs procedures. Some nations require that importers of foreign goods obtain licenses. By restricting the issuance of licenses, imports can be restricted. Although many nations carefully inspect imported agricultural products to prevent the introduction of potentially harmful insects, some countries use lengthy inspections to impede imports.

A **voluntary export restriction (VER)** is a trade barrier by which foreign firms "voluntarily" limit the amount of their exports to a particular country. Exporters agree to a VER, which has the effect of an import quota, to avoid more stringent trade barriers. In the late 1990s, for example, Canadian producers of softwood lumber (fir, spruce, cedar, pine) agreed to a VER on exports to the United States under the threat of a permanently higher U.S. tariff.

Export subsidies consist of government payments to domestic producers of export goods. By reducing production costs, the subsidies enable producers to charge lower prices and thus to sell more exports in world markets. Example: The United States and other nations have subsidized domestic farmers to boost the domestic food supply. Such subsidies have lowered the market price of agricultural commodities and have artificially lowered their export prices.

export subsidies
Government payments to domestic producers to enable them to reduce the price of a product to foreign buyers.

Economic Impact of Tariffs

Tariffs, quotas, and other trade restrictions have a series of economic effects predicted by supply and demand analysis and observed in reality. These effects vary somewhat by type of trade protection. So to keep things simple, we will focus on the effects of tariffs.

Direct Effects Because tariffs raise the price of goods imported to the United States, U.S. consumption of those goods declines. Higher prices reduce quantity demanded, as indicated by the law of demand. A tariff prompts consumers to buy fewer of the imported goods and reallocate a portion of their expenditures to less desired substitute products. U.S. consumers are clearly injured by the tariff.

U.S. producers—who are not subject to the tariff—receive the higher price (pre-tariff foreign price + tariff) on the imported product. Because this new price is higher than before, the domestic producers respond by producing more. Higher prices increase quantity supplied, as indicated by the law of supply. So domestic producers increase their output. They therefore enjoy both a higher price and expanded sales; this explains why domestic producers lobby for protective tariffs. But from a social point of view, the greater domestic production means the tariff allows domestic producers to bid resources away from other, more efficient, U.S. industries.

Foreign producers are hurt by tariffs. Although the sales price of the imported good is higher, that higher amount accrues to the U.S. government as tariff revenues, not to foreign producers. The after-tariff price, or the per-unit revenue to foreign producers, remains as before, but the volume of U.S. imports (foreign exports) falls.

Government gains revenue from tariffs. This revenue is a transfer of income from consumers to government and does not represent any net change in the nation's economic well-being. The result is that government gains a portion of what consumers lose by paying more for imported goods.

Indirect Effects Tariffs have a subtle effect beyond those just mentioned. They also hurt domestic firms that use the protected goods as inputs in their production process. For example, a tariff on imported steel boosts the price of steel girders, thus hurting firms that build bridges and office towers. Also, tariffs reduce competition in the protected industries. With less competition from foreign producers, domestic firms may be slow to design and implement cost-saving production methods and introduce new products.

Because foreigners sell fewer imported goods in the United States, they earn fewer dollars and so must buy fewer U.S. exports. U.S. export industries must then cut production and release resources. These are highly efficient industries, as we know from their comparative advantage and their ability to sell goods in world markets.

Tariffs directly promote the expansion of inefficient industries that do not have a comparative advantage; they also indirectly cause the contraction of relatively efficient industries that do have a comparative advantage. Put bluntly, tariffs cause resources to be shifted in the wrong direction—and that is not surprising. We know that specialization and world trade lead to more efficient use of world resources and greater world output. But protective tariffs reduce world trade. Therefore, tariffs also reduce efficiency and the world's real output.

ORIGIN OF THE IDEA

O 12.2

Mercantilism

Net Costs of Tariffs

Tariffs impose costs on domestic consumers but provide gains to domestic producers and revenue to the federal government. The consumer costs of trade restrictions are calculated by determining the effect the restrictions have on consumer prices. Protection raises the price of a product in three ways: (1) The price of the imported product goes up; (2) the higher price of imports causes some consumers to shift their purchases to higher-priced domestically produced goods; and (3) the prices of domestically produced goods rise because import competition has declined.

Study after study finds that the costs to consumers substantially exceed the gains to producers and government. A sizable net cost or efficiency loss to society arises from trade protection. Furthermore, industries employ large amounts of economic resources to influence Congress to pass and retain protectionist laws. Because these efforts divert resources away from more socially desirable purposes, trade restrictions also impose that cost on society.

Conclusion: The gains that U.S. trade barriers produce for protected industries and their workers come at the expense of much greater losses for the entire economy. The result is economic inefficiency, reduced consumption, and lower standards of living.

So Why Government Trade Protections?

In view of the benefits of free trade, what accounts for the impulse to impede imports and boost exports through government policy? There are several reasons—some legitimate, most not.

Misunderstanding the Gains from Trade It is a commonly accepted myth that the greatest benefit to be derived from international trade is greater domestic sales and employment in the export sector. This suggests that exports are "good" because they increase domestic sales and employment, whereas imports are "bad" because they reduce domestic sales and deprive people of jobs at home. Actually, the true benefit created by international trade is the extra output obtained from abroad—the imports obtained for a lower opportunity cost than if they were produced at home.

A recent study suggests that the elimination of trade barriers since the Second World War has increased the income of the average U.S. household by at least $7000 and perhaps by as much as $13,000. These income gains are recurring; they happen year after year.[2]

Political Considerations While a nation as a whole gains from trade, trade may harm particular domestic industries and particular groups of resource suppliers. In our earlier comparative-advantage example, specialization and trade adversely affected the U.S. avocado industry and the Mexican soybean industry. Understandably, those industries might seek to preserve their economic positions by persuading their respective governments to protect them from imports—perhaps through tariffs.

Those who directly benefit from import protection are relatively few in number but have much at stake. Thus, they have a strong incentive to pursue political activity to achieve their aims. Moreover, because the costs of import protection are buried in the price of goods and spread out over millions of citizens, the cost borne by each individual citizen is quite small. However, the full cost of tariffs and quotas typically greatly exceeds the benefits. It is not uncommon to find that it costs the public $250,000 or more a year to protect a domestic job that pays less than one-fourth that amount.

---

[2]Scott C. Bradford, Paul L.E. Grieco, and Gary C. Hufbauer, "The Payoff to America from Globalization," *The World Economy*, July 2006, pp. 893–916.

In the political arena, the voice of the relatively few producers and unions demanding *protectionism* is loud and constant, whereas the voice of those footing the bill is soft or nonexistent. When political deal making is added in—"You back tariffs for the apparel industry in my state, and I'll back tariffs for the steel industry in your state"—the outcome can be a network of protective tariffs.

ILLUSTRATING THE IDEA

Buy American?

Will "buying American" make Americans better off? No, says Dallas Federal Reserve economist W. Michael Cox:

> A common myth is that it is better for Americans to spend their money at home than abroad. The best way to expose the fallacy of this argument is to take it to its logical extreme. If it is better for me to spend my money here than abroad, then it is even better yet to buy in Texas than in New York, better yet to buy in Dallas than in Houston . . . in my own neighborhood . . . within my own family . . . to consume only what I can produce. Alone and poor.[*]

[*]"The Fruits of Free Trade," 2002 Annual Report, by W. Michael Cox and Richard Alm, p. 16, Federal Reserve Bank of Dallas. Used with permission.

Three Arguments for Protection

Arguments for trade protection are many and diverse. Some—such as tariffs to protect "infant industries" or to create "military self-sufficiency"—have some legitimacy. But other arguments break down under close scrutiny. Three protectionist arguments, in particular, have persisted decade after decade in the United States.

Increased-Domestic-Employment Argument

Arguing for a tariff to "save U.S. jobs" becomes fashionable when the economy encounters a recession (such as the severe recession of 2007–2009 in the United States). In an economy that engages in international trade, exports involve spending on domestic output and imports reflect spending to obtain part of another nation's output. So, in this argument, reducing imports will divert spending on another nation's output to spending on domestic output. Thus domestic output and employment will rise. But this argument has several shortcomings.

While imports may eliminate some U.S. jobs, they create others. Imports may have eliminated the jobs of some U.S. steel and textile workers in recent years, but other workers have gained jobs unloading ships, flying imported aircraft, and selling imported electronic equipment. Import restrictions alter the composition of employment, but they may have little or no effect on the volume of employment.

The *fallacy of composition*—the false idea that what is true for the part is necessarily true for the whole—is also present in this rationale for tariffs. All nations cannot simultaneously succeed in restricting imports while maintaining their exports; what is true for one nation is not true for all nations. The exports of one nation must be the imports of another nation. To the extent that one country is able to expand its economy through an excess of exports over imports, the resulting excess of imports over exports worsens another economy's unemployment problem. It is no wonder that tariffs and import quotas meant to achieve domestic full employment are called "beggar my neighbor" policies: They achieve short-run domestic goals by making trading partners poorer.

Moreover, nations adversely affected by tariffs and quotas are likely to retaliate, causing a "trade-barrier war" that will choke off trade and make all nations worse off. The **Smoot-Hawley Tariff Act** of 1930 is a classic example. Although that act was meant to reduce imports and stimulate U.S. production, the high tariffs it authorized prompted adversely affected nations to retaliate with tariffs equally high. International trade fell, lowering the output and income of all nations. Economic historians generally agree that the Smoot-Hawley Tariff Act was a contributing cause of the Great Depression.

Finally, forcing an excess of exports over imports cannot succeed in raising domestic employment over the long run. It is through U.S. imports that foreign nations earn dollars for buying U.S. exports. In the long run a nation must import in order to export. The long-run impact of tariffs is not an increase in domestic employment but, at best, a reallocation of workers away from export industries and to protected domestic industries. This shift implies a less efficient allocation of resources.

Cheap-Foreign-Labor Argument

The cheap-foreign-labor argument says that government must shield domestic firms and workers from the ruinous competition of countries where wages are low. If protection is not provided, cheap imports will flood U.S. markets and the prices of U.S. goods—along with the wages of U.S. workers—will be pulled down. That is, the domestic living standards in the United States will be reduced.

This argument can be rebutted at several levels. The logic of the argument suggests that it is not mutually beneficial for rich and poor persons to trade with one another. However, that is not the case. A relatively low-income mechanic may fix the Mercedes owned by a wealthy lawyer, and both may benefit from the transaction. And both U.S. consumers and Chinese workers gain when they "trade" a pair of athletic shoes priced at $30 as opposed to U.S. consumers being restricted to a similar shoe made in the United States for $60.

Also, recall that gains from trade are based on comparative advantage, not on absolute advantage. Again, think back to our U.S.-Mexico (soybean-avocado) example in which the United States had greater labor productivity than Mexico in producing both soybeans and avocados. Because of that greater productivity, wages and living standards will be higher for U.S. labor. Mexico's less productive labor will receive lower wages.

The cheap-foreign-labor argument suggests that, to maintain American living standards, the United States should not trade with low-wage Mexico. Suppose it forgoes trade with Mexico. Will wages and living standards rise in the United States as a result? Absolutely not! To obtain avocados, the United States will have to reallocate a portion of its labor from its relatively more-efficient soybean industry to its relatively less-efficient avocado industry. As a result, the average productivity of U.S. labor will fall, as will real wages and living standards for American workers. The labor forces of both countries will have diminished standards of living because without specialization and trade they will have less output available to them. Compare column 4 with column 1 in Table 12.4 to confirm this point.

Protection-against-Dumping Argument

The protection-against-dumping argument contends that tariffs are needed to protect domestic firms from "dumping" by foreign producers. **Dumping** is the sale of a product in a foreign country at prices either below cost or below the prices commonly charged at home.

Smoot-Hawley Tariff Act
Legislation passed in 1930 that established very high U.S. tariffs designed to reduce imports and stimulate the domestic economy. Instead, the law resulted only in retaliatory tariffs by other nations and a decline in trade worldwide.

dumping
The sale of products in a foreign country at prices either below costs or below the prices charged at home.

Economists cite two plausible reasons for this behavior. First, with regard to below-cost dumping, firms in country A may dump goods at below cost into country B in an attempt to drive their competitors in country B out of business. If the firms in country A succeed in driving their competitors in country B out of business, they will enjoy monopoly power and monopoly prices and profits on the goods they subsequently sell in country B. Their hope is that the longer-term monopoly profits will more than offset the losses from below-cost sales that must take place while they are attempting to drive their competitors in country B out of business.

Second, dumping that involves selling abroad at a price that is below the price commonly charged in the home country (but which is still at or above production costs) may be a form of price discrimination, which is charging different prices to different customers. As an example, a foreign seller that has a monopoly in its home market may find that it can maximize its overall profit by charging a high price in its monopolized domestic market while charging a lower price in the United States, where it must compete with U.S. producers. Curiously, it may pursue this strategy even if it makes no profit at all from its sales in the United States, where it must charge the competitive price. So why bother selling in the United States? Because the increase in overall production that comes about by exporting to the United States may allow the firm to obtain the per unit cost savings often associated with large-scale production. These cost savings imply even higher profits in the monopolized domestic market.

Because dumping is an "unfair trade practice," most nations prohibit it. For example, where dumping is shown to injure U.S. firms, the federal government imposes tariffs called *antidumping duties* on the goods in question. But relatively few documented cases of dumping occur each year, and specific instances of unfair trade do not justify widespread, permanent tariffs. Moreover, antidumping duties can be abused. Often, what appears to be dumping is simply comparative advantage at work.

Trade Adjustment Assistance

A nation's comparative advantage in the production of a certain product is not forever fixed. As national economies evolve, the size and quality of their labor forces may change, the volume and composition of their capital stocks may shift, new technologies may develop, and even the quality of land and the quantity of natural resources may be altered. As these changes take place, the relative efficiency with which a nation can produce specific goods will also change. Also, new trade agreements can suddenly leave formerly protected industries highly vulnerable to major disruption or even collapse.

Shifts in patterns of comparative advantage and removal of trade protection can hurt specific groups of workers. For example, the erosion of the United States' once strong comparative advantage in steel has caused production plant shutdowns and layoffs in the U.S. steel industry. The textile and apparel industries in the United States face similar difficulties. Clearly, not everyone wins from free trade (or freer trade). Some workers lose.

The **Trade Adjustment Assistance Act** of 2002 introduced some innovative policies to help those hurt by shifts in international trade patterns. The law provides cash assistance (beyond unemployment insurance) for up to 78 weeks for workers displaced by imports or plant relocations abroad. To obtain the assistance, workers must participate in job searches, training programs, or remedial education. There also are relocation allowances to help displaced workers move geographically to new jobs within the United States. Refundable tax credits for health insurance serve as payments to help workers maintain their insurance coverage during the retraining and job search period. Also, workers who are 50 years of age or older are eligible for "wage insurance," which replaces some of the difference in pay (if any) between their old and new jobs.

Trade Adjustment Assistance Act A U.S. law passed in 2002 that provides cash assistance, education and training benefits, health care subsidies, and wage subsidies (for persons age 50 or more) to workers displaced by imports or plant relocations abroad.

Many economists support trade adjustment assistance because it not only helps workers hurt by international trade but also helps create the political support necessary to reduce trade barriers and export subsidies.

But not all economists are keen on trade adjustment assistance. Loss of jobs from imports or plant relocations abroad is only a small fraction (about 4 percent in recent years) of total job loss in the economy each year. Many workers also lose their jobs because of changing patterns of demand, changing technology, bad management, and other dynamic aspects of a market economy. Some critics ask, "What makes losing one's job to international trade worthy of such special treatment, compared to losing one's job to, say, technological change or domestic competition?" There is no totally satisfying answer.

APPLYING THE ANALYSIS

offshoring
The practice of shifting work previously done by American workers to workers located in other nations.

Is Offshoring of Jobs Bad?

Not only are some U.S. jobs lost because of international trade, but some are lost because of globalization of resource markets. In recent years U.S. firms have found it increasingly profitable to outsource work abroad. Economists call this business activity **offshoring:** shifting work previously done by American workers to workers located in other nations. Offshoring is not a new practice but traditionally has involved components for U.S. manufacturing goods. For example, Boeing has long offshored the production of major airplane parts for its "American" aircraft.

Recent advances in computer and communications technology have enabled U.S. firms to offshore service jobs such as data entry, book composition, software coding, call-center operations, medical transcription, and claims processing to countries such as India. Where offshoring occurs, some of the value added in the production process occurs in foreign countries rather than the United States. So part of the income generated from the production of U.S. goods is paid to foreigners, not to American workers.

Offshoring is obviously costly to Americans who lose their jobs, but it is not generally bad for the economy. Offshoring simply reflects a growing international trade in services, or, more descriptively, "tasks." That trade has been made possible by recent trade agreements and new information and communication technologies. As with trade in goods, trade in services reflects comparative advantage and is beneficial to both trading parties. Moreover, the United States has a sizable trade surplus with other nations in services. The United States gains by specializing in high-valued services such as transportation services, accounting services, legal services, and advertising services, where it still has a comparative advantage. It then "trades" to obtain lower-valued services such as call-center and data entry work, for which comparative advantage has gone abroad.

Offshoring also increases the demand for complementary jobs in the United States. Jobs that are close substitutes for existing U.S. jobs are lost, but complementary jobs in the United States are expanded. For example, the lower price of offshore maintenance of aircraft and reservation centers reduces the price of airline tickets. That means more domestic and international flights by American carriers, which in turn means more jobs for U.S.-based pilots, flight attendants, baggage handlers, and check-in personnel. Moreover, offshoring encourages domestic investment and expansion of firms in the United States by reducing their costs and keeping them competitive worldwide. Some observers equate "offshoring jobs" to "importing competitiveness."

QUESTION: What has enabled white-collar labor services to become the world's newest export and import commodity even though such labor itself remains in place?

Multilateral Trade Agreements and Free-Trade Zones

Being aware of the overall benefits of free trade, nations have worked to lower tariffs worldwide. Their pursuit of free trade has been aided by the growing power of free-trade interest groups: Exporters of goods and services, importers of foreign components used in "domestic" products, and domestic sellers of imported products all strongly support lower tariffs. And, in fact, tariffs have generally declined during the past half-century.

General Agreement on Tariffs and Trade

Following the Second World War, the major nations of the world set upon a general course of liberalizing trade. In 1947 some 23 nations, including the United States, signed the **General Agreement on Tariffs and Trade (GATT)**. GATT was based on the principles of equal, nondiscriminatory trade treatment for all member nations and the reduction of tariffs and quotas by multilateral negotiation. Basically, GATT provided a continuing forum for the negotiation of reduced trade barriers on a multilateral basis among nations.

Since 1947, member nations have completed eight "rounds" of GATT negotiations to reduce trade barriers. The *Uruguay Round* agreement of 1993 phased in trade liberalizations between 1995 and 2005.

World Trade Organization

The Uruguay Round of 1993 established the **World Trade Organization (WTO)** as GATT's successor. In 2011, 153 nations belonged to the WTO, which oversees trade agreements and rules on disputes relating to them. It also provides forums for further rounds of trade negotiations. The ninth and latest round of negotiations—the **Doha Round**—was launched in Doha, Qatar, in late 2001. (The trade rounds occur over several years in several geographic venues but are named after the city or country of origination.) The negotiations are aimed at further reducing tariffs and quotas, as well as agricultural subsidies that distort trade.

GATT and the WTO have been positive forces in the trend toward liberalized world trade. The trade rules agreed upon by the member nations provide a strong and necessary bulwark against the protectionism called for by the special-interest groups in the various nations. For that reason and because current WTO agreements lack strong labor standards and environmental protections, the WTO is controversial.

European Union

Countries have also sought to reduce tariffs by creating regional *free-trade zones*—also called *trade blocs*. The most dramatic example is the **European Union (EU)**. In 2007, the addition of Bulgaria and Romania expanded the EU to its present size of 27 nations.[3]

The EU has abolished tariffs and import quotas on nearly all products traded among the participating nations and established a common system of tariffs applicable to all goods received from nations outside the EU. It has also liberalized the movement of capital and labor within the EU and has created common policies in other economic matters of joint concern, such as agriculture, transportation, and business practices. The EU is now a strong **trade bloc:** a group of countries having common identity, economic interests, and trade rules. Of the 27 EU countries, 17 used the **euro** as a common currency in 2011.

---

[3]The other 25 are France, Germany, United Kingdom, Italy, Belgium, the Netherlands, Luxembourg, Denmark, Ireland, Greece, Spain, Portugal, Austria, Finland, Sweden, Poland, Hungary, Czech Republic, Slovakia, Lithuania, Latvia, Estonia, Slovenia, Malta, and Cyprus.

General Agreement on Tariffs and Trade (GATT)
An international accord reached in 1947 in which 23 nations agreed to give equal and nondiscriminatory treatment to one another, to reduce tariffs through multinational negotiations, and to eliminate import quotas.

World Trade Organization (WTO)
An organization of 153 nations (as of 2008) that oversees the provisions of the current world trade agreement, resolves disputes stemming from it, and holds forums for further rounds of trade negotiations.

Doha Round
The latest, uncompleted (as of 2011) sequence of trade negotiations by members of the World Trade Organization; named after Doha, Qatar, where the set of negotiations began.

European Union (EU)
An association of 27 European nations that has eliminated tariffs and quotas among them, established common tariffs for imported goods from outside the member nations, reduced barriers to the free movement of capital, and created other common economic policies.

trade bloc
A group of nations that lower or abolish trade barriers among themselves.

euro
The common currency unit used by 17 (as of 2011) European nations in the European Union.

EU integration has achieved for Europe what the U.S. constitutional prohibition on tariffs by individual states has achieved for the United States: increased regional specialization, greater productivity, greater output, and faster economic growth. The free flow of goods and services has created large markets for EU industries. The resulting economies of large-scale production have enabled those industries to achieve much lower costs than they could have achieved in their small, single-nation markets.

North American Free Trade Agreement

North American Free Trade Agreement (NAFTA)
A 1993 agreement establishing, over a 15-year period, a free-trade zone composed of Canada, Mexico, and the United States.

In 1993 Canada, Mexico, and the United States formed a major trade bloc. The **North American Free Trade Agreement (NAFTA)** established a free-trade zone that has about the same combined output as the EU but encompasses a much larger geographic area. NAFTA has eliminated tariffs and other trade barriers between Canada, Mexico, and the United States for most goods and services.

Critics of NAFTA feared that it would cause a massive loss of U.S. jobs as firms moved to Mexico to take advantage of lower wages and weaker regulations on pollution and workplace safety. Also, there was concern that Japan and South Korea would build plants in Mexico and transport goods tariff-free to the United States, further hurting U.S. firms and workers.

In retrospect, critics were much too pessimistic. Since the passage of NAFTA in 1993, employment in the United States has increased by more than 20 million workers. Increased trade between Canada, Mexico, and the United States has enhanced the standard of living in all three countries.

Not all aspects of trade blocs are positive. By giving preferences to countries within their free-trade zones, trade blocs such as the EU and NAFTA tend to reduce their members' trade with non-bloc members. Thus, the world loses some of the benefits of a completely open global trading system. Eliminating that disadvantage has been one of the motivations for liberalizing global trade through the World Trade Organization. Its liberalizations apply equally to all 153 nations that belong to the WTO.

Recent U.S. Trade Deficits

As shown in Figure 12.2 the United States has experienced large and persistent trade deficits in recent years. These deficits rose rapidly between 2002 and 2006 before declining when consumers and businesses greatly curtailed their purchase of imports

FIGURE 12.2 U.S. trade deficits, 2002–2010.
The United States experienced large deficits in *goods* and in *goods and services* between 2002 and 2010. These deficits steadily increased until the recession of 2007–2009. Despite the decline, large trade deficits are expected to continue for many years to come.
Source: Bureau of Economic Analysis, **www.bea.gov.**

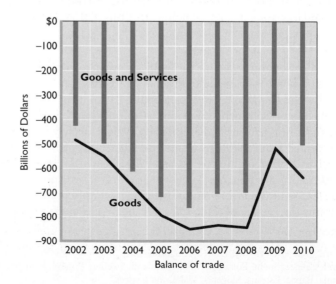

Balance of trade

during the recession of 2007–2009. Even in 2009, however, the trade deficit on goods was still at $517 billion and the trade deficit on goods and services was $379 billion. As the economy began to recover, the trade deficit on goods rose to $646 billion in 2010, and the trade deficit on goods and services rose to $500 billion. Economists expect the trade deficits to continue to expand, absolutely and relatively, toward prerecession levels when the economic recovery strengthens and U.S. income and imports rise at a faster pace.

Causes of the Trade Deficits

The large U.S. trade deficits have several causes. First, the U.S. economy expanded more rapidly between 2001 and 2007 than the economies of several U.S. trading partners. The strong U.S. income growth that accompanied that economic growth enabled Americans to greatly increase their purchases of imported products. In contrast, Japan and some European nations suffered recession or experienced relatively slow income growth over that same period. So consumers in those countries increased their purchases of U.S. exports much less rapidly than Americans increased their purchases of foreign imports.

Another factor explaining the large trade deficits is the enormous U.S. trade imbalance with China. In 2007 the United States imported $257 billion more of goods and services than it exported to China. Even in the recession year 2009, the trade deficit with China was $220 billion. That deficit was double the combined deficits with Mexico ($43 billion), Germany ($37 billion), and Japan ($28 billion). The United States is China's largest export market, and although China has greatly increased its imports from the United States, its standard of living has not yet risen sufficiently for its households to afford large quantities of U.S. products. Adding to the problem, China's government has fixed the exchange rate of it currency, the yuan, to a basket of currencies that includes the U.S. dollar. Therefore, China's large trade surpluses with the United States have not caused the yuan to appreciate much against the U.S. dollar. Greater appreciation of the yuan would have made Chinese goods more expensive in the United States and reduced U.S. imports from China. In China a stronger yuan would have reduced the dollar price of U.S. goods and increased Chinese purchases of U.S. exports. That combination—reduced U.S. imports from China and increased U.S. exports to China—would have reduced the large U.S. trade imbalance.

Another factor underlying the large U.S. trade deficits is a continuing trade deficit with oil-exporting nations. For example, in 2010 the United States had a $96 billion trade deficit with the OPEC countries.

Finally, a declining U.S. saving rate (= saving/total income) also contributed to the large U.S. trade deficits. Up until the recession of 2007–2009, the U.S. saving rate declined substantially, while its investment rate (= investment/total income) increased. The gap between U.S. investment and U.S. saving was filled by foreign purchases of U.S. real and financial assets. Because foreign savers were willing to finance a large part of U.S. investment, Americans were able to save less and consume more. Part of that added consumption spending was on imported goods. That is, the inflow of funds from abroad may be one cause of the trade deficits, not just a result of those deficits.

Implications of U.S. Trade Deficits

The prerecession U.S. trade deficits were the largest ever run by a major industrial nation. Whether the large trade deficits should be of significant concern to the United States and the rest of the world is debatable. Most economists see both benefits and costs to trade deficits.

Increased Current Consumption At the time a trade deficit or a current account deficit is occurring, American consumers benefit. A trade deficit means that the United States is receiving more goods and services as imports from abroad than it is sending out as exports. Taken alone, a trade deficit allows the United States to consume outside its production possibilities curve. It augments the domestic standard of living. But here is a catch: The gain in present consumption may come at the expense of reduced future consumption.

Increased U.S. Indebtedness A trade deficit is considered "unfavorable" because it must be financed by borrowing from the rest of the world, selling off assets, or dipping into foreign currency reserves. Trade deficits are financed primarily by net inpayments of foreign currencies to the United States. When U.S. exports are insufficient to finance U.S. imports, the United States increases both its debt to people abroad and the value of foreign claims against assets in the United States. Financing of the U.S. trade deficit has resulted in a larger foreign accumulation of claims against U.S. financial and real assets than the U.S. claim against foreign assets. In 2008, foreigners owned about $3.5 trillion more of U.S. assets (corporations, land, stocks, bonds, loan notes) than U.S. citizens and institutions owned of foreign assets.

If the United States wants to regain ownership of these domestic assets, at some future time it will have to export more than it imports. At that time, domestic consumption will be lower because the United States will need to send more of its output abroad than it receives as imports. Therefore, the current consumption gains delivered by U.S. current account deficits may mean permanent debt, permanent foreign ownership, or large sacrifices of future consumption.

We say "may mean" above because the foreign lending to U.S. firms and foreign investment in the United States increase the stock of American capital. U.S. production capacity might increase more rapidly than otherwise because of a large inflow of funds to offset the trade deficits. We know that faster increases in production capacity and real GDP enhance the economy's ability to service foreign debt and buy back real capital, if that is desired.

Downward Pressure on the Dollar Finally, the large U.S. trade deficits place downward pressure on the exchange value of the U.S. dollar. The surge of imports requires the United States to supply dollars in the currency market in order to obtain the foreign currencies required for purchasing the imported goods. That flood of dollars into the currency market causes the dollar to depreciate relative to other currencies. Between 2002 and 2008, the dollar depreciated against most other currencies, including 43 percent against the European euro, 27 percent against the British pound, 37 percent against the Canadian dollar, 15 percent against the Chinese yuan, and 25 percent against the Japanese yen. Since 2008, the U.S. dollar has continued to depreciate against the Canadian dollar, the Chinese yuan, and the Japanese yen but has appreciated relative to the euro and the pound. Some of this depreciation was fueled by the expansionary monetary policy (reduced real interest rates) undertaken by the Fed beginning in 2007 and carrying into 2011 (discussed in Chapter 10). The subsequent appreciation of the U.S. dollar relative to the European euro and British pound is largely attributed to continued economic weakness in part of the euro zone and the United Kingdom.

Economists feared that the decline in the dollar would contribute to inflation as imports became more expensive to Americans in dollar terms. Traditionally the Fed would need to react to that inflation with a tight monetary policy that raises real interest rates in the United States. However, because of the financial crisis and recession that began in 2007, the Fed chose to aggressively reduce interest rates, hoping to halt the downturn in the economy. In effect, it gambled that its actions would not ignite inflation because of the dampening effect of the severe economic recession on rising prices.

Summary

1. The United States leads the world in the volume of international trade, but trade is much larger as a percentage of GDP in many other nations.

2. Mutually advantageous specialization and trade are possible between any two nations if they have different domestic opportunity-cost ratios for any two products. By specializing on the basis of comparative advantage, nations can obtain larger real incomes with fixed amounts of resources. The terms of trade determine how this increase in world output is shared by the trading nations. Increasing costs lead to less-than-complete specialization for many tradable goods.

3. The foreign exchange market establishes exchange rates between currencies. Each nation's purchases from abroad create a supply of its own currency and a demand for foreign currencies. The resulting supply-demand equilibrium sets the exchange rate that links the currencies of all nations. Depreciation of a nation's currency reduces its imports and increases its exports; appreciation increases its imports and reduces its exports.

4. Currencies will depreciate or appreciate as a result of changes in their supply or demand, which in turn depend on changes in tastes for foreign goods, relative changes in national incomes, relative changes in inflation rates, changes in interest rates, and the extent and direction of currency speculation.

5. Trade barriers and subsidies take the form of protective tariffs, quotas, nontariff barriers, voluntary export restrictions, and export subsidies. Protective tariffs increase the prices and reduce the quantities demanded of the affected goods. Sales by foreign exporters diminish; domestic producers, however, gain higher prices and enlarged sales. Consumer losses from trade restrictions greatly exceed producer and government gains, creating an efficiency loss to society.

6. Three recurring arguments for free trade—increased domestic employment, cheap foreign labor, and protection against dumping—are either fallacies or overstatements that do not hold up under careful economic analysis.

7. Not everyone benefits from free (or freer) trade. The Trade Adjustment Assistance Act of 2002 provides cash assistance, education and training benefits, health care subsidies, and wage subsidies (for persons 50 years old or more) to workers who are displaced by imports or plant relocations abroad. But less than 4 percent of all job losses in the United States each year result from imports, plant relocations, or the offshoring of service jobs.

8. In 1947 the General Agreement on Tariffs and Trade (GATT) was formed to encourage nondiscriminatory treatment for all member nations, to reduce tariffs, and to eliminate import quotas. The Uruguay Round of GATT negotiations (1993) reduced tariffs and quotas, liberalized trade in services, reduced agricultural subsidies, reduced pirating of intellectual property, and phased out quotas on textiles.

9. GATT's successor, the World Trade Organization (WTO), had 153 member nations in 2011. It implements WTO agreements, rules on trade disputes between members, and provides forums for continued discussions on trade liberalization. The latest round of trade negotiations—the Doha Development Agenda—began in late 2001 and as of 2011 was still in progress.

10. Free-trade zones (trade blocs) liberalize trade within regions but may at the same time impede trade with non-bloc members. Two examples of free-trade arrangements are the 27-member European Union (EU) and the North American Free Trade Agreement (NAFTA), comprising Canada, Mexico, and the United States. Seventeen of the EU nations (as of 2011) have abandoned their national currencies for a common currency called the euro.

11. U.S. trade deficits have produced current increases in the living standards of U.S. consumers. But the deficits have also increased U.S. debt to the rest of the world and increased foreign ownership of assets in the United States. This greater foreign investment in the United States, however, has undoubtedly increased U.S. production possibilities. The trade deficits also place extreme downward pressure on the international value of the U.S. dollar.

Terms and Concepts

comparative advantage

terms of trade

foreign exchange market

exchange rates

depreciation

appreciation

tariffs

import quotas

nontariff barriers (NTBs)

voluntary export restriction (VER)

export subsidies

Smoot-Hawley Tariff Act

dumping

Trade Adjustment Assistance Act

offshoring

General Agreement on Tariffs and Trade (GATT)

World Trade Organization (WTO)

Doha Round

European Union (EU)

trade bloc

euro

North American Free Trade Agreement (NAFTA)

Questions ![Mc Graw Hill] connect™ ECONOMICS

1. Quantitatively, how important is international trade to the United States relative to its importance to other nations? What country is the United States' most important trading partner, quantitatively? With what country does the United States have the largest current trade deficit? LO1

2. What effect do rising costs (rather than constant costs) have on the extent of specialization and trade? Explain. LO2

3. What is offshoring of white-collar service jobs, and how does it relate to international trade? Why has it recently increased? Why do you think more than half of all offshored jobs have gone to India? Give an example (other than that in the textbook) of how offshoring can eliminate some U.S. jobs while creating other U.S. jobs. LO2

4. Explain why the U.S. demand for Mexican pesos is downsloping and the supply of pesos to Americans is upsloping. Indicate whether each of the following would cause the Mexican peso to appreciate or depreciate: LO3
    a. The United States unilaterally reduces tariffs on Mexican products.
    b. Mexico encounters severe inflation.
    c. Deteriorating political relations reduce American tourism in Mexico.
    d. The U.S. economy moves into a severe recession.
    e. The United States engages in a high-interest-rate monetary policy.
    f. Mexican products become more fashionable to U.S. consumers.
    g. The Mexican government encourages U.S. firms to invest in Mexican oil fields.

5. Explain why you agree or disagree with the following statements: LO3
    a. A country that grows faster than its major trading partners can expect the international value of its currency to depreciate.
    b. A nation whose interest rate is rising more rapidly than interest rates in other nations can expect the international value of its currency to appreciate.
    c. A country's currency will appreciate if its inflation rate is less than that of the rest of the world.

6. If the European euro were to depreciate relative to the U.S. dollar in the foreign exchange market, would it be easier or harder for the French to sell their wine in the United States? Suppose you were planning a trip to Paris. How would depreciation of the euro change the dollar cost of your trip? LO3

7. What measures do governments take to promote exports and restrict imports? Who benefits and who loses from protectionist policies? What is the net outcome for society? LO4

8. Speculate as to why some U.S. firms strongly support trade liberalization while other U.S. firms favor protectionism. Speculate as to why some U.S. labor unions strongly support trade liberalization while other U.S. labor unions strongly oppose it. LO4

9. Explain: "Free-trade zones such as the EU and NAFTA lead a double life: They can promote free trade among members, but they pose serious trade obstacles for nonmembers." Do you think the net effects of trade blocs are good or bad for world trade? Why? How do the efforts of the WTO relate to these trade blocs? LO5

Problems

1. Assume that the comparative-cost ratios of two products—baby formula and tuna fish—are as follows in the nations of Canswicki and Tunata:

    Canswicki: 1 can baby formula ≡ 2 cans tuna fish
    Tunata: 1 can baby formula ≡ 4 cans tuna fish

    In what product should each nation specialize? Which of the following terms of trade would be acceptable to both nations: (a) 1 can baby formula ≡ $2\frac{1}{2}$ cans tuna fish; (b) 1 can baby formula ≡ 1 can tuna fish; (c) 1 can baby formula ≡ 5 cans tuna fish? LO2

2. The accompanying hypothetical production possibilities tables are for New Zealand and Spain. Each country can produce apples and plums. Plot the production possibilities data for each of the two countries separately. Referring to your graphs, answer the following: LO2

**New Zealand's Production Possibilities Table
(Millions of Bushels)**

Product	Production Alternatives			
	A	B	C	D
Apples	0	20	40	60
Plums	15	10	5	0

**Spain's Production Possibilities Table
(Millions of Bushels)**

Product	Production Alternatives			
	R	S	T	U
Apples	0	20	40	60
Plums	60	40	20	0

a. What is each country's cost ratio of producing plums and apples?

b. Which nation should specialize in which product?

c. Show the trading possibilities lines for each nation if the actual terms of trade are 1 plum for 2 apples. (Plot these lines on your graph.)

d. Suppose the optimum product mixes before specialization and trade were alternative B in New Zealand and alternative S in Spain. What would be the gains from specialization and trade?

3. The following hypothetical production possibilities tables are for China and the United States. Assume that before specialization and trade the optimal product mix for China is alternative B and for the United States is alternative U. **LO2**

Product	China Production Possibilities					
	A	**B**	**C**	**D**	**E**	**F**
Apparel (in thousands)	30	24	18	12	6	0
Chemicals (in tons)	0	6	12	18	24	30

Product	U.S. Production Possibilities					
	R	**S**	**T**	**U**	**V**	**W**
Apparel (in thousands)	10	8	6	4	2	0
Chemicals (in tons)	0	4	8	12	16	20

a. Are comparative-cost conditions such that the two areas should specialize? If so, what product should each produce?

b. What is the total gain in apparel and chemical output that would result from such specialization?

c. What are the limits of the terms of trade? Suppose that the actual terms of trade are 1 unit of apparel for $1\frac{1}{2}$ units of chemicals and that 4 units of apparel are exchanged for 6 units of chemicals. What are the gains from specialization and trade for each nation?

4. Refer to the following table, in which Q_d is the quantity of yen demanded, P is the dollar price of yen, Q_s is the quantity of yen supplied in year 1, and Q_s' is the quantity of yen supplied in year 2. All quantities are in billions and the dollar-yen exchange rate is fully flexible. **LO3**

Q_d	P	Q_s	Q_s'
10	125	30	20
15	120	25	15
20	115	20	10
25	110	15	5

a. What is the equilibrium dollar price of yen in year 1?

b. What is the equilibrium dollar price of yen in year 2?

c. Did the yen appreciate or did it depreciate relative to the dollar between years 1 and 2?

d. Did the dollar appreciate or did it depreciate relative to the yen between years 1 and 2?

e. Which one of the following could have caused the change in relative values of the dollar and yen between years 1 and 2: (1) more rapid inflation in the United States than in Japan, (2) an increase in the real interest rate in the United States but not in Japan, or (3) faster income growth in the United States than in Japan.

5. Suppose that the current Canadian dollar (CAD) to U.S. dollar exchange rate is $.85 CAD = $1 US and that the U.S. dollar price of an Apple iPhone is $300. What is the Canadian dollar price of an iPhone? Next, suppose that the CAD to U.S. dollar exchange rate moves to $.96 CAD = $1 US. What is the new Canadian dollar price of an iPhone? Other things equal, would you expect Canada to import more or fewer iPhones at the new exchange rate? **LO3**

FURTHER TEST YOUR KNOWLEDGE AT
www.mcconnellbrief2e.com

At the text's Online Learning Center, **www.mcconnellbrief2e.com**, you will find one or more web-based questions that require information from the Internet to answer. We urge you to check them out, since they will familiarize you with websites that may be helpful in other courses and perhaps even in your career. The OLC also features multiple-choice quizzes that give instant feedback and provides other helpful ways to further test your knowledge of the chapter.

Visit your mobile app store and download the McConnell Brief Edition: Study Econ app today!

ability-to-pay principle   The idea that those who have greater income (or wealth) should pay a greater proportion of it as taxes than those who have less income (or wealth).

actual reserves   The funds that a bank has on deposit at the Federal Reserve Bank of its district (plus its vault cash).

aggregate   A collection of specific economic units treated as if they were one. For example, all prices of individual goods and services are combined into a price level, or all the units of output are aggregated into gross domestic product.

aggregate demand   A schedule or curve that shows the total quantity of goods and services demanded (purchased) at different price levels.

aggregate demand–aggregate supply model   The macroeconomic model that uses aggregate demand and aggregate supply to determine and explain the price level and the real domestic output.

aggregate supply   A schedule or curve showing the total quantity of goods and services supplied (produced) at different price levels.

aggregate supply shocks   Sudden unanticipated large changes in resource costs that shift an economy's aggregate supply curve.

allocative efficiency   The apportionment of resources among firms and industries to obtain the production of the products most wanted by society (consumers); the output of each product at which its marginal cost and price or marginal benefit are equal.

anticipated inflation   Increases in the price level (inflation) that occur at the expected rate.

appreciation (of the dollar)   An increase in the value of the dollar relative to the currency of another nation, so a dollar buys a larger amount of the foreign currency and thus of foreign goods.

asset   Anything of monetary value owned by a firm or individual.

asset demand for money   The amount of money people want to hold as a store of value; this amount varies inversely with the interest rate.

average tax rate   Total tax paid divided by total (taxable) income, as a percentage.

balance sheet   A statement of the assets, liabilities, and net worth of a firm or individual at some given time.

bank deposits   The deposits that individuals or firms have at banks (or thrifts) or that banks have at the Federal Reserve Banks.

bankers' bank   A bank that accepts the deposits of and makes loans to depository institutions; in the United States, a Federal Reserve Bank.

bank reserves   The deposits of commercial banks and thrifts at Federal Reserve Banks plus bank and thrift vault cash.

barter   The exchange of one good or service for another good or service.

base year   The year with which other years are compared when an index is constructed; for example, the base year for a price index.

benefits-received principle   The idea that those who receive the benefits of goods and services provided by government should pay the taxes required to finance them.

Board of Governors   The seven-member group that supervises and controls the money and banking system of the United States; also called the *Board of Governors of the Federal Reserve System* and the *Federal Reserve Board*.

bond   A financial device through which a borrower (a firm or government) is obligated to pay the principal and interest on a loan at a specific date in the future.

budget constraint   The limit that the size of a consumer's income (and the prices that must be paid for goods and services) imposes on the ability of that consumer to obtain goods and services.

budget deficit   The amount by which the expenditures of the federal government exceed its revenues in any year.

budget line   A line that shows the different combinations of two products a consumer can purchase with a specific money income, given the products' prices.

budget surplus   The amount by which the revenues of the federal government exceed its expenditures in any year.

built-in stabilizer   A mechanism that increases government's budget deficit (or reduces its surplus) during a recession and increases government's budget surplus (or reduces its deficit) during expansion without any action by policymakers. The tax system is one such mechanism.

Bureau of Economic Analysis (BEA)   An agency of the U.S. Department of Commerce that compiles the national income and product accounts.

business   A firm that purchases resources and provides goods and services to the economy.

business cycles   Recurring increases and decreases in the level of economic activity over periods of years; a cycle consists of peak, recession, trough, and expansion phases.

business firm   (See **firm**.)

capital   Human-made resources (buildings, machinery, and equipment) used to produce goods and services; goods that do not directly satisfy human wants; also called *capital goods* and *investment goods*.

capital gain The gain realized when securities or properties are sold for a price greater than the price paid for them.

capital goods (See **capital.**)

capitalism An economic system in which property resources are privately owned and markets and prices are used to direct and coordinate economic activities.

capital stock The total available capital in a nation.

cartel A formal agreement among firms (or countries) in an industry to set the price of a product and establish the outputs of the individual firms (or countries) or to divide the market for the product geographically.

ceiling price (See **price ceiling.**)

central bank A bank whose chief function is the control of the nation's money supply; in the United States, the Federal Reserve System.

central economic planning Government determination of the objectives of the economy and how resources will be directed to attain those goals.

ceteris paribus **assumption** (See **other-things-equal assumption.**)

change in demand A change in the quantity demanded of a good or service at every price; a shift of the demand curve to the left or right.

change in quantity demanded A change in the amount of a product that consumers are willing and able to purchase because of a change in the product's price; a movement from one point to another on a fixed demand curve.

change in quantity supplied A change in the amount of a product that producers offer for sale because of a change in the product's price.

change in supply A change in the quantity supplied of a good or service at every price; a shift of the supply curve to the left or right.

checkable deposit Any deposit in a commercial bank or thrift institution against which a check may be written.

check clearing The process by which funds are transferred from the checking accounts of the writers of checks to the checking accounts of the recipients of the checks.

checking account A checkable deposit in a commercial bank or thrift institution.

circular flow diagram The flow of resources from households to firms and of products from firms to households. These flows are accompanied by reverse flows of money from firms to households and from households to firms.

Coase theorem The idea, first stated by economist Ronald Coase, that externality problems may be resolved through private negotiations of the affected parties.

coincidence of wants A situation in which the good or service that one trader desires to obtain is the same as that which another trader desires to give up and an item that the second trader wishes to acquire is the same as that which the first trader desires to surrender.

command system A method of organizing an economy in which property resources are publicly owned and government uses central economic planning to direct and coordinate economic activities; command economy; communism.

commercial bank A firm that engages in the business of banking (accepts deposits, offers checking accounts, and makes loans).

commercial banking system All commercial banks and thrift institutions as a group.

communism (See **command system.**)

comparative advantage A situation in which a person or country can produce a specific product at a lower opportunity cost than some other person or country; the basis for specialization and trade.

compensation of employees Wages and salaries plus wage and salary supplements paid by employers to workers.

competition The presence in a market of independent buyers and sellers competing with one another along with the freedom of buyers and sellers to enter and leave the market.

complementary goods Products and services that are used together. When the price of one falls, the demand for the other increases (and conversely).

constant opportunity cost An opportunity cost that remains the same for each additional unit as a consumer (or society) shifts purchases (production) from one product to another along a straight-line budget line (production possibilities curve).

consumer goods Products and services that satisfy human wants directly.

Consumer Price Index (CPI) An index that measures the prices of a fixed "market basket" of some 300 goods and services bought by a "typical" consumer.

consumer sovereignty Determination by consumers of the types and quantities of goods and services that will be produced with the scarce resources of the economy; consumers' direction of production through their dollar votes.

consumer surplus The difference between the maximum price a consumer is (or consumers are) willing to pay for a product and the actual price paid.

contractionary fiscal policy A decrease in government purchases for goods and services, an increase in net taxes, or some combination of the two, for the purpose of decreasing aggregate demand and thus controlling inflation.

corporate income tax A tax levied on the net income (accounting profit) of corporations.

corporation A legal entity ("person") chartered by a state or the federal government that is distinct and separate from the individuals who own it.

cost-benefit analysis A comparison of the marginal costs of a government project or program with the marginal benefits to decide whether or not to employ resources in that project or program and to what extent.

cost-of-living adjustment (COLA) An automatic increase in the incomes (wages) of workers when inflation occurs; guaranteed by a collective bargaining contract between firms and workers.

cost-push inflation Increases in the price level (inflation) resulting from an increase in resource costs (for example, raw-material prices) and hence in per-unit production costs; inflation caused by reductions in aggregate supply.

Council of Economic Advisers (CEA) A group of three persons that advises and assists the president of the United States on economic matters (including the preparation of the annual *Economic Report of the President*).

creative destruction The hypothesis that the creation of new products and production methods simultaneously destroys the market power of existing monopolies.

credit union An association of persons who have a common tie (such as being employees of the same firm or members of the same labor union) that sells shares to (accepts deposits from) its members and makes loans to them.

crowding-out effect A rise in interest rates and a resulting decrease in investment caused by the federal government's increased borrowing to finance budget deficits or debt.

currency Coins and paper money.

cyclical asymmetry The potential problem of monetary policy successfully controlling inflation during the expansionary phase of the business cycle but failing to expand spending and real GDP during the recessionary phase of the cycle.

cyclical deficit A federal budget deficit that is caused by a recession and the consequent decline in tax revenues.

cyclically adjusted budget A measure of what the federal budget deficit or budget surplus would be with the existing tax and government spending programs if the economy had achieved full-employment GDP in the year.

cyclical unemployment A type of unemployment caused by insufficient total spending (or by insufficient aggregate demand).

deflating Finding the real gross domestic product by decreasing the dollar value of the GDP for a year in which prices were higher than in the base year.

deflation A decline in the economy's price level.

demand A schedule showing the amounts of a good or service that buyers (or a buyer) wish to purchase at various prices during some time period.

demand curve A curve illustrating demand.

demand-pull inflation Increases in the price level (inflation) resulting from an excess of demand over output at the existing price level, caused by an increase in aggregate demand.

demand shocks Sudden, unexpected change in demand.

demand-side market failures Underallocations of resources that occur when private demand curves understate consumers' full willingness to pay for a good or service.

dependent variable A variable that changes as a consequence of a change in some other (independent) variable; the "effect" or outcome.

depository institutions Firms that accept deposits of money from the public (businesses and persons); commercial banks, savings and loan associations, mutual savings banks, and credit unions.

depreciation (of the dollar) A decrease in the value of the dollar relative to another currency, so a dollar buys a smaller amount of the foreign currency and therefore of foreign goods.

determinants of aggregate demand Factors such as consumption spending, investment, government spending, and net exports that, if they change, shift the aggregate demand curve.

determinants of aggregate supply Factors such as input prices, productivity, and the legal-institutional environment that, if they change, shift the aggregate supply curve.

determinants of demand Factors other than price that locate the position of the demand curve.

determinants of supply Factors other than price that locate the position of the supply curve.

developing countries Many countries of Africa, Asia, and Latin America that are characterized by lack of capital goods, use of nonadvanced technologies, low literacy rates, high unemployment, rapid population growth, and labor forces heavily committed to agriculture.

direct relationship The relationship between two variables that change in the same direction, for example, product price and quantity supplied.

discount rate The interest rate that the Federal Reserve Banks charge on the loans they make to commercial banks and thrift institutions.

discretionary fiscal policy Deliberate changes in taxes (tax rates) and government spending by Congress to promote full employment, price stability, and economic growth.

discrimination The practice of according individuals or groups inferior treatment in hiring, occupational access, education and training, promotion, wage rates, or working conditions even though they have the same abilities, education, skills, and work experience as other workers.

disinflation A decline in the annual rate of inflation from the previous year.

dividends Payments by a corporation of all or part of its profit to its stockholders (the corporate owners).

division of labor The separation of the work required to produce a product into a number of different tasks that are performed by different workers; specialization of workers.

Doha Round The latest, uncompleted (as of 2011) sequence of trade negotiations by members of the World Trade Organization; named after Doha, Qatar, where the set of negotiations began.

dollar votes The "votes" that consumers and entrepreneurs cast for the production of consumer and capital goods, respectively, when they purchase those goods in product and resource markets.

dumping   The sale of products in a foreign country at prices either below costs or below the prices charged at home.

durable good   A consumer good with an expected life (use) of 3 or more years.

easy money policy   Federal Reserve System actions to increase the money supply to lower interest rates and expand real GDP.

economic cost   A payment that must be made to obtain and retain the services of a resource; the income a firm must provide to a resource supplier to attract the resource away from an alternative use; equal to the quantity of other products that cannot be produced when resources are instead used to make a particular product.

economic efficiency   The use of the minimum necessary resources to obtain the socially optimal amounts of goods and services; entails both productive efficiency and allocative efficiency.

economic growth   (1) An outward shift in the production possibilities curve that results from an increase in resource supplies or quality or an improvement in technology; (2) an increase of real output (gross domestic product) or real output per capita.

economic law   An economic principle that has been tested and retested and has stood the test of time.

economic model   A simplified picture of economic reality; an abstract generalization.

economic perspective   A viewpoint that envisions individuals and institutions making rational decisions by comparing the marginal benefits and marginal costs associated with their actions.

economic policy   A course of action intended to correct or avoid a problem.

economic principle   A widely accepted generalization about the economic behavior of individuals or institutions.

economic problem   The choices necessitated because society's economic wants for goods and services are unlimited but the resources available to satisfy these wants are limited (scarce).

economic profit   The total revenue of a firm less its economic costs (which include both explicit costs and implicit costs); also called *pure profit* and *above-normal profit.*

economic resources   The land, labor, capital, and entrepreneurial ability that are used in the production of goods and services; productive agents; factors of production.

economics   The study of how people, institutions, and society make economic choices under conditions of scarcity.

economic system   A particular set of institutional arrangements and a coordinating mechanism for solving the economizing problem; a method of organizing an economy, of which the market system and the command system are the two general types.

economic theory   A statement of a cause-effect relationship; when accepted by nearly all economists, an economic principle.

economies of scale   Reductions in the average total cost of producing a product as the firm expands the size of plant (its output) in the long run; the economies of mass production.

efficiency (deadweight) loss   A reduction in combined consumer and producer surplus caused by an underallocation or overallocation of resources to the production of a good or service.

efficient allocation of resources   That allocation of an economy's resources among the production of different products that leads to the maximum satisfaction of consumers' wants, thus producing the socially optimal mix of output with society's scarce resources.

entrepreneurial ability   The human resource that combines the other resources to produce a product, makes nonroutine decisions, innovates, and bears risks.

equilibrium price   The price in a competitive market at which the quantity demanded and the quantity supplied are equal, there is neither a shortage nor a surplus, and there is no tendency for price to rise or fall.

equilibrium price level   The price level at which the aggregate demand curve intersects the aggregate supply curve.

equilibrium quantity   The quantity demanded and supplied at the equilibrium price in a competitive market.

equilibrium real output   The gross domestic product at which the total quantity of final goods and services purchased (aggregate expenditures) is equal to the total quantity of final goods and services produced (the real domestic output); the real domestic output at which the aggregate demand curve intersects the aggregate supply curve.

euro   The common currency unit used by 17 European nations as of 2011 (Austria, Belgium, Cyprus, Estonia, Finland, France, Germany, Greece, Ireland, Italy, Luxembourg, Malta, the Netherlands, Portugal, Slovakia, Slovenia, and Spain).

European Union (EU)   An association of 27 European nations (as of 2011) that has eliminated tariffs and quotas among them, established common tariffs for imported goods from outside the member nations, eliminated barriers to the free movement of capital, and created other common economic policies.

excess reserves   The amount by which a bank's or thrift's actual reserves exceed its required reserves; actual reserves minus required reserves.

exchange rate   The rate of exchange of one nation's currency for another nation's currency.

exchange-rate appreciation   An increase in the value of a nation's currency in foreign exchange markets; an increase in the rate of exchange for foreign currencies.

exchange-rate depreciation   A decrease in the value of a nation's currency in foreign exchange markets; a decrease in the rate of exchange for foreign currencies.

excise tax   A tax levied on the production of a specific product or on the quantity of the product purchased.

expansion   The phase of the business cycle in which output, income, and business activity rise.

expansionary fiscal policy   An increase in government purchases of goods and services, a decrease in net taxes, or some combination of the two, for the purpose of increasing aggregate demand and expanding real output.

expectations The anticipations of consumers, firms, and others about future economic conditions.

expected rate of return The increase in profit a firm anticipates it will obtain by purchasing capital (or engaging in research and development); expressed as a percentage of the total cost of the investment (or R&D) activity.

exports Goods and services produced in a nation and sold to buyers in other nations.

export subsidies Government payments to domestic producers to enable them to reduce the price of a good or service to foreign buyers.

external benefit A benefit obtained without compensation by third parties from the production or consumption of sellers or buyers. Example: A beekeeper benefits when a neighboring farmer plants clover.

external cost A cost imposed without compensation on third parties by the production or consumption of sellers or buyers. Example: A manufacturer dumps toxic chemicals into a river, killing the fish sought by sport fishers.

externality A benefit or cost from production or consumption, accruing without compensation to nonbuyers and nonsellers of the product (see **external benefit** and **external cost**).

external public debt Public debt owed to foreign citizens, firms, and institutions.

factors of production Economic resources: land, capital, labor, and entrepreneurial ability.

fallacy of composition The false idea that what is true for the individual (or part) is necessarily true for the group (or whole).

Federal Deposit Insurance Corporation (FDIC) The federally chartered corporation that insures deposit liabilities (up to $250,000 per account) of commercial banks and thrift institutions (excluding credit unions, whose deposits are insured by the National Credit Union Administration).

Federal funds rate The interest rate banks and other depository institutions charge one another on overnight loans made out of their excess reserves.

federal government The government of the United States, as distinct from the state and local governments.

Federal Open Market Committee (FOMC) The 12-member group that determines the purchase and sale policies of the Federal Reserve Banks in the market for U.S. government securities.

Federal Reserve Banks The 12 banks chartered by the U.S. government to control the money supply and perform other functions. (See **central bank, quasi-public bank,** and **bankers' bank.**)

Federal Reserve Note Paper money issued by the Federal Reserve Banks.

Federal Reserve System A central component of the U.S. banking system, consisting of the Board of Governors of the Federal Reserve and 12 regional Federal Reserve Banks.

final goods and services Goods and services that have been purchased for final use and not for resale or further processing or manufacturing.

financial capital Money available to purchase capital; simply money, as defined by economists.

financial services industry The broad category of firms that provide financial products and services to help households and businesses earn *interest*, receive *dividends*, obtain *capital gains*, insure against losses, and plan for retirement.

firm An organization that employs resources to produce a good or service for profit and owns and operates one or more plants.

fiscal policy Changes in government spending and tax collections designed to achieve a full-employment and noninflationary domestic output; also called *discretionary fiscal policy.*

flexible prices Product prices that freely move upward or downward when product demand or supply changes.

foreign exchange market A market in which the money (currency) of one nation can be used to purchase (can be exchanged for) the money of another nation.

foreign exchange rate (See **exchange rate.**)

fractional reserve A reserve requirement that is less than 100 percent of the checkable-deposit liabilities of a commercial bank or thrift institution.

fractional reserve banking system A banking system in which banks and thrifts are required to hold less than 100 percent of their checkable-deposit liabilities as reserves.

freedom of choice The freedom of owners of property resources to employ or dispose of them as they see fit, of workers to enter any line of work for which they are qualified, and of consumers to spend their incomes in a manner that they think is appropriate.

freedom of enterprise The freedom of firms to obtain economic resources, to use those resources to produce products of the firm's own choosing, and to sell their products in markets of their choice.

free-rider problem The inability of a firm to profitably provide a good because everyone, including nonpayers, can obtain the benefit.

free trade The absence of artificial (government–imposed) barriers to trade among individuals and firms in different nations.

frictional unemployment A type of unemployment caused by workers voluntarily changing jobs and by temporary layoffs; unemployed workers between jobs.

full employment (1) The use of all available resources to produce want-satisfying goods and services; (2) the situation in which the unemployment rate is equal to the full-employment unemployment rate and where frictional and structural unemployment occur but not cyclical unemployment (and the real GDP of the economy equals potential output).

full-employment unemployment rate The unemployment rate at which there is no cyclical unemployment of the labor force; equal to between 4 and 5 percent in the United States because some frictional and structural unemployment is unavoidable.

gains from trade   The extra output that trading partners obtain through specialization of production and exchange of goods and services.

GDP   (See **gross domestic product.**)

GDP gap   Actual gross domestic product minus potential output; may be either a positive amount (a positive GDP gap) or a negative amount (a negative GDP gap).

General Agreement on Tariffs and Trade (GATT)   The international agreement reached in 1947 in which 23 nations agreed to give equal and nondiscriminatory treatment to one another, to reduce tariff rates by multinational negotiations, and to eliminate import quotas. It now includes most nations and has become the World Trade Organization.

government purchases   Expenditures by government for goods and services that government consumes in providing public goods and for public capital that has a long lifetime; the expenditures of all governments in the economy for those final goods and services.

government transfer payment   The disbursement of money (or goods and services) by government for which government receives no currently produced good or service in return.

gross domestic product (GDP)   The total market value of all final goods and services produced annually within the boundaries of the United States, whether by U.S.- or foreign-supplied resources.

gross private domestic investment   Expenditures for newly produced capital goods (such as machinery, equipment, tools, and buildings) and for additions to inventories.

growth accounting   The bookkeeping of the supply-side elements that contribute to changes in real GDP over some specific time period.

household   An economic unit (of one or more persons) that provides the economy with resources and uses the income received to purchase goods and services that satisfy economic wants.

human capital   The accumulation of knowledge and skills that make a worker productive.

human capital investment   Any expenditure undertaken to improve the education, skills, health, or mobility of workers, with an expectation of greater productivity and thus a positive return on the investment.

hyperinflation   A very rapid rise in the price level; an extremely high rate of inflation.

hypothesis   A tentative explanation of cause and effect that requires testing.

immediate short-run aggregate supply curve   An aggregate supply curve for which real output, but not the price level, changes when the aggregate demand curve shifts; a horizontal aggregate supply curve that implies an inflexible price level.

import quota   A limit imposed by a nation on the quantity (or total value) of a good that may be imported during some period of time.

imports   Spending by individuals, firms, and governments for goods and services produced in foreign nations.

income   A flow of dollars (or purchasing power) per unit of time derived from the use of human or property resources.

increase in demand   An increase in the quantity demanded of a good or service at every price; a shift of the demand curve to the right.

increase in supply   An increase in the quantity supplied of a good or service at every price; a shift of the supply curve to the right.

increasing returns   An increase in a firm's output by a larger percentage than the percentage increase in its inputs.

independent goods   Products or services for which there is little or no relationship between the price of one and the demand for the other. When the price of one rises or falls, the demand for the other tends to remain constant.

independent variable   The variable causing a change in some other (dependent) variable.

industry   A group of (one or more) firms that produce identical or similar products.

inferior good   A good or service whose consumption declines when income rises, prices held constant.

inflation   A rise in the general level of prices in an economy.

inflationary expectations   The belief of workers, firms, and consumers about future rates of inflation.

inflationary output gap   (See **positive GDP gap.**)

inflation premium   The component of the nominal interest rate that reflects anticipated inflation.

inflexible prices   Product prices that remain in place (at least for a while) even though supply or demand has changed; stuck prices or sticky prices.

information technology   New and more efficient methods of delivering and receiving information through use of computers, fax machines, wireless phones, and the Internet.

infrastructure   The capital goods usually provided by the public sector for the use of its citizens and firms (for example, highways, bridges, transit systems, wastewater treatment facilities, municipal water systems, and airports).

interest   The payment made for the use of money (of borrowed funds).

interest rate   The annual rate at which interest is paid; a percentage of the borrowed amount.

intermediate goods   Products that are purchased for resale or further processing or manufacturing.

internally held public debt   Public debt owed to citizens, firms, and institutions of the same nation that issued the debt.

inventories   Goods that have been produced but remain unsold.

inverse relationship   The relationship between two variables that change in opposite directions, for example, product price and quantity demanded.

investment Spending for the production and accumulation of capital and additions to inventories.

investment demand curve A curve that shows the amounts of investment demanded by an economy at a series of real interest rates.

investment goods (See **capital.**)

investment in human capital (See **human capital investment.**)

"invisible hand" The tendency of firms and resource suppliers that seek to further their own self-interests in competitive markets to also promote the interest of society.

labor People's physical and mental talents and efforts that are used to help produce goods and services.

labor force Persons 16 years of age and older who are not in institutions and who are employed or are unemployed and seeking work.

labor-force participation rate The percentage of the working-age population that is actually in the labor force.

labor productivity Total output divided by the quantity of labor employed to produce it; the average product of labor or output per hour of work.

labor union A group of workers organized to advance the interests of the group (to increase wages, shorten the hours worked, improve working conditions, and so on).

Laffer Curve A curve relating tax rates and tax revenues and on which a particular tax rate (between zero and 100 percent) maximizes tax revenues.

land Natural resources ("free gifts of nature") used to produce goods and services.

law of demand The principle that, other things equal, an increase in a product's price will reduce the quantity of it demanded, and conversely for a decrease in price.

law of increasing opportunity costs The principle that as the production of a good increases, the opportunity cost of producing an additional unit rises.

law of supply The principle that, other things equal, as price rises, the quantity supplied rises, and as price falls, the quantity supplied falls.

learning by doing Achieving greater productivity and lower average total cost through gains in knowledge and skill that accompany repetition of a task; a source of economies of scale.

legal tender A legal designation of a nation's official currency (bills and coins). Payment of debts must be accepted in this monetary unit, but creditors can specify the form of payment, for example, "cash only" or "check or credit card only."

liability A debt with a monetary value; an amount owed by a firm or an individual.

limited liability Restriction of the maximum loss to a predetermined amount for the owners (stockholders) of a corporation. The maximum loss is the amount they paid for their shares of stock.

liquidity The ease with which an asset can be converted quickly into cash with little or no loss of purchasing power. Money is said to be perfectly liquid, whereas other assets have a lesser degree of liquidity.

liquidity trap A situation in a severe recession in which the Fed's injection of additional reserves into the banking system has little or no additional positive impact on lending, borrowing, investment, or aggregate demand.

long run In macroeconomics, a period in which output prices, wages, and other input prices are all flexible.

long-run AD-AS model A model in which the equilibrium price level and level of real GDP are determined by the intersection of the AD curve and the vertical long-run AS curve.

long-run aggregate supply curve The aggregate supply curve associated with a time period in which input prices (especially nominal wages) are fully responsive to changes in the price level.

long-run vertical Phillips Curve The Phillips Curve after all nominal wages and other input prices have adjusted to changes in the rate of inflation; a line emanating straight upward at the economy's natural rate of unemployment, indicating that over long periods of time there is no trade-off between inflation rates and unemployment rates.

M1 The most narrowly defined money supply, equal to currency in the hands of the public and the checkable deposits of commercial banks and thrift institutions.

M2 A more broadly defined money supply, equal to M1 plus noncheckable savings accounts (including money market deposit accounts), small-denominated time deposits (deposits of less than $100,000), and individual money market mutual fund balances.

macroeconomics The part of economics concerned with the economy as a whole; with such major aggregates as the household, business, and government sectors; and with measures of the total economy.

marginal analysis The comparison of marginal ("extra" or "additional") benefits and marginal costs, usually for decision making.

marginal benefit The extra (additional) benefit of consuming 1 more unit of some good or service; the change in total benefit when 1 more unit is consumed.

marginal cost The extra (additional) cost of producing 1 more unit of output; equal to the change in total cost divided by the change in output (and, in the short run, to the change in total variable cost divided by the change in output).

marginal tax rate The tax rate paid on an additional dollar of income.

market Any institution or mechanism that brings together buyers (demanders) and sellers (suppliers) of a particular good or service.

market economy An economy in which only the private decisions of consumers, resource suppliers, and firms determine how resources are allocated; the market system.

market failure   The inability of a market to bring about the allocation of resources that best satisfies the wants of society; in particular, the overallocation or underallocation of resources to the production of a particular good or service because of spillovers or informational problems or because markets do not provide desired public goods.

market for externality rights   A market in which firms can buy rights to discharge pollutants. The price of such rights is determined by the demand for the right to discharge pollutants and a perfectly inelastic supply of such rights (the latter determined by the quantity of discharges that the environment can assimilate).

market system   All the product and resource markets of a market economy and the relationships among them; a method that allows the prices determined in those markets to allocate the economy's scarce resources and to communicate and coordinate the decisions made by consumers, firms, and resource suppliers.

Medicare   A federal program that is financed by payroll taxes and provides for (1) compulsory hospital insurance for senior citizens, (2) low-cost voluntary insurance to help older Americans pay physicians' fees, and (3) subsidized insurance to buy prescription drugs.

medium of exchange   Any item sellers generally accept and buyers generally use to pay for a good or service; money; a convenient means of exchanging goods and services without engaging in barter.

microeconomics   The part of economics concerned with such individual units as a household, a firm, or an industry and with individual markets, specific goods and services, and product and resource prices.

minimum wage   The lowest wage employers may legally pay for an hour of work.

monetary multiplier   The multiple of its excess reserves by which the banking system can expand checkable deposits and thus the money supply by making new loans (or buying securities); equal to 1 divided by the reserve requirement.

monetary policy   A central bank's changing of the money supply to influence interest rates and assist the economy in achieving price stability, full employment, and economic growth.

money   Any item that is generally acceptable to sellers in exchange for goods and services.

money income   (See **nominal income**.)

money market   The market in which the demand for and the supply of money determine the interest rate (or the level of interest rates) in the economy.

money market deposit account (MMDA)   An interest–earning account (at a bank or thrift) consisting of short-term securities and on which a limited number of checks may be written each year.

money market mutual funds (MMMFs)   Interest-bearing accounts offered by investment companies, which pool depositors' funds for the purchase of short-term securities. Depositors may write checks in minimum amounts or more against their accounts.

money supply   Narrowly defined, *M*1; more broadly defined, *M*2. (See **M1, M2**.)

monopoly   A market structure in which the number of sellers is so small that each seller is able to influence the total supply and the price of the good or service.

moral hazard   The possibility that individuals or institutions will change their behavior as the result of a contract or agreement.

mortgage-backed securities   Bonds that represent claims to all or part of the monthly mortgage payments from the pools of mortgage loans made by lenders to borrowers to help them purchase residential property.

mortgage debt crisis   The period beginning in late 2007 when thousands of homeowners defaulted on mortgage loans when they experienced a combination of higher mortgage interest rates and falling home prices.

multiple counting   Wrongly including the value of intermediate goods in the gross domestic product; counting the same good or service more than once.

multiplier   The ratio of a change in the equilibrium GDP to the change in *investment* or in any other component of *aggregate expenditures* or *aggregate demand*; the number by which a change in any such component must be multiplied to find the resulting change in the equilibrium GDP.

multiplier effect   The effect on equilibrium GDP of a change in *aggregate expenditures* or *aggregate demand* (caused by a change in the *consumption schedule*, *investment*, government expenditures, or *net exports*).

national bank   A commercial bank authorized to operate by the U.S. government.

National Credit Union Administration (NCUA)   The federally chartered agency that insures deposit liabilities (up to $100,000 per account) in credit unions.

national income   Total income earned by resource suppliers for their contributions to gross domestic product (plus taxes on production and imports); the sum of wages and salaries, rent, interest, profit, and proprietor's income.

national income accounting   The techniques used to measure the overall production of the economy and other related variables for the nation as a whole.

national income and product accounts   The national accounts that measure overall production and income of the economy and other related aggregates for the nation as a whole.

natural rate of unemployment   The full-employment unemployment rate; the unemployment rate occurring when there is no cyclical unemployment and the economy is achieving its potential output; the unemployment rate at which actual inflation equals expected inflation.

near-money   Financial assets, the most important of which are noncheckable savings accounts, time deposits, and U.S. short-term securities and savings bonds, which are not a medium of exchange but can be readily converted into money.

negative externalities A cost imposed without compensation on third parties by the production or consumption of sellers or buyers. Example: A manufacturer dumps toxic chemicals into a river, killing the fish sought by sports fishers; an external cost or a spillover cost.

negative GDP gap A situation in which actual gross domestic product is less than *potential output*. Also known as a recessionary output gap.

negative relationship (See **inverse relationship**.)

net exports Exports minus imports.

net taxes The taxes collected by government less government transfer payments.

network effects Increases in the value of a product to each user, including existing users, as the total number of users rises.

net worth The total assets less the total liabilities of a firm or an individual; for a firm, the claims of the owners against the firm's total assets; for an individual, his or her wealth.

nominal GDP Gross domestic product measured in terms of the price level at the time of the measurement; GDP that is unadjusted for inflation.

nominal income The number of dollars received by an individual or group for supplying resources during some period of time; income that is not adjusted for inflation.

nominal interest rate The interest rate expressed in terms of annual amounts currently charged for interest and not adjusted for inflation.

nominal wage The amount of money received by a worker per unit of time (hour, day, etc.); money wage that is not adjusted for inflation.

nondiscretionary fiscal policy (See **built-in stabilizer.**)

nondurable good A consumer good with an expected life (use) of less than 3 years.

nonexcludability The inability to keep nonpayers (free riders) from obtaining benefits from a certain good; a public goods characteristic.

nonmarket transactions The value of the goods and services not included in the measurement of the gross domestic product because they are not bought and sold.

nonproduction transaction The purchase and sale of any item that is not a currently produced good or service.

nonrivalry The idea that one person's benefit from a certain good does not reduce the benefit available to others; a public goods characteristic.

nontariff barriers All barriers other than protective tariffs that nations erect to impede international trade, including import quotas, licensing requirements, unreasonable product-quality standards, and unnecessary bureaucratic detail in customs procedures.

normal good A good or service whose consumption increases when income increases and falls when income decreases, price remaining constant.

North American Free Trade Agreement (NAFTA) A 1993 agreement establishing, over a 15-year period, a free-trade zone composed of Canada, Mexico, and the United States.

offshoring The practice of shifting work previously done by American workers to workers located abroad.

OPEC (See **Organization of Petroleum Exporting Countries.**)

open-market operations The buying and selling of U.S. government securities by the Federal Reserve Banks for purposes of carrying out monetary policy.

opportunity cost The value of the good, service, or time forgone to obtain something else.

optimal reduction of an externality The reduction of a negative externality such as pollution to a level at which the marginal benefit and marginal cost of reduction are equal.

Organization of Petroleum Exporting Countries (OPEC) A cartel of oil-producing countries (Algeria, Angola, Ecuador, Indonesia, Iran, Iraq, Kuwait, Libya, Nigeria, Qatar, Saudi Arabia, Venezuela, and the UAE) that attempts to control the quantity and price of crude oil exported by its members and that accounts for 60 percent of the world's export of oil.

other-things-equal assumption The assumption that factors other than those being considered are held constant; *ceteris paribus* assumption.

partnership An unincorporated firm owned and operated by two or more persons.

patent An exclusive right given to inventors to produce and sell a new product or machine for 20 years from the time of patent application.

payroll tax A tax levied on employers of labor equal to a percentage of all or part of the wages and salaries paid by them and on employees equal to a percentage of all or part of the wages and salaries received by them.

per capita GDP Gross domestic product (GDP) per person; the average GDP of a population.

per capita income A nation's total income per person; the average income of a population.

personal consumption expenditures The expenditures of households for durable and nondurable consumer goods and services.

personal income tax A tax levied on the taxable income of individuals, households, and unincorporated firms.

per-unit production cost The average production cost of a particular level of output; total input cost divided by units of output.

Phillips Curve A curve showing the relationship between the unemployment rate (on the horizontal axis) and the inflation rate (on the vertical axis).

political business cycle   The alleged tendency of Congress to destabilize the economy by reducing taxes and increasing government expenditures before elections, and by raising taxes and reducing expenditures after elections.

positive GDP gap   A situation in which actual gross domestic product exceeds *potential output*. Also known as an inflationary output gap.

positive relationship   A direct relationship between two variables.

potential output   The real output (GDP) an economy can produce when it fully employs its available resources.

poverty   A situation in which the basic needs of an individual or family exceed the means to satisfy them.

poverty rate   The percentage of the population with incomes below the official poverty income levels that are established by the federal government.

price   The amount of money needed to buy a particular good, service, or resource.

price ceiling   A legally established maximum price for a good or service.

price floor   A legally determined price above the equilibrium price.

price index   An index number that shows how the weighted-average price of a "market basket" of goods changes over time.

price level   The weighted average of the prices of all the final goods and services produced in an economy.

price-level stability   A steadiness of the price level from one period to the next; zero or low annual inflation; also called *price stability*.

price support   A minimum price that government allows sellers to receive for a good or service; a legally established or maintained minimum price.

price war   Successive and continued decreases in the prices charged by firms in an oligopolistic industry. Each firm lowers its price below rivals' prices, hoping to increase its sales and revenues at its rivals' expense.

prime interest rate   The benchmark interest rate that banks use as a reference point for a wide range of loans to businesses and individuals.

principal-agent problem   A conflict of interest that occurs when agents (workers or managers) pursue their own objectives to the detriment of the principals' (stockholders') goals.

principles   Statements about economic behavior that enable predictions of the probably effects of certain actions.

private good   A good or service that is individually consumed and that can be profitably provided by privately owned firms because they can exclude nonpayers from receiving the benefits.

private property   The right of private persons and firms to obtain, own, control, employ, dispose of, and bequeath land, capital, and other property.

private sector   The households and business firms of the economy.

producer surplus   The difference between the actual price a producer receives (or producers receive) and the minimum acceptable price.

production possibilities curve   A curve showing the different combinations of two goods or services that can be produced in a full-employment, full-production economy where the available supplies of resources and technology are fixed.

productive efficiency   The production of a good in the least costly way; occurs when production takes place at the output at which average total cost is a minimum and marginal product per dollar's worth of input is the same for all inputs.

productivity   A measure of average output or real output per unit of input. For example, the productivity of labor is determined by dividing real output by hours of work.

productivity growth   The increase in productivity from one period to another.

product market   A market in which products are sold by firms and bought by households.

progressive tax   A tax whose average tax rate increases as the taxpayer's income increases and decreases as the taxpayer's income decreases.

property tax   A tax on the value of property (capital, land, stocks and bonds, and other assets) owned by firms and households.

proportional tax   A tax whose average tax rate remains constant as the taxpayer's income increases or decreases.

proprietor's income   The net income of the owners of unincorporated firms (proprietorships and partnerships).

protective tariff   A tariff designed to shield domestic producers of a good or service from the competition of foreign producers.

public debt   The total amount owed by the federal government to the owners of government securities; equal to the sum of past government budget deficits less government budget surpluses.

public good   A good or service that is characterized by nonrivalry and nonexcludability; a good or service with these characteristics provided by government.

public investments   Government expenditures on public capital (such as roads, highways, bridges, mass-transit systems, and electric power facilities) and on human capital (such as education, training, and health).

public sector   The part of the economy that contains all government entities; government.

purchasing power   The amount of goods and services that a monetary unit of income can buy.

quantity demanded   The amount of a good or service that buyers (or a buyer) desire to purchase at a particular price during some period.

quantity supplied The amount of a good or service that producers (or a producer) offer to sell at a particular price during some period.

quasi-public bank A bank that is privately owned but governmentally (publicly) controlled; each of the U.S. Federal Reserve Banks.

quasi-public good A good or service to which excludability could apply but that has such a large spillover benefit that government sponsors its production to prevent an underallocation of resources.

rate of return The gain in net revenue divided by the cost of an investment or an R&D expenditure; expressed as a percentage.

rational behavior Human behavior based on comparison of marginal costs and marginal benefits; behavior designed to maximize total utility.

real capital (See **capital.**)

real GDP (See **real gross domestic product.**)

real GDP per capita Real output (GDP) divided by population.

real gross domestic product (GDP) Gross domestic product adjusted for inflation; gross domestic product in a year divided by the GDP price index for that year, the index expressed as a decimal.

real income The amount of goods and services that can be purchased with nominal income during some period of time; nominal income adjusted for inflation.

real interest rate The interest rate expressed in dollars of constant value (adjusted for inflation) and equal to the nominal interest rate less the expected rate of inflation.

recession A period of declining real GDP, accompanied by lower real income and higher unemployment.

recessionary output gap (See **negative GDP gap.**)

refinancing the public debt Selling new government securities to owners of expiring securities or paying them money gained from the sales of new securities to others.

regressive tax A tax whose average tax rate decreases as the taxpayer's income increases and increases as the taxpayer's income decreases.

required reserves The funds that banks and thrifts must deposit with the Federal Reserve Bank (or hold as vault cash) to meet the legal reserve requirement; a fixed percentage of the bank's or thrift's checkable deposits.

reserve ratio The specified minimum percentage of its checkable deposits that a bank or thrift must keep on deposit at the Federal Reserve Bank in its district or hold as vault cash.

resource A natural, human, or manufactured item that helps produce goods and services; a productive agent or factor of production.

resource market A market in which households sell and firms buy resources or the services of resources.

rule of 70 A method for determining the number of years it will take for some measure to double, given its annual percentage increase. Example: To determine the number of years it will take for the price level to double, divide 70 by the annual rate of inflation.

sales tax A tax levied on the cost (at retail) of a broad group of products.

saving Disposable income not spent for consumer goods; equal to disposable income minus personal consumption expenditures.

savings account A deposit that is interest-bearing and that the depositor can normally withdraw at any time.

savings institution (See **thrift institution.**)

scarce resources The limited quantities of land, capital, labor, and entrepreneurial ability that are never sufficient to satisfy people's virtually unlimited economic wants.

scientific method The procedure for the systematic pursuit of knowledge involving the observation of facts and the formulation and testing of hypotheses to obtain theories, principles, and laws.

secular trend A long-term tendency; a change in some variable over a very long period of years.

securitization The process of aggregating many individual financial debts into a pool and then issuing new securities (financial instruments) backed by the pool. The holders of the new securities are entitled to receive debt payments made on the individual financial debts in the pool.

self-interest The most-advantageous outcome as viewed by each firm, property owner, worker, or consumer.

service An (intangible) act or use for which a consumer, firm, or government is willing to pay.

shocks Sudden, unexpected changes in *demand* (or *aggregate demand*) or *supply* (or *aggregate supply*).

shortage The amount by which the quantity demanded of a product exceeds the quantity supplied at a particular (below-equilibrium) price.

short run In macroeconomics, a period in which prices of output are flexible but wages and other input prices are inflexible.

short-run aggregate supply curve An aggregate supply curve relevant to a time period in which input prices (particularly nominal wages) do not change in response to changes in the price level.

simultaneous consumption A product's ability to satisfy a large number of consumers at the same time.

slope of a straight line The ratio of the vertical change (the rise or fall) to the horizontal change (the run) between any two points on a line. The slope of an upward-sloping line is positive, reflecting a direct relationship between two variables; the slope of a downward-sloping line is negative, reflecting an inverse relationship between two variables.

Smoot-Hawley Tariff Act Legislation passed in 1930 that established very high tariffs. Its objective was to reduce imports and stimulate the domestic economy, but it resulted only in retaliatory tariffs by other nations.

Social Security The federal program, financed by compulsory payroll taxes, that partially replaces earnings lost when workers retire, become disabled, or die.

Social Security trust fund A federal fund that saves excessive Social Security tax revenues received in one year to meet Social Security benefit obligations that exceed Social Security tax revenues in some subsequent year.

sole proprietorship An unincorporated firm owned and operated by one person.

specialization The use of the resources of an individual, a firm, a region, or a nation to concentrate production on one or a small number of goods and services.

speculation The activity of buying or selling with the motive of later reselling or rebuying for profit.

stagflation Inflation accompanied by stagnation in the rate of growth of output and an increase in unemployment in the economy; simultaneous increases in the inflation rate and the unemployment rate.

start-up (firm) A new firm focused on creating and introducing a particular new product or employing a specific new production or distribution method.

sticky prices (See **inflexible prices.**)

stock (corporate) An ownership share in a corporation.

store of value An asset set aside for future use; one of the three functions of money.

structural unemployment Unemployment of workers whose skills are not demanded by employers, who lack sufficient skill to obtain employment, or who cannot easily move to locations where jobs are available.

subprime mortgage loans High-interest-rate loans to home buyers with above-average credit risk.

subsidy A payment of funds (or goods and services) by a government, firm, or household for which it receives no good or service in return. When made by a government, it is a government transfer payment.

substitute goods Products or services that can be used in place of each other. When the price of one falls, the demand for the other product falls; conversely, when the price of one product rises, the demand for the other product rises.

supply A schedule showing the amounts of a good or service that sellers (or a seller) will offer at various prices during some period.

supply curve A curve illustrating the direct relationship between the price of a product and the quantity of it supplied, other things equal.

supply shocks Sudden, unexpected changes in *aggregate supply*.

supply-side economics A view of macroeconomics that emphasizes the role of marginal tax rates and other factors that affect long-rung aggregate supply and therefore affect inflation, unemployment, and economic growth.

supply-side market failures Overallocations of resources that occur when private supply curves understate the full cost of producing a good or service.

surplus The amount by which the quantity supplied of a product exceeds the quantity demanded at a specific (above-equilibrium) price.

tariff A tax imposed by a nation on an imported good.

tax An involuntary payment of money (or goods and services) to a government by a household or firm for which the household or firm receives no good or service directly in return.

tax incidence The degree to which a tax falls on a particular person or group.

technological advance New and better goods and services and new and better ways of producing or distributing them.

technology The body of knowledge and techniques that can be used to combine economic resources to produce goods and services.

terms of trade The rate at which units of one product can be exchanged for units of another product; the price of a good or service; the amount of one good or service that must be given up to obtain 1 unit of another good or service.

thrift institution A savings and loan association, mutual savings bank, or credit union.

tight money policy Federal Reserve System actions that contract, or restrict, the growth of the nation's money supply for the purpose of reducing or eliminating inflation.

time deposit An interest-earning deposit in a commercial bank or thrift institution that the depositor can withdraw without penalty after the end of a specified period.

token money Bills or coins for which the amount printed on the *currency* bears no relationship to the value of the paper or metal embodied within it; for currency still circulating, money for which the face value exceeds the commodity value.

total cost The total expense to a firm of producing a particular level of output.

total demand for money The sum of the transactions demand for money and the asset demand for money.

total revenue The total number of dollars received by a firm (or firms) from the sale of a product; equal to the total expenditures for the product produced by the firm (or firms); equal to the quantity sold (demanded) multiplied by the price at which it is sold.

Trade Adjustment Assistance Act A U.S. law passed in 2002 that provides cash assistance, education and training benefits, health care subsidies, and wage subsidies (for persons age 50 or more) to workers displaced by imports or plant relocations abroad.

trade balance The export of goods (or goods and services) of a nation less its imports of goods (or goods and services).

trade bloc A group of nations that lower or abolish trade barriers among members. Examples include the European Union and the nations of the North American Free Trade Agreement.

trade deficit The amount by which a nation's imports of goods (or goods and services) exceed its exports of goods (or goods and services).

trademark A legal protection that gives the originators of a product an exclusive right to use the brand name.

trade-off The sacrifice of some or all of one economic goal, good, or service to achieve some other goal, good, or service.

trade surplus The amount by which a nation's exports of goods (or goods and services) exceed its imports of goods (or goods and services).

transactions demand for money The amount of money people want to hold for use as a medium of exchange (to make payments); varies directly with nominal GDP.

transfer payment A payment of money (or goods and services) by a government to a household or firm for which the payer receives no good or service directly in return.

Troubled Asset Relief Program (TARP) A 2008 federal government program that authorized the U.S. Treasury to loan up to $700 billion to critical financial institutions and other U.S. firms that were in extreme financial trouble and therefore at high risk of failure.

unanticipated inflation Increases in the price level (inflation) at a rate greater than expected.

unemployment The failure to use all available economic resources to produce desired goods and services; the failure of the economy to fully employ its labor force.

unemployment compensation (See **unemployment insurance**.)

unemployment insurance The social insurance program that in the United States is financed by state payroll taxes on employers and makes income available to workers who become unemployed and are unable to find jobs.

unemployment rate The percentage of the labor force unemployed at any time.

unfulfilled expectations Situations in which households and businesses were expecting one thing to happen but instead find that something else has happened; unrealized anticipations or plans relating to future economic conditions and outcomes.

unit of account A standard unit in which prices can be stated and the value of goods and services can be compared; one of the three functions of money.

unlimited wants The insatiable desire of consumers for goods and services that will give them satisfaction or utility.

U.S. securities Treasury bills, Treasury notes, Treasury bonds, and U.S. savings bonds issued by the federal government to finance expenditures that exceed tax revenues.

utility The want-satisfying power of a good or service; the satisfaction or pleasure a consumer obtains from the consumption of a good or service (or from the consumption of a collection of goods and services).

value of money The quantity of goods and services for which a unit of money (a dollar) can be exchanged; the purchasing power of a unit of money; the reciprocal of the price index.

vault cash The currency a bank has in its vault and cash drawers.

voluntary export restrictions Voluntary limitations by countries or firms of their exports to a particular foreign nation to avoid enactment of formal trade barriers by that nation.

wage (or wage rate) The price paid for the use or services of labor per unit of time (per hour, per day, and so on).

Wall Street Reform and Consumer Protection Act of 2010 A law that gave authority to the Federal Reserve to regulate all large financial institutions, created an oversight council to look for growing risk to the financial system, established a process for the federal government to sell off the assets of large failing financial institutions, provided federal regulatory oversight of asset-backed securities, and created a financial consumer protection bureau within the Fed.

wealth Anything that has value because it produces income or could produce income. Wealth is a stock; income is a flow. Assets less liabilities; net worth.

wealth effect The tendency for people to increase their consumption spending when the value of their financial and real assets rises and to decrease their consumption spending when the value of those assets falls.

World Trade Organization (WTO) An organization of 153 nations (as of 2011) that oversees the provisions of the current world trade agreement, resolves trade disputes stemming from it, and holds forums for further rounds of trade negotiations.